Transport Law in India

Transport Law in India

Second Edition

Talat Fatima

This book was originally published as a monograph in the International Encyclopaedia of Laws/Transport Law.

Founding Editor: Roger Blanpain
General Editor: Frank Hendrickx
Volume Editor: Eric Van Hooydonk

Wolters Kluwer

Published by:
Kluwer Law International B.V.
PO Box 316
2400 AH Alphen aan den Rijn
The Netherlands
E-mail: international-sales@wolterskluwer.com
Website: lrus.wolterskluwer.com

Sold and distributed by:
Wolters Kluwer Legal & Regulatory U.S.
7201 McKinney Circle
Frederick, MD 21704
United States of America
E-mail: customer.service@wolterskluwer.com

ISBN 978-94-035-4004-7

e-Book: ISBN 978-94-035-4005-4
web-PDF: ISBN 978-94-035-4010-8

The Author

Born and brought up in the City of Joy, Calcutta, Talat Fatima passed her higher secondary with distinction and she was a rank holder in the state of West Bengal. She passed her graduation in English Honours in first class from the Aligarh Muslim University, Aligarh. She is a Gold Medallist in Law, and her star-studded academic career received a boost when she cleared her Master of Laws from the same University with flying colours. She joined the bar at the prestigious Calcutta High Court for about three years and thereafter joined as a lecturer in Government Law College, Dholpur from where she retired as Principal recently.

Dr Fatima is a prolific writer. Her doctoral thesis has been published in the form of a reference cum textbook entitled *Cybercrimes* which is a pioneer work in India. The same book has been translated by her in Hindi, a dominant language of India and which has the credit of being the first book in the language on the subject of cyber law which has been published by the prestigious Eastern Book Company, Lucknow.

Dr Fatima is also associated with the prestigious Kluwers for more than a decade now and has also authored Cyber Law in India.

The Author

Table of Contents

Table of Contents

Table of Contents

List of Abbreviations

AIMTC	All-India Motor Transport Congress
AIR	All-India Reporter
ALHW	Andaman Lakshadweep Harbour Works
AMTOI	Association of Multimodal Transporters of India
ASAs	Air Services Agreements
ASTRU	Association of State Road Transport Undertakings
AWR	All-Weather Roads
BOT	Build, Operate and Transfer by Rail
CBM	Coal Bed Methane
CIM	Convention Concerning International Carriage by Rail
CIRT	Central Institute of Road Transport
CIWTC	Central Inland Water Transport Corporation Limited
CLC	International Convention on Civil Liability for Oil Pollution
CMI	Comite' Maritime International
CMR	Convention on the Contract for the International Carriage of Collisions at Sea
COLREG	Convention on the International Regulations for Preventing Collisions at Sea, 1972
CRF	Central Road Fund
CRZ	Control Resource Zone
CSC	International Convention for Safe Containers
CTD	Combined Transport Document Damage
DGLL	Director General Light Houses and Lightships
DGS	Director General of Shipping
EEE	Engineers Enforcement Education
EEZ	Exclusive Economic Zone
FAL	Convention on Facilitation of International Maritime Traffic
FDI	Foreign Direct Investment
GAGAN	GPS Aided Geo Augmentation Navigation

List of Abbreviations

GAIL	Gas Authority of India Limited
HP	Hindustan Petroleum
IBM	India–Bangladesh–Myanmar
ICC	International Chamber of Commerce
ICD	Inland Container Depot
IIM	Institute of Management
IMA	International Monetary Organization
IMF	International Monetary Fund
IMO	International Maritime Organization
INMARSAT	Convention on the International Mobile Satellite Organization
IPA	Indian Ports Authority Act
IPI	Iran–Pakistan–India
ISC&EI	Interstate Connectivity and Economic Importance
ISPS	Security of Ships and Port Facility
ISSC	International Ship Security Certificate
IWAI	Inland Waterways Authority of India
IWT	Inland Water Transport
IWT	Indus Waters Treaty
LHB	Linke Hofmann Busch
LJ	Law Journal
LL	International Convention of Load Line
LLMC	Limitation of Liability for Maritime Claims
MARPOL	International Convention for the Prevention of Pollution from ships
MEMA	Monthly Ex-Gratia Monetary Assistance
MEPC	Marine Environment Protection Committee
MMSCMD	Million Standard Cubic Metres
MMTG	The Multimodal Transportation of Goods Act 1993
MoU	Memorandum of Understanding
MoRTH	Ministry of Road Transport and Highways
MT	Million Tonnes
MMT	Million Metric Tonnes
MP	Madhya Pradesh
MS	Merchant Shipping
MTD	Multimodal Transport Document
MTOs	Multimodal Transport Operators
MTPA	million tonnes per annum
NG	Natural Gas

NGO	Non-Governmental Organization
NH	National Highways
NHDP	National Highways Development Project
NSTC	North-South Transport Corridor
NW	National Waterway
OPRC	International Convention on Oil Pollution Preparedness, Response and Cooperation
PSSA	Particular Sensitive Sea Area
PSU	Public Sector Undertakings
RIC	Regulation Concerning the International Carriage of Containers
RID	Regulation Concerning the International Carriage of Dangerous Goods by Rail
RIP	Regulation Concerning International Haulage of Private Owners' Wagons by Rail
ROB	Rail Over Bridges
RSD	River Service Division
RT	Road Transport
SAM	Safety of Maritime Navigation
SAR	International Convention on Maritime Search and Rescue
SCC	Supreme Court Cases
SDRs	Special Drawing Rights
SRTCs	State Road Transport Corporations
STCW	International Convention on Standards of Training, Certification
STP	Special Trade Passenger
SUA	Convention for the Suppression of Unlawful Acts against the
SWFS	Seafarer's Welfare Fund Society
TAPI	Turkmenistan–Afghanistan–Pakistan–India
TONNAGE	International Convention on Tonnage Measurement of Ships
TOR	Terms of Reference
TW	Territorial Waters
UNCLOS	United Nations Convention on The Law of the Sea
UPU	Universal Postal Union
VLCC	Very Large Crude Carrier

List of Abbreviations

Preface

Overhauling the entire legal mesh along modern lines and in conformity with the Information Technology sweep is the latest trend in India. It saw enormous legal activity and a bent to revamp the legal machinery along the path of practicability and progress. The transport law is among the very first ones which have geared up for a change, a replacement, with an aim to adopt energy-efficient technologies and a customer-focused approach. The Admiralty (Jurisdiction and Settlement of Maritime Claims) Act 2017 fulfils the long-awaited need for comprehensive legislation in the area of admiralty jurisdiction regarding vessels and their arrest. The years 2017 and 2020 also proved to be years of construction as it was a year of ambitious rollouts and engineering marvels. On the road, a state-of-the-art project namely *Bharatmala Pariyojna*, India's largest-ever highway development programme optimizes the efficiency of road traffic. The National Waterways Act 2016 has turned a new leaf by giving a boost to the potential of navigability, cargo availability and by connecting the hinterland to the progressive urban ports. The civil aviation market is the third-largest one in the world with more than 144.17 million passengers flying in the year 2019. Though burdened with more than a billion population and crippled by the deadly coronavirus pandemic, it has modified its entire transportation system along the COVID Guidelines. The country has the audacity to include bullet trains with a speed of 325 kmph in its transportation fold by 2022. From the seabed to the aviation arena, the vision has been inclusive, to take the fruits of technology to the remotest village and the efforts are untiring.

June 2021
Talat Fatima
India

General Introduction

§1. General Background of the Country

I. Geography

1. India is a naturally gifted land with all the characteristics of a continent. The physical features of India are heterogeneous in nature and it has all the natural landscapes. It is surrounded by land in the north while it has a peninsula in the south surrounded on three sides by water. In the northwest, it shares its borders with Pakistan and Afghanistan; in the north, borders are partially common with Nepal and Bhutan while in the east, Bangladesh and Myanmar are its neighbours. The Great Himalayas stand as the caretaker of the larger part of Indian borders in the north. The Palk Strait and the Gulf of Mannar separate Sri Lanka from India. The southern peninsula, having the shape of a triangle, is bounded by the Indian Ocean and Bay of Bengal in the east and the Arabian Sea in the west. The Indian mainland extends between latitudes 8.4' and 37.6' North and longitudes 68.7' and 97.25' East. The total length of the coastline including Lakshadweep, Andaman and Nicobar Islands is 7,516.6 km. India is the seventh-largest country in the world covering an area of 32,87,263 sq. km which is equivalent to 2.42% of the world area. The land is enriched by mighty rivers like the Indus, the Brahmaputra, the Narmada, the Tapti and the Holy Ganges which forms the lifeline not only of physical India but also of spiritual and ethnic India. Climate of India is basically tropical monsoon type and it also experiences the extreme climates of winter and summer while the monsoon is almost equally distributed over the entire country and is by and large satisfactory. The political division of India comprises twenty-eight states and eight Union territories. The Jammu & Kashmir Reorganization Act 2019 was enacted in November 2019 which provided for the reorganization of the erstwhile state of Jammu & Kashmir into the two Union territories– one to be eponymously called Jammu & Kashmir and the other Ladakh. This makes up twenty-eight States and eight Union territories in the country (INDIA – YEAR BOOK 2021).

II. Demography

2. The final population data of India was released on 30 April 2013. It is one of the densely populated countries in the world and stands second to China sharing about 16% of the world's population. It has a sizeable tribal population with more than fifty tribal groups.

It is studded with more than two thousand ethnic groups and two religions namely, Hinduism (79.8%) and Islam (14.2%) which form the major faiths of the country. India also has the majority of the world's Zoroastrians (0.01%), Sikhs (1.7%) and Jains (0.5%) while there are about 2.5% Christians, 2.3% (The World Factbook, 2021) Jews and Bahá'ís. Though India occupies only 2.4% of the world's land, yet it houses over 16% of the world's total population.

Census 2011 was the fifteenth Census of the country since 1872. The fifteenth Census was held in two Phases: House Listing and House Census (April to September 2010) and Population Enumeration (9 February–28 February 2011 with Revisional round during 1 March–5 March 2011). The reference date was 00.00 hours of 1 March 2011. In snow-bound areas, the Population Enumeration was conducted from 11 September–30 September 2010. The final population data was released on 30 April 2013.[1] The Population of India as of March 2011 stood at 1,210.9 million (632.2 million males and 587.6 million females). Although India accounts for a meagre 2.4% of the world surface area of 135.79 million sq. km., yet it sustains a whooping percentage of the world population. The population of India as of 3 June 2021 is 1,392,457,088 (UN Worldometer). Thus, India is the seventh-largest country in the world by area and by population, it is the second-most populous country in the world.

Languages

3. Four major families of languages namely, Indo-European, Dravidian, Austro-Asiatic and Tibeto-Burman are spoken in the country while two other languages isolate namely, Nihali and the Burushaski are spoken in the disputed parts of Jammu & Kashmir. Interestingly enough English remains the dominating language of not only the educated class but as a reminiscence of the British rule, the English language dominates the official work and is exclusively the language of the Supreme Court of India. The Hindi language is the constitutionally recognized National language of India, and it is also the language of the major part of the population especially in North India. Thus, the percentage of languages as spoken in India is as follows: (World Factbook, 19 May 2021)

Hindi 43.6%
Bengali 8%
Telugu 6.7%
Marathi 6.9%
Tamil 5.7%
Urdu 4.2%
Gujarati 4.6%
Kannada 3.6%
Malayalam 2.9%
Oriya 3.1%
Punjabi 2.7%
Assamese 1.3%

1. INDIA 2018 – Publications Division – Government of India – New Delhi.

Maithili 1.1%
Others 5.6% (2011 estimate).

The population growth rate is at 1.04% (2021 est.) whereas the birth rate is 17.53 births/1000 population (2021 est.) and the death rate is 7.1% /1000 population (2021 est.) The ethnic census is not done in the country. Thus as per the CIA World Factbook (2021), the demographic structure of the country is as follows:

Age structure: (2020 est.)	
0-14 years	27.34% (male 186,087,665/female 164,398,204)
15-24 years:	17.51% (male 123,423,531/female 108,739,780)
25-54 years:	41.56% (male 285,275,667/female 265,842,319)
55-64 years:	7.91% (male 52,444,817/female 52,447,038)
65 years and over:	6.72% (male 42,054,459/female 47,003,975) (2020 est.)

As per the Indian Census 2011 the Age structure is as follows:

0–14 years:	26.31% (male 185,017,089, female 163,844,572)
15–64 years:	64.9% (male 398,757,331, female 372,719,379)
65 years and over:	5.5% (male 30,831,190, female 33,998,613)
Median Age; (2011 est.)	
Total	28.7 years
Male	25.6 years
Female	26.9 years

The birth rate as per the latest Census is 20.97 births/1,000 population and the population growth rate is 1.344%. Significantly enough, there is a gradual decrease in the rate of population growth which was increasing at the rate of 2.2% from 1951 to 1980 and at 2.1% between 1981 and 1990. The rate fell to 1.8% annually between 1991 and 2000 (when the population reached an estimated 1.016 billion people). The population numbered 1.112 billion in 2006 and the growth rate is projected at just 1.5% annually by 2010. However, India also shows a favourable demographic profile as the country has more than 400 million people, less than 15 years old, and over 10 million people are added to this every year. However, more than 70% of this population lives in poverty. However, poverty has been reduced in the past fifteen years as there has been an increase in per capita income. Life expectancy has gone up from less than 60 years in 1991 to close to 65 years at present. Literacy rates have gone up from 52% in 1991 to 62% in 2006. The literacy rate has been recorded at 74.04 % in 2011 which is a rise of 22% in females and 9% in males and the total rise is at 14%. As for females, it has gone from 53.67% (in 2001) to 65.46% (in 2011) while for males it has gone from 75.26% (in 2001) to 82.14% (in 2011) (Registrar General of India; Census 2011).

Indian Population Clock:

> The population of India as of 3 June 2021 was 1,392,457,088 as per the Worldometer of the United Nations Data. Thus the population in 2021 stands at about 1.39 billion.

COVID-19 Impact on Indian Demography

The killer pandemic gripping the entire world in its deadly clutches will be far from over even when mankind becomes mask-free. Its destructive effect ripples over generations to come and has the potency to uproot world demography including India. Unemployment, educational losses, health deterioration, commercial degradation and physical impairment and undoing decades of progress stand as a big threat. It is estimated that in India about 1.8% of the population is hit by coronavirus while 98% still remains vulnerable while those who perished are about 3.4 million. (18 May 2021). In India, the pandemic affects the population in an uneven and disproportionate manner in the sense that some states are more affected than others while the state of Maharashtra bears the hardest brunt. The State has 19% of infection and 33% of total deaths in the country as of 23 December 2020. (Vasishtha, G., Mohanty, S. K., Mishra, U. S. et al. 'Impact of COVID-19 Infection on Life Expectancy, Premature Mortality, and DALY in Maharashtra', India. *BMC Infect Dis* **21,** 343 (2021). https://doi.org/10.1186/s12879-021-06026-6.)

The demographic structure after the COVID-19 attack reveals that the males are more affected (76%) than females (24%). The most affected are among the age group below 40 years (47%) while 34% of the age group of 40-60 years and 19% affected are in the age group of 60 and above. 63% of fatalities are found in people above 60 years out of which 73% are males.(Updates on COVID-19 – Ministry of Health and Family Welfare, Government of India– Posted April 6, 2020. Release ID: 1611676).

Literacy Rate

The literacy rate in India as per the Census 2011 has shown an upward trend. It is 73.0%– 80.9% for males and 64.6% for females. It is nevertheless increasing every year. Thus as per the recent survey, it has risen to 80%.[2] The state of Kerala has the highest literacy at 94% while it is closely followed by Lakshadweep Island which has 91.9%. Bihar is at the lowest rung of literacy at 61.8%.

III. Information on the Political and Legal System of the Country: Form of Government

4. India has travelled from a colonial dependency to a robust and resilient nation. The year 1600 marked the stepping of the Englishmen on Indian lands in the guise of the erstwhile East India Company which later acceded to the ruling apex in the

2. India will gain 100% literacy in the next five years Javadekar – Hindustan Times, 5 Aug. 2017.

country after the transition of Indian into colonialism in 1757. The entire national political scene is structured along the historic and political upheavals. The rising of the Indian nation against the foreign rule in 1857 also known as the First War of Independence, the sporadic revolutionary movements by some nationalist leaders for Home Rule, the appearance of the Mahatma (Mohan Das Karamchand Gandhi) who solicited world sympathy in the battle of right against might (5 April 1930) bloodlessly culminated into the birth of free India on 15 August 1947. India asserted itself as a sovereign and free nation and the country was restored to the natives. Political stability was achieved and the nation heralded its entry into the league of truly democratic nations of the world. Centuries-old aspirations, wishes and dreams saw the light of the day when India wrote its constitution on 26 November 1949 which became fully operative on 26 January 1950, also celebrated as Republic Day. The constitution of India is the Mother Law of the country and acts as a touchstone for all the laws. It is a written constitution, the lengthiest in the world and envisages the federal type of government for the country. It declares India as a Union of states (Article 1 of the Constitution) comprising twenty-eight states and seven Union Territories (Schedule 1 of the Constitution). Being a federation, the constitution includes the scheme of distribution of powers between the Centre and the states (Schedule VII), upholds the supremacy of the constitution and the independence of the judiciary. Part III of the constitution embodies the Fundamental Rights which subsume the doctrine of rule of law, equality of status and of opportunity, liberty of belief, expression, thought and worship and justice, social, economic and political. The Directive Principles of State Policy are given in Part IV which provides guidelines to the state while laying down certain policies, making laws or passing orders. Also in Part IV A, the Fundamental Duties of the citizens are given.

A. Type of Government

5. Indian constitution recognizes the federal type of government where there is a two-tier government; one for the Centre known as the Union Government and the other for each state known as State Governments and both of which are autonomous in their spheres of administration, lawmaking and judicial system. As India is a motley of religions, languages, culture and racial groups, hence to avoid any kind of alienation tendencies, the Union has been endowed with more powers to control the states by assuming the administration of the states in case of emergency (Articles 352, 356 of the constitution) which is why often the Indian governmental system is regarded as quasi-federal by some critics. India is a Republic where the head of the state namely the President of India is selected through an indirect election, on the basis of proportional representation by means of a single transferable vote. The Indian Parliament is a bicameral legislature where the lower house known as the Lok Sabha has 545 members where all are elected on the basis of direct election which recognizes universal adult suffrage. The Prime Minister of India is the leader of the majority party in the Lok Sabha and also heads the council of ministers. The constitution recognizes the responsible type of government where the prime minister together with all the ministers is answerable to the Lok Sabha. The Upper House known as the Rajya Sabha is a permanent body and is the council of

states whereas the members are elected by the states legislatures on the basis of proportional representation. Two members from the Anglo-Indian community and twelve on the basis of special contribution in the fields of science, literature, social work and art are nominated by the President in the Lok Sabha and Rajya Sabha respectively.

B. Legal System

6. The Indian legal system reflects the heterogeneous origin and is a mosaic of Hindu, Islamic and British laws. The biggest chunk of the legal infrastructure owes its origin to the British period where civil, penal and commercial laws were mostly formulated by the English while the religion-based family laws govern the family matters of Hindus, Muslims and other religions like the Parsis and Christians. Reminisces of the Mughal period are also found in the lower courts where the language and some customs still reflect the Mughal pattern.

7. The legal matrix consists of a well-defined hierarchy with the Supreme Court of India at the apex down to the court of the munsif magistrate; all upholding the rule of law. The Supreme Court seated at Delhi enjoys the place of the interpreter of the constitution and the arbiter between the Union and the constituent states which are the important components of the Indian federation. The Supreme Court has original, appellate, civil, criminal and constitutional jurisdiction, advisory jurisdiction and extraordinary jurisdiction where it can hear and dispose of any case of any nature from any court in India (Article 136, Appeal by Special Leave) and is also a Court of Record. The most sacred jurisdiction of the Supreme Court is regarding the Fundamental Rights of the citizens where it acts as the guardian of the rights where a citizen from any part of India can approach the Supreme Court directly and where the speedy remedy is provided by it by passing orders, directions or by issuing writs like the writ of habeas corpus, mandamus, certiorari, prohibition or quo warranto (Article 32). The Supreme Court is the court of ultimate appeal in the country and the system of sending final appeal out of India (Privy Council) came to an end in 1949.

8. Besides Supreme Court there are High Courts for each state. The origin of High Courts dates back to 1862 when three High Courts each at Bombay, Calcutta and Madras were established by the Indian High Courts Act 1861 and later High Courts continue to be established for each state and there are twenty-one High Courts at present some of which have concurrent jurisdiction for two states. High Courts stand at the apex of the state judiciary and are powerful institutions subordinate only to the Supreme Court of India. The High Courts enjoy original, appellate, civil, criminal, admiralty and extraordinary jurisdiction. Article 226 of the Constitution gives elaborate powers to High Courts whereas these courts have powers to issue orders, directions and writs and are very much similar to the power of Supreme Court regarding Fundamental Rights and are also Courts of Record. Apart from the High Court, each state has a network of subordinate courts enjoying both civil and criminal jurisdictions of local nature and the district level courts also have appellate jurisdiction. Tribunals also dispense justice and work as courts in matters of taxation, foreign exchange, industrial and labour disputes, elections and some other specialized fields established under the constitutional provisions (Article 323 A and 323 B). The law establishing these tribunals excludes the jurisdiction of all courts except the Supreme Court of India. Quite recently in India, Lok Adalats (people's courts) were also established under the Legal Services Authorities Act 1987 which aim at the summary disposal of small causes through reconciliation and taking justice to the doors of the needy.

IV. Population and Employment: Social and Cultural Values

A. Population

9. The Indian society, however, is sharply divided on social parameters of income and education. The literacy rate is 73% (2018 est.) while 22% (2006 est.) of the Indian population was below the poverty line. However, India is no longer a country housing the largest number of poor population, from the top position it has come down to third, and the study shows that there are 73 million poor people in India at present. (May 2018 US-based Brookings Study).[3] The unemployment rate is 9.2%. However, as per the International Labour Organization (ILO) Report of 2018, there is an increase in the unemployment population which shot from 3.51 % in 2017 (18.3 million) to 3.52% in 2018 (18.6 million). The National Consensus of India does not recognize the racial groups while it does recognize certain tribal groups under the heading Schedule Caste and Schedule Tribes. According to the Joshua Project, there are 2,334 ethnic groups in India. The origin of the Indians can be traced back to the Caucasoid groups of Dravidians, the Indo-Aryans, Iranians, Bactrians, the Europeans, Greeks, Hephthalites, Arabs, the Australoid Austro-Asiatics, the Mongoloid Tibeto-Burmans, Kushans, Turks, Mughals and a few African Siddis. The Indian culture of today owes much to these ethnic groups though some of these dominate the Indian culture like the Mughals.

10. When the British left India, it was an economically viable country with enough industrialization, with an English-based education system and well-developed administrative, civil and legal set-up though there was a low rate of literacy and the population at that time was marred by poverty. All this contributed to the sorry state of unemployment. However, the contribution of industry to national income was low and in 1950–1951, the share of the primary sector in total Gross Domestic Product (GDP) was as high as 57% and that of the secondary sector was 14%, with the tertiary sector amounting to 29%. Thereafter India has made long strides in economic growth when the National Planning Committee implemented the Five-Year-Plans scheme and the GNP showed an upward movement. The year 1991 marked the economic renaissance and governmental reforms brought a friendly environment for trade and investment. Indian firms started raising funds abroad through instruments like Global Depository Receipts (GDRs) and American

3. *Indian No longer a Poor Nation with World's largest Poor Population*-Report. PTI – 27 Jun. 2018.

Depository Receipts (ADRs). All this led to entrepreneurship and more employment opportunities were created especially in the knowledge services sector.

11. According to an International Labour Organization (ILO) study, the labour participation rate in India was 62% (between 15–64 age group) in 2005 and was far behind China's 82%. The unorganized sector employs close to 925 of the national workforce and produces 60% of GDP. The economic reforms showed tremendous results in the area of the Information Technology (IT) services industry. India's IT and IT Enabled Services (ITES) exports have grown from a mere USD 150 million in 1991–1992 to USD 24 billion in 2005–2006 and was projected to reach USD 60 billion by 2010. This industry employs close to 1.3 million and offers indirect employment to over 3 million people. According to a recent survey, by CLSA, by 2010–2011, India's IT sector including exports and domestic services will employ about [illegible] million people. Thus unemployment has come down and today the top three Information Technology services companies namely Infosys, TCS and Wipro alone employed around 250,000 people in March 2007.

12. However, the ILO has rated that the unemployment rate which is 3.5% in India in 2018 will stay in spite of population explosion constraints. The report says that though there is strong job creation in the Information and Communication Technology (ICT) sectors, the low-value-added services and vulnerable forms of employment are unabating.

13. The Ministry of Labour and Employment (MoLE) has taken major steps and even legislative initiatives to reduce the rate of unemployment in both organized and unorganized labour sectors.[4] As per the recommendations of the Second National Commission on Labour, the Ministry has taken steps for the codification of present Central labour laws into four Codes by simplifying, amalgamating and rationalizing these laws.

14. India as per the Central Statistics Organization (CSO) and International Monetary Fund (IMF) India is emerging as one of the fastest-growing economies and within 10–15 years, it will rise to one of the top three economic powers. India's GDP had reached 6.6 % in 2017–2018 and 7.3% in 2018–2019. The year 2018 had been a year when the three-layered reforms of 2017 namely, bank recapitalization, insolvency resolution and Goods and Services Tax (GST) had started showing positive results. The GST, a new experience in the field, has done indirect tax expansion and removal of interstate check posts ensuring faster movement of goods across internal borders. The Government of India (GOI) effort has been to make growth more inclusive and the key reform pillars are rural economy, infrastructure, social security and employment.

---

4. Annual Report 2017–2018 – Ministry of Labour & Employment – Government of India – New Delhi.

B. Social and Cultural Values

15. India came to be called so after the name of one of its mighty rivers the Indus or Sindhu which gave shelter and entertained a number of races, tribes, caravans and armies for thousands of years. India is a closely knit society and the social and cultural values delve deep down its roots. The Indian society is dotted with long-standing traditions, classical music, art, folkdance, language, scripts, local dialects, religious festivals. The mythological epics of Ramayana and Mahabharata form the backbone of Indian culture, myth, philosophy, history and common belief. In fact, India lives on its culture and can be well called a squeamish society.

16. The Mohenjodaro and Harappa ruins are reflectors of the Indus Valley Civilization (IVC) which were highly developed though some of the inscriptions are still not deciphered. It is believed that the first great cultural synthesis and fusion took place between the incoming Aryans and the Dravidians who are said to be the representatives of the IVC. Out of this synthesis grew the Indian races and the basic Indian culture. The incoming of Iranians, Greeks, Parthians, Bactrians, Scythians, Huns, Turks (before Islam), early Christians, Jews, and Zoroastrians explain the diversity and variety in the Indian culture which according to Dodwell was 'infinitely absorbent like the ocean'. The Vedas, believed to exist before the IVC, are the earliest records of Indian culture. Unlike many countries of the world, India has lingual heterogeneity and has two major linguistic families; Indo-Aryan and Dravidians. Indo-Aryan languages, which are eleven in number, are derived from Sanskrit and are spoken by nearly 75% people out of which Hindi is spoken by nearly 42% people. The Dravidian languages are spoken by 24% people mostly in south India. These languages are a rich fountain of Indian culture. Article 344 of the Indian Constitution declares Hindi as the official language. The Official Languages Act 1963 declares that the English language should continue to be used as an official language in addition to Hindi. Twenty-two languages are constitutionally recognized under Schedule VIII.

17. The Indian dances have strong mythological and religious overtones and occupy a place of pride in Indian life. Gods like Shiva, Krishna and Kali were dancers. The common root of all classical dance is Bharat's Natyasastra which is a commendable work on the science and technique of dance, drama and music. Bhangra of Punjab and Rouf of Kashmir are the dances of the modern age and are socially acclaimed. Indian folk theatres are also a rich source of Indian culture where prior to the fourteenth century, the dramas were mainly in Sanskrit. These theatres mainly deal with mythological heroes, medieval romances and social and political events and are patronized by the National School of Drama. From the prehistoric period to date, Indians have shown great interest in painting and sculpture. The art was patronized by rulers during the Guptas and the Mughals and consists of mural and miniature paintings. The paintings at Ajanta and Ellora Caves are good pieces of creativity and art and reflect the cycle of birth and death. The Indian Cinema is the mirror of the changing social and cultural values of Indian society. It is the largest film producing country in the world with at least 1,200 movies every year made in sixteen languages. It is estimated that around 15 million people see movies every day in about 13,000 cinema houses every day.

V. General Introduction Relating to Transportation

18. India is a country where heterogeneity is a way of life. The vast country is connected by well-developed rail and road infrastructure showing a wide variety of conveyance systems from hackney carriages and bullock carts to the metro trains and sky buses all existing together. Transport and communication facilities cannot be underrated though inland waterways and water transport have scope for development. Ocean waterways are already well-developed. Railways share the largest burden of transport and communication accounting for three-fourth of the passenger traffic and four fifth of the freight traffic and are the most popular means of movement. The country can boast of having the largest railway system in Asia and the fourth largest in the world.

19. Indian railways from a start-up in 1853 from Bombay to Thane with a distance of 21 miles and in 1854 from Howrah to Hooghly for about a distance of 24 miles now has burgeoned into Asia's largest and world's second-largest network. It is the country's largest network and premier transport organization. It is a multi-gauge, multi-traction system. The network area covered by the Railways is about 67,415 km with a fleet of 12,147 locomotives and 67,597 passenger service vehicles and is divided into 17 zones. In its eventful history of about 165 years, the growth and contribution of railways in the economy and social development of the country have been phenomenal.[5]

COVID-19 Pandemic Preparedness: Railways

The Railways geared up to face the deadly pandemic. Under the Disaster Management Act 2005, many alterations have been done in the entire railways' system conforming to the Guidelines and Advisories issued by the Ministry of Health and Family Welfare to contain the pandemic and to minimize losses. While it suffered unprecedented financial losses, it ran COVID Special trains in conformity with strict COVID Guidelines.

IT enablement

India became the first developing country and the fifth country in the world to roll out the first indigenously built 'state-of-the-art' high horsepower three-phase electric locomotive. Another, Diesel Locomotive Works, Varanasi produced a state-of-the-art 4000HP AC/AC diesel locomotive in April 2018.

Roads

5. INDIA –Year Book 2021 – Government of India. New Delhi.

20. The country has seen a phenomenal and unprecedented proliferation of Road construction work which is still untiring. It comprised national highways, expressways, state highways major district roads, other district roads and village roads. The huge network spreads to about 58.98 lakh km (2018–2019).

21. The year 2018–2019 is regarded as the year of construction whereas the Ministry achieved the highest ever construction of 10,855 km of Highways as against 9,829 km in the year 2017–2018. The Government of India lays more stress on award and construction which depends on demand, land availability and management of contracts. March 2018–2019 can be recorded as the year of highest awards at 18,385 km and construction at 8,741 km. The following Table explains the construction activity over the years.

Year	*Award (km)*	*Construction*
2014-2015	7972	4410
2015-2016	10098	6061
2016-2017	15948	8231
*2018-2019	18385	8741

Courtesy: Ministry of Road Transport & Highways, Government of India– Posted 1 January 2018.

*Annual Report 2018-2019, Ministry of Road Transport and Highways, Government of India.

22. The RT goes into the heartland and connects the villages and rural spots with big cities. It is one of the largest in the world aggregating to about 3.3 million km at present. The National Highway Development Project (NHDP) changed the entire road map with the introduction of the Golden Quadrilateral (GQ) connecting the four metros of Kolkata, Mumbai, Delhi and Chennai and the NS & EW corridors connecting other remote corners of the country. India also signed a historic agreement for constructing Asian Highway Network (AHN) and the North-South Transport Corridor (NSTC).

23. India's communication system also extends to the inland waterways and ports. It has about 5,600 km of the main coastline served by twelve major ports and about 184 other ports. Civil Aviation is well structured along three functional divisions; regulatory, infrastructural and operational. On the operational side, Indian Airlines, Alliance Air, private scheduled airlines and non-scheduled operators provide domestic air services while Air India and Indian Airlines provide international air services. Pavan Hans Limited provides basically helicopter support services to the oil sector; hill stations and remote areas. The liberalization process in April 1990 opened the doors to private air taxis. In the pipeline is also the project of starting Sky Buses by the Konkan Railway Corporation and the first one is proposed to run between Andheri and Ghatkopar, an 8.3 km stretch in the city of Mumbai. The year 2017 also registers the multimodal transport system gaining ground in the country. The 2017-18 Union Budget was comprehensive having big plans in the area of road transport. It organized the India integrated Transport Logistics Summit in March 2017 and planned the promotion of multimodal transport with increased synergy in investments in railways, roads, waterways and civil aviation. The Multimodal Transportation Act 1993 is gearing up for a replacement aiming at including domestic trade and to reduce the cost of all businesses and not only international trade.

VI. Inland Waterways and Ports

24. In India, the inland waterways extend to about 14,500 km (9,000 miles) which include rivers, lakes, canals, creeks, backwaters, and so on, though the potential of these has not been utilized to the fullest. The Inland Waterways Authority of India (IWAI), established in 1986 under the IWAI Act 1985, is the statutory body which takes care of the development and regulation of inland waterways for the purposes of shipping and navigation. The Inland Water Transport (IWT) is a cost-effective and climate-friendly mode of transport to carry heavy cargo. For long, the transport system in this area remained neglected though now considerable steps are being taken to improve the infrastructure. In the country, the National Waterways (NWs) come under the purview of the Government of India while the other waterways remain under the control of the various State Governments.

25. For the regulation and development of waterways for the purposes of shipping and navigation the Government of India passed the National Waterways Act 2016(17 of 2016)[6] which makes major changes in the field of shipping and navigation and which also consolidates the legal regime in the said field. The Act repeals the following five Acts:

a) The National Waterway (Allahabad–Haldia stretch of the Ganga–Bhagirathi–Hooghly River) Act 1982.
b) The National Waterway (Sadiya–Dhubri Stretch of Brahmaputra River) Act 1988.
c) The National Waterway (Kollam–Kottapuram Stretch of West Coast Canal and Champakara and Udyogmandal Canals) Act 1992.
d) The National Waterway (Talcher–Dhamra Stretch of Rivers, Goenkhali Charbatia Stretch of East Coast Canal, Charbatia–Dhamra Stretch of Matai River and Mahanadi Delta Rivers) Act 2008
e) The National Waterway (Kakinada–Puducherry Stretch of Canals and the Kaluvelly Tank, Bhadrachalam–Rajamundry Stretch of River Godavari and Wazirabad Vijayawada Stretch of River Krishna) Act 2008.

26. A good number of studies are being carried out which cover the potential of navigability, cargo availability, cost of development, etc.

---

6. The Gazette of India – Extraordinary-Part II – Section 1-New Delhi, the 26 Mar. 2016/Chaitra 6,1938 *(Saka)*.

A. New Waterways Network

27. The National Waterways Act 2016 has made major changes in the field of National Waterways and has declared 111 waterways as national waterways. These are:

National Waterway 1: *Allahabad –Haldia Stretch of the Ganga-Bhagirathi–Hooghly Rivers*:
The Limits are:
From road bridge at Allahabad across the River Ganga, about 2 km upstream of the confluence of the rivers Ganga and Yamuna at Triveni to the inland waterway limit on the tidal waters of the River Hooghly from a line drawn between No. 1 Refuge house at the entrance to Baratola River commonly called Channel Creek, to a position 2.5 km due south of Saugor lighthouse, and then connected to the right or south bank at the entrance to the Hijili or Russulpore River, through River Ganga, lock canal and feeder canal at Farakka, River Bhagirathi and River Hooghly.

National Waterway 2. *Sadiya–Dhubri Stretch of Brahmaputra River.* The Limits are:

From a line drawn across the Brahmaputra River from the point on the north bank of the Kundil River at its confluence with the Brahmaputra River near Sadiya to the beginning of the river island Majuli and therefrom through all the channels of the Brahmaputra River on either side of the river island Majuli up to the end of the river island Majuli and then up to the international border downstream of Dhubri.
National Waterway 3. *Kollam–Kozhikode Stretch of West Coast Canal and Champakara and Udyogmandal Canal:* The limits are: The northern limit of the West Coast Canal shall be Kozhikode at Lat 11°13'39" N, Lon 75°46'44" E and the southern limit shall be a line drawn across the Ashtamudi Kayal at a distance of 100 m south of Kollam jetty. The Champakara Canal starting from the confluence with the West Coast Canal and ending at the railway bridge (railway siding for Cochin Oil Refinery) near Fertilisers and Chemicals Travancore Limited, boat basin. The Udyogmandal Canal starting from the confluence with West Coast Canal and ending at the Padalarn road bridge (Eloor–Edayar).
National Waterway 4. *Kakinada-Puducherry Stretch of Canals and the Kaluvelly Tank, Nashik–Bhadrachalam–Rajahmundry Stretch of River Godavari and Bridge near village Galagali–Wazirabad–Vijayawada Stretch of River Krishna:* The limits are: Kakinada-Puducherry Stretch of Canals and the Kaluvelly Tank, Nashik–Bhadrachalam–Rajahmundry Stretch of River Godavari and Bridge near village Galagali–Wazirabad–Vijayawada Stretch of River Krishna with the following limits, namely: Kakinada–Puducherry Canal (Canal system consisting of Kakinada Canal, Eluru Canal, Commamur Canal and North Buckingham canal, portion of the Cooum River linking North and South Buckingham Canals, South Buckingham Canal and Kaluvelly Tank); Northern

limit: A line drawn across the Kakinada Canal parallel to the Jagannadhapuram road bridge, Kakinada at a distance of 500 m downstream at Lat 16° 56' 24" N, Lon 82° 14'20" E; Southern limit: Junction of East Coast Highway and Chinnakalawari–Kanakachettikulam road at Kanakachettikulam which is the end point of the artificial canal link to Kaluvelly tank at Lat 20° 0' 07" N, Lon 79° 52' 12" E. River Godavari Western limit: Road bridge on Mumbai–Agra Highway at Nashik across River Godavari at Lat 20°0' 07" N, Lon 73°48' 12" E; Eastern limit: Sir Arthur Cotton barrage across River Godavari at Dowlaiswaram, Rajahmundry at Lat 16° 56' 05" N, Lon 81° 45' 32" E. River Krishna Western limit: Bridge near village Galagali Lat 16° 25' 28" N, Lon 75° 26'19" E. Eastern limit: Prakasam barrage across River Krishna at Vijayawada at Lat 16° 30' 18" N, Lon 80° 36' 23" E.

National Waterway 5. *Talcher–Dhamra Stretch of Brahmani–Kharsua–Tantighai–Pandua Nala–Dudhei Nala–Kani–Dhamra river system, Geonkhali–Charbatia Stretch of East Coast Canal, Charbatia–Dhamra Stretch of Matai River and Mahanadi Delta Rivers:* The limits are: East Coast Canal and Matai River (Consisting of old Hijli tidal canal, Orissa Coast anal and Matai River); Northern limit: Confluence point of Hooghly River and Hijli tidal canal at Geonkhali at Lat 22° 12' 20" N, Lon 88° 03' 07" E; Southern limit: Confluence of Matai River and Dhamra River near Dhamra Fishing harbour at Lat 20° 47' 42" N, Lon 86° 53' 03" E. Brahmani–Kharsua–Dhamra river system (Consisting of Brahmani–Kharsua–Tantighai–Pandua Nala–Dudhei Nala–Kani–Dhamra Rivers)

North-Western limit: Samal barrage across River Brahmani, Talcher at Lat 21° 04' 26" N, Lon 86° 08' 05" E; South-eastern limit: An imaginary line drawn across Dhamra River at East Point of Kalibhanj Dian Reserved Forest near Chandnipal at Lat 20° 46' 26" N, Lon 86° 57' 15" E. Mahanadi delta Rivers (Consisting of Hansua river, Atharabanki Creek, Nuna nala, Gobri nala, Kharnasi River and Mahanadi River) (Alternate route-Hansua River enters into the Bay of Bengal through the northern point of False point bay, then enters River Kharnasi at the southern end of False point bay, River Atharabanki, a northernly distributory of River Mahanadi) Northern limit: Confluence of Kharsua River with Brahmani River at Ramchandrapur at Lat 20° 36' 55" N, Lon 86° 45' 05" E; Southern limit: An imaginary line in continuation to the Northern break water structure across the entrance channel at Paradip Port at Lat 20° 15'38" N, Long 86°' 40' 55" E.

National Waterway 6. *Aai River:* Upstream of Bridge at Adalguri No. 3 at Lat 26°33'32" N, Lon 90°34'01" E to confluence with Brahmaputra River at Lat 26°12'50" N, Lon 90°36'24" E (4.7 km upstream of Naranarayan Setu at Jogighopa).

National Waterway 7. *Ajoy (Ajay) River*: Bridge on Morgram–Panagarh State Highway No. 14 at Illambazar Lat 23°36'56" N, Lon 87°31'58" E to the confluence of River Ajoy with River Bhagirathi at Lat 23°39'23" N, Lon 88°07'57" E at Katwa.

National Waterway 8. *Alappuzha–Changanassery Canal*-Boat Jetty, Alappuzha at Lat 9°30'03" N, Lon 76°20'37" E to Changanassery Jetty at Lat 9°26'42" N, Lon 76°31'42" E.

National Waterway 9. *Alappuzha–Kottayam Athirampuzha Canal*-Boat Jetty, Alappuzha at Lat 9°30'03" N, Lon 76°20'37" E to Athirampuzha market Lat 9°40'04" N, Lon 76°31'54" E.

National Waterway 10. *Amba River–Arabian Sea*, Dharamtaar creed near village Revas at Lat 18°50'15" N, Lon 72°56'31" E to a Bridge near Nagothane ST Stand at Lat 18°32'20" N, Lon 73°08'0" E.

National Waterway 11. *Arunawati Aran River System*-Bridge on State Highway No. 211 at Lat 20°13'33" N, Lon 77°33'23" E to the confluence of Arunawati and Aran rivers near Ratanapur village at Lat 19°59'31" N, Lon 78°09'38" E to the confluence of Aran and Penganga rivers near Chimata village at Lat 19°54'08" N, Lon 78°12'36" E.

National Waterway 12. *Asi River*: Ganga River confluence at Assi Ghat, Varanasi at Lat 25°17'19" N, Lon 83° 0'25" E to near Newada, Varanasi at Lat 25°16'37" N, Lon 82°58'18" E.

National Waterway 13. *AVM Canal*: Poovar Beach at Lat 8°18'30" N, Lon 77°04'45" E to Erayumanthurai Bus Stop at Lat 8°14'54" N, Lon 77°09'34" E.

National Waterway 14. *Baitarni River:* Dattapur village at Lat 20°51'45" N, Lon 86°33'30" E to confluence with Dhamra River near Laxmiprasad Dia at Lat 20°45'13" N, Lon 86°49'15" E.

National Waterway 15. *Bakreswar Mayurakshi River System:* Bakreswar River from Nil Nirjan Dam at Lat 23°49'31" N, Lon 87°24'59" E to the confluence of Bakreswar and Mayurakshi Rivers near Talgram village at Lat 23°51'58" N, Lon 88°02'21" E. Mayurakshi River from Talgram village to confluence with Dwarka River near Dakshin Hijal village at Lat 23°58'22" N, Lon 88°09'21" E.

National Waterway 16. *Barak River*: Lakhipur Ferry Ghat Lat 24°47'18" N, Lon 93°01'16" E to Tuker Gram Lat 24°52'34" N, Lon 92°29'21" E.

National Waterway 17. *Beas River*: Talwara Barrage at Lat 31°57'22" N, Lon 75°53'37" E to the confluence of Beas and Sutlej rivers near Harike at Lat 31°09'09" N, Lon 74°58'08" E.

National Waterway 18. *Beki River:* Elenagamari Lat 26°38'37" N, Lon 90°59'02" E to Brahmaputra confluence at Lat 26°14'24" N, Lon 90°47'21" E.

National Waterway 19. *Betwa River*: Rirwa Buzurg Dariya at Lat 25°54'17" N, Lon 79°45'06" E to the confluence of Betwa and Yamuna Rivers near Merapur Daria village at Lat 25°55'11" N, Lon 80°13'08" E.

National Waterway 20. *Bhavani River*: Bhavani Sagar Dam, Sathyamangalam at Lat 11°28'16" N, Lon 77°06'49" E to the confluence of Bhavani and Kaveri Rivers at Kaveri river bridge on Salem–Coimbatore Highway: " National Highway-47 Lat 11°25'54" N, Lon 77°41'02" E.

National Waterway 21. *Bheema River:* Barrage (approx. 1 km from Hippargi village) at Lat 17°09'05" N, Lon 76°46'34" E to the confluence of Bheema and Krishna Rivers at Gundloor Lat 16°24'28" N, Lon 77°17'13" E.

National Waterway 22. *Birupa Badi Genguti Brahmani River System*: Birupa Barrage at Choudwar at Lat 20°30'49" N, Lon 85°55'20" E to Confluence of Birupa and Brahmani rivers near Upperkai Pada village at Lat 20°37'36" N,

Lon 86°24'19" E including the alternative route from, Samaspur village Lat 20°35'41" N, Lon 86°06'32" E to near Kharagpur village Lat 20°38'28" N, Lon 86°17'32" E. Brahmani River from the confluence of Birupa and Brahmani Rivers near Upperkai Pada village at Lat 20°37'36" N, Lon 86°24'19" E to Brahmani River at Katana Lat 20°39'26" N, Lon 86°44'53" E.

National Waterway 23. *Budha Balanga River:* Barrage (approx. 300 m from Patalipura village) at Lat 21°38'13" N, Lon 86°50'53" E to the confluence of Budha Balanga River with Bay of Bengal at Chandipur Fishing Port Lat 21°28'12" N, Lon 87°04'12" E.

National Waterway 24. *Chambal River*: Chambal road bridge on National Highway-92 Lat 26°41'56" N, Lon 78°56'09" E to the confluence of Chambal and Yamuna Rivers at Charakpura village Lat 26°29'30" N, Lon 79°15'01" E.

National Waterway 25. *Chapora River*: Bride at State Highway No. 124 (1 km from Maneri village) Lat 15°42'47" N, Lon 73°57'23" E to the confluence of Chapora River with the Arabian Sea at Morjim Lat 15°36'33" N, Lon 73°44'01" E.

National Waterway 26. *Chenab River*: Chenab road bridge at Lat 33°05'07" N, Lon 74°48'06" E to Bridge near Bhardakalan at Lat 32°48'12" N, Lon 74°34'53" E.

National Waterway 27. *Cumberjua River*: Confluence of Cumberjua and Zuvari Rivers near Cortalim ferry terminal Lat 15°24'40" N, Lon 73°54'48" E to confluence of Cumberjua and Mandovi rivers near Sao Martias Vidhan Parishad Lat 15°31'26" N, Lon 73°55'34" E.

National Waterway 28. *Dabhol Creek Vashishti River:* The Arabian Sea at Dabhol Lat 17°34'51" N, Lon 73°09'18" E to bridge at Pedhe Lat 17°32"39" N, Lon 73°30'36" E.

National Waterway 29. *Damodar River*: Krishak Setu, Bardhman on State Highway No. 8 at Lat 23°12'40" N, Lon 87°50'54" E to the confluence with Hooghly River near Purbha Basudebpur at Lat 22°21'01" N, Lon 88°05'19" E.

National Waterway 30. *Dehing River*: Rail Bridge at Merbil Majuli No. 1 Lat 27°19'25" N, Lon 95°18'45" Eto the confluence of Dehing and Brahmaputra Rivers near village Lachan at Lat 27°15'10" N, Lon 94°40'01" E.

National Waterway 31. *Dhansiri/Chathe River:* Bridge near Morongi T. E. village Lat 26°24'41" N, Lon 93°53'47" E to Numaligarh Lat 26°42'01" N, Lon 93°35'15" E.

National Waterway 32. *Dikhu River:* Bridge at Nazira on State Highway No 1 Lat 26°55'18" N, Lon 94°44'27" E to the confluence of Dikhu and Brahmaputra rivers at Lat 26°59'58" N, Lon 94°27'42" E.

National Waterway 33. *Doyans River*: Bridge near Sialmari Lat 26°10'47" N, Lon 93°59'10" E to confluence of Doyans and Subansiri rivers at Lat 26°26'53" N, Lon 93°57'12" E.

National Waterway 34. *DVC Canal*: Durgapur Barrage Lat 23°28'47" N, Lon 87°18'19" E to Confluence point of DVC canal with Hooghly River near Tribeni Lat 23°0'31" N, Lon 88°24'55" E.

National Waterway 35. *Dwarakeswar River*: Bridge near Abantika Lat 23°06’55” N, Lon 87°18’47” E to the confluence of Dwarakeswar and Silai rivers at Pratappur Lat 22°40’17” N, Lon 87°46’43” E.

National Waterway 36. *Dwarka River*: Bridge at Tarapith at Lat 24°06’58” N, Lon 87°47’51” E to the confluence with Bhagirathi River near Maugram village at Lat 23°43’53” N, Lon 88°10’51” E.

National Waterway 37. *Gandak River*: Bhaisaslotal Barrage near Triveni Ghat at Lat 27°26’22” N, Lon 83°54’24” E to Gandak and Ganga Rivers confluence at Hajipur Lat 25 39°18’N, Lon 85°10’28” E.

National Waterway 38. *Gangadhar River*: Pakriguri Bridge on National Highway-31C at Lat 26°27’30” N, Lon 89°51’25” E to Bangladesh Border at Binnachara Point III Lat 26°0’32” N, Lon 89°49’57” E.

National Waterway 39. *Ganol River*: Bangladesh Border at Mankachar Lat 25°31’47” N, Lon 89°51’24” E to bridge near Dolbari at Lat 25°34’20” N, Lon 90°03’46” E.

National Waterway 40. *Ghaghra River:* Faizabad at Lat 26°47’51” N, Lon 82°06’46” E to Ghaghra and Ganga River confluence at Manjhi Ghat Lat 25°44’13” N, Lon 84°42’03” E.

National Waterway 41. *Ghataprabha River:* Barrage near Malali Lat 16°20’01” N, Lon 75°11’23” E to the confluence with River Krishna at Chicksangam Lat 16°20’13” N, Lon 75°47’54” E.

National Waterway 42. *Gomti River:* Bara Imambara, Lucknow Lat 26°52’21” N, Lon 80°54’58” E to the confluence of River Gomti with River Ganga Lat 25°30’31” N, Lon 83°10’17” E.

National Waterway 43. *Gurupur River:* Confluence of Netravathi River at Lat 12°50’44” N, Lon 74°49’45” E to confluence of Mangalore Port Bridge at Lat 12°55’35” N, Lon 74°49’37” E.

National Waterway 44. *Ichamati River*: Bridge on Border Main Road at Gobra near Bangladesh Border at Lat 22°53’50” N, Lon 88°53’49” E to near Bangladesh Border at Bansjhari Mallikpur Lat 22°39’07” N, Lon 88°55’35” E.

National Waterway No. 45. *Indira Gandhi Canal:* Harike Barrage at Lat 31°08’33” N, Lon 74°56’57” E to near Mohangarh Lat 27°18’37” N, Lon 71°09’10” E.

National Waterway 46. *Indus River*: Bridge on the highway at Upshi village Lat 33°49’43” N, Lon 77°48’56” E to Bridge on Shey–Chuchol road near Shey village Lat 34°03’35” N, Lon 77°38’33” E.

National Waterway 47. *Jalangi River:* Bridge on State Highway No. 14 near Plashipara at Lat 23°47’47” N, Lon 88°27’09” E to the confluence of Jalangi with Hooghly/Bhagirathi Rivers at Nabadwip Lat 23°24’39” N, Lon 88°22’48” E.

National Waterway 48. *Jawai-Luni Rivers and Rann of Kutch:* Jawai River from Jalore at Lat 25°20’37” N, Lon 72°41’09” E to Luni River near Gandhav village to Rann of Kutchh at Lat 23°32’54” N, Lon 68°22’27” E.

National Waterway 49. *Jhelum River*: Bridge on the highway at Lat 33°49’26” N, Lon 75°03’50” E to Wuler lake, Srinagar at Lat 34°21’37” N, Lon 74°36’36” E.

National Waterway 50. *Jinjiram River:* Confluence with Brahmaputra River at Tumni Lat 25°51'51" N, Lon 89°58'57" E to Fulerchar Point. III at Brahmaputra River Lat 25°44'15" N, Lon 89°52'53" E.
National Waterway 51. *Kabini River:* Kabini Dam Lat 11°58'25" N, Lon 76°21'10" E to Beeramballi at Lat 11°56'10" N, Lon 76°14'18" E.
National Waterway No. 52. *Kali River*: Kodasalli Dam Lat 14°55'08" N, Lon 74°32'07" E to the confluence of Kali River with the Arabian Sea near Sadashivgad bridge at Lat 14°50'31" N, Lon 74°07'21" E.
National Waterway 53. *Kalyan–Thane–Mumbai Waterway, Vasai Creek and Ulhas River*: the Arabian Sea at Navi Mumbai Lat 18°55'50" N, Lon 72°53'22" E via Ulhas River to bridge on State Highway No. 76 near Malegaon T. Waredi Lat 19°02'38" N, Lon 73°19'54" E; Bridge on Kalyan–Badlapur road near Kalyan railway yard at Kalyan Lat 19°14'06" N, Lon 73°08'49" E to Kalyan Lat 19°15'35" N, Lon 73°09'28" E; Vasai Creek from Lat 19°18'54" N to Lon 72°47'30" E to Kasheli at Lat 19°13'23" N, Lon 73°0'21" E.
National Waterway 54. *Karamnasa River:* Bridge at Kakarait Lat 25°18'11" N, Lon 83°31'38" E to the confluence of Karamnasa and Ganga Rivers at Kutubpur Lat 25°31'06" N, Lon 83°52'47" E.
National Waterway 55. *Kaveri Kollidam River*: Uratchikottai Barrage at Lat 11°29'03" N, Lon 77°42'14" E to the confluence of River Kollidam with the Bay of Bengal at Pazhaiyar Lat 11°21'38" N, Lon 79°49'53" E.
National Waterway 56. *Kherkai River:* Dam near Gangia village at Lat 22°45'12" N, Lon 86°05'09" E to the confluence with Subarnrekha River at Jamshedpur Lat 22°50'13" N, Lon 86°09'37" E.
National Waterway 57. *Kopili River:* Bridge at Banthai Gaon Tinali Bus Stop at Lat 26°10'41" N, Lon 92°13'05" E to the confluence with Brahmaputra River at Chandrapur No. 2 Lat 26°15'07" N, Lon 91°56'49" E.
National Waterway 58. *Kosi River*: Kosi Barrage at Hanuman Nagar Lat 26°31'40" N, Lon 86°55'29" E to the confluence of River Kosi with Ganga River at Kursela Lat 25°24'40" N, Lon 87°15'14" E.
National Waterway 59. *Kottayam–Vaikom Canal:* Kottayam, near Kodimatha at Lat 9°34'39" N, Lon 76°31'08" E to Vechoor joining National Waterway No. 3 at Lat 9°40'0" N, Lon 76°24'11" E.
National Waterway 60. *Kumari River*: Dam near Amruhasa village at Lat 23°06'37" N, Lon 86°15'51" E to Mukutmanipur Dam at Chiada Lat 22°57'18" N, Lon 86°44'43" E.
National Waterway 61. *Kynshi River:* Bangladesh Border near Mawpyllum Lat 25°12'07" N, Lon 91°15'21" E to bridge on Nonghyllam-Maweit road at Lat 25°19'35" N, Lon 91°04'07" E.
National Waterway 62. *Lohit River*: Parasuram Kund at 27°52'40" N, Lon 96°21'40" E to Saikhowa Ghat, Sadiya Lat 27°47'49" N, Lon 95°38'14" E.
National Waterway 63. *Luni River*: Dam at Jaswantpura Lat 26°13'35" N, Lon 73°41'20" E to Barrage near Malipura Lat 24°57'04" N, Lon 71°38'02" E.
National Waterway 64. *Mahanadi River*: Sambalpur Barrage at Lat 21°27'34" N, Lon 83°57'50" E to Paradip at Lat 20°19'38" N, Lon 86°40'17" E.

National Waterway 65. *Mahananda River*: Bridge near Gosaipur at Lat 25°26’41” N, Lon 88°05’26” E to Bangladesh Border near Adampur at Lat 24°57’17” N, Lon 88°10’59” E.
National Waterway 66. *Mahi River*: Kadana Dam Lat 23°18’22” N, Lon 73°49’37” E to the confluence with Gulf of Khambhat near Kavi railway station Lat 22°10’35” N, Lon 72°30’36” E.
National Waterway 67. *Malaprabha River*: Jakanuru at Lat 15°49’51” N, Lon 75°38’54” E to the confluence with River Krishna at Kudalasangama Lat 16°12’30” N, Lon 76°04’16” E.
National Waterway No. 68. *Mandovi River:* Bridge at Usgaon at Lat 15°26’42” N, Lon 74°03’12” E to the confluence of Mandovi River with the Arabian Sea at Reis Magos Lat 15°28’32” N, Lon 73°46’46” E.
National Waterway No. 69. *Manimutharu River*: Manimutharu Dam Lat 8°39’14” N, Lon 77°24’47” E to the confluence with Tamaraparani River near Aladiur Lat 8°41’03” N, Lon 77°26’07” E.
National Waterway 70. *Manjara River*: Singur Dam at Lat 17°44’58” N, Lon 77°55’41” E to the confluence with River Godavari at Kandakurthi at Lat 18°49’07” N, Lon 77°52’20” E.
National Waterway 71. *Mapusa/Moide River*: Bridge on National Highway-17 at Mapusa Lat 15°35’21” N, Lon 73°49’17” E to the confluence point of Mapusa and Mandovi Rivers at Porvorim Lat 15°30’20” N, Lon 73°50’42” E.
National Waterway 72. *Nag River*: Bridge near NIT Colony, Nagpur Lat 21°06’17” N, Lon 79°06’03” E to the confluence with River Kanhan near Sawangi village at Lat 21°05’38” N, Lon 79°27’54” E.
National Waterway 73. *Narmada River*: Pandhariya at Lat 21°57’10” N, Lon 74°08’27” E to the confluence of Narmada with the Arabian Sea at Gulf of Khambhat Lat 21°38’27” N, Lon 72°33’28” E.
National Waterway 74. *Netravathi River*: Netravathi Dam, Dharmsthala Lat 12°57’55” N, Lon 75°22’10” E to confluence with the Arabian sea at Bengre Lat 12°50’43” N, Lon 74°49’29” E.
National Waterway 75. *Palar River*: Rail bridge at Virudampattu, Vellore at Lat 12°56’14” N, Lon 79°07’30” E to the confluence with Bay of Bengal at Sadurangapattinam Lat 12°27’52” N, Lon 80°09’13” E.
National Waterway 76. *Panchagungavali (Panchagangoli) River*: Panchagangavali (Panchagangoli) River: Gangoli Port at Lat 13°38’01” N, Lon 74°40’08” E to Bridge at Badakere at Lat 13°44’50” N, Lon 74°39’15” E.
National Waterway 77. *Pazhyar River*: Pazhyar River: Bridge near Veeranarayana Mangalam village at Lat 8°13’49” N, Lon 77°26’27” E to the confluence with the Arabian Sea at Manakudi at Lat 8°05’15” N, Lon 77°29’08” E.
National Waterway 78. *Penganga Wardha River System:* Confluence of Aran and Penganga Rivers near Chimata village at Lat 19°54’08” N, Lon 78°12’36” E to the confluence of Wardha and Pranahita Rivers near Ravalli village at Lat 19°33’59” N, Lon 79°49’0” E.
National Waterway 79. *Pennar River*: Penna Barrage, Pothireddypalem at Lat 14°28’08” N, Lon 79°59’09” E to the confluence with the Bay of Bengal near Kudithipalem at Lat 14°35’37” N, Lon 80°11’31” E.

National Waterway 80. *Ponniyar River:* Sathanur Dam at Lat 12°11’0” N, Lon 78°51’01” E to Cuddalore at the confluence of the Bay of Bengal at Lat 11°46’22” N, Lon 79°47’42” E.

National Waterway 81. *PunpunRiver*: Bridge on National Highway-83 near Pakri village Lat 25°29’50” N, Lon 85°06’19” E to the confluence with River Ganga at Fatuha Lat 25°30’50” N, Lon 85°18’17” E.

National Waterway 82. *Puthimari River*: Bridge on National Highway-31 near village Ghopla at Lat 26°22’01” N, Lon 91°39’11” E to the confluence with Brahmaputra River near Bamunbori at Lat 26°15’28” N, Lon 91°20’35” E.”.

National Waterway 83. *Rajpuri Creek*: The Arabian Sea at Rajpuri Lat 18°18’03” N, Lon 72°56’43” E to Mhasala at Lat 18°08’15” N, Lon 73°06’45” E.

National Waterway 84. *Ravi River*: Dam at Gandhiar Lat 32°35’51” N, Lon 75°50’05” E to Ranjeet Sagar Dam at Basoli Lat 32°26’36” N, Lon 75°43’45” E.

National Waterway 85. *Revadanda Creek Kundalika River System:* The Arabian Sea at Revadanda Lat 18°32’20” N, Lon 72°55’33” E to bridge on Roha–Astami Road near Roha Nagar Lat 18°26’32” N, Lon 73°07’11” E.

National Waterway 86. *Rupnarayan River*: Confluence of Dwarakeswar and Silai Rivers at Pratappur Lat 22°40’17” N, Lon 87°46’43” E to the confluence with Hooghly River at Geonkhali Lat 22°12’42” N, Lon 88°03’14” E.

National Waterway 87. *Sabarmati River*: Barrage near Sadoliya Lat 23°26’50” N, Lon 72°48’35” E to the confluence with Gulf of Khambhat near Khambhat Lat 22°09’18” N, Lon 72°27’28” E.

National Waterway 88. *Sal River*: Orlim Deusa Bridge Lat 15°13’11” N, Lon 73°57’30” E to confluence with the Arabian Sea at Mobor Lat 15°08’32” N, Lon 73°57’0” E.

National Waterway 89. *Savitri River (Bankot Creek):* Bridge near Sape at Lat 18°05’54” N, Lon 73°20’09” E to the Arabian Sea at Bankot Lat 17°58’47” N, Lon 73°01’45” E.

National Waterway 90. *Sharavati River*: Honnavar Port Sea Mouth at Lat 14°17’56” N, Lon 74°25’27” E to link at the highway at Gersoppa Lat 14°14’15” N, Lon 74°39’06” E.

National Waterway 91. *Shastri River Jaigad Creek*: Sangmeshwar at Lat 17°11’16” N, Lon 73°33’03” E to the confluence with the Arabian Sea at Jaigad Lat 17°19’12” N, Lon 73°12’39” E.

National Waterway 92. *Silabati River:* Barrage near Shimulia village at Lat 22°34’53” N, Lon 87°38’31” E to the confluence of Dwarakeswar and Silai Rivers at Pratappur Lat 22°40’17” N, Lon 87°46’43” E.

National Waterway 93. *Simsang River*: Bangladesh Border at Lat 25°11’05” N, Lon 90°39’25” E to bridge on National Highway-62 near Nongalbibra Lat 25°27’20” N, Lon 90°42’22” E.

National Waterway 94. *Sone River*: Sone Barrage near Dehri at Lat 24°50’14” N, Lon 84°08’03” E to the confluence of Sone and Ganga Rivers at Lat 25°42’15” N, Lon 84°52’02” E.

National Waterway 95. *Subansiri River:* Gerukamukh Lat 27°27'03" N, Lon 94°15'16" E to Brahmaputra confluence at Lat 26°52'25" N, Lon 93°54'31" E.

National Waterway 96. *Subarnrekha River:* Chandil Dam at Lat 22°58'29" N, Lon 86°01'14" E to confluence with the Bay of Bengal at Lat 21°33'29" N, Lon 87°22'59" E.

National Waterway 97. *Sunderbans Waterways:* (i) Namkhana at Lat 21°45'46" N, Lon 88°13'06" E to Athara Banki Khal Lat 21°56'57" N, Lon 89°05'32" E; (ii) Bidya River: Lot No. 124 at Lat 21°54'43" N, Lon 88°41'08" E to near Uttar Danga at Lat 22°11'48" N, Lon 88°51'55" E; (iii) Chhota Kalagachi (Chhoto Kalergachi) River: Near Rajani ferry ghat Lat 22°19'57" N, Lon 88°54'21" E to near Nazat at Lat 22°26'05" N, Lon 88°50'12" E; (iv) Gomar River: Near Ramkrishnapur Lat 22°11'53" N, Lon 88°44'42" E to near Gosaba Kheya ghat at Lat 22°10'05" N, Lon 88°47'37" E; (v) Haribhanga River: Bangladesh Border Lat 21°53'19" N, Lon 89°01'24" E to confluence with Jhila River at Lat 21°58'18" N, Lon 88°55'08" E;(vi) Hogla (Holgal-)–Pathankhali River: Near Parandar Lat 22°12'22" N, Lon 88°40'43" E to near Sandeshkhai Ferry Ghat at Lat 22°21'12" N, Lon 88°52'48" E; (vii) Kalindi (Kalandi) River: Bangladesh Border at Hingalganj Lat 22°28'08" N, Lon 88°59'46" E to Bangladesh Border near Khosbash at Lat 22°24'41" N, Lon 88°58'21" E; (viii) Katakhali River: Bangladesh Border near Barunh at Lat 22°30'31" N, Lon 88°58'25" E to Lebukhali ferry at Lat 22°21'45" N, Lon 88°57'30" E; (ix) Matla River: Bay of Bengal at Lat 21°33'04" N, Lon 88°38'26" E to Canning ferry ghat at Lat 22°18'39" N, Lon 88°40'43" E; (x) Muri Ganga (Baratala) River: Bay of Bengal near Bisalakshmipur Lat 21°37'52" N, Lon 88°10'0" E to near Kakdwip at Lat 21°52'17" N, Lon 88°09'08" E; (xi) Raimangal River: Hemnagar at Lat 22°11'41" N, Lon 88°58'01" E to Rajnagar at Lat 22°33'57" N, Lon 88°56'17" E;(xii) Sahibkhali (Sahebkhali) River: Near Ramapur Lat 22°17'52" N, Lon 88°56'35" E to Bangladesh Border near Khosbash at Lat 22°24'41" N, Lon 88°58'21" E; (xiii) Saptamukhi River: Bay of Bengal at Henry Island Lat 21°34'57" N, Lon 88°19'08" E to near Chintamanipur at Lat 21°51'14" N, Lon 88°18'41" E; (xiv) Thakurran River: Bay of Bengal at Lat 21°33'32" N, Lon 88°27'45" E to Madhabpur at Lat 22°02'52" N, Lon 88°33'28" E; 98.

National Waterway 98. *Sutlej River:* Sunni Road Bridge at Lat 31°14'45" N, Lon 77°07'34" E to Harike Dam at Lat 31°08'33" N, Lon 74°56'57" E.

National Waterway 99. *Tamaraparani River:* Sulochana Mudalir bridge, Tirunelveli Lat 8°43'43" N, Lon 77°42'54" Eto the confluence with the Bay of Bengal near Punnaikayal at Lat 8°38'25" N, Lon 78°07'38" E.

National Waterway 100. *Tapi River*: Hatnur Dam Near Mangalwadi Lat 21°04'22" N, Lon 75°56'45" E to Gulf of Khambhat (Arabian Sea) at Lat 21°02'16" N, Lon 72°39'30" E.

National Waterway 101. *Tizu and Zungki Rivers:* Longmatra at Lat 25°46'12" N, Lon 94°44'35" E to Avanghku at Myanmar border Lat 25°35'03" N, Lon 94°53'06" E and in Zungki River from the bridge at Lat 25°48'26" N, Lon 94°46'36" E to the confluence of Zungki and Tizu Rivers at Lat 25°46'58" N, Lon 94°45'21" E.

National Waterway 102. *Tlwang (Dhaleswari River):* Khamrang near National Highway-54 Lat 23°55’22” N, Lon 92°39’08” E to Bridge on National Highway-154 at Gharmura Lat 24°17’19” N, Lon 92°31’0” E.

National Waterway 103. *Tons River:* Bridge on National Highway-27 near Chakghat at Lat 25°02’05” N, Lon 81°43’45” E to Ganga confluence at Sirsa Lat 25°16’32” N, Lon 82°05’0” E.

National Waterway 104. *Tungabhadra River*: Bridge on State Highway No. 29 near Chikka Jantakal village at Lat 15°24’33” N, Lon 76°35’13” E to the confluence with River Krishna near village Murva Konda at Lat 15°57’20” N, Lon 78°14’30” E.

National Waterway 105. *Udayavara River*: Arabian Sea Mouth at Malpe Lat 13°20’57” N, Lon 74°41’28” E to Bridge near Manipura Lat 13°17’33” N, Lon 74°46’26” E.

National Waterway 106. *Umngot (Dwuki) River:* Arabian Sea Mouth at Malpe Lat 13°20’57” N, Lon 74°41’28” E to Bridge near Manipura Lat 13°17’33” N, Lon 74°46’26” E.

National Waterway 107. *Vaigai River:* Barrage near Anai Patti at Lat 10°05’19” N, Lon 77°51’10” E to Viragnoor Dam at Lat 9°53’52” N, Lon 78°10’34” E.

National Waterway 108. *Varuna River*: Road bridge near Kuru at Lat 25°23’15” N, Lon 82°44’07” E to Ganga confluence at Saray Mohana, Varanasi Lat 25°19’45” N, Lon 83°02’41” E.

National Waterway 109. *Wainganga Pranahita River System*: Bridge near Chandapur village at Lat 20°0’30” N, Lon 79°47’08” E to the confluence of River Godavari at Kaleshwaram Lat 18°49’33” N, Lon 79°54’33” E.

National Waterway 110. *Yamuna River:* Jagatpur (6 km upstream of Wazirabad Barrage) Delhi Lat 28°45’28” N, Lon 77°13’50” E to the confluence of Yamuna and Ganga Rivers at Sangam, Allahabad at Lat 25°25’24” N, Lon 81°53’20” E.

National Waterway 111. *Zuari River*: Sanvordem bridge Lat 15°16’15” N, Lon 74°07’11” E to Marmugao Port Lat 15°25’55” N, Lon 73°48’13” E.

B. New National Waterways Law

28. The Parliament has passed the National Waterways Act 2016 declaring 111 waterways as National Waterways.

C. Protocol on Inland Water Transit and Trade

29. There exists a strong commercial bond between India and Bangladesh via the water route. This is reflected in the Protocol which was first signed between the two countries in 1972, renewed in 2015 with a provision for its automatic renewal for a period of five years. Both the countries entered into institutional arrangements regarding the Protocol in 2018(India) and in 2019(Bangladesh). This resulted in the signing of the Second Addendum to the Protocol which aims at the improvement of inland waterways trade between the two countries. The second Addendum to the Protocol was signed between India and Bangladesh on 20 May 2020 in which some path-breaking developments were initiated. To the five Ports of Call were added six more Ports of Call and two more extended Ports of Call making it to a total of eleven Ports of Call. As per Article 1.3 of the Protocol shallow draft mechanized vessels if registered under Inland Shipping Ordinance 1976 of Bangladesh or Inland Vessels Act 1917 of India are introduced to facilitate trade. The Protocol also allows plying of Inland vessels of both the countries on the designated protocol route.(Release ID: 1625342 – Press Information Bureau, Ministry of Ports, Shipping and Waterways, Government of India).

Consequently, the inland water transit and trade between the two countries also improved by using National Waterways -1 and National Waterways -2 which is also destined to connect the landlocked countries like Bhutan, Nepal and Myanmar to facilitate commercial relations between these countries as per the Ministry of Ports and Shipping. (D. Nag.: Indo-Bangladesh Protocol on Inland Water Transit and Trade to Improve trading between the two nations; Details. Financial Express– 5 February 2021).

VII. Ports

30. The country's long coastline of around 7,517 km belted around the western, eastern and southern ends is a natural gift and has strong potential for the country's trade and tourism development. Around 95% by volume and 70% by value of the country's external merchandise trade is carried out through maritime transport. Ports play a key role between ocean transport and land-based transport. Along with major ports some non-major ports have also witnessed growth in traffic. There has been an increase in the cargo handled at Indian ports from a level of 19.38 million tonnes (major ports in 1950–1951 to around 575 million tonnes by 2005–2006 and to around 722.93 million tonnes by 2007–2008 (major and non-major ports). In the Financial Year 2018, the cargo traffic was reported at 679.36 million tonnes (MT) showing a growth of 4.77% over the same period last year. The ports handle almost 95% of trade volumes in India which is a significant contribution to the cargo traffic of the country. Capacity at major Indian ports reached 1,451 MT by March 2018. The cargo capacity of major ports has increased from 599.47 MTPA in 2014 to 1514.09 MTPA in 2019. The cargo handling capacity of non-major ports has increased from 599.47 MTPA in 2014 to 863.50 in 2019. The cargo traffic handled by non-major ports during April–December 2019 was around 447.21 MT which recorded growth of over 4.8% over the same period in the previous year (Annual Report 2019–2020 – Ministry of Shipping, Government of India).

31. There are twelve major ports and 200 non-major ports administered by Port Trusts which are autonomous bodies except the newly constructed Ennore Port which is run by a company named Ennore Port Limited registered under Companies Act 1956. There are twelve major ports out of which on the Eastern coast are Kolkata (including Dock complex at Haldia) – established in 1870 is the only major riverine major port of India; Paradip – established in 1966 is the only major sea port in the state of Orissa; Visakhapatnam – a port of natural harbour was opened to commercial shipping in 1933 and today it has emerged as a multi commodity Port with variegated cargo; Chennai – is an all-weather artificial harbour with one Outer Harbour and an Inner Harbour with a Wet Dock and a Boat Basin established in 1875; Tuticorin – situated on the east coast was declared as a major port in 1974; on the Western Coast are; Cochin – the modern port formally opened for vessels in 1930–1931; New Mangalore – the port having a modern all-weather artificial lagoon was established in 1974; Mormugao – though it is a century-old port but it has modern infrastructural facilities and is one of the finest ports in the world and was established as a major port in 1963; Jawaharlal Nehru at Nhava – established in the mid-1980s it is a world class international container handling port; Mumbai – it is the second-oldest port after Kolkata and it is a multipurpose port; Kandla – established in 1955 is a natural harbour and is a gateway to the North-western states.

32. The Andaman Lakshadweep Harbour Works (ALHW) is a subordinate office under the Department of Shipping which is entrusted with the work of formulating and implementing the programme for providing port and harbour facilities in Andaman & Nicobar Islands. Two Training Institutes namely, National Maritime Academy and Indian Institute of Port Management, registered as autonomous societies impart training, consultancy and research in the Port, Shipping and related sectors.

VIII. Rail Roads

33. In order to improve infrastructure to facilitate the transportation of raw materials, the British established railways in India in the year 1853 between Bombay and Thane. Major rail networks connected the major harbours at the port cities of Madras, Bombay and Calcutta which carried the majority of the foreign trade. By 1947, the Indian Railways became one of the world's largest networks and according to the railways' statistics, the total route miles increased from 838 in 1860 to over 42,000 by 1947 and the number of passengers carried increased from less than 50 million in 1870 to over 600 million by 1940. Railways provide a good alternative to the roadways as it reduces the average cost of transportation in terms of money and time.

34. The network of railways has seen constant expansion and is tirelessly trying to cater to the burgeoning population needs. The route length of the railways by March 2020 was 67, 956 km (42,226 mi) as of 31 March 2020. Out of these, Broad Gauge is 63,950 km. Meter Gauge 2,402 km and Narrow Gauge is at 1,809 km. The total track has steadily progressed from 77,609 km in 1951 since the Independence of India to 1,26,366 km in 2019–2020*(Indian Railways Year Book 2019–2020 at p. 60).* The entire system is run by 12,729 locomotives (2018–2019) with 70,236 passenger service vehicles. The Indian Railways (IR) runs three types of locomotives, steam (939), diesel, (5,898) and 12,729 electric units. There are about 7, 325 railway stations all over the country. As of 31 March 2020, the IR owns about 4.81 hectares of land. Electrification of the railway tracks is to achieve modern and eco-friendly targets and to minimize the country's dependence on petroleum in order to achieve energy security. 57.87% of the railway tracks have been electrified and the cumulative electrified routes stand at 39, 329 in 2020. From the viewpoint of safety and modernization, the old Multi Cabin Mechanical Signalling System has been done away with which is now replaced by Modern Signalling systems comprising of Panel Interlocking/Route Relay Interlocking/and Electronic Interlocking. To avoid collisions and accidents Train Collision Avoidance System has been developed. For safety purposes, the IR has provided interlocking with Signals at 11, 639 Level Crossing Gates as of 31 March 2020. The Railways have also made massive use of modern telecommunication systems. As of March 2020, the IR has about 59,105 km of Optical Fibre Cable (OFC) that is carrying Gigabytes of traffic. In view of the Digital India Programme of the Government of India, the passengers are provided with a WiFi internet facility at 5,819 stations as of 31 March 2020. On this date, 5,655 stations were live with Rail Tel's Railwire which stands as the largest and fastest public network in the world. For security purposes, the Railway Protection Force was constituted under the Railway Protection Force Act 1957 which was amended in 1985 and 2003. The RPF is empowered under the Railway Property (Unlawful Possession) Act 1966 to deal with cases of theft, dishonest misappropriation and unlawful possession of railway property. On 14 August 2019, the Government introduced Railway Commando Force for railways or Commandos for Railway Security or CORAS.[7]

IX. Road Systems

35. India's road transport network has burgeoned into an era which is not only widely constructive but also has been modernized as never before. RT in India forms as a link service to railways, shipping and air traffic. Under the Tenth Five Year Plan period, it is estimated that passenger traffic would account for 87% of RT and freight traffic for 65%. Starting from the pugdandis (mud roads) of prehistoric times to the express highways of today the roads form the most cost-effective and popular means of national transport. Though the NH totalling around 259 comprise only 2% of the entire road network, they carry about 40% of the freight and passengers and they are assuming bigger dimensions with modern technological introductions. The biggest reason for the popularity of roads in the country is that where no means of national transport reaches, buses and trucks make their presence felt. RT acts as a feeder service to railways, shipping and air traffic. However, compared to the requirements of the country the roadways are still to be improved. It is the conveyance system which dominates the other systems. The country has a road network of 3.32 million km, consisting of NH, expressways, state highways, major district roads and other district roads and village roads which have the following length distribution: [8]

---

7. Indian Railways Year Book 2019–2020 – Published by Directorate of Statistics and Economics-Ministry of Railways(Railway Board), Government of India, New Delhi.
8. INDIA 2018-Publications Division-Ministry of Information and Broadcasting-Government of India – New Delhi.

National Highways/ Express Ways	1,03,933 km
State Highways	1,61,487 km
Major and Other District Roads	52,07,044 km
Total	54,72,464 km

On the basis of the carriageway width of a highway, the National Highways have been classified as under:

Single Lane/Intermediate Lane	17,752 km (25%)
Double Lane	36,995 km (52%)
Four Lane/Six Lane/Eight Lane	16,187 km (23%)

36. The Department of RT and Highways under the Ministry of Shipping, RT and Highways has been entrusted primarily with the functions of construction and maintenance of National Highways (NH), administration of Motor Vehicles Act and Central Motor Vehicles Rules. The Department also lays policies regarding RT environmental issues and automotive norms, and so on, and it also makes arrangements for movements of vehicular traffic with neighbouring countries. The road systems form the lifeline of passenger and goods movement in India. It has been the Government's effort to expand this infrastructure and to make highways free of Railway crossings by building over bridges and underpasses. To achieve this aim bridges like Dhaula Sadia in the Assam region and state-of-the-art tunnel namely Chenani–Nashriin the State of Jammu and Kashmir and many others are being built to not only shorten the distances in difficult terrains but to speed up the travel time. World Class Expressways are now becoming common. The Ministry of Road Transport can be credited with path-breaking and modernized achievements some of which are as follows:

National Registry of Vehicles and License Records

About twenty crore vehicle records under the plan named VAHAN and ten crore driving licences are being listed under the SARATHI registry scheme. A hundred percent automation of Regional Transport Offices pan India has been achieved under Transport Mission Mode Project.

Road Safety

SETU BHARATAM is the programme which ensures road safety by making highways free of railways level crossings by 2019. The government has approved National Road Safety Policy to minimize road accidents. A general awareness programme regarding road safety is being implemented on a large scale.

e-Tolling

In order to get rid of traffic jams at toll plazas and free movement of vehicles, the Government has also implemented a pan India Electronic Toll Collection based on passive Radio Frequency Identification (RFID) conforming to EPC Gen-2, ISO

18000-6C standards. It is done through the electronic collection of toll through FASTags. The project was launched in 2015.

National Green Highways Project

This project aims at eco-friendly National Highways. To achieve this has been solicited services of farmers, NGOs and the private sector. Thus plantation drive on 1,500 km of national highways is taken at a cost of 300 crore rupees and was launched in 2016 under the Green Highways (Plantation, Transplantation, Beautification and Maintenance) Policy 2016.

37. Thus the quick expansion of the road network is being planned to accommodate future traffic and to provide accessibility to the hinterland. For this, the Government of India has the National Highways Development Project (NHDP) which looks after the RT needs for better energy efficiency, lesser pollution and enhanced road safety and has taken up the largest highways project ever undertaken by the country. The major achievements of the NHDP are that the Golden Quadrilateral of about a total length of 5,864 km connects four metro cities of Delhi, Mumbai, Kolkata and Chennai. The North-South-East-West (NSEW) Corridor comprising a length of 7,142 km connects Srinagar in the North to Kanyakumari in the South including a spur from Salem to Kochi and Silchar in the East to Porbandar in the West, respectively. The NHDP also includes the Port Connectivity Project comprising a length of 380 km for improvement of roads connecting twelve major ports in the country and Other Projects involving a length of 962 km. India is a signatory to the proposed Global Transport Corridor Project. The agreement has two important projects:

A. The Project proposes to cover an area of 140,000 km-long highway. Pakistan, China, Iran, Indonesia, Japan, Mongolia, Kazakhstan, South Korea, Turkey and Vietnam are also its signatories.
B. North-South Transport Corridor (NSTC)– an intergovernmental agreement on North–South Transport was signed for ten years by India. Russian Federation and Iran will regulate international transport and transit of goods and passengers from the Western port of Mumbai to Russia through Chahbahar and the Caspian Sea.

38. The Acts/Rules envisaging the policy relating to motor vehicles and State Road Transport Corporations (SRTCs) are as follows:

National Acts:

- The National Highways Act 1956.
- The National Highways Fee (Determination of Rates and collection) Rules 2008 as amended 2017.
- The Central Road Fund Act 2000 as amended by the Finance at 2016 (28 of 2016).
- The Central Road Funds (State Roads) Rules 2014 as amended by (Amendment) Rules 2017.

- The Control of National Highways (Land and Traffic) Act 2002 (13 of 2003) as amended by the Finance Act 2017 (7 of 2017).
- Motor Vehicles Act 1988.
- Central Motor Vehicles Rules 1989.
- RT Corporations Act 1950.
- Carriers Act 1865 (Repealed, 2007).
- The Carriage by Road Act 2007 (41 of 2007).
- The Carriage by Road Rules 2011.

The Motor Vehicles Act 1988 is undergoing major changes for which a Bill has been introduced in the Indian Parliament to amend the said Act. The Bill has been passed by the Lok Sabha (the Lower House) of the Parliament in April 2017 and is now pending in the Rajya Sabha (Upper House). The ultimate aim of the Bill is to enhance road safety in the country. To achieve this aim the Bill proposes to establish a Vehicle Accident Fund and also provides for cashless treatment of the road accident victims. There is a provision for the Golden Hour Scheme for immediate treatment of such victims without wasting valuable time in legal formalities. It also provides for a National Road Safety Board.

X. Airport Numbers

39. India has a well-established civil aviation system to serve both international and domestic traffic which is third in passenger movement and fourth in freight movement in comparison to other means of transport in India. The Ministry of Civil Aviation is responsible for national policies, management and control of the civil aviation industry in the country. It is also responsible for the administration of the Civil Aviation Act 1934, Aircraft Rules 1937 and other related legislations, apart from the implementation of various governmental policies and monitoring of civil aviation activities. A new Integrated Civil Aviation Policy was notified in 2016 which aims at creating an ecosystem, takes initiatives for the growth of the civil aviation sector including expansion of tourism. A Regional Connectivity Scheme – UDAN – was envisaged in National Civil Aviation Policy in 2016 which aimed at taking the flying facilities to the masses and for upgrading unserved and under-served airports and airstrips in the country.

The Airports Authority of India (AAI) came into being in April 1995. New additions of flights and domestic aerodromes are made regularly. The air transport sector can be termed as the fastest-growing sector of transport in India.

Passenger traffic, both international and domestic grows annually at the rate of 15.6% which is well above the world growth rate of 5%. It is expected to continue to grow up to 2025 at 7.7% against 4.5% of the world growth rate. To affirm India's commitment to future developments, steps are taken towards the development of technology in this field. The GPS Aided Geo Augmentation Navigation (GAGAN) system in the country is an augmentation system to enhance the accuracy and integrity of GPS signals to meet precision approach requirements in civil aviation. It is operational since May 2015 and is available on a 24×7 basis. Growth of the airport sector is important for overall transport growth hence there has been a continuous rise in this means of transport and airports in the country including the international and domestic airports out of which 125(2017) are managed by the AAI.

40. The number of various categories of Airports in the country are as follows: (2021)[9]

125 Airports maintained by AAI (96 operational and 29 non-operational)

- Twenty-one International airports(three Civil Enclaves).
- Eight Custom Airports(four Civil enclaves).
- Seventy-seven Domestic Airports
- Nineteen Domestic Civil Enclaves

AAI has completed the upgradation and modernization of sixty airports including two metro airports at Kolkata and Chennai creating an additional capacity of 102 million passengers per annum (MPPA). The present capacity of Indian airports is 282 MPPA (2018). The AAI also provides communication, navigation and surveillance infrastructure and Air Tariff Management at ten airports not managed by it. These are Delhi, Mumbai, Bangalore, Hyderabad, Cochin, and domestic ones being Lengpui, Diu, Puttaparthi, Jamshedpur, Vidyanagar airports (Annual Report, 2008, Ministry of Civil Aviation).

The Ministry of Civil Aviation has divided civil aviation routes which consist of:

(a) Category I – Metros.
(b) Category II – North-eastern Region, Jammu & Kashmir, Andaman & Nicobar and Lakshadweep.
(c) Category III – Routes not covered by Category I & II.

A. International

41. There are more than thirty (2018) international airports in India the major ones being Indira Gandhi International Airport, Delhi; Dumdum Airport, Kolkata; Santacruz Airport, Mumbai; Meenambakkam Airport, Chennai; Thiruvananthapuram Airport, Kerala; Begumpet Airport, Hyderabad; Cochin International Airport, Kochi; HAL Airport, Bangalore. At present, fifty-seven international flights are operated on different routes.

---

9. INDIA 2021 – Publications Division. Ministry of Information and Broadcasting – Government of India – New Delhi.

B. Domestic

42. The domestic airline network in the country is also expanding and both government and private operators are providing domestic services. Apart from Air India, Indian Airlines, Alliance Air and Air India Charters Ltd., there are at present seven private scheduled operators, viz. Jet Airways (India) Ltd., Jetlite Airlines, Go Airlines (India) Pvt. Ltd., Spicejet Ltd., Paramount Airways Pvt. Ltd. and Inter Globe Aviation Ltd. (IndiGo). These airlines operate in the domestic sector providing a wide choice of flights and connectivity to various parts of the country. Competition among these private companies, however, enhances the quality of services and facilities to the passengers. The market share of these companies stands as follows as of April 2018:[10]

Domestic Airlines	*Market Share (%)*
Air India	13.3
Jet Airways & Jet Lite	16.2
IndiGo	39.8
Spice Jet	12.4
Go Air	8.8
Others	9.5

Apart from these a new category of Scheduled airlines, a scheduled Air Transport (Regional) service has been introduced to enhance connectivity to smaller cities.

There are also three cargo airlines viz., Blue Aviation Private Limited, Deccan Cargo and Express Logistics (Pvt.) Ltd., operating scheduled cargo services in the country.

XI. Pipelines

43. Energy plays a pivotal role in the sustainability and economic growth of a country. India being both a massive and fastest-growing economy requires a large amount of energy. However the energy resources of India are not in proportion to its population needs yet it supports 17% of the world population and has only 0.3% of oil, 0.8% of natural gas and 6.8% of the world's oil, gas and coal reserves respectively. Thus India strives to increase its energy supply by exploiting all possible sources of conventional and non-conventional energy. In India like many other industries, natural gas (NG) has not only gained importance but is on constant move particularly in the last decade so much so that it is being termed as the fuel of the twenty-first century. The transportation of this highly inflammable and volatile gas through pipelines is an environment-friendly and cost-effective means.

10. Director General of Civil Aviation(DGCA).

44. Natural Gas Pipeline Networks in India is continuously expanding and as of 1 April 2018, there are reported presently three major pipeline entities engaged in natural gas transportation across India namely GAIL, RGTIL/RGPL and GSPL. GAIL is operating about 11,410 km of trunk pipelines in India comprising 68% of the pan India pipeline network. This includes HVJ, DVPL, DUPL/DPPL, Dadri–Bawana–Nangal and Dabhol–Bengaluru trunk pipelines to evacuate domestic gas as well as imported RLNG. In addition, GAIL also operates regional gas pipeline networks in Maharashtra, K. G. Basin, Cauvery Basin and Gujarat. RGTIL and RGPL are operating 1,784 km of pipelines (about 11% of pan India network), namely the East-West Pipeline (EWPL) to evacuate gas from the KG-D6 field in Andhra Pradesh and the Shadol–Phulpur Pipeline respectively. GSPL is mainly focused in the state of Gujarat consisting of about 2,618 km gas pipelines (about 16% of total).

45. Production of NG in India was negligible at the time of independence (1947) but is at present at the level of around 87 million standard m^3 per day (MMSCMD). Its transportation and distribution take place through pipelines which are operated by GAIL, Hindustan Petroleum (HP) and Oil India Ltd. India is new to the NG market as compared to the NG-based economies like Japan, Korea and the United States. The country is expected to rival Japan and China in having the largest NG demand in Asia by 2025. Most of the gas pipeline infrastructure is concentrated in the Western-Northern part of India. In the VIth Asia Gas Partnership Summit, the Government assured that soon in tandem with the increasing supplies the network will be taken to all parts of India. India leads globally with a planned and announced pipeline length of 29,612 km from 2021–2025.[11]

46. The main producers of NG are ONGC, Oil India Ltd., and JVs of Tapti, Panna–Mukta and Ravva. The government under the New Exploration Licensing Policy (NELP) has offered blocks to private and public companies.

47. To develop the NG availability in the country, the Petroleum and Natural Gas Ministry has launched a programme for exploring coal bed methane (CBM). The CBM policy plans to put in place an internationally competitive fiscal and contractual regime to promote this new source of energy. There are several gas pipeline projects launched by the government. The operational output of pipelines was recorded at 65.01 million metric tonnes during 2009–2010 and the offshore terminals of Indian Oil at Vadinar, Mundra and Paradip have handled 218 tankers including 128 Very Large Crude Carriers (VLCCs) during the year. The Euro-IV grade high-quality fuel was first transported to the National Capital Region of Delhi in January 2010 and thereafter, it is being transported through the pipelines to all the metros.

48. The Iran–Pakistan–India (IPI) project was originally conceived in 1989 which involves laying in a 2,500 km pipeline between India and Iran via Pakistan.

---

11. Global Data's latest report, 'Global Length and Capital Expenditure Outlook for Oil and Gas Pipelines, 2021–2025 – India and the US Lead Global Pipelines Growth' 7 May, 2021. https://www.offshore-technology.com/comment/india-leads-global-upcoming-pipeline/.

Iran–Pakistan working group was formed in 2003 and Indi joined the group in 2005. Iran–Pakistan (IP) pipeline project was aimed at constructing a 1,724 miles (2775 km) pipeline from Iran's South Pars fields in the Persian Gulf to Pakistan's major cities of Karachi and Multan and then further to Delhi, India. India had withdrawn from the project in 2009 over pricing issues though subsequently in March 2010, India called on Pakistan and Iran to hold talks regarding it in Tehran in May 2010. The IPI pipeline also known as the peace pipeline has geopolitical significance for the three partner countries. However, the IPI pipeline has many hurdles like pricing, trade and transit issues, security situation in Baluchistan, sovereignty issues, etc. On 21 July 2014, the Ministry of Petroleum & Natural Gas Pipeline tried to solve these issues in which the proposal was to supply 60MMSCMD in Phase I to be shared equally between India and Pakistan. In Phase II, 90MMSCMD of gas supply is proposed. However, the issue of pricing and international seat of arbitration, etc., is yet to be resolved.[12] However, the Construction work of the Iran-Pakistan pipeline is proposed to be completed by 2017.[13]

49. The Turkmenistan–Afghanistan–Pakistan–India (TAPI Gas Pipeline)– It is a natural gas pipeline being developed by Asian Development Bank. It was originally expected to start in 2012 and come on stream in 2016. It proposed to construct a 1,680 km pipeline with a total gas capacity of 90MMSCMD. Under the scheme, 38 MMSCMD would go to Pakistan and India each while 14MMSCMD would go to Afghanistan. The construction work began in Turkmenistan on 13 December 2015 and was expected to be operational by 2019 but it is facing many hurdles. The Afghan section of the pipeline was reportedly under construction in 2018 and the construction of the Pakistan section was supposed to start in 2019.[14] Recently (April 2021), India discussed security measures for pipeline builders with Afghanistan and it is for such hurdles that the project is still unexecuted. The issues are expected to be resolved and the project to restart in 2021. The project has great importance for India as it will allow gas reserves for India to run its power plants, a share of about 15-25% of natural gas would mean large investments in the manufacturing sector in Gujarat, Rajasthan and Punjab regions. India will be getting gas at competitive prices and the entry of Turkmenistan as an energy exporter in South Asia would be greatly beneficial for Indian markets. The project is passing through many hurdles.

50. Energy Security for India – South Asia Gas Enterprise (SAGE) has undertaken a path-breaking project to build the Deepest Underwater Transnational Gas Pipeline also known as the Middle East to India Deepwater Pipeline (MEIDP). Qatar, Iran, Iraq and Turkmenistan have joint gas reserves to the tune of 2,000 cubic feet. For supply to India, a distance of 1,300 km will be covered and the gas be supplied through the Arabian Sea underwater to the coast of Gujarat and Maharashtra.

---

12. Press Information Bureau, Government of India-Ministry of Petroleum & Natural Gas. 21 Jul. 2014.
13. Pakistan on Wednesday said the construction of Iran–Pakistan gas pipeline was currently in progress and would be completed by the end of 2016 or early 2017, but the first shipment of liquefied natural gas (LNG) expected by 31 Mar. this year would be provided to the transport sector. Published in Dawn Daily, 29 Jan. 2015.
14. Pakistan–Turkmenistan to discuss TAPI gas pipeline groundbreaking in August, Business Recorder, 8 Jul. 2019.

Known as the Energy Corridor it has the advantage of bypassing Pakistan and it is even secure and shorter in distance. The Gas pipeline is designed to transport up to 1.1 BSCFD gas into the Indian energy market over the next twenty years. Undersea pipelines can bring cheaper gas to India.[15]

51. Tri-Nation Pipeline: There has been two-decade-old planning to rope the three countries, India, Bangladesh and Myanmar into the arrangement of a pipeline for the supply of natural gas. First mooted in 2005, there was an agreement to source natural gas from Myanmar via Bangladesh to India. It was meant to deliver 5 billion cubic metres of gas from the Swe field in Myanmar covering a distance of 900 km. However, due to political considerations, the plan could not be materialized. On 13 September 2017, Bharat Petroleum (BPCL) revived talks with the Bangladesh Government to set up around a million-tonne product pipeline to the country and also planned to set up another pipeline with Myanmar.

XII. Important Data Relating to Transport Activity

52. There has been enormous effort and activity by the Government of India to improve transport in the country. Special focus is made on the construction of roads and in increasing their efficiency. The Highlights of the Build, Operate and Transfer (BOT) projects are as under. Under the BOT model, till early 2016, big projects were taken up by those who could invest in large amounts.

53. Now the National Highways Authority of India (NHAI) and the Ministry of Road Transport and Highways have rolled out smaller projects and have changed the chief bidding models from BOT to the less capital-intensive EPC (engineering, procurement and construction). In the financial year 2014 (FY14), the mid-sized project was 15% of all the contracts while in FY18, the figure went up to 40%. Besides giving smaller projects to the small developers in 2016, the Government introduced the hybrid annuity model (HAM) where the developer gets 40% of the project cost in five instalments linked to the project's progress. The rest is borne by the developer but can be recovered from NHAI as an annuity.

54. In the Budget 2018–2019, the transport field got a big boost. The Government of India gave priority to rail and road sectors with an all-time high allocation in the Union Budget 2018–2019. It aims to increase infrastructure projects which could support the economy and with an aim to connect and integrate the nation with a network of roads, airports, railways, ports and inland waterways. The main investment fields are; Smart roads (115 projects to be implemented in 60 cities) and a capital investment of INR 1.48 trillion (USD 23.5 billion) to the railway sector among many other. There is an investment towards track improvement, towards rolling stock (12,000 wagons, 5,160 coaches and 700 locomotives)). There is also Government's plan to construct Rapid Regional Transit System (RRTS). Suburban

15. Updated – 6 Sep. 2017.

Railway is a passenger rail transport service to carry loads of city passengers, vendors, etc. The Government also unveiled the Metro Rail Policy 2017 to boost investment in the Urban Rail sector. Also, a subsidy of INR 2.60 billion (USD 42 million) has been allocated towards Faster Adoption and Manufacturing of Electric (& Hybrid) Vehicles (FAME Scheme) in 2018–2019 (source: International Union of Public Transport (UITP India).

XIII. Ministry or Department Responsible for Transportation Policy

55. In India, as the varied means of transport are governed under different ministries hence policy regarding each is laid down and implemented by the respective ministries.

56. R*ailways* – The route length of the railways by March 2020 was 67,956 km (42,226 mi) as of 31 March 2020. Out of these, Broad Gauge is 63,950 km. Meter Gauge 2,402 km and Narrow Gauge is at 1,809 km. The Railways are exclusively managed by a separate ministry, the Ministry of Railways and the Railway Board which comes under it. It is the principal mode of transportation and can be termed as the popular mode of travel for the masses. It is the best option to explore the country as it is spread over Great Indian Plains, the Thar Desert, the Deccan Plateau, the coastal plains and the Northern states. It serves as the true kaleidoscope to have a look into the real India.

57. Roadways– The Ministry of Road Transport and Highways is the nodal authority in respect of maintenance and construction of Highways and for implementation of various Acts related to it, formulation of broad policies relating to road transport, environmental issues, automotive norms and safety matters. The Ministry works through various arms like the National Highways Authority of India (NHAI), National Highways & Infrastructure Development Corporation Ltd. (NHIDCL). For the north-east region, there is a Special Accelerated Road Development Programme for the North-east Region (SARDP_NE) which takes care of the improvement of road connectivity in remote areas.

*58. Civil Aviation–*The Ministry of Civil Aviation is the main authority in the area of civil aviation in the country which not only formulates policies regarding national policies for regulation and maintenance of air travel in the country but it also implements various legislations connected with it. It also provides guidance to the organization in implementing the policies and guidelines and also evaluates their activities and provides for their interface with the Parliament. The Ministry of Civil aviation has come up with several national policies like National Civil Policy 2016 which aims at creating an ecosystem to accelerate civil aviation, promote tourism, increase employment and lead to balanced regional growth. It also aims at taking flying to the masses by providing cheaper, affordable and convenient procedures for air travel. This is done with the help of the Regional Connectivity Scheme. Another initiative of the Ministry taken in 2016 is *Air Sewa* to provide travellers with a hassle-free and convenient air travel experience. The Director General of Civil Aviation (DGCA) and Bureau of Civil Aviation are the various wings of the Ministry to regulate air transport services in the country and also to take care of safety measures.

59. Shipping– The Department of Shipping – Ministry of Shipping, RT and Highways of the Government of India undertakes the job of formulation of policies and maintenance and regulation of transport in the country, apart from making arrangements of movement of vehicular traffic with the adjoining countries.

60. The National Shipping Board established in 1959 is a permanent body which undertakes to advise the Government of India on matters related to shipping including development thereof. The Directorate General of Shipping (DGS) was an attached office of the Ministry of Shipping RT and Highways and was established in 1949 which administered all matters relating to shipping policy and legislation, implementation of various international conventions, promotion of maritime education and training; examination and certification. However, as Maritime Transport is a critical infrastructure for the economic development of a country, a comprehensive policy package is necessary to address the diverse issues facing it. Thus, the Ministry of shipping was separately formed as an independent Ministry in 2009. It is no longer combined with the RT and Highways. The vision of the Ministry of shipping is to ensure vibrant, efficient, viable and safe ports and shipping services. The Ministry encompasses within its fold shipping and port sectors which also include shipbuilding, ship repair, major ports and IWT. India joined the 1998 Agreement of WP-29 (World Forum for harmonization of vehicles regulations) on 21 April 2006. This has given a boost to the international practices regarding environment-friendly, road safety and fuel efficiency in India and has helped the country to follow global norms in these fields.

61. A Bill to repeal Carriers Act 1865 and to enact new Carriage by Road law which pressed the need for redefining the common carrier, regulation of common carriers by state and provision of a transparent framework of rights and liabilities to govern the transactions between the common carriers and the customers were introduced in the Rajya Sabha (Upper House of the Parliament) on 7 December 2005 with the object of having an exclusive law for the RT. The Standing Committee on Transport, Tourism and Culture submitted its report regarding the said Bill on 21 March 2006. On the basis of the recommendations made by the Standing Committee, a revised Bill namely, Carriage by Road Bill 2006 was finalized in consultation with the Ministry of Law. Thereafter the Government set up another Committee under the chairmanship of the Director, Association of State Road Transport Undertakings (ASTRU) comprising members from Central Institute of Road Transport (CIRT), erstwhile Ministry of Surface Transport, representatives of All-India Motor Transport Congress (AIMTC) which made recommendations for the repeal of the archaic Carriers Act 1865 and re-enactment of the road law. After a big deal of negotiations and parleys the long-awaited Carriage by Road Act 2007 (41 of 2007) has been passed (29 September 2007) thereby also repealing the Carriers Act 1865 which was considered obsolete in the present modern communication scenario.

Part I. Introduction

Chapter 1. Definitions and Notions

§1. Limitations of the Subject Matter

I. Maritime Law and Transport Law

A. Maritime Law

62. Maritime law in India dates back to the middle of the nineteenth century when need-based legislation was made and thus sporadic legislative activity in this field led to a bundle of laws thereby making their application very difficult. Thus, today in India, the law relating to admiralty, shipping, carriage by sea and maritime matters is in most deplorable, degrading and chaotic condition.

63. Article 372 of the Constitution of India permits the continuance of pre-constitutional laws unless repealed by active legislation. During the British period, often the English Acts were directly adopted making their application difficult in Indian situations. Bombay Coasting Vessels Act of 1838 was the first law on maritime shipping and attempts were made in 1867, 1882, 1893 and 1896 to revise these laws but no positive result was achieved. Limited legislative power of the Indian legislature at that time and the condition that an Indian law had to be in harmony with the UK law was responsible for such legal uncertainty.

64. After India gained independence on 15 August 1947 another law namely the Merchant Shipping (MS) Laws (Extension to Acceding States and Amendment) Act 1949 was passed. The MS Act 1923 repealed some thirty Acts, was amended from time to time and was replaced by the MS Act 1958 (hereinafter called the 'MS Act') by the Indian Parliament. The 1958 Act, however, has since been amended several times: in 1966, 1970, 1976, 1978, 1979, 1981, 1983, 1984 1987, 1988, 1993, 1998 and in 2002. In 1966, the Act was amended to subsume the recommendations of the International Convention for the Safety of Life at Sea 1960; in 1970, the Act was amended to give effect to the International Convention for the Prevention of Pollution of the Sea by Oil 1954 (as amended 1962), the International Convention on Limitation of Liability of Owners of Sea-going Ships 1957 and the International Convention on Load Lines 1966. The 1976 amendment in the 1958 Act was made to subsume the provisions of two international instruments; The Special Trade Passenger Ships Agreement 1971 and the Protocol and Space Requirements for Special

Trade Passenger Ships 1973. The 1978 amendment makes considerable changes in the 1958 Act concerning the Shipping Development Fund, its constitution, amount of loans, and so on. The 1979 amendment is concerned with the training of the Merchant Navy personnel. The 1981 amendment is concerned with the change in the law of acquisition of ship; the 1983 amendment is related to pollution of the sea by oil; the 1984 amendment was made with a view to include the recommendations of the National Shipping Board and to adopt the provisions of the Prevention of Accidents (Seafarers) Convention 1970; the 1986 amendment was done with the object of adopting the International Convention in the Standards of Training, Certification and Watch keeping for Seafarers which was adopted in 1978 and came into force on 18 April 1984. The amendment made in 1987 was done with the aim of amending Part VI of the 1958 Act.

65. The 1988 amendment amended Part XB of the 1958 Act. The 1993 amendment was made in order to simplify the loans. Lastly, in 2002, the amendment was considerable which was done with the aim of including the Civil Liability Convention (CLC) provisions and the Fund Convention 1992 recommendations. However, these amendments were made either to give effect to the international instruments or to include the experiences gained from the implementation of the 1958 Act.

66. As India was without a comprehensive law on the subject of maritime shipping for more than a century hence the 1958 Act being a new one is not a time-tested law and there is ample scope for its development. Law Commission of India in its 151st Report submitted in 1994 made scathing remarks on the admiralty jurisdiction of courts and on the plight of maritime law in the country pressing the urgent need to refurbish law on this subject. One drawback of the MS Act is that it does not deal with the admiralty jurisdiction. A good number of international agreements, protocols and conventions to which India is a party or signatory or assenting state are yet to be compiled and consolidated.

B. Transport Law

67. Though having multiple means of transport in the country, this area of law needs to be developed. It encompasses sea, road, rail, air, inland waterways and a number of traditional means of transportation like the tonga, rickshaw, bullock cart, camel cart which are the only means on the muddy road, exist in good number even today in rural India. In each sphere of conveyance, transportation is dealt with by the special law of that area and there is no exclusive law regarding transportation in India.

II. Law of the Sea

68. Oceans are friends of man since times immemorial. Obviously, the claim of all the coastal countries of the world over the boundless oceans covering three-fourth of the globe has been made evident oft and on. Hugo Grotius was one such great writer (Mare Liberum, 1609) who first emphasized the freedom of the Sea and its universal character. Sea trade and navigation are the oldest source of commercial activities and have attracted all the human beings on earth irrespective of their race or origin. The United Nations thus organized Law of the Sea Conferences several times (UNCLOS I-1958, UNCLOSII-1960, UNCLOSIII-1982) for shaping a suitable policy for unifying various interests and coming out with a solution which should be acceptable to all the nations of the world. India is one such country which has a major area of its land surrounded by water and as Hindu scriptures show that for about thirty centuries India has been regarded as a place of commercial activities which are mainly sea trade with nations like Phoenicians, Jews, Assyrians, Greeks, Egyptians and Romans in ancient period besides maritime trade with Portuguese, Dutch and English, and so on, in modern times. Legally speaking some jurists regard the high seas as *res nullius* while others regard it as *res communis*. The Indian law on the subject of the Law of the Sea developed in stages though in the beginning there was no explicit provision governing it. The Constitution of India refers to the territorial waters (TW) at two places: Article 297 and entry 57 in List I of the Seventh Schedule. Article 297 substituted by the Constitution (Fourteenth Amendment) Act 1976 (w. E. F. 27 May 1976) titled 'Things of value within territorial waters or continental shelf and resources of the Exclusive Economic Zone (EEZ) to vest in the Union' vests all lands, minerals and other things of value underlying the ocean within the TW, or the continental shelf, or the EEZ of India in the Union and is declared to be held for the purposes of the Union. It also declares to vest in the Union all other resources of the EEZ of India. List I which envisages the subjects on which the Parliament can legislate includes within the list at entry 57, 'fishing and fisheries beyond territorial waters'.

69. Though the constitution is silent on the exact limit of TW of India, Article 73 of the Constitution extends the executive the President of India to matters with respect to which Parliament has the power to legislate. Thus the President of India, by virtue of Article 73 issued a Proclamation on 22 March 1956 declaring that the '– the territorial waters of India extend into the sea to a distance of six nautical miles measured from the appropriate base-line, a declaration which implicitly recognized that until the issue of the said Proclamation, India had a three mile maritime belt' (Vide, PC Rao; The Law of Maritime Zone, 1983 Ed., 63–64).

70. However, another Proclamation in super session of the earlier one was passed by the President of India on 30 September 1967 in which the extent of the TW of India was declared to be twelve nautical miles. Later the parliament passed the Maritime Zones Act 1976 which further clarified the Indian position regarding its TW. Section 3 of the Act reaffirms the extent of TW to a distance of twelve nautical miles yet it also enables the Central Government to alter the limit, by notification in the official gazette having regard to the international law and state practice.

71. Thus section 3 gives due recognition to the principles of international law. In India, the TW, Continental Shelf, EEZ and other Maritime Zones Act 1976 provides for the use of its TW by foreign ships. Article 4 of the Act provides that all foreign ships (other than warships including submarines and other underwater vehicles) shall have the right of innocent passage through the TW.

Chapter 2. Main Sources of Transport Law

§1. Maritime Law

I. Treaties and National Legislation

A. Treaties

72. The first Indian MS Act was enacted in 1923 which was in line with the UK MS Act 1894. After India gained independence on 15 August 1947, a comprehensive maritime law called the MS Act 1958 was passed. India has ratified the International Convention but has not statutorily enacted it. Goods transported by sea are governed by the Carriage of Goods by Sea Act 1925 and the (Indian) Bills of lading Act 1856. Apart from this, the Marine Insurance Act is also applicable. Important changes were made in maritime law in 2002. Amendments in 2002 to MS Act 1958 helps India's accession to the International Convention on Limitation of Liability for Maritime Claims (LLMC). Hitherto the Indian shipping industry was subjected to unlimited claims entailing high insurance costs. India was following the 1957 Convention on LLMC where the system of computing claims was based on the French Formula in terms of gold. In view of the increasing perils at Sea and the growing insecurity in the context of terrorism and piracy and other crimes committed on the high seas, India decided to legislate on the long-awaited subject of maritime security. To bring India in line with the International Code for the Security of Ships and Port Facility (ISPS Code) the MS (Amendment) Act 2007 (40 of 2007) was passed by the Parliament. The Act also makes relevant amendments to the Indian Ports Act 1908 (15 of 1908).

73. The Merchant Shipping Act 1958 looks forward to a total replacement by the Merchant Shipping Bill 2016. It was introduced in the Lower House of the Parliament on 16 December 2016. The Bill seeks to bring reforms in the shipping sector and has as its aim to promote ease of doing business and to develop Indian Coastal shipping. It proposes to repeal the archaic Coastal Vessels Act 1838. However, the Bill is still pending. The Merchant Shipping Act 1958 has been amended by the Finance Act 2016(28 of 2016).

74. In March 2011, India acceded to the protocol of 1996 which amends the Convention on Limitation of Liability for Maritime Claims, 1976 and which prescribes a higher limit.

75. The LLMC 1976 lays down the limits for claiming compensation in terms of Special Drawing Rights (SDRs), as determined by the International Monetary Fund (IMF). One of the Acts passed is Suppression of Unlawful Acts against Safety of Maritime Navigation and Fixed Platforms (In Continental shelf of India) 2002 which deals with acts of terrorism in India's TW. It is based on the International Maritime Organization (IMO) convention on suppression of Unlawful acts Against

Safety of Maritime Navigation 1988 and the IMO Protocol for the Suppression of Unlawful Acts against Safety of Fixed Platforms located on the Continental Shelf 1988.

76. The Law Commission in its 151st Report tabled in the Indian Parliament in August 1995 recommended for enacting a new Admiralty Act of India. Thus, the proposed 'Admiralty Bill 2005' includes all such recommendations. The object of the proposed Bill is to consolidate and amend the law relating to Admiralty jurisdiction of Courts, legal proceedings in connection with ships, their arrest, detention and sale and related matters. It also proposes to enlarge the scope of the legislation to cover claims pertaining to pollution damages, loss of life, personal injury, towage of ships, pilotage of ships, port dues, disbursement made by the shipowners and agents of ships.

77. The bill, *inter alia,* also proposes the vesting of civil jurisdiction in respect of various types of claims pertaining to the shipping industries in High Courts, power of the Supreme Court to transfer cases from one High Court to another and power of the High Court to confer admiralty jurisdiction in consultation with the Chief Justice of India on any principal civil court of the state. The Bill also proposes admiralty jurisdiction and the mode of exercising it, condition in respect of claims in an action in rem, jurisdiction in personam, restriction on the entertainment of actions in cases pertaining to action in personam in the collision of ships. The Proposed Bill apart from the above matters contains a number of proposals regarding vesting of rights on sale of ships, maritime lien and matters connected thereto other than taking into account the needs of the maritime industry and the application of the Code of Civil Procedure 1908 (5 of 1908).

78. The Government of India has come up with a Sagarmala Programme under whichsome 577 Projects have been identified which aim at port modernization, port development, port connectivity enhancement, port-linked industrialization and coastal community development. The Programme spreads over a period of 2015–2035. As of 31 March 2018, 492 Projects were under various stages of implementation, development and completion.

79. List of IMO Instruments ratified by India.

1. Conventions

80.

- Hong Kong International Convention for the Safe and Environmentally Sound Recycling of Ships, 2009.
- International Convention for the Safety of Life at Sea 1974 as amended (SOLAS amended 1974).
- Convention on the International Regulations for Preventing Collisions at Sea, 1972 as amended (COLREG amended 1972).

- International Convention for the Prevention of Pollution from Ships 1973 as modified by the Protocol of 1978 relating thereto (MARPOL (amended) 73/78) (Annex I, II, III, IV & V).
- Convention on Facilitation of International Maritime Traffic (FAL) 1965 as amended (FAL (amended) 1965).
- International Convention of Load Line 1966 (LL 1966).
- International Convention on Tonnage Measurement of Ships 1969 (TONNAGE 1969).
- International Convention Relating to Intervention on the High Seas in Cases of Oil Pollution Casualties 1969 (INTERVENTION 1969).
- International Convention on Civil Liability for Oil Pollution Damage 1969 (CLC 1969) (Denounced).
- International Convention on the Establishment of an International Fund for Compensation of Oil Pollution Damage 1971 (FUND 1971) (Denounced).
- International Convention for Safe Containers (CSC), 1971 as amended (CSC (amended) 1972).
- Convention on the International Mobile Satellite Organization (INMARSAT) as amended (INMARSAT C (amended)).
- Convention of Limitation of Liability for Maritime Claims 1976 (LLMC 1976).
- International Convention on Standards of Training, Certification and Watch Keeping for Seafarers 1978 (STCW 1978).
- International Convention on Maritime Search and Rescue 1979 (SAR 1979).
- Convention for the Suppression of Unlawful Acts against the Safety of Maritime navigation 1988 (SUA 1988).
- International Convention on Oil Pollution Preparedness, Response and Cooperation 1990 (OPRC 1990).
- Fund Convention 1992.
- IMO Convention.

2. Protocols

81.

- Protocol of 1978 relating to the International Convention for the Safety of Life at Sea 1974 as amended (SOLAS PROT (amended) 1978).
- Protocol to the International Convention on Civil Liability for Oil Pollution Damage 1969 (CLC PROT 1976) (Denounced).
- Protocol on Space Requirement for Special Trade Passenger Ships 1972 (SPACE STP 1973).
- Protocol to the International Convention on the Establishment of an International Fund for Compensation for Oil Pollution Damage 1971 (FUND PROT 1976) (Denounced).
- Protocol for Suppression of Unlawful Acts against the Safety of Maritime Navigation (SUA PROT 1988).
- Protocol of 1992 to amend the International Convention on Civil Liability for Oil Pollution Damage 1969 (CLC PROT 1992).

- Protocol of 1992 to amend the International Convention on the Establishment of an International Fund for compensation of Oil Pollution Damage 1971 (FUND PROT 1992).
- Protocol of 1988 relating to the International Convention for the Safety of Life at Sea 1974 (SOLAS PROT (HSSC) 1988).
- Protocol of 1988 relating to the International Convention on Load Lines 1966 (LL PROT (HSSC) 1988).
- The Protocol on FUND PROT 2000 has been ratified by tacit approval.
- The Protocol of 1996 was ratified by India in 2011.

a. Agreement Ratified

82. Special Trade Passenger Ships Agreement 1971 (STP 1971)

b. Operating Agreement Ratified

83. Operating Agreement on the International Mobile Satellite Organization (INMARSAT), as amended (INMARSAT OA (amended)).

3. Memorandum of Understanding[16]

84.

A. Memorandum of Understanding For Cooperation in Inland, Coastal and Maritime Technology was signed between India and Germany on 1 November 2019.
B. Joint Declaration of Intent regarding the cooperation in the field of prevention of marine litter was made between India and Germany on 1 November 2019.
C. Agreement between India and Sweden on Recognition of Seafarer Certificates pursuant to Regulation I/10 of the International Convention on Standards of Training, Certification and Watch was signed between the two countries on 2 December 2019.
D. MoU for the Establishment of Passenger and Cargo Services by Sea between Ministry of Shipping, Government of India and Ministry of Transport and Civil Aviation and Government of Maldives on June 8, 2019.
E. A MoU between India and Maldives signed on 8 June 2019 shall pave the way for ferry and cargo services between Maldives and Kerala.
F. A Memorandum of Understanding (MoU) between the Government of the Republic of India and the Government of the United Arab Emirates on Institutional Cooperation on Maritime Transport was signed on 25 January 2017.
G. A Memorandum of Understanding between Federal Transport Authority-Land and Maritime in the United Arab Emirates and the Director General of Shipping

16. Ministry of Shipping 2017 – Year of Consolidation-Posted on 20 Dec. 2017 by PIB Delhi.

in the Republic of India on the Mutual Recognition of certificates of competency as per the provisions of the Standards of Training, Certification and Watchkeeping (STCW, 78) and amendments thereof was signed on 25 January 2017.

H. An Agreement on Merchant Shipping between the Government of the Republic of India and the Government of the Republic of Cyprus was signed on 28 April 2017.

I. A Memorandum of Understanding between India and Netherlands for bilateral cooperation in the fields of ports, maritime transport and logistics which was originally signed on 12 February 2008 and subsequently renewed on 10 May 2011 and 11 May 2014 was further extended on 11 October 2017 for a period of three years, till 10 October 2020 as per the renewal clause mentioned in the said MoU.

J. A Memorandum of Understanding signed between India and Austria on 3 October 2012 on Technology Cooperation in the Shipping and Ports infrastructure sector was valid for a period of five years till 2 October 2017 and was further renewed for another period of five years beginning from 3 October 2017 as per the renewal clause mentioned in the said MoU.

B. National Legislation

1. Constitutional Provisions

85. India being a federal state recognizes the scheme of distribution of powers between the Union and the states under three heads of legislative, administrative and financial distribution. The Constitution spells out the nature of relations between the Union and the states meticulously (Part XI Chapters 1 & 2 and Part XII Chapter 1). There are three lists: (Union List – 97 Items; State List 66 Items; Concurrent List – 47 Items) which subsume the various items on which the Union, the states or both of these can legislate and are given in full detail in Schedule VII of the Constitution of India.

86. The following Items are given in the Union List on which only the Indian Parliament can legislate to the exclusion of state legislatures:

(1) Shipping and navigation on inland waterways declared by Parliament by law to be NWs; as regards mechanically propelled vessels; the rule of the road on such waterways (Item No. 24).
(2) Maritime shipping and navigation; provisions of education and training for the mercantile marine (Item No. 25).
(3) Lighthouses including lightships, beacons and other provisions for the safety of shipping and aircraft (Item No. 26).
(4) Ports declared or under law made by Parliament or existing law to be a major port, including their destination and the constitution and powers of port authorities therein (Item No. 27).
(5) Port quarantine, including hospitals (Item No. 28).

(6) Carriage of passengers and goods by NWs in mechanically propelled vessels (Item No. 30).
(7) Regulation and development of interstate rivers and river valleys to the extent of public interest (Item No. 56).
(8) Fishing and fisheries beyond TW (Item No. 57).

2. National Acts

87. Following are the Acts which have pan India application in the area of merchant shipping and related matters:

(1) Indian Bills of Lading Act 1856.
(2) The Obstruction in Fairways Act 1881
(3) The Indian Ports Act 1908 (15 of 1908)(Amended 2007).
(4) Maritime Convention Act 1911.
(5) Indian Carriage of Goods by Sea Act 1925 (XXVI of 1925).
(6) The Indian Light House Act 1927 (17 of 1927).
(7) The Marking of Heavy Packages Act 1951.
(8) The MS Act 1958 (amended 2003).
(9) The MS (Amendment) Act 2007 (40 of 2007).
(10) The Merchant Shipping Act 1958 (Amended by Finance Act 2016(28 of 2016))
(11) The Merchant Shipping (Recruitment and Placement of Seafarers) Rules 2016
(12) The Merchant Shipping (Civil Liability for Oil Pollution Damage) Rules 2008
(13) The Merchant Shipping (International Fund for Compensation for Oil Pollution Damage) Rules 2008
(14) The Merchant Shipping (Prevention of Pollution by Garbage from Ships) Rules 2009
(15) The Merchant Shipping (Prevention of Pollution by Sewage from Ships) Rules 2010
(16) The Merchant Shipping (Prevention of Pollution from Harmful Substances carried by Sea in Packaged Form) Rules 2010
(17) The Merchant Shipping (Control of Pollution by Noxious Liquid Substances in Bulk) Rules 2010.
(18) The Merchant Shipping (Prevention of Pollution by Oil from Ships) Rules 2010.
(19) The Merchant Shipping (Regulation of Entry of Ships into Ports Anchorages and Offshore Facilities) Rules 2012.
(20) The Merchant Shipping (Standards of Training, Certification and Watchkeeping for Seafarers) Rules 2014.
(21) The Merchant Shipping (Limitation of Liability for Maritime Claims) Rules 2015 as amended by Rules 2017.
(22) The Merchant Shipping (Control of Anti-Fouling Systems) Rules 2016.
(23) The Merchant Shipping (Seafarers Bio-metric Identity Document) Rules 2016.
(24) The Merchant Shipping ((Continuous Discharge Certificate) Rules 2017.

(25) Marine Insurance Act 1963.
(26) The Major Port Trusts Act 1963 (38 of 1963).
(27) The Seamen's Provident Fund Act 1966 (4 of 1966).
(28) The Sailing Vessels (Members of Crew) Rules, 1967.
(29) Maritime Zones of India (Regulation of Fishery by Foreign Vessels) Act 1981.
(30) The Admiralty Act 2017 (22 of 2017).
(31) Recycling of Ships Act 2019.

88. Indian Maritime Law has been in a scattered form for centuries. Limitation of Indian Legislature to legislate on shipping and the imposition of British Statute Law on the subject including parts of the MS Act 1894 caused hindrances in the way of achieving a unified code on Indian maritime law. An attempt was made in 1921–1922 to consolidate some of the then-existing twenty-one acts on the subject and as a result, the Indian MS Act 1923 was passed. The said Act is amended once in 1933 to implement the provisions of the International Convention on Load Lines 1930 and then in 1953 so as to implement the International Convention on Safety of Life at Sea held in 1948 and both of which were ratified by India.

89. By virtue of Article 372 of the Constitution of India, some of the UK Acts are still continuing in India but the results are unsatisfactory. The main lacuna of the Indian law on the subject is that it is silent on many important legal points, for instance, there is no provision dealing with the registration of sea-going vessels except the Coasting Vessels Act 1838 and the Indian Registration of Ships Act 1841 under which only sailing vessels are being registered; the other ships are still registered under the United Kingdom MS Act 1894 and are being technically regarded as British ships. Soon after the independence of India, MS Laws (Extension to Acceding States and Amendment) Act the British MS 1894 to 1938 were extending to the Acceding states and by which certain powers of the Indian consular Officers were enlarged. The Control of Shipping Act 1947 was another temporary measure which continued the wartime control over Indian Shipping and controlled the coastal trade by a system of licensing.

90. The International Convention for the Safety of Life at Sea 1948 was later reviewed by the International Conference on Safety of Life at Sea in 1960 which also evaluated and examined the experiences of various countries who were signatories in the 1948 Convention. As India was also a signatory to the 1960 Conference as well it thus became necessary that the present law on the subject must be reviewed in the light of the new Conference. The 1958 Act was thus amended to the extent of embodying the new changes indicated by the said Conference. In view of the increased sabotaging and destructive activities on sea and in view of the increased number of piracy and other crimes on Indian ships the government has become alert and to deal with the safety of its ships and men aboard suitable measures have been taken. It is the effort to legalize some of these measures for which the MS (Amendment) Act 2007 (40 of 2007) has been passed.

II. Inland Navigation

A. *Treaties*

91. For centuries, the rivers of India not only have mythological importance in the Indian fraternity but the rich river network facilitates the movement of men and goods within the national borders of India. Steam vessels were in vogue in the early days but they are gradually being replaced by 'mechanically propelled vessels'. Treaties and National Legislation Treaties International Treaties in Relation to Indian Waterways and Rivers Agreement on the Kosi Project 1954 Agreement on the Gandak Irrigation and Power Project 1959 Indus Waters Treaty 1960 Farakka Treaty 1996 National Legislation.

92. There has been an Indo-Nepal Statement on New Connectivity through Inland Waterways signed by the Prime Ministers of the two respective countries (April 7, 2018). The object is to facilitate traffic-in-transit and there was mutual agreement on finding out the modalities for including inland waterways as an additional means of transport in the protocol to the treaty of Transit between India and Nepal.[17] The target is to recognize the untapped potential of the inland waterways.

93. An Agreement on a coastal shipping line was signed between Bangladesh and India in June 2015. India is of the view that 'connectivity through the inland waterways and the coastal shipping line is an important part of our objective to create multimodal transport links between India and Bangladesh'.[18] The first cargo ship under this agreement sailed from Chittagong to Vishakhapatnam in March 2016.

B. *National Legislation*

1. Constitutional Provisions

94. The Indian states forming the units of the federation are autonomous in their legislative and administrative fields. List II or the State List enumerates the subjects on which the state legislatures can make laws to the exclusion of Parliament. The list given in Schedule VII of the Constitution envisages the following items related to inland waterways which compared to the items in the Union List are very limited. These are:

- Communication including roads, bridges, ferries and other means of communication not specified in List I; municipal tramways; roadways; inland waterways and traffic-related thereto.
- Water, that is to say, water supplies, irrigation and canals, drainage and embankments water storage and water power subject to the provisions of entry 56 of List I.

---

17. Media Center – Ministry of External Affairs-Government of India.
18. Harsh Vardhan Shringla-Indian High Commissioner to Bangladesh.

– Fisheries.

Thus laws are often passed by the state legislatures but which always remain subject and subservient to the law passed by the Parliament on the same subject (Articles 45 and 46 of the Constitution of India).

2. National Acts

95.

– The Northern India Ferries Act 1878 (Act XVII of 1878).
– The Inland Vessels Act 1917 (1 of 1917).
– The IWAI Act 1985.
– National Waterways Act 2016(Act 17 of 2016).

The Northern India Ferries Act 1878

96. Bengal Regulation VI which regulated the ferries in the Punjab province was repealed by the Punjab Laws Act leaving no law for the regulation of government ferries in Punjab and to prevent any unlicensed person from setting up a rival ferry in competition of government ferries. The Northern India Ferries Act 1878 was thus passed. The Act is based upon the Burma Ferries Act 1873 (Act II of 1873) and extends to Uttar Pradesh, Punjab, the Central Provinces, Assam, Delhi and Ajmer.

97. The Inland Vessels Act 1917 is the major Act which governs the navigation activities in the Indian rivers. The Act was not found adequate as it did not give power to the State Governments to take action to clear navigable channels. It did not have any arrangement for insurance of passengers against accidents and other hazards which might come their way during navigation. Thus in 1977 elaborate amendments were made and the Steam Vessels (Amendment) Act 1977 was passed to amend the Indian Vessels Act 1917.

The Inland Waterways Authority of India Act 1985

98. Recommendations from various Committees including the National Transportation Policy Committee supported the establishment of an IWAI which could work for the development, maintenance and regulation of national rivers for shipping and navigation. The IWAI Act 1985 (82 of 85) was enacted to carry out the recommendations and also to declare certain waterways as NWs.

99. National Waterways Act 2016(Act 17 of 2016)-The Inland waterways transport witnessed major changes with the passing of the National Waterways Act 2016 which repeals previous Acts namely: The National Waterways Act 1982, the National Waterway Act 1988, the National Waterway Act 1992 and the two Acts passed as the National Waterway Act 2008. This has been done with the aim of consolidating the various Acts in the same field and giving uniformity to the legal regime. The National Waterway Act 2016 has also made big changes in identifying the waterways and has declared 111 waterways as National Waterways.

III. Rail Transport

100. In the beginning, the railways in India were owned and conducted by private companies. The role of the Government of India was in the form of a coordinating authority. It was a regulating authority in matters of inter-railway movement of traffic, fixation of rates, sharing of revenue earnings, apportionment of claims, liability amongst the railways, providing facilities to passenger and goods traffic, and so on, which was reflected in the Railways Act 1890. At present, there is a monopoly of the Government of India in the field of railways commercials. This necessitated a big change in the rail law as many provisions of the Railways Act 1890 became superfluous, redundant and irrelevant. In 1989 the law was therefore changed and the Railways Act 1989 which is a Central Act was passed.

A. *Treaties and National Legislation*

1. National Acts

101.

(1) The Railways Act 1989.
(2) The Railways (Amendment) Act 1994 (28 of 1994).
(3) The Railways (Amendment) Act 2003 (56 of 2003).
(4) The Railways (Second Amendment) Act 2003 (51 of 2003).
(5) The Railways (Amendment) Act 2005 (47 of 2005).
(6) Carriage Act 1965.
(7) Carriage Act 1934.
(8) Railways Act 1890.
(9) Railways Act 1989.
(10) Railway and Canal Tariff Act 1888.
(11) Railways Claims Tribunal Act 1987.
(12) Railway Protection Force Act 1957.
(13) The Railway Property (Unlawful Possession) Act 1966 (29 of 1966).
(14) The Statutory Investigation into Railway Accidents Rules 1998.
(15) The Railway (Notices of and Inquiries into Accidents) Rules 1998.
(16) The Railway servants (Hours of Work and Period of Rest) Rules 2005.
(17) The Railway Passengers Manner of Investigation of Untoward Incidents).
(18) Rules 2003.
(19) The Railway (Punitive Charges for Overloading of Wagon).

B. Treaties

Agreement between India and Nepal

102. India will build a strategic rail link between Raxaul in Bihar (India) and Kathmandu in Nepal. This was agreed upon by the Premiers of the two countries in April 2018. This is to enhance connectivity between people of the two countries and to allow bulk cargo movement with the landlocked neighbour.

IV. Road Transport

103. The Year 2017 can be termed as the watershed year in the history of road transport in India as the MoRTH has taken formidable steps to improve and refurbish the entire transportation system in the country. RT system is well-developed in India and heavy activity is on to make further improvements utilizing modern technology. The government is also taking steps to give incentives to the private sector so as to encourage its participation in the Highway Sector. The Central Government has created a dedicated fund called CRF from the collection of cess on petrol and high-speed diesel (HSD) oil. The fund is utilized for the development and maintenance of NH, state roads, rural roads and for the construction/development of railway over bridges, under bridges and other safety features. The Department of Road Transport and Highways under the Ministry of Shipping also recognizes the need for improving the country's road safety record which has three aspects; Engineering, Enforcement and Education (Three Es).

A. Treaties and National Legislation

1. Treaties and MoU

104. An MoU has been signed between India and Nepal in August 2017 for laying down implementation arrangements o cost-sharing schedules and safeguard issues for the construction of a new bridge over River Mechi at the Indo-Nepal border. The new bridge is part of the upgradation of Kakarvitta (Nepal) to Panitanki Bypass (India).

MoU between India and United Arab Emirates (UAE)

India and UAE signed an MoU in January 2017 to foster bilateral cooperation in the Road Transport & Highways sector. The MoU envisages cooperation, exchange and collaboration between India and UAE for promoting increased investment in infrastructure development and logistics efficiency.

Agreement between India and Afghanistan

India and Afghanistan signed a Motor Vehicles Agreement (MVA) in September 2017 for the regulation of passenger, personal and cargo vehicular traffic. This will enhance regional connectivity through road transport and for promoting cross-border road transportation for increased trade with Afghanistan via the land route.

Agreement Between IAHE, India and IFEER

A Cooperation Framework Agreement between the Indian Academy of Highway Engineers (IAHE), India and the Institute of Training in Engines and Road Maintenance (IFEER) Morocco has been signed on 14 December 2017. The Agreement envisages bilateral cooperation in the field of training in Engines and Road Maintenance of Moroccan Engineers.

2. National Acts

105.

(1) The Carriers Act 1865 (3 of 1865) Now Repealed (2007).
(2) The RT Corporations Act 1950 (64 of 1950).
(3) The National Highways Act 1956 (48 of 1956).
(4) The Motor Vehicles Act 1988 (59 of 1988) A Bill to amend the Act is pending (2018).
(5) Central Motor Vehicles Rules 1989.
(6) The National Highways Authority of India Act 1988 (69 of 1988).
(7) The Central Road Fund Act 2000 as amended by the Finance Act 2016 (28 of 2016).
(8) The Central Road Funds (State Roads) Rules 2014 as amended by (Amendment) Rules 2017.
(9) The Control of National Highways (Land & Traffic) Act 2002 (13 of 2003) as amended by the Finance Act 2017(7 of 2017).
(10) The Carriage by Road Act 2007 (41 of 2007).
(11) The Carriage by Road Rules 2011.

3. Projects

106.

(1) Global Transport Corridor Project (GTCP).
(2) NHDP – The Project extends over seven phases and it comprises four laning and six laning of important NH on a BOT basis apart from overall upgrading of the roads.

4. Government Schemes

107. The year 2017 has been a year of Ambitious Rollouts and Engineering Marvels in the country. There have been never seen before great planning and schemes to upgrade the entire road map. The year 2017 is a turning point for transport planning in the country as it also boosted the multimodal transportation system. The landmark Schemes and Plans are as follows:

Bharatmala Pariyojana Phase I

A new umbrella programme which aims to fulfil the connectivity needs of areas like places of economic activity, places of religious and tourist interest, border areas, backwards and tribal areas. Multimodal integration is the key focus of this scheme. A total of 53,000 km of NHs have been identified to improve National Corridor efficiency of which 24,500 km. will be taken up in Phase I which will be implemented over a period of five years spreading over 2017-2018 and 2021-2022.

Chenani–Nashri Tunnel

It is an ideal presentation of the 'Make in India' and 'Skill India' initiatives of the Government. It is a 9 km-long twin-tube all-weather tunnel between Udhampur and Ramban in the State of Jammu & Kashmir. It is not only India's but Asia's longest bi-directional tunnel. It is part of the 286 km-long project for fourlaning of the Jammu-Srinagar National Highway. It not only saves a distance of 41 km but also cuts down travel time by two hours.

Dhola–Sadiya Bridge

Yet another engineering marvel over the River Brahmaputra and is graded as the longest bridge of the country having a length of 9.15 km and bridges the distance between upper Assam and Eastern part of Arunachal Pradesh. It will clearly steer out of flood miseries, only day connectivity and cuts down travel time from six hours to one hour only.

Extra-dosed Bridge

The bridge across the Narmada River at Bharuch is a cable-stayed bridge bringing relief to the people on the Vadodara–Surat section of NH-8.

Apart from these major marvels, there has been considerable activity in the area of road transportation like speeding up the languished and stalled projects. This is done by the One Time Fund Infusion Scheme (OTFIS) to complete these projects at the earliest.

The RT ministry has also taken up an initiative named Indian Bridge Management System (IBMS) under which it inventorizes all structures like bridges and culverts constructed on National Highways.

Setu Bharatam

The RT Ministry has also planned replacement of Level Crossings on National Highways with Road Over Bridge (ROB) and Road Under Bridge (RUB) under the Scheme Setu Bharatam. This is to ensure smooth uninterrupted and safe movement of traffic.

Toll-Operate Transfer (ToT)

Under this Scheme, the ministry is monetizing its road assets constructed with public funds through toll-operate transfer. The scheme envisages bidding of bundled National Highways for a concession period of 30 years.

Masala Bonds

For mobilization of funds, NHAI launched an issue of Masala Bonds at the London Stock Exchange in May 2017. It received an overwhelming response from investors. The initial benchmark issue of rupees 1500 crore was upsized to 3000 crores. Asia contributed 60% and Europe 40% of subscription. The amount is from fund managers or insurance funds, 18 from banks and 14% from private banks is 61%.

Road Safety

In the latest Government Schemes, road safety has been given priority as never before. This entails New Accident Reporting Format, the rectification of black spots, training of drivers, model automated Centres for checking fitness of vehicles. There are planned special safety measures for two-wheelers as two-wheelers are major victims of road accidents on highways. Thus all the two-wheelers are mandated to be fitted with Anti-Lock Brake System (ABS) from 1 April 2019. There have been made provisions for a free eyecheck-up at various toll plazas. To ensure the safety of women and children, all public conveyances are mandated to be fitted with GPS devices. There is a proposal to amend the Motor Vehicles Act 1988 with a view to addressing road safety, stiffer penalties for the defaulters, permitting electronic enforcement, improving fitness certification, recognition of IT enabled enforcement systems. An important and long-overdue provision to be included in the said Act is to provide quick relief to the accident victims in the Golden Hour without wasting time.

Green Initiatives

There has been a constant effort to give a natural look to the Highways and to make them more environmentally friendly. For this, about twenty-five million trees have been planted on Highway dividers and even water conservation bodies are being constructed at the road embankment. Even there is a Scheme for the revival of existing ponds and construction of water bodies especially in the drought-hit areas and nearby villages.

e-Tolling

This is the flagship scheme of the Government which has been implemented on a pan India basis. This is mainly to ensure the smooth running of vehicles and avoiding bottlenecks at toll plazas by introducing Electronic toll Collection (ETC). Banks have been mandated to issue FASTags to road users. This is made possible by reserving one lane for FASTag users.

V. Air Transport

A. Treaties and National Legislation

108. Civil Aviation started in India in 1953 and the entire activity is increasing day by day with the increase of international traffic and domestic burden as well. India is a signatory to the Warsaw Convention of 1929 which is an International Agreement governing the liability of the air carrier regarding international carriage of passengers, baggage and cargo. The Warsaw Convention was first given effect in India by the enactment of the Indian Carriage by Air Act 1934 (20 of 1934) in respect of international carriage and the Act is also extended to domestic carriage with certain modifications. Later after the Protocol 1955, the 1934 Act was replaced by The Carriage by Air Act 1972 (69 of 1972) subsuming the Hague Protocol. A big change has been made in the air law in India to make the carrier more liable towards the consumer and to safeguard the interest of the consumer. For this India became a signatory (91st) to the Montreal Convention and to subsume its provisions the Carriage by Air Act 1972 has been amended in which Schedule III has been added to include the rules to raise the liability of the carrier towards the consumer in respect of death or injury of the passenger or the loss, delay or damage of baggage or cargo. It also makes the registration of common carriers compulsory and has brought them within the tax net by requiring them to submit annual returns. The Carriage by Air Act was amended in 2015 in which there is a provision to revise the liability of the carrier and to include it in the Principal Act. By this amendment after section 8, another section, section 8A, has been added which gives power to the Central Government to make Rules to give effect to the provisions of the Principal Act regarding limits of liability of the carrier. India's aviation sector, which was not promising for so long, was audited by the UN aviation watchdog International Civil Aviation Organization (ICAO) in November 2017 and gave 'satisfied' with the safety system remark.

The legal framework in India regarding civil aviation does not exist in one single Act and it partakes of certain other laws in the field of contract and company laws and by Indian Foreign Exchange Regulations.[19] Moreover, a ratification by India of any Convention has the force of law without any specific act for the same.

1. National Acts

109.

(1) The Carriage by Air Act 1972 (69 of 1972).
(2) The Carriage by Air (Amendment Act) 2015 (12 of 2016).
(3) The Carriage by Air (Amendment Act) 2016(12 of 2016).
(4) Aircraft (Investigation of Accidents and Incidents) Rules 2012.
(5) Aircraft (Security) Rules 2011.

19. INSOl International-Aircraft repossession upon a Default – a review of the issues in the United kingdom, USA, India and Nigeria – November 2019 – Technical Paper Series 45.9.

(6) The Airports Authority of India Act 1994.
(7) The Airports Authority of India (Amendment) Act 2003.
(8) Airports Economic Regulatory Authority of India (AERA) Act 2008.
(9) The Carriage by Air (Amendment) Act 2009 (28 of 2009).

2. Conventions

110.

(1) The Warsaw Convention 1929 – Amended by Hague Protocol 1955.
(2) Convention Supplementary to Warsaw Convention 1961.
(3) International Conference at Montreal 1975.
(4) The Montreal Convention 1999.

3. Treaties/Agreements

111.

(1) Open Skies Agreement – India signed MoU with twelve countries in December 2016. The major issues were solved as per the National Civil Aviation Policy (NCAP2016). The Policy allows an unlimited number of flights to six metro airports namely Delhi, Mumbai, Hyderabad, Kolkata Bengaluru and Chennai. The Agreement was signed with six countries namely Jamaica, Guyana, Czech Republic, Finland, Spain and Sri Lanka. [20]
(2) Air Service Agreement was signed with Jamaica and Guyana (2016).
(3) Delegation of European Community and Government of India on 8 April 2008 in Brussels signed a horizontal Aviation Agreement to store legal certainty to the bilateral services between India and the EU Member States.
(4) Second India–US Aviation Partnership Summit was held in the US from 7 December–9 December 2009.
(5) Meeting of Joint Aviation Steering Committee Working Group Meetings on 7 December–9 December 2009 on modernization and security measures in the field of civil aviation.
(6) Three Memorandums of Understanding (MoUs) were signed between the Director General of Civil Aviation of India and Bureau of Enquiry and Analysis for Civil Aviation Safety (BEA of France on 11 February 2010) relating to Aircraft Accident and Incident Investigation.
(7) In 2010 consultations were held with Zimbabwe, Indonesia, Ireland, Brazil, UK and Iran and amendments were made in the Air Services Agreements (ASAs).
(8) Technical cooperation agreements were signed between the Director General of Civil Aviation and Airports Authority of India with Nepal and Afghan.

---

20. Press information Bureau – Ministry of Civil Aviation – Government of India –New Delhi.

(9) Under the Joint Action Plan between India and the European Union, a Civil Aviation Cooperation Project II has been agreed and Terms of Reference (TOR) have been finalized.
(10) Two MoU on the deployment of Air Marshals and Cooperation in airport Technical Visits were signed between the Government of India and the Government of United States of America on 20 January–21 January 2010.

VI. Multimodal Transportation

112. The Multimodal Transportation of Goods (MMTG) was introduced to facilitate the exporters and to give them a feeling of security in the matter of transportation of goods. The Act is inspired by and is based on the universally accepted principles as given in the United Nations Conference on Trade and Development (UNCTAD) and International Chamber of Commerce (ICC). India was a signatory to the Convention on the International Multimodal Transport of Goods on 24 May 1980 and is one of the rare countries that have their separate law for multimodal transportation. For this, the Act not only defines and explains certain terms but also lays down some basic rules which regulate the activities in this field. It is for the first time that India is going to have National Transport Master Plan (2017). The Plan will be jointly developed by ministries of road transport and highways, shipping, aviation and railways. The Plan includes the construction of multimodal transport hubs that will have railway stations, light railway stations (metro) and bus terminals under one roof. Consequently, ten multimodal transport hubs are likely to come up across India.

A. Treaties and National Legislation
  (1) National Acts
    (1) The Multimodal Transportation of Goods Act 1993 (MMTG) (28 of 1993).
    (2) The Multimodal Transport Document Rules, 1994.
  (2) Convention

Convention on the International Multimodal Transport of Goods on 24 May 1980.

Chapter 3. Jurisdiction and Courts

113. Though courts in India have common and general jurisdiction regarding most of the matters yet so far the matters connected with transportation are concerned the jurisdiction is different in respect of shipping matters which usually involves foreign nationals and vessels registered in foreign countries and railway matters as these are the oldest means of transportation and cover a considerably large area of transportation cases. The matter is thus dealt with under separate heads.

§1. Jurisdiction and Courts in Admiralty Matters

114. The admiralty jurisdiction of the three High Courts namely, the Calcutta, Bombay and Madras High Court continue to be governed by the 1891 Act. The inadequacy of admiralty jurisdictional power of these High Courts was discussed several times. It was held that in view of the Admiralty Court Act 1861 the jurisdiction of the Calcutta High Court was limited (*Jayaswal Shipping Co. v. S. S. Leelawati* AIR 1954 Cal 413). Similar views were expressed by the Bombay and Madras High Courts in which doubt was expressed regarding the extent of admiralty jurisdiction of these High Courts in the post-constitution period. Thus the 151st Report of the Law Commission of India presented in 1994 recommended that India has no 'Admiralty Law' of its own and felt that the issues regarding jurisdiction of courts and applicable law are still unattended in the country.

115. This was inspired by the observations of the Supreme Court of India regarding admiralty jurisdiction of the Andhra Pradesh High Court where Sahay J. expressed his surprise that even in 1991 the admiralty jurisdiction of the Indian High Courts is governed by the English Admiralty Courts Act 1861 (*M. V. Elizabeth v. Harwan Investment and Trading Private Limited*, JT 1992 (2) SC 165). However, the admiralty jurisdiction of the High Courts in India originated in the Charters of 1774 and 1798. Such jurisdiction was from time to time expanded and modified by the Letters Patent of 1823, 1862 and 1965 read with the Admiralty Court Act 1861, the Colonial Courts of Admiralty Act 1890 and the Colonial Courts of Admiralty (India) Act 1891. This was further preserved by section 106 of the Government of India Act 1915, section 223 of the Government of India Act 1935 and by Article 225 of the Constitution of India.

116. The Colonial Courts of Admiralty (India) Act 1891 conferred admiralty jurisdiction on the High Court of Judicature at Fort Williams in Calcutta and also on the Colonial Courts in Bombay and Madras. These courts were also endowed with the power to regulate their procedure and practice in matters of admiralty jurisdiction in accordance with the rules made for the purpose. As vessels are given legal personality of their own in admiralty matters the claimant is allowed to bring an action in rem that is, against the cargo or ship as different from a right in personam to proceed against the owner. The admiralty jurisdiction also symbolizes the territorial sovereignty of a state and hence the laws are exercised by the High Court as the superior Courts of Records.

§2. Jurisdiction in Railway Matters

117. The entire Indian Railways come under the control and administration of the Government of India through the ministry of Railways. In a vast democracy like that of India answerability of the Government before the masses calls for more viable machinery which would exclusively deal with public grievances regarding railway matters. As Article 323A (Part XIV-A) of the Constitution of India makes provision for the establishment of tribunals for adjudication of certain disputes; the Government of India proposed for the establishment of a Railway Claims Tribunal for loss, damage, deterioration or non-delivery of goods or animals entrusted to it to be carried by railway or for the refund of fares or freight or for compensation for death or injury to passenger occurring as a result of railway accidents.

118. With this object, the Railway Claims Tribunal Bill was introduced in the Lok Sabha on 23 November 1987 and became an Act after receiving President's assent. The substantive liability of the railway administration is given in the Indian Railways Act 1890. Till now the consignors, consignee, and passengers or their representatives preferred claims for compensation against the railway administration. Those who claim compensation for loss of and damage to booked goods and are dissatisfied with the decisions of the railway administration filed suits in the courts of law. Claims for compensation for death of or injury or loss, and so on, to passengers in train accidents are at present settled by Claims Commissioners. However, this process being protracted, one took too much time and entailed extra expenses. Keeping this in view the specialized tribunals to provide speedy remedy are established by the Railways Claims Tribunal Act 1987 and are chaired by a Judge of a High Court (section 5) and all the matters which were previously dealt with by the regular courts or by the Claims Commissioner came within the jurisdiction of the Railway Tribunal. Such Claims Tribunal also has Benches in various parts of the country. The Railway Claims Tribunal is made to give legal aid to a person who is indigent and is unable to bear the legal expenses. The Supreme Court has ruled that the Tribunal should follow Order 33 of the Code of Civil Procedure 1908 (5 of 1908) and be just towards the indigent person and cannot refuse jurisdiction on this basis (*A. A. Muniuddin v. Indian Railways*, AIR 1993 SC 361). From the decision of the Railway Tribunal, the appeal is taken to the respective High Court.

Chapter 4. State Immunity and Transport Law

119. State immunity is envisaged in Articles 299 and 300 of the Constitution of India under which the state is not made liable regarding matters which are strictly sovereign in nature. Consequently, where the state is engaged in commercial activities like plying of buses (*Amulya Patnaik v. State of Orissa* AIR 1967 Ori 116) running of railways, and any accident or loss of property is caused then the state is liable to compensate the aggrieved like any other common entity. In *State of Rajasthan v. Vidyawati* (AIR 1962 SC 633), the Supreme Court refused to give immunity to the state on the ground that the deceased was killed by a car which belonged to the state. The court held that the state was vicariously liable for the negligence of its driver and the car at that time was not engaged in a work of sovereign nature. Again transportation of records, ranging machines and other equipment in a military truck from the workshop to the School of Artillery was held to be of non-sovereign nature and the state was denied immunity (*Union of India v. Sughra Bai* AIR 1969 Bom 13).

120. In matters connected with the railways, the provisions of the Railways Act 1890 provide immunity to the state in matters of losses arising out of causes enumerated in the Railways Act 1890 (section 73). Immunity can be claimed by the railways on the basis that reasonable care and foresight had been used and for which evidence will be given by it (*Punjab National Bank v. Beniprasad Maheshwari* AIR 1981 MP 95 (1981) MP LJ 380).

121. The burden is on the Railways administration to plead immunity by giving proof that reasonable care had been taken to avoid the loss (*Union of India v. Orissa Textile Mills* AIR 1979 Ori 165). Act of God can also be taken as a plea for immunity where the loss has been caused due to natural causes. The immunity in this matter is granted mainly depending on the nature of the activity undertaken by the state and not as per the vehicles or means of transportation used.

Chapter 5. Transport Intermediaries

122. Transport of goods and carriage of passengers takes place under a contract. At times, such a contractual relationship is achieved directly when the consignor and the consignee stand face to face. However, often, the relation is created through the agency of a third person. An 'agent' is a person employed to do any act for another or to represent another, in dealings with third persons. The person for whom such act is done, or who is so represented is called the 'principal' (section 182 The Indian Contract Act 1872). The main function of an agent is over once such a contractual tie is achieved. He can neither sue nor be sued on contracts entered into by him on his principal's behalf on the basis of the principle of the agent's immunity from personal liability (*Marine Container Services South P Ltd v. Go Go Garments* (1998) 3 SCC 247). Agents are of different varieties who acts as an intermediary between the principal and the third party and who represent the agent may be in following situations called as 'mercantile agent' (The Indian Contract Act 1872).

§1. Factor

123. A factor is an agent entrusted with the possession of goods for the purpose of selling them 'He is a mercantile agent whose ordinary course of business is to dispose of goods, of which he is entrusted with the possession or control by his principal.'

§2. Broker

124. A broker is also a kind of mercantile agent. He is appointed to negotiate and make contracts for the sale or purchase of property on behalf of this principal but is not given the possession of goods.

§3. Del Credere Agent

125. It is yet another kind of mercantile agent who undertakes to be liable to the principal in case the third party fails to perform and his extra commission for the guarantee is known as del credere commission. It was held that in such kind of agency, the agent has a personal interest in the contract and they are liable by reason of their charging a del credere though they have no guaranteed by writing (*Couturier v. Hastie* (1856) 5 HLC 673.).

126. The agent of a contractor who was charged under the Consumer Protection Act 1986 for deficient services was held to be entitled to raise the defence of immunity and that defence could not be brushed aside without due consideration. An agent, however, may contract to undertake personal liability. An agent may be given the authority to sell goods, as a mercantile agent to sell goods without having possession of it. The principle of agency of necessity was first applied to cases of marine adventures. Due to emergent situations during the voyage, a marine adventure may threaten the goods and the master of the ship is unable to communicate with the principal. In such a situation the master gets the authority to sell the goods and the sale will bind the cargo owner. This principle was later extended to carriers by land. In the field of transportation, the agency plays a major role as travel agents are instrumental in making contracts either for consignment of goods or for the carriage of passengers on behalf of the principals.

127. Though all the above-mentioned agents work for the principal in the normal course of business, they often act as intermediaries in matters of transport and consignment of goods and as such their duties and rights accrue from the law of agency under the Indian Contract Act 1872.

Part II. Maritime Law

Chapter 1. The Vessel

§1. Definition and Legal Status of Vessels

128. The legal importance of vessels lies in the fact that the law takes within its ambit vessels which are registered in India and those which are required by the Act to be registered and also those which are owned by either by a citizen of India or by a company registered in India or by a cooperative society registered in India. According to section 3(55) of the MS Act 1958 (44 of 1958), a 'vessel' includes any ship, boat, sailing vessel, or other description of vessel used in navigation. Thus a specific meaning of the term 'vessel' is important for the application of maritime law.

129. Again referring to the definition of 'ship' under Indian Statutes section 3(55) of the General Clauses Act which follows the definition of the term given in section 742 of the (English) MS Act provides that a 'ship' includes vessels not exclusively propelled by oars. Section 48 of the Indian Penal Code 1860 defines 'vessels' as 'anything made for the conveyance by water of human beings or property'. This would thus include vessels propelled by oars. Section 3(45) of the Indian MS Act 1958 enacts that a ship does not include sailing vessels. This definition is only for the purpose of that Act and it is declared in the Act itself that but for the specific provision contained in this Act, the word 'ship' would include sailing vessels.

130. The Admiralty Act 2017 defines 'vessel' as including a ship, boat, sailing vessel, or other description of vessel used or constructed for use in navigation by water, whether it is propelled or not. It also includes a barge, lighter or other floating vessel, a hovercraft, an offshore industry mobile unit, a vessel that has sunk or is stranded or abandoned and the remains of such vessel [section 2(l)]. However, the explanation further explains that a broken vessel which is incapable of navigation when certified by a surveyor does not fall under the definition of vessel.

131. As there was a demand from the thinkers in South India where such vessels are in considerable use to include the sailing vessels in the definition of the terms 'ship' and hence the Twenty-First Report of the Law Commission of India in section 2(h) declares formally that a 'ship' includes a sailing vessel. It also includes any type of vessel used in navigation not propelled by oars and will include a hopper barge with rudder and navigating lights but without means of propulsion.

132. By the Judicature (Consolidation) Act 1925 the term 'ship' includes any description of vessel used in navigation not propelled by oars, and by this description, the jurisdiction of the High Court over salvage claims would also include services rendered to vessels not propelled by oars. Again the Admiralty Court Act 1861 defines 'Ship' under section 2 of the act as to include any description of vessel used in navigation not propelled by oars. Under the 'Dead vessel' doctrine, a vessel permanently withdrawn from use for navigational purposes is not a vessel. Moreover, where a vessel is kept to alter it or for making it fit for maritime service then also it is not a 'dead vessel'. Also, a ship will be considered as a 'live ship' not a 'dead vessel' when it is in a dry dock. While the Indian law is nearer the definition of 'vessel' given under the UK MS Acts the American law is slightly different as it gives importance to the fact that the watercraft must be used for business irrespective of its size or capacity. Thus, rafts and pump boats are vessels while aircraft, and so on, may not be so as they are not used in waters for navigation purposes.

133. Thus under the Indian law according to the latest judicial pronouncement regarding the meaning of the term 'vessel' or 'ship' it is expressed in the light of the judgment of the *Queen's Bench Division in Steedman v. Scofield* ((1992) 2 Lloyd's Rep 163) that the expression is meant to indicate a 'vessel' or 'ship' which must be necessarily capable of being navigated. Main contention in the case was regarding the arrest of the ship. It was argued that since the vessel was arrested in an action in rem and since the respondents had appeared in the court, the court should entertain the suit against the respondents by way of action in personam. This would have been true had the current owner namely the respondent had come to the court and submitted to the jurisdiction by providing security for release from the arrest warrant. But the respondents had moved the court for vacating the arrest warrant on the ground that the arrest warrant itself could not have been issued to arrest an entity which was neither a 'ship' nor 'vessel'. Justice Sheen says 'a vessel is usually a hollow receptacle for carrying goods or people. In common parlance "vessel" is a word used to refer to craft larger than rowing boats and it includes every description watercraft used or capable of being used as a means of transportation on water' (*Ocean Marine Mutual Insurance Association Ltd v. M. V. WOHFU & Others*, AIR 1999 Bom 18). The term vessel is also defined in the Indian Ports Act 1908 to include anything made for the conveyance (mainly) by water of human beings or property (section 3(7)). Vessel status is important in determining the jurisdictional issues as acts occurring aboard a vessel are considered to meet the maritime relationship requirement. Moreover, the status of the vessel is also useful in determining a salvage award, liability of unseaworthiness or a maritime lien under the maritime law.

134. A vessel is also not considered as a person. For the purposes of the Recovery of Debts due to Banks and Financial Institutions Act 1993 a 'vessel' cannot be treated as a person and therefore when a financial institution brings an action in rem against a vessel in an admiralty court then it cannot be said that the claim that the bank or financial institution is making is a debt within the meaning of section 2(g) of the said Act and as such the DRT will not have jurisdiction to entertain that suit in terms of the provisions of section 17 of the said Act and the admiralty jurisdiction of the High Court would not be ousted (*ICICI Ltd v. MFV Shilpa on Indian Vessel* AIR 2002 Bom 371).

§2. Registration and Nationality of Ocean-Going Vessels

135. The MS Act 1958 provides for the registration of sea-going vessels and ships in different provisions as under.

I. Registration of Sailing Vessels

136. Part XV of the MS Act provides for the registration of sea-going vessels owned by a citizen of India whether the vessel is owned by an individual, or a company or a cooperative society. In case of any dispute arising as to the point whether any vessel is a sailing vessel or not, the decision of the Director General of Shipping (DGS) would be final.

A. Certificate of Registry

137. Every sailing vessel other than a sailing vessel solely engaged in fishing for profit shall be registered according to the procedure given in this Part. The owner of every sailing vessel shall make an application in a prescribed form to the registrar, causing the tonnage of the vessel to be ascertained in the prescribed manner, for the grant to him of a certificate of registry. The registrar after making inquiry as regarding the particulars made in the application shall enter into the prescribed register; the name of the sailing vessel, the place she was built and the port to which she belongs; the rig, type and tonnage of the vessel; the name, occupation and residence of the owner of the vessel; the number assigned to the vessel; the mortgages, if any effected by the owner in respect of the vessel, and so on. Thereafter, the registrar shall grant a certificate of registry to the applicant in the prescribed form.

138. The owner of every sailing vessel is required to pay the fee as prescribed by the Central Government but in no case exceeding INR 1 per tonne of its gross tonnage. A sailing vessel which is required to be registered but which is not so registered may be detained by a proper officer until the owner or tindal produces a certificate of registry in respect of the vessel (section 417).

II. Registration of Ships

139. The flag state has exclusive jurisdiction over its flagships on the high seas. That makes it necessary that every ship which is lawfully on the high seas should have a nationality and in order to give it a nationality, it should be registered in a state. Registration gives a right to the ship to fly the flag of the country where she is registered. Articles 91, 92 and 94 of the Law of the Sea Convention 1982 are relevant to the question of registration. These articles enumerate the principles of international law. While Article 91 enumerates the rules that every State must specify the conditions for the grant of registration and of its nationality to the ships, Article 92 says that ships should sail under the flag of one country only and shall be subject to its exclusive jurisdiction except when otherwise provided by some international treaty or convention. Article 94 declares the jurisdiction, and control in administrative, technical and social matters of States over ships flying their flag.

140. Every State shall maintain a register of ships containing the detail of the ships and assume jurisdiction under its internal law over each ship flying its flag and its master, officers and crew in respect of administrative, technical and social matters concerning the ship (Cl 2. Article 94). Every State should also take measures regarding the safety of the ship at sea in respect of the construction; equipment and seaworthiness of ships, the manning of ships, labour conditions and the training of crews, taking into account the applicable international instruments, and so on. By registration, the members of the crew are given protection against injuries and loss of life and it is easier for them to get compensation under Indian law.

A. *Indian Law Regarding Registration of Ships*

141. The Indian Law regarding registration of ships is given in Part V of the MS Act which for the first time entails the provisions of the Law of the Sea Convention of 1982. Part V not only deals with the procedure of registration and prescribes the methods of proof of national character but also establishes a clear link between the Indian State and the ships registered in India as required by the Law of the Sea. Part XV of the Act deals with the registration of sailing vessels while XVA deals with the registration of shipping boats.

142. The law is explicit in establishing a link between ownership and the law of the flag so as to avoid the application of different considerations in the determination of the proper applicable law in respect of any matter concerned with shipping. The legal provisions concerning registration of ships clarify fully that the law of the flag State shall grant protection to the ship and will determine jurisdiction and control in administrative, technical and social matters.

1. Procedure

143. The registration procedure of the registration of Indian ships within the State of India is given in Part V of the said Act and are supplemented by the MS (Registration of Indian Ships) Rules 1960 as amended in 1966, 1970, 1994 and 1997. The registration of ships will be made only at the notified ports which are the ports of Bombay, Calcutta, Madras, Cochin and Murmagao at present and the principal officers of Mumbai, Calcutta and Madras and Surveyor in charge of Murmagao and Cochin have been notified as Registrar of an Indian ship.

144. Such other ports in India as the Central Government may, by notification in the Official Gazette, can be declared to be ports of registry under the Act (section 23). At each of the ports of Bombay, Calcutta and Madras, the principal officer of the Mercantile Marine Department and at any other port where such authority as the Central Government may, by notification in the Official Gazette, appoint, shall be the registrar of Indian Ships at that port (section 24). Under the MS Act, only ships which have mechanical means of propulsion are required to be registered. The conditions to be satisfied by a ship for being treated as an Indian ship are laid down in section 21 of the MS Act 1958 as amended in 1993. A ship shall not be deemed an Indian ship unless it is owned wholly by persons who are; citizens of India, or a company of body established by or under any Central or State Act which has a principal place of business in India, or a cooperative society which is registered or deemed to be registered under the Cooperative Societies Act 1912 or any other law relating to cooperative societies for the time being in force in India. The 1993 amendment has dispensed with the earlier requirement in respect of a company which was to have at least 60% of share capital, Chairman, Managing Director and 3/4th of the number of Directors of the company to be citizens of India.

145. Application for registry of an Indian ship shall be made by: a person requiring to be registered as an owner where there is more than one individual requiring to be so registered by someone or more of the persons so requiring or by his or their agent and in the case of a company or cooperative society requiring to be so registered, by its agent. Sea-going ships fitted with mechanical means of propulsion of 15 tonnes net and above and those of less than 15 tonnes net employed otherwise than solely on the Indian coasts are qualified for registration under Part V. The owner of a ship is required to submit to the registrar the following documents namely: a declaration of ownership in the prescribed forms; a certificate by the shipbuilder giving full details of proper denomination and tonnage of the ship and the time and place of shipbuilding; notice in fourteen days advance to the Registrar of the name proposed and prior approval by the DGS will be taken by the registrar regarding the name of the ship. The Registrar then arranges for the survey of the ship in accordance with the MS (Tonnage Measurement) Rules 1987.

146. The Registrar then issues a carving and marking note which is then duly carried out in the ship engraving the name of the ship on its bows and other details. The Registrar then enters the particulars of the ship like the name of the ship and the port to which she belongs, details given in the Surveyor Certificate, particulars regarding the origin of the ship, the name and description of the registered owner, name of the master in the register meant for it.

2. Formalities Regarding Registration of Indian Ship When Acquired Abroad

147. When a ship is built or acquired out of India and is owned by an Indian then the owner or master of the ship is required to apply to the nearest Indian Consular Officer on proof of ownership for the issue of a provisional certificate which remains valid for a period of six months from or until the ship arrives at a port where there is a Registrar.

3. Registration of Government Ships

148. Apart from the regular procedure, a government ship is required to have some additional formalities to complete the registration. Secretary of the Ministry or the Head of the Department to whom the management of the ship is entrusted or any other officer specially appointed for the purpose shall apply with such particulars as name and description of the ship, time and place of the construction of the ship, statement regarding the nature of the title to the said ship, name of the master.

The registrar on completion of such formalities shall enter the name of the ship in the registry book with the mentioning of the fact as to whether the ship belongs to the Central or State Government. In case the ship is to be transferred then the sale deed should be in the prescribed form and is required to be signed by an official of the said government.

4. New Guidelines by the DGS

149. To simplify the law of registration of ships and of mortgages, and realizing that the shipping industry needs guidelines for registration of ships including entry of mortgages easily and urgently on the register book, to enable and satisfy the banks or financial institutions in India and abroad, lending money for acquisition of Indian ships; realizing that maritime administrations all over the world are very swift in according registration so that the shipowners can choose their flag and attract all the benefits connected thereto in a short time; realizing that the Indian practice of registration has protracted the registration of ships thereby subjecting the shipowners to unnecessary hardships; realizing also that the Indian Shipping companies finding the registration formalities very complicated and prolonged often are tempted to acquire ships abroad through their foreign subsidiaries where they are benefited by the simple and brief registration procedure and entry of mortgage; (Government of India, Ministry of Shipping issued Office Memorandum No. SD 11018/197 – MD dated 15 June 2001 thereafter dated 5 March 2002) required the DGS to issue detailed guidelines on registration of Indian Ships and the Central Government by virtue of clause (1) of section 456 of the MS Act 1958 read with notification issued vide S. O. No. 3144 dated 17 December 1960 delegated to him to pass necessary order as required by the circumstances of the case; as a result of this, the DGS issued an order comprising some revised and new guidelines for registration of Indian ships, provisional registration of Indian ships and entry of mortgage.

150. The order thus says that: on receipt of all the documents required for registration of the ship, the Registrar shall ensure grant of certificate of permanent registration to the ship immediately within three working days., that permission of the DGS to register a ship built in a Shipyard other than an Indian shipyard is being dispensed with that the tonnage measured in accordance with the MS (Tonnage Measurement Ships) Rules 1987 as applicable or tonnage certificate issued by the previous maritime administration shall be accepted for the purpose of registration. When the ship is acquired abroad then the present practice of provisional registry to the ship by the Indian consular Officer shall continue. The registrar of Ships shall send a detailed message to Indian High Commission/Embassy about the provisional registration.

151. The sighting of Carving and Marking on the ship and the endorsement of the Carving and Marking note should be done by a Surveyor of Mercantile Marine Department or of a Recognized Classification Society. For the provisional registry of ships, a page shall be fixed by the Registrar in the Register and whenever the permanent registration is confirmed then the same page shall be used where the word 'provisional' shall be replaced by 'permanent'. The serial number of the ship shall be the same and two different dates should be given, one for provisional and the other for permanent registration (Director General of MS Order No. 2 of 2002 dated 2 May 2002 No. SD-13/POL (5) 2001). A ship which is required to be registered in India but has not been so registered shall not be recognized as an Indian ship. The provisions of the MS Act also provide safeguards against the wrongful assumption of Indian character by foreign-owned ships and concealment of Indian character by Indian ships (sections 63, 65). The law also requires the registered ships to hoist proper and prescribed national colours (section 66).

5. Certificate of Registry

152. Certificate of registry is the proof of the nationality of the ship and it is almost like a title deed. Being a public document it also shows the privileges of the ship and the obligations of an Indian ship also showing that the master is the lawfully appointed master. Any change in the master or owner shall be endorsed on the certificate by the Registrar or by any other duly authorized person. The certificate also becomes useful in the event of the ship becoming lost or ceasing to be Indian owned, the certificate shall be returned to the Registrar for closing the registry. Every Registrar of ships, Principal officer and the Surveyors incharge are required to maintain a complete record of ships on register entering the date, person or persons, either in their individual capacity or as joint owners or as a corporate body. Not more than ten individuals are entitled to be registered as the owner of a fractional part of a share in a ship or of any share and shares therein. The certificate of registry, issued by the Registrar of Indian ships of the port of registry contains the following particulars; the name of the ship and the name of the port to which she belongs, the details contained in the surveyor's certificate, the particulars respecting her origin stated in the declaration of ownership and the name and description of her registered owner or owners and, if there are more owners than one, the number of shares owned by each of them and the name of the Master.

§3. Acquisition and Ownership

153. Part V of the MS Act deals with the transfer of ownership or interest in an Indian ship. Section 42 deals with the transfer of ships or shares and says that no person shall transfer or acquire any Indian ship or any share or interest therein without the previous approval of the Central Government. According to this provision the Indian shipowners if they wanted to build a ship whether in India or abroad or if they want to buy a second-hand ship whether Indian or foreign, must take the previous approval of the Government of India.

154. With a view to liberalize policy so that the Indian shipowners could take on the spot advantage of the shipping market, section 42 was amended in 1993 as under: (1) No person shall transfer or acquire any Indian ship or any share or interest therein at any time during which the security of India or of any part of the territory thereof is threatened by war or external aggression and during which a proclamation of emergency under clause (1) of Article 352 of the Indian Constitution is in operation (2A). No transfer or acquisition of any Indian ship shall be valid unless: (i) all wages and other amounts due to seamen in connection with their employment on that ship have been paid in accordance with the provisions of this Act; (ii) the owner of the ship has given notice of such transfer or acquisition of the ship to the DGS. The said amendment has simplified the acquisition, sale or creating mortgage on Indian ships as no prior approval is now necessary.

155. However, the amendment intends to safeguard the interests of the crew of Indian ships so sold by requiring settlement of their wages or other dues before the actual sale of Indian ships. The transfer of an Indian ship or share therein shall be through a written instrument. Such instrument shall contain such description of the ship as is contained in the surveyor's certificate or some other description sufficient to identify the ship to the satisfaction of the registrar and shall be in the prescribed form or as near thereto as circumstances permit and shall be executed by the transferor in the presence of and be attested by at least two witnesses (section 42). Every such instrument after its execution shall be registered with the registrar of her port of registry and the registrar shall enter in the register book the name of the transferee as the owner of the ship or share and shall make an endorsement on the instrument the fact of entry having been made with the day and hour thereof (section 43).

I. Transmission of Property in Indian Ship on Death, Insolvency

156. Where the property in an Indian ship or share therein is transmitted to a person on the death or insolvency of any registered owner or by any lawful means other than by a transfer under the MS Act then the person shall authenticate the transmission by making and signing a declaration in the prescribed form identifying the ship and the manner of transmission. In case of transmission as a result of insolvency, the declaration should contain the proof of such claim and in case of transmission consequent upon death, the declaration should contain a succession certificate, probate or letters of administration under the Indian Succession Act 1925. The registrar while registering the declaration of transmission shall, if there are two or more persons register them as one and no one shall be regarded as the owner of the fraction but as joint owners of an undivided part (section 44).

II. Transmission of Proprietary Interest in Indian Ship

157. Transmission of interest in Indian ships can take place by operation of law. As a consequence, the ownership passes to a foreigner and the ship may cease to be an Indian ship. With the purpose of conserving Indian tonnage, the law provides for the sale of such ships through High Court to any citizen of India or any company or a statutory body of cooperative society which satisfies the requirements specified in section 21 of the MS Act 1958. The new owner being a foreigner will be paid from the proceeds of such sale after deducing the expenses thereof. Usually, ships are owned by limited companies where there is no effect of the death or marriage and the liquidator of such ship is an Indian and thus the eventuality of the ship losing its nationality hardly arises in such cases. Thus by this way, the transfer of ownership or creation of property interest in an Indian ship arises and when a court orders sale of any ship or share therein, the court order declares a named person to have the right to own the ship or a share therein. If the person is an Indian then, the Indian Registrar of ships honours the court order and registers the ship or share it in the name of such person. If the new owner is a foreigner and the ship ceases to be an Indian ship, the registrar of ships in the other country likewise accepts the claim of that country's owner of the ship and grants registry to that ship in accordance with its law (sections 44–46).

III. Transfer Procedure

158. Transfer can be effected only by a written instrument containing the full description of the ship as is generally contained in the Surveyor's Certificate (Registration Form No. 9 MS (Registration of Ships) Rules 1960) Where such transfer takes place in India then the instrument shall be accompanied by a declaration of ownership and presented to the registrar of ships who shall then make relevant entries in the registration document. The DGS is required to be kept informed of such transfers. As regarding the transfer of interest in an Indian ship which occurs due to the death or insolvency of the registered owner or by any other lawful means then an application is to be made to the Registrar giving out full details of the ship and the manner of transmission. As when transmission takes place on the basis of insolvency then the proof of such claim must also be given with it and in case of transmission on the basis of death the declaration of transmission shall be accompanied by a succession certificate, probate or letters of administration under the Indian Succession Act 1925 or a duly certified copy thereof. The Registrar is then required to make relevant entries thereof. In the case where as a result of such transmission the ship ceases to be an Indian ship then the Registrar of her port of Registry shall inform the Central Government through the DGS about the circumstances in which it has ceased to be an Indian ship. The Central Government can then apply to the relevant High Court within sixty days of the receipt of such information for a direction for the sale of such ship to an Indian or to an Indian Company.

IV. Sistership

159. There has been considerable deliberation by the courts regarding the ownership of a sistership. A ship in the same 'beneficial ownership' is called a 'sistership'. The Bombay High Court observed in *m. v. Mariner IV v. Videsh Sanchar Nigam Limited* ((1998) 1 Mah LJ 751) that 'In view of the decision of the Supreme Court in M. Elizabeth we are of the clear view that the High Court does have jurisdiction to arrest a "sistership" for securing any maritime claim'. In *m. v. Sea Success I-v-Liverpool and London Steamship Protection and Indemnity Association Ltd*, the Bombay High Court held that a subsidiary company and a parent company are two separate entities. The Appeal Court is of the opinion that 'In maritime law worldwide ownership of a ship is denoted by the concept of the owner of the shares in a ship. Fundamentally each company incorporated in law in a distinct legal entity and mere incorporation of 100% subsidiary company by its parent company cannot lead to the conclusion that the assets of the former belong to and are owned by parent company'. In *m v. Mariner IV* the Division Bench of the Bombay High Court held that 'The admiralty jurisdiction could be invoked not only against the offending but also against a sistership in regard to which the claim arose'. Ships are said to be in the same ownership when all the shares are owned by the same person or persons Article 3(2) of 1952 Brussels Arrest Convention) and thus the court concluded that the defendant No. 1 vessel is a sistership of the two vessels in question namely 'Sea Glory' and 'Sea Ranger' in view of the beneficial ownership.

Chapter 2. Maritime Liens and Mortgages

§1. Maritime Liens

I. General Concepts: Introduction

160. Maritime lien is a concept which can be traced back to the sixteenth and seventeenth centuries when maritime commerce formed the hub of trading activities in Europe. It evolved as part of international customary law and came to be recognized by all the nations of the world though it has not yet been formally defined. It is a charge upon maritime property, having the force of law and binds the property even in the hands of a bona fide purchaser for value and without notice. It can, however, only be enforced by admiralty claim in rem. A ship as a rule represents a usually large proportion of the owner's general property. It may cause unenforceable damage by collision or otherwise and such perils are unpredictable in the sea surroundings.

161. A ship can also be termed as an evasive sort of property which can be slipped out of the hands of a person when the owner remains unaware as he is far away from it whereas his financial strength is also unknown or untraceable. The foreign courts may prove expensive or unapproachable. Contracts of carriage and repairs done and other services rendered to the ship are customary practice. It was also seen that such services remained unpaid while the ship or the vessel slipped away leaving no remedy to the persons engaged in maritime activities as there was no means to get the assets of these foreigners attached. All these factors gave birth to the concept of maritime lien by which the aggrieved party is able to treat the vessel as a security for his claim.

162. The concept of maritime lien regards the ship as a person whereas whenever the charges in respect of any services rendered to it remain due then in such a case the ship or the vessel itself is presumed under an obligation to satisfy the claim and in case of the sale of the vessel the proceeds are to be appropriated to the satisfaction of maritime lien. No public undertakings having the authority to sell the vessel can sell it without the lien attached to it.

163. Some thinkers define maritime lien as: (i) a right to a part of property in the res; and (ii) a privileged claim upon a ship, aircraft or other maritime property in respect of services rendered to or injury caused by that property. A maritime lien is attached to the property at the moment the cause of action arises and remains attached (rather like a leech to human skin), travelling with it through changes of ownership. It is of, however, minimal value unless enforced by action in rem (Saurabh Singh – A Comment on the Concept of Maritime Lien, Journal of the Indian Law Institute, New Delhi. Vol. 48 No. 4 2006 at 572).

164. The underlying idea in a maritime concept is that since the vessel is regarded as a person and the services have been rendered to the vessel then the claims attached to the vessel are to be discharged by it. The concept of maritime lien differed from other types of liens in the sense that; it was independent of possession, that even if bona fide purchaser purchased it even then it did not extinguish, and that the lien rests itself irrespective of the owner. In *M. v. Elizabeth*, the Supreme Court of India made a comment on the justification of maritime lien by saying that:

> Merchant ships of different nationalities travel from port to port carrying goods or passengers. They incur liabilities in the course of their voyage and they subject themselves to the jurisdiction of foreign States when they enter the waters of those States. They are liable to be arrested for the enforcement of maritime claims, or seized in execution or satisfaction of judgments in legal actions arising out of collisions, salvage, loss of life or personal injury, loss or damages to goods and the like.

165. As maritime lien is a common law concept hence most of the countries including India do not have specific legislation. In this regard, India has been following the laws of the UK and in this regard courts in India having admiralty jurisdiction are competent to deal with cases of maritime liens. The MS Act 1958, Admiralty Courts Act 1861 and the judicial decisions recognize and confirm the international practice in this respect. Sections 439–445 of MSA provides detailed provisions for seamen wages, section 402 of MSA provides for maritime lien for salvage. Section 7 of the Admiralty Court Act 1861 provide for maritime lien in respect of claims for damage done by any ship.

166. The Admiralty Bill 2005 proposed under Article 13 that maritime lien shall attach to a ship for its property in respect of the following:

1. Claim for salvage of life, ship or its property.
   The salvage services for saving life, from a vessel registered in India or assisting a vessel or saving the cargo or equipment of a vessel which is wrecked, stranded or in distress at any place on or near the coasts of India, or the services in saving a wreck are the amounts of money due to the salvor and operate as liens. The salvage in saving life has a preference over all other claims for salvage. Moreover, where services are rendered by or on behalf of the Government or the Indian Navy or of the Coast Guard or any other member working therein shall also get the same rights and remedies as the normal salvors (section 402 MSA).

(2) Wages and other sums due to the master or members of the crew of the ship in respect of their employment on the ship; the master of a ship is under obligation to deliver an account of wages to be paid off to seamen. No objection can be raised with regard to the payment of wages to the master that the company was merely an agent of the owner of the ship and as such, it cannot be made liable for making payment under section 129(2) of the MS Act.

(3) Claim for loss of life or personal injury having a direct connection with the operation of the ship.

(4) Claim for contribution to general average; Claim to general average contribution can be made when there is a common danger which is real and not apprehended the sacrifice is necessitated, and it is voluntary and real and the imperil led property is saved and the mission is successful. The measure of indemnity is governed by 'contributory value' which is its arrived value less any expenses or charges incurred after the general act which would not have been incurred had this proved abortive (section 73 IMA).

(5) Port, canal and other waterway dues and pilotage dues.

Amount, as directed by the Government in the prescribed manner, shall be levied on vessels entering the port and the rate of such dues is subject to changes made by the Government. The amount as port dues shall be collected by the officers appointed by the Government. No port clearance is to be granted until the port charges are paid and any person failing to pay the port dues shall be liable to pay a fine which may extend to five times the amount of the sum (sections 33, 34, 43 and 45 The Indian Ports Act 1908). Fees may be charged for pilotage, hauling, mooring, remooring, hooking, measuring and other services rendered to vessels at such rates as the Government may direct (section 35 The Indian Ports Act 1908).

(6) Claim based on tort arising out of physical loss or damage caused by the operation of the ship other than the loss or damage to cargo, containers and passengers' effects carried on the ship, the date of accrual of such maritime lien being the date on which he operation giving rise to the said claim were performed.

167. The Supreme Court of India in *M. V. AL Quamar v. Tsavliris Salvage (International) Ltd* (2000) (8) SCC 278) and *MV. Elizabeth v. Harwan Investment and Trading ((P) Ltd* (1993 Supp. (2) SCC 433) declared that there are two attributes to maritime lien; first, a right over a part of the property in the res and second, a privileged claim upon the ship in respect of services rendered to or injury caused by that property. In *Epoch Enterrepots v. MV Won Fu* ((2003) 1 SCC 305), the court listed salvage, wages of seamen, collision, general average and port canal and other waterway dues as situations where maritime lien will arise reflecting the international practice in this respect. In the recent judgment in *O. Konavalov v. Commander Coast Guard region and Others* ((2006) 4 SCC 620), the Supreme Court gave the ruling regarding the seamen wages as given in section 144 of the MSA which gives the unfettered right to seamen for wages. In this case, the vessel Klobe Queen I which was carrying steel into the TW was seized by the customs department because it violated section 30 (the section provides that any vessel entering the TW of India is required to show their import manifestation and in event of non-compliance the vessel will be arrested) of the Indian Customs Act 1962.

168. Later under section 115 (the power to confiscate a vessel absolutely in the event of any contraband being brought to India and 115(2) provides relief against confiscation if it is established by the owner or the person in charge of the conveyance that the conveyance has been used for the prohibited purpose without their knowledge or connivance) of the said Act, the custom's commissioner confiscated the vessel absolutely and later the cargo and the vessel were sold. On the demand by the owner of the ship regarding the wages of the seamen to be paid out of the proceeds of the sale, the customs department responded by saying that the res of the confiscated vessel is the property of the Central Government and hence the principle of sovereign immunity applied and there can thus be no lien on the vessel.

169. This section depicts contradiction with sections 138, 140, 141 and 144 of the MSA which envisage a scheme of statutory rights of wages of seamen which could be enforced under section 145 of the Act. Rights to wages of seamen are declared unfettered under section 144 of MSA. The right of seamen regarding their wages is recognized internationally and it is ruled that a seaman has 'a right to cling to the last plank of the ship in satisfaction of the wages or part of them' as declared in The Neptune (1 Hagg 227) and Ruta ((2000) 1 Lloyd's Rep 359).

170. The Supreme Court of India thus envisages the international judicial thought regarding seamen's wages and in the light of such judgments invoked Article 21 of the Constitution of India (fundamental right to life and personal liberty to all irrespective of the nationality of a person) Interpreting both the provisions the Court held that Article 21 also includes the right to livelihood (Olga Tellis (1985) 3 SCC 545) and thus section 144 of the MSA is in consonance with Article 21 and upheld the international practice of recognizing the payment of seamen's wages.

II. Categories of Maritime Liens

171. The national laws of maritime countries on maritime liens and mortgages differ from country to country and consequently, the categories of claims also differ. Some of the national laws recognize certain rights in ships, not being maritime liens, for example, the possessory lien of shipwrights and port authorities which under certain conditions rank higher than all maritime claims. Even some countries discriminate against the rights of foreign creditors and protect their own nationals. A maritime lien takes precedence over the claim of a mortgagee in respect of a mortgaged ship mainly because it has a possessory claim on the ship. The claims which are usually accepted as maritime liens are wages and other sums, due to the officers and crew of a vessel in respect of their employment on the vessel, public charges like tonnage dues, harbour dues, and pilotage dues, remuneration for assistance, salvage and contribution to general average and claims in respect of loss of life or personal injury occurring in connection with the operation of the vessel and claims for damage, and so on, arising from tort.

172. The seller of a ship may have a possessory lien for the unpaid purchase price and a ship repairer may have a similar lien for repairs done on the vessel. In *Epoch Enterrepots v. M. V. Won Fu* (2003 1 SCC 305), it was held by the Supreme Court of India that the Admiralty Courts Act 1961 read with International Convention for Unification of Certain Rules Relating to Maritime Rules Relating to Maritime Liens and Mortgages at Brussels 1926 read with the Brussels' Arrest for (of

Sea-going Ships) Convention 1952 and the Brussels Maritime Liens Convention 1967 indicates that a claim arising out of an agreement relating to use or hire of the ship although a maritime claim cannot be called as a maritime lien. Thus a maritime lien exists in the following cases:

- Any claim for damage done by any ship – The High Court on its Admiralty side has exclusive jurisdiction in respect of damage done by a ship to property on the high seas, causing loss of life or personal injury as a result of collision which falls under section (d) by virtue of the Maritime Conventions Act 1911. But this Convention so far as it extended and operated as part of Indian law was repealed by section 46(2) of the MS Act 1958 (w. E. F. 1 January 1961) and it depends on the judicial interpretation whether from such date claim for damages for loss of life or personal injuries will still come under the purview of the section.
- Any claim for damage received by any ship or sea-going vessel – It does not make any difference whether such ship was in India or upon the high seas when the damage was done but any such claim being made by a ship or sea-going vessel is a maritime claim.
- Whenever there is any claim for the ownership of the ship or to the ownership of any share therein then it is a maritime claim.
- Any claim in the nature of salvage services rendered to a ship, whether such ship or vessel was within India or the high seas at the time when its services were rendered. Section 402 of the MS Act enumerates the services as follows: service rendered in assisting a vessel or saving the cargo or equipment of a vessel which is wrecked, stranded or in distress at any place on or near the coast of India; or service rendered by any person to save the wreck; salvage in respect of the preservation of life when payable by the owner of the vessel shall be payable in priority to all other claims for salvage; when services are rendered by or on behalf of the Government or by any vessel belonging to the Indian Navy then their rights and liabilities are recognized as that of a salvor; any dispute regarding the amount under the present section.
- Any claim by a master or crew for wages or for any money or property which under any statutory provisions is recoverable as such.
- Any claim by a master in respect of disbursements made on account of a ship.
- Any claim arising out of bottomry. The last judicial pronouncement in this regard was in 1967 (*m. v. Kali Elpis*) and is almost obsolete in practice.

III. Employment of Maritime Liens

173. A maritime lien is a claim against a ship or other maritime property which can be made effective by the seizure of the property in question. It exists independently of the possession of the object over which it is claimed but is attached to it in the sense that it is unaffected by change of ownership or of registration, in fact, it is a right in rem and is enforceable against the world at large. There have been many attempts at the international level to unify the rules regarding priorities and manner of enforcing maritime liens. The 151st Report of the Law Commission recommends the situations in which maritime liens would be attached to a ship or a property (section 13, at 151.92). The date of accrual of such maritime lien shall be the date on which the operations giving rise to the said claim were performed. These are:

(a) Claims for salvage of life, ship or property.
(b) Wages and other sums due to the master or the members of the crew of the ship in respect of their employment on the ship.
(c) Port and canal and other waterway dues and pilotage dues.
(d) Claims for loss of life or personal injury having a direct connection with the operation of the ship.
(e) Claims for contribution to general average.
(f) Claims based on tort arising out of physical loss or damage caused by the operation of the ship other than the loss or damage due to cargo, containers and passengers' effects carried on the ship.

174. A maritime lien shall stand extinguished on the expiry of one year from the date on which the lien has attached to the ship or property. The Claim if not barred by limitation may be enforced by an action in personam. The period of one year may be further extended if the claimant was unable to commence an action due to some reason beyond his control. Any person who has a right to lien can enforce it.

IV. Concurrent Liens

A. *Custom and Port Authorities*

175. The officer who is under a duty to take the port charges and other customs authorities has a lien.

B. *Agent's Lien*

176. An Agent has a lien over the property of the principal. Unless barred by a contract, an agent is entitled to retain goods, paper and other property whether movable and immovable of the principal received by him, until the amount due to himself for commission, disbursements and services in respect of the same has been paid or accounted for to him. In this case, it is to be seen that the agent exercises such lien over a property which belongs to the principal and the agent is lawfully entitled to receive from the principal a sum of money by way of commission or disbursements made or services rendered in the proper execution of the business or agency (section 221 The India Contract Act 1872). The Agent, however, loses such right of lien when the possession is lost, when he waives his right of lien and a contract to the contrary exists.

C. Bottomry Bond

177. A bottomry bond or contract is a maritime bond which is often entered into by the master of a ship. It is the maritime bond in the form of a mortgage or hypothecation of a ship whereby the keel or bottom is pledged in order to secure a loan. It creates a lien. Similarly, there can be hypothecation of cargo by the master of the ship without transfer of possession. The lender advances in good faith with the hope to get possession of the goods in case the payment of loan is not made. The master of a ship, as an agent of necessity, has the power to pledge the goods on behalf of the owner in order to meet the exigencies to complete the voyage. Such exigencies are: the expenses must be reasonably necessary for the completion of the voyage; there are no other ways by which the master can raise the funds; the expenditure is safety for both the cargo and the ship; and the master is unable to communicate with the cargo owner.

V. Ranking

178. The 151st Report of the Law Commission recommends the following order of priority of claims (section 12, at 151.91).

The order of claim determining *inter se* priority in an admiralty action shall be as follows:

(a) A claim where there is a maritime lien on any ship or other property including bunker against which the action is proceeded with.
(b) Mortgages and charges on the ship or other property against which action is proceeded with.
(c) All other claims. The priority among the claims *inter se* in clause (a) shall be as follows:
  - Claims for salvage of life, ship or property provided that salvage of life shall take priority over other salvages.
  - Wages or other sums due to the master or the members of the crew of the ship in respect of their employment in the ship not exceeding six month's wages.
  - Port, canal and other waterway dues and Pilotage dues.
(d) Balance of wages and other sums due to the master or the members of the crew of the ship in respect of their employment on the ship after deducting the amount paid under clause (ii) above.
  - Claims in respect of the loss of life or personal injury in direct connection with the operation of the ship.
  - Claims for the contribution of general average.
  - Claims based on tort arising out of physical damage or damage caused by the operation of the ship other than loss or damage to cargo containers and passengers' effects carried on the ship.
  - Bottomry.

The rules regarding the determination of priority claims *inter se* are that:

(a) the claims in order of priority shall exclude subsequent ones;
(b) if there are more claims than one in any category of priority, they shall rank *pari passu*;
(c) claims for various salvages shall rank in reverse order of time (when the claim secured thereto accrued) claims for salvage, port dues, wages and claims in the nature of general average shall take priority over all other claims mentioned in clause (e) above which are attached to ship prior to the time when the operations giving rise to the said claims were performed.

VI. Choice of Law

179. Often when in one case more than one national laws clash with each other uncertainties and ambiguity in the litigation process is bound to arise. Arbitration comes out as the common remedy and choice of law plays a crucial role in the international arena. Four separate choices of law issues arise in respect of international arbitration which are: (1) the substantive laws governing contract, (2) the substantive law governing the parties' arbitration agreement, (3) the procedural law applicable to the arbitration proceedings, and (4) the conflict of law rules. India too has accepted the choice of law option to some extent. In the early 1920s under the League of Nations, the Geneva Convention of 1923 was adopted and it was ratified by a number of countries including India. The Protocol was augmented by the Geneva Convention for the Execution of Foreign Arbitral Awards of 1927 which expanded the enforceability of arbitration awards pursuant to arbitration awards and subject to the Geneva Protocol.

180. As there were many limitations in these conventions hence they were not widely ratified. After the Geneva Convention in 1958, the United Nations Convention on the Recognition and Enforcement of Foreign Arbitral Awards was signed. The convention is regarded as 'the cornerstone of current international commercial arbitration'.

181. During the last decade, India ratified the New York convention and even a good number of countries have adopted supportive legislation to provide a stable framework for international arbitration. Courts in such countries have not shown a positive attitude towards such conventions and have often held such arbitration agreements or awards invalid. In *Union of India v. McDonnell Douglas Corporation* (30 July 1987) Article 11 of the agreement provided that it was to be governed, interpreted and construed in accordance with the laws of India. In the agreement Article 8 envisaged the arbitration clause which said that '. … In the event of a dispute or difference arising out of or in connection with this Agreement which cannot be resolved by amicable settlement, the same shall be referred to an Arbitration Tribunal consisting of three members. Either Party shall give notice to the other regarding its decision to refer the matter to arbitration … .' The clause contained certain procedural rules regarding referring the matter to arbitration whereas it was agreed that the President of the ICC shall be requested to nominate the third Arbitrator who shall not be the citizen of either country. It was also agreed that the arbitration shall be conducted with the procedure provided in the Indian Arbitration Act 1940 and the seat of arbitration shall be London, cost of it to be equally borne by both the parties.

182. Thus the law of India having many similarities with the English law on the subject was chosen to govern the arbitration proceedings. Under Article 11 the parties chose to govern not only the arbitration proceedings but also the commercial bargaining is agreed to be done on the basis of Indian law. Drastic varieties in the national laws make the issues crucial. The dispute regarding the application of a particular substantive law is usually decided by international arbitrators ('choice of law clauses').

183. Often the national laws are in contradiction of private contractual agreements. The arbitral tribunal often selects a law. Traditionally the national conflict of laws rules of the arbitral situs is applied while some authorities appear to be moving towards recognition of an international body of conflict of laws rules. Instances are also there where the arbitral tribunal's 'direct' application of substantive rules of law.

184. Arbitration agreements are 'separable' from the actual contract as often the law governing the arbitration agreement and the law governing the contract are of different nationals. This happens often as a result of the parties' express choice of law or by the application of conflict of law rules. There are four alternatives of law governing an arbitration agreement; the law chosen by the parties to govern the arbitration agreement itself, the law of the arbitral *situs*, the law governing the parties' underlying contract and the law of the forum in which the agreement is to be judicially enforced. The examples are FAA in US court and IACA in India. The arbitration proceedings are subject to legal rules like the procedural law of arbitration, the curial law, the law arbitri, or the loi de l'arbitrage. Laws of different nations take different approaches to such rules, some are narrow in their approach while others give importance to universal rules like 'due process' or 'natural justice'. Under Indian rules of conflict of laws a foreign maritime lien may not be recognized by Indian courts, for example, a preferred ship's mortgage, necessaries, repairs, supplies, towage, use of dry dock though they are recognized under the United States law as a maritime lien. For this in the case of the owner's bankruptcy before applying for the arrest of the ship, the claimant is required to ascertain maritime liens such as for wages, damage, salvage and the like. Thus if a claim is clearly outside the admiralty jurisdiction of the court then the courts will reject in limine an application for the arrest of the ship.

§2. Ship Mortgages

I. General Concepts

185. Making vessel a security is done by way of mortgage. The charge or encumbrance is created in favour of the lender or the mortgagee by the mortgagor.

In this way, the mortgagee becomes a secured creditor and obtains a hold on the property mortgaged preventing all the general creditors from selling the ship in satisfaction of their claims and enables the mortgagee to recoup himself for the mortgagor's failure to repay the loan or to pay the interest thereon by the sale of the ship or by taking possession of her while the ship remains in the mortgagor's possession and use. Thus the mortgagee constitutes an ideal form of security since it allows the mortgagor to carry on his business activities but at the same time, it allows the mortgagee to have some control over the mortgaged ship. In this way, the mortgagee is able to take possession and realize the security as soon as the owner-debtor defaults or jeopardizes the security.

186. Mortgages are visible claims because national laws generally provide for the registration of mortgages with the Registrar of ships and when a ship is mortgaged to more than one party, the priority between them is determined by the date of registration, the mortgagee is protected against all unregistered mortgages or charges as well as against his trustee in bankruptcy. A mortgage, however, ranks only after maritime liens arising from various special contingencies.

II. Creation of the Ship Mortgage

187. A registered ship can be made a security for a loan. For this, according to section 47 of the MS Act 1958, this can be done by an instrument called mortgage which shall either be in a prescribed form or as near thereto as possible. On the production of such instrument, the registrar of the ship's port of registry shall record it in the register book. The mortgages shall be recorded by the registrar in the order in time in which they are produced to him for that purpose, and the registrar shall, by memorandum under his hand, notify on each mortgage that it has been recorded by him stating the day and hour of that record. In India, sections 47 to 54 of the MS Act 1958 and the MS (Registration of Indian Ships) Rules 1960 contain provisions relating to mortgages of ships. Thus a registered ship or a share therein may be mortgaged as security for a loan or other valuable consideration. The MS Act also apart from registration of mortgages provides for entry or discharge of mortgages by the registrar, priority of mortgages according to the date of registration of each mortgage, transfer of mortgage to third parties, transmission of interest in mortgage in certain circumstances, and so on.

188. Under section 51 (as amended 1993) if there is only one registered mortgagee of a ship or share he is entitled to recover the amount due under the mortgage deed by selling the mortgaged ship or share without approaching the High Court. If there are two or more registered mortgagees, they are entitled to enforce the mortgage and recover the amount due to him through a High Court in India. In this respect, Indian law conforms to the law in other countries like the UK.

III. Formalities Relating to the Creation of Mortgage

189. Section 47 of the MS Act lays down the basic formalities relating to the mortgage of a ship or share. Thus a registered ship or share stands as a security for a loan. The instrument of mortgage is required to be in a prescribed form whereas, on production of such instrument, the registrar of the ship's port of registry shall record it in the register book. Mortgages are recorded by the registrar in the order in which they are produced to him for that purpose, and he shall, by a memorandum in his hand, notify on each mortgage that it has been recorded by him and he should also state the exact timing of that record.

A. *Formalities*

190. The Order of the DGS issued in 2002 revises the formalities related to the creation of ship mortgage making it at par with the same rules in other parts of the world. The new guidelines say that the mortgage shall be entered on the provisional registry of ships. The Registrar shall issue a letter to the Bank or Financial institution stating, that once the mortgage is entered on provisional registration, the said mortgage will continue to remain in force even after the said ship has been granted permanent registration. When the registered mortgage is discharged, the Registrar shall, on the production of the mortgage deed with discharge duly signed, after satisfying himself that the discharge on the mortgage instrument is in order and that it is properly witnessed enter it in the register book.

191. When a joint mortgage is created in favour of two or more mortgagees and when the mortgage is released by one of the mortgagees, the Registrar shall on production of evidence relating to the release of mortgage, make the entry relating to the discharge of the mortgage by one of the mortgagees in the register book by way of modification of the mortgage. The registration of creation, modification or discharge of the mortgage with the Registrar of Companies shall not be a pre-requisite to entering a mortgage in the Register. The fees for entering every mortgage will be 10 paise for every INR 1,000 of the value of the mortgage for the entry of mortgage on the first ship. If the loan amount involves the creation of a mortgage on more than one vessel, the fee chargeable for entering the mortgage on the second and subsequent vessel would be INR 500 only. In case of an additional amount being sanctioned by the same mortgage leading to additional mortgage, the fee for registration shall be charged only for the additional amount (DIRECTOR GENERAL OF MERCHANT SHIPPING ORDER No. 2 of 2002 dated 2 May 2002 No. SD-13/POL (5) 2001).

1. Mortgage Deed

192. A mortgage deed is proof of a valid mortgage and its registration with the registrar. The mortgage deed is to be presented with a receipt for the mortgage money endorsed thereon, duly signed and attested at the time of the discharge of mortgage (section 48).

2. Recording and Registration

193. On receiving the mortgage instrument to the Registrar of the ship's port of registry, the Registrar shall proceed to record the mortgage transaction in the register book with the date and hour of acceptance and shall also endorse on it the fact of recording and the date and hour of acceptance. Mention should also be made by the Registrar that on the permanent registry of the ship, the mortgage will be automatically transferred on the permanent registry. The second and any subsequent mortgage on a ship will be recorded in the register of the ships only after No Objection Certificate (NOC) from the first or any existing mortgagee has been obtained.

IV. Ranking

194. Though a mortgagee is also a secured creditor, he ranks only after maritime liens arising from various special contingencies. In case there are more mortgages than one recorded in respect of the same ship or share, the mortgagees shall notwithstanding any express, implied or constructive notice, have priority according to the date on which each mortgage is recorded in the register book and not according to the date of each mortgage itself (section 49 MS Act). The mortgagee, however, continues to be the creditor and in no case shall be deemed to be the owner (section 50 MS Act).

V. Validity Period of Mortgage

195. There is no specified validity period of mortgage given under the MS Act or even under the regular Transfer of Property Act 1882.

VI. Assignment of Mortgage

196. A registered mortgagee of a ship or share may be transferred to any person and the instrument affecting the transfer shall be in the prescribed form or as near thereto as circumstances permit. The Registrar shall complete all the formalities of such transfer by entering in the register book the name of the transferee as mortgagee of the ship or share and by notifying on the instrument of transfer that it is recorded by him by also mentioning the date and time on it (section 53 MSA).

A. Transmission of Interest in Mortgage

197. An interest of a mortgagee in a ship or share may be transmitted on death, insolvency or by any lawful means but not by a transfer under MSA. Such transmission is to be authenticated by a declaration of the person to whom the interest is transmitted containing a statement of the manner in which and the person to whom the property has been transmitted and shall be accompanied by the like evidence as is by this Act required in case of a corresponding transmission of the ownership of a ship or share. On receiving the declaration and on production of the evidence aforesaid, the Registrar shall enter the name of the person entitled under the transmission in the register book as mortgagee of the ship or share (section 54 MSA).

VII. Ship Mortgage and International Law

198. Legal mortgages are usually allowed in favour of complete ships which are duly registered. As an international practice, most of the countries are allowing legal mortgages of ships which are under construction so as to facilitate the financing of new ships. In such cases, if the mortgage is not when the completed ship is registered, the mortgage is transferred to the ordinary ship's register. In India, the MS Act permits statutory mortgages only in respect of registered ships. However, there is nothing to prevent ships under construction from being accepted as a security by the builders or financers for the payment of purchase price. In such cases, the ship under construction and the material and equipment purchased by the builder for construction are hypothecated to him or the financer by the prospective owner by agreement between the parties concerned which forms a reasonably good security.

§3. Extinction of Ship Mortgages and Liens

199. When a registered mortgage is discharged, the registrar shall, on the production of the mortgage deed with a receipt for the mortgage money endorsed thereon duly signed and attested, make an entry in the register book to the effect that the mortgage has been discharged. When such entry is made the estate if there is any which passed to the mortgagee shall vest in the person in whom having regard to intervening acts and circumstances if any, it would have vested, if the mortgage had not been made (section 48 MS Act).

I. Extinction of the Main Claim

200. The mortgage normally ends when the debt is satisfied and the ship is relieved. This is regulated by the terms covered by the parties. In case there is and dispute and the matter goes to court, then the verdict of the court puts an end to all the claims.

II. Claim Waiver by the Creditor

201. When a ship is mortgaged there is a charge or encumbrance which the borrower of money, the mortgagor creates in favour of the lender or the mortgagee. The mortgagee becomes a secured creditor and obtains a hold on the property mortgaged which prevents the general creditor of the owner from selling the ship in satisfaction of their claims and enables the mortgagee to recoup himself for the mortgagor's failure to repay the loan or to pay the interest thereon by the sale of the ship or by taking possession of it.

III. Forced Public Sale

A. Order for Sale Where Ship Has Ceased to Be An Indian Ship

202. In all cases where by reason of the transmission of any property in a ship or a share therein on death, insolvency or otherwise, a ship ceases to be an Indian ship the Registrar of her port of registry shall send a report regarding it to the Central Government. Thereafter on receipt of such report, the Central Government may make an application to the High Court for a direction for the sale to any citizen of India, or to any company or body established by or under any Central or State Act which has its principal place of business in India (section 21(b) MSA) or cooperative society which is registered or deemed to be registered under the Cooperative societies Act 1912 (2 of 1912) or any other law relating to cooperative societies for the time being in force in India (section 21(c) MSA).

203. The High Court is also authorized to take evidence in support of the application and pass an order accordingly or it may also reject the application. In case the High Court finds that the ship has not ceased to be an Indian ship and in case the ship or share is ordered to be sold, then it shall direct that the proceeds of the sale after deducting the necessary expenses thereof, be paid to the person entitled under such transmission. Every application for sale must be made within prescribed time and in case of delay beyond such period if the Central Government satisfies the High Court regarding the reason of such delay then the High Court may admit such application.

IV. Voluntary Sale of the Encumbered Vessel

204. It has been recognized as the right of the mortgagee that when there is only one registered mortgagee under the mortgaged ship or share then he shall be entitled to recover the due amount under the mortgaged ship without approaching the High Court. When such mortgagee intends to sell the mortgaged ship or share then he is required to give an advance notice of fifteen days relating to such sale to the registrar of the ship's port of registry. The notice should be accompanied with the proof of payment of the wages and a declaration that other amounts as given under section 42(2A)(a) … due to seamen in connection with their employment on that ship have been paid in accordance with the provisions of MS Act (section 51 MS Act). In case there are two or more registered mortgagees of s ship or share they shall be entitled to recover the amount due under the mortgage in the High Court and when passing a decree or thereafter the High Court may direct that the mortgaged ship or share be sold in execution of the decree. The admiralty court has jurisdiction to exercise jurisdiction of the High Court. The provisions of the Recovery of Debts due to Banks and Financial Institutions Act 1993 do not oust the jurisdiction of the High Court to entertain the suit filed by a bank or financial institution of recovery of its claim against a vessel in its admiralty jurisdiction (*ICICI Ltd v. MFV Shilpa an Indian Vessel*, AIR 2002 Bom 37). Such High Court can also direct the sale of the ship in the execution of the decree.

V. Modification of the Vessel's Nationality

205. Whenever the ownership of any Indian ship is changed then the registrar of the port at which the ship is registered may on the application of the owner of the ship register the ship anew. The registrar of a ship shall deposit the certificate of the first registry and may require some other documents before the second registry is completed. Once the new registry is done the old registry stands closed. The MS Act prohibits the unlawful assumption of Indian character by a foreign ship except for the purpose of capture by the enemy or by a foreign ship of war in the exercise of some belligerent right. It also prohibits the concealment of Indian or assumption of foreign character by a ship with the intent to deceive any authority (sections 59, 64, 65, MS Act).

Chapter 3. Master and Crew

§1. Master

206. The master is the most important person aboard. He is the centre point of all the activities and sits at the helm of affairs in the ship. The rights and the liabilities of the master are extensive and give many dimensions to his position; like he is the representative of the owner, he is the person who is contacted by the passengers during normal times and at the time of peril, he is also contacted by the shippers, consignors, consignees and by the authorities.

I. Appointment of the Master

207. According to section 3(22) of the Indian Merchants Shipping Act 1958 'master' includes any person (except a pilot or harbour master) having command or charge of a ship. This was reiterated by the Supreme Court of India (*Karan Vaswani v. Union of India & Others* AIR 2000 SC 1447). Master of the ship is supposed to be an officer in rank than seamen. There is an absence of provision which equals seamen and master of the ship (AIR 1985 SC 760). The owner appoints the master on the basis of a contract concluded between the two.

Section 3(2) of the Indian Ports Act 1908 too defines 'master' when used as in relation to any vessel (or any aircraft making use of any port) any person (except a pilot or harbour master ((of the port) having for the time being the charge or control of the vessel (or the aircraft, as the case may be).

II. Public Functions of the Master

208. The public functions of the master of a ship under Indian law are many. The MS Act enjoins upon the master a number of duties and obligations which in fact make the master the most sought after person on board. Most of his functions are in the nature of duties the violation of which gives rise to both civil and criminal liability.

A. *Taking Charge of the Effects of Deceased Seamen*

209. According to the Act, any seaman or apprentice engaged on any ship, the voyage of which is to terminate in India, dies during that voyage, the master of the ship shall report the death to the next of kin of the deceased and to the shipping master at the port of engagement (section 152 MS Act). He shall also take charge of any money or effects belonging to the seaman or apprentice which are on board the ship. The master then should also enter in the official logbook the following particulars, namely; a statement of the amount of money and a detailed description of the other effects.

He should also enter a statement of the sum due to the deceased for wages and of the amount of deduction, if any, to be made from the wages.

B. Dealing With and Account of Property of Seamen Who Die During Voyage

210. Whereas any seaman or apprentice engaged on any ship, the voyage of which is to end in India dies during the voyage and the ship remains for about forty-eight hours at some place in India then the master should contact the Indian consular at such port and make him abreast of the details of the voyage.

III. Private Functions of the Master

211. The relation of the master with the owner gives rise to certain duties which may not be found in the law provisions but which come from the employment agreement between the owner and the master. Most of the private functions have evolved on the basis of tradition and usage. The nature of such functions and the authority of the master as the agent of the owner also vary according to the usage of the trade. Though he is a servant of the owner of the ship yet for a good number of functions he also acts as the agent of the owner. During the voyage, his position becomes all the more important in the absence of the owner and in the loss of any contact with him.

A. Binding the Owner

212. The master has the implied authority to bind the owner by a charter party and when he is away in the sea and cannot contact the owner.

B. Supplying Goods

213. His authority may also extend to contracts for the supply of certain important things related to the ship, like the anchors, cables, rigging, fuel, provisions and clothing for the crew, copper sheathing, a screw propeller or for the advance of money to pay for the necessaries.

C. To Tranship

214. The master also has the authority to transship the cargo to another vessel to be forwarded to its original destination.

D. To Jettison Cargo

215. He is also entitled to throw away any dangerous goods where such goods are not properly marked and well packed according to their nature. When there is peril in the sea the master is the person who decides the goods and cargo to be jettisoned to mitigate the danger to the ship. He is also entitled to throw away any dangerous goods where such goods are not properly marked and well packed according to their nature. When there is peril in the sea the master is the person who decides the goods and cargo to be jettisoned to mitigate the danger to the ship.

E. Legal Representation

216. He also has the authority to sell the goods. In legal matters, the master represents the owner.

IV. Main Duties of the Master

217. The master of a ship is to discharge the following duties under the Maritime Shipping Act 1958.

A. Renewal of Running Agreements in Certain Cases

218. The master of a ship, with the previous sanction of the shipping master, renew the agreement with the crew when a running agreement has been made with the crew of a foreign-going Indian ship and the ship arrives after the expiration of a period of six months from the date on which it was executed at a port of destination in India which is not the port at which the crew have agreed to be discharged. When such renewal is required by the shipping master to be made by the master of a ship and the master refuses to so renew it then all the expenses arising out of the subsistence of the crew and their conveyance to the port at which they have agreed to be discharged incurred by the Government shall be a charge upon the ship (section 104).

B. Changes in Crew to Be Reported

219. The master of every foreign-going ship and of every home-trade Indian ship of two hundred tonnes gross or more, the crew of which has been engaged before a shipping master, shall before finally leaving the port where the engagement took place, sign and send to the nearest shipping master a full and accurate statement in the prescribed, of every change which has taken place in his crew, and that statement shall be admissible in evidence. A copy of such a statement is to be sent to the seamen's employment office (section 105).

C. Duties in Respect of Seamen and Apprentice

220. The master shall, in the event of a seaman or apprentice being left behind must keep a record of the amount due to the seaman or apprentice and of the property left behind by him and must take charge of such property. He shall then hand over the due amount and the property to the shipping master (section 122 MS Act).

D. Certificate as to Agreement with Crew

221. The master of a ship is under a duty to produce before the customs collector, a certificate granted to it by the shipping master regarding the renewal of the running agreement or regarding the execution of an agreement with the crew of a foreign-going ship or a home trade Indian ship of two hundred tonnes gross or more. The master shall also, within forty-eight hours after the ship's arrival at the port in India at which the crew is to be discharged, deliver such agreement to a shipping master at the port who will then give to the master a certificate of such delivery. Copy of such agreement shall be made accessible to the crew whereas the master is required to cause a legible copy of the agreement and if necessary a certified translation thereof, to be placed or posted up in such part of the ship so as to make it accessible to the crew (section 107).

E. Repatriation of Seamen on Termination of Service

222. When the services of the seaman or apprentice are without his consent at a port outside India, then the master shall not only take care of the terminated servant as per his status but should also arrange for the return of him to some proper port (section 122).

F. Master to Deliver Account of Wages

223. When a seaman is paid off or discharged under the Act then the master has a duty to deliver a full and true account in the form prescribed, of the seaman's wages and of all deductions to be made therefrom either to the seaman himself or to the shipping master (section 122).

G. Disrating of Seamen

224. When the master of a ship disrates a seaman, he shall forthwith enter or cause to be entered in the official logbook a statement of the disrating and hand over a copy of the entry to the seaman whereas no reductions in the wages shall be done unless such copy is delivered (section 126).

H. Deductions from Wages

225. The master shall keep a record of the various matters in respect of which the deductions are made during the voyage regarding a seaman in a book kept for it. Such book shall be produced by him during payment of wages or before any competent authority if so required (section 127).

I. Time of Payment of Wages

226. The master, owner or agent is under obligation to pay his wages within four days after the seaman is discharged. Failure to do so shall entitle the discharged seaman to an increased amount (section 129).

J. Master to Give Facilities to Seaman

227. Where the seaman expresses his desire to the master that any due amount of his wages be remitted to any savings bank or near relative then the master is under a duty to do so (section 131).

K. Inspection by Master of Provisions, and so on

228. The Master of an Indian ship which is at sea shall, once in every ten days cause an inspection to be made of the provisions and water provided for the seamen. He should also ascertain whether such items are supplied in accordance with the standards set by the MS Act (section 177).

L. Duty of Master of Ship to Assist

229. Whenever there is a collision between two ships it shall be the duty of the master or any other person who is in charge of each ship to render to his own ship, crew and passengers, or to the other ship such assistance as may be practicable and may be necessary to save them from any danger and to stay with the other ship unless it is assured by it that there is no further need for such assistance and to give to the masters or persons in charge of the other ships the name of his own ship and of the port to which she belongs and also the names of the ports from which she comes and to which she is bound (section 348 MS Act).

M. Maintenance of Log Books Entries to Be Made by the Master

230. The official logbook shall be kept in a prescribed form in every Indian ship except a home-trade ship of less than two hundred tonnes gross. The official log will at the discretion of the master be kept distinct from or united with the ordinary ship's log (section 212).

N. Duties in Respect of Official Log Books

231. All entries in the official logbook shall be made promptly and dated punctually and should be signed by the master and by the mate or some other member of the crew and by other authorities as prescribed. All such entries are admissible as evidence in law courts (section 213).

O. Entries to Be Made by the Master

232. The master of a ship shall enter or cause to enter in the official logbook the following matters, namely:

(a) every conviction by a legal tribunal of a member of his crew and the punishment inflicted;
(b) every offence committed by a member of his crew for which it is intended to prosecute or to enforce forfeiture or exact a fine;
(c) every offence for which punishment is inflicted on board and the punishment inflicted;
(d) a report on the quality of work of each member of his crew and in case he declines to give such report then a statement mentioning the reason for so declining;
(e) every case of illness, hurt or injury happening to a member of the crew with nature thereof and the medical treatment adopted;
(f) every case of death onboard and the cause thereof;
(g) every birth happening on board, with the sex of the child, name of parents and other particulars;
(h) every marriage taking place on board with the names and ages of the parties;
(i) the name of every seaman or apprentice who ceases to be a member of the crew otherwise than by death, with the place, time, manner and cause thereof;
(j) the wages due to any seaman or apprentice who dies during the voyage and the gross amount of all deductions to be made therefrom;
(k) the money or other property taken over of any seaman or apprentice who dies during the voyage;
(l) any other matter which is to be or maybe prescribed for entry in the official log (section 214).

P. Master to Report Arrival

233. The master of a ship is under a duty to report, within twenty-four hours after the arrival, within the limits of any port of any vessel which is liable to the payment of port –dues to report her arrival to the conservator of the port (section 39 The Indian Ports Act 1908).

Q. Master to Hoist Number of Vessel

234. The master of every inward of outwards bond vessel, on arriving within a signal distance of any signal station established within the limits of the River Hooghly or within the limits of any part of a river or channel leading to a port which is subject to the Indian law, on requisition from the pilot in charge of the vessel, signifies the name of the vessel by hoisting the number by which she is known, or by adopting such other means to this end as may be practicable and usual and shall keep the signal flying until it is answered from the signal station (section 51 The Indian Ports Act 1908).

V. Liability of the Master

235. Liability of the master arises on several occasions; often when he fails to discharge his duties under the MS Act and often along with the owner or in place of the owner. Apart from this, his liability arises also under the Indian Ports Act 1908. All the liabilities here are almost criminal in nature as he is required to undergo imprisonment on several occasions (sections under which charges are given in brackets. All sections are of the MS Act). The section relevant to penalties and procedure is 436.

A. Liability of the Master Alone

236.

- Failing to deliver provisional certificate (36(4)) – Fine up to INR 500.
- Failing to deliver certificate of registry (38(3)).
- Master fails to notify about the lost ship (39(2)) – Fine up to INR 1000.
- Failing to produce contract of apprenticeship (94) – Fine up to INR 100.
- Taking a seaman to sea without a contract (100) – Fine up to INR 100 for each seaman so taken.
- Failing to renew the running agreements (104), failing to report changes in the crew (105) and failing to give agreement to the shipping master (106(4)) – Fine up to INR 50.
- Refusing or neglecting to produce certificate of fitness (General) – Fine up to INR 50.
- Failing to keep the register of young persons (General) – Fine up to INR 200.

- Master of a non-Indian ship engages a seaman in India without following the law (114) – Fine up to INR 100 for every such seaman.
- Fails to return certificate of competency to the officer concerned – (119) – Fine up to INR 200.
- Failing to deliver to the shipping master certificate of discharge of seaman –(120)
- Fine up to INR 100.
- Fails to deliver account of wages (125) – Fine up to INR 50.
- Failing to take charge of the deceased men (154(1)) – Fine up to three times the value of property, if not ascertained then up to INR 500.
- Refusing to receive distressed seamen on his ship – (163(1)) – Fine up to INR 1,000 in respect of each seaman.
- Using bad quality water for the crew (168(3)) – Fine which may extend to INR 200.
- Failing to allow inspection of water (168(6)) Fine up to INR 500.
- Failing to furnish provisions to a seaman – Fine up to INR 500.
- Failing to furnish weight and measures on board (171) – Fine up to INR 100.
- Failing to give facility to seaman to complain (184) – Fine up to INR 100.
- Failing to report about desertion and absence of seaman -(197) – Imprisonment up to one month or fine up to INR 100 or both.
- Failure to deduct fine from the wages of seaman (202) – Fine which may extend to six times the amount of the fine retained.
- Failing to deliver or transmit documents (209) – Fine up to INR 500.
- Discharging seaman outside India (210(1)) – Imprisonment up to three months or fine up to INR 1,000.
- Failing to report about birth or death on board to DGC (214) – Fine up to INR 100.
- Failing to deliver official logs to shipping master (216) – Fine up to INR 200.
- Contravenes the prescribed number of passengers (249) – Fine up to INR 1,000.
- Filing to produce certificates to the custom collector (307) – Fine up to INR 100 for each passenger.
- Failing to insert particulars (320) – Fine up to INR 100.
- Master of a nuclear ship failing to notify authorities (344F) – Fine up to INR 10,000.
- Failing to give notice about the accident and condition of a nuclear ship (344 G(1) (2)& (5)) – Imprisonment up to one year or fine up to INR 10,000.
- Failure to comply with 344G(3)(5) – Imprisonment up to one year or fine up to INR 10,000.
- Failing to assist in collision (348) – Imprisonment up to three months or fine up to INR 3,000.

  Failing to enter the report in the logbook (349) – Fine up to INR 100.
- Failing to give report of danger to authorities onshore (354) – Fine up to INR 500.
- Failure to render assistance at the time of distress (355(1)(2)) – Imprisonment up to six months or fine up to INR 1,000.
- Failing to register the reason of non-compliance to distress signal (355(5)) – Fine up to INR 1,000.

- Failing to render assistance to men in danger (355A) – Imprisonment up to six months or fine up to INR 1,000.
- Sailing into the sea without the international oil pollution certificate (356C(1)) – Fine up to INR 500,000.
- Sailing of an Indian ship carrying noxious liquid without a proper certificate (356C(2)) – Fine up to INR 500,000.
- When the discharge is by a foreign ship (356C(2)) – Fine up to INR 500,000.
- Master of an offshore installation, for discharge of oily mixture (356C(3)) – Fine up to INR 500,000.
- Failing to maintain an oil record book (356F) – Fine up to INR 5,000.
- Refuses to certify a copy of oil record book entry (356G(2)) – Fine up to INR 500.
- Proceeding to sea in spite of detention (444(2)) – Five up to INR 1,000.

B. Liability of the Master Along with the Owner

237.

- Failing to mark the ship (28(2)) – Fine up to INR 1,000.
- Certificate of registry which is not legal (35(4)) – Fine up to INR 1,000.
- Owner fails to notify about the lost ship (39(1)) – Fine up to INR 1,000.
- Owner fails to apply for renewal of registry (56) – Fine up to INR 1,000.
- Concealing the Indian character of the ship (65) – Imprisonment up to two years or fine up to INR 5,000.
- Failing to record properly contract of apprenticeship (93) – Fine up to INR 200.
- Wilfully disobeys prohibition to engage seamen (116) – Imprisonment up to three months or fine up to INR 1,000 or both.
- Failing to make the discharge of a seaman as per law (118) – Fine up to INR 100.
- Pays wages to a seaman without the presence of the shipping master – (128(1)) Fine which may extend to INR 100.
- Failing to follow the working hours of the seamen (138A) – Fine which may extend to double the average wages per hour payable to the seaman for working beyond forty-eight hours.
- Owner alters conditions of service of seamen (151) – Imprisonment up to six months or fine which may extend to INR 1,000 or both.
- Fails to deposit wages (206(b)) – Fine up to INR 500.
- Failing to send official logbook to the shipping master (217) – Fine up to INR 100.
- Failing to notify about the alteration in the ship (229) – Fine up to INR 500.
- Failing to deliver the expired certificate (230) – Fine up to INR 100.
- Failing to notify about the day of sailing (238) – Fine up to INR 200.
- Failing to exhibit certificate A – (246) – Fine up to INR 200.
- Omitting to supply food, and so on, on board (247) – Fine up to INR 30 for every passenger.
- Making voyage in contravention of contract (252) – Fine up to INR 1,000.

- Failing to advertise about the date of sailing, and so on, (255) – Fine up to INR 200.
- Failing to comply with directions under 255 – (255(1)) – Fine up to INR 200.
- Failing to carry medical attendants on board (259) – Fine up to INR 500.
- Bringing passengers from a foreign place beyond the prescribed number (260) – Fine up to INR 1,000.
- Failing to install radiotelegraph service on board (291) – Fine up to INR 1,000.
- Failing to carry radio direction finder (292) – Fine up to INR 200.
- Failing to provide with signalling lamp (297) – Fine up to INR 200.
- Failure to give information about ship's stability (298) – Fine up to INR 1,000.
- Altering structural arrangements in a ship (309A) – Fine up to INR 500.
- Proceeding to sea without marking of deck line and load line, and so on, (312) – Fine up to INR 1,000.
- Loading of the ship in such a manner as to cause its submersion (313) – Fine up to INR 10,000.
- Failing to maintain load line marks (314) – Fine up to INR 1,000.
- Failing to deliver certificate (317) – Fine up to INR 100.
- Failing to deliver certificate to custom collector (318) – Fine up to INR 1,000.
- Failing to follow grain loading plan (331A) – Fine up to INR 100.
- Failing to take precautions for loading the grain, failing to deliver notice, making a false statement in such notice (332(1)(3)(3)) – Fine up to INR 100.
- Failing to send the report of collision to authorities (350) – Fine up to INR 500.
- Failing to give notice about the lost ship to the Central Government (351) – Fine up to INR 500.
- Indian ship not fitted with equipment prescribed (356E) – Fine up to INR 10,000.
- Failing to deliver cancelled certificate to Central Government, marine board, and so on, (378) – Fine up to INR 500.
- Failing to furnish information as required by the DGS (413) – Imprisonment up to six months or fine up to INR 500 or both.
- Proceeding to sea in spite of detention with the authorized person (444(3)) – Fine up to INR 1,000.

C. Liability of the Master under the Indian Ports Authority Act (IPA)

238.

(a) Where a master of a ship fails to make a report of the arrival of the ship within the given time of twenty-four hours, then every such offence will be punishable with a fine which may extend to INR 100.
(b) The master of a vessel when under the duty to signify the name of the vessel by hoisting the number, by which she is known, offends against it then he is liable to be punished for every such offence with a fine which may extend to INR 1,000.
(c) Where any vessel belonging to any Indian or Commonwealth citizen, or which is sailing under the Indian or British colours; hoists, carries or wears, within the limits of the application of any Indian law, any flag, jack, pennant or colours

the use of which is prohibited by the MS Act or any other Indian statute then for such offence the master of the vessel shall, for every such offence, be punishable with fine which may extend to INR 50. Such a fine shall be in addition to any other penalty recoverable in respect of such an offence (section 62 Indian Ports Act 1908).

D. *Power of Court*

239. Any court making a formal investigation into a shipping casualty may inquire into any charge of incompetency or misconduct arising, in the course of the investigation, against master, mate or engineer as well as into any charge of a wrongful act or default on his part causing the shipping casualty (section 362).

§2. Crew

240. The entire staff on board employed by the master forms the crew of the ship for the journey and it remains under the command and authority of the master. Due importance is given to the crew members under the law and their life and limb and welfare has been taken proper care of. A good number of Rules are devised for their welfare as labourers or workers. These are:

– The MS (Crew Accommodation) Rules 1960 GSR No. 1568.
– The Sailing Vessels (Statement of Crew) Rules 1960 GSR No. 1554.
– The MS (Distress Seamen) Rules 1960 GSR No. 1552.
– The MS (Seamen's Levy of Fees) Rules 1974 GSR No. 80.
– The National Welfare (Board of Seafarers) Rules 1963 GSR No. 1187.
– The Merchant Shipping (Recruitment and Placement of Seafarers) Rules 2016.
– The Merchant Shipping (Seafarer's Bio-metric identity Document) Rules 2016.

I. Contract of Employment for Crew Members

A. *Agreement with Crew in India*

241. 'Seamen' as defined in section 3(42) of the MS Act 1958 includes persons employed or engaged in accordance with the provisions of the Act. Section 100 of the Act says that master of every Indian ship, except a home-trade ship of less than two hundred tonnes gross, shall enter into an agreement in accordance with the provisions of the Act with every seaman whom he engages in, and carries to sea as one of his crew from any port in India. When certain fishermen had not entered into an agreement under section 100, it could not exclude the application of section 150 (Power to refer disputes between seamen and their employers to tribunals). The tribunal could go into the details to find out whether the employees that is, fishermen had been employed or engaged as members of the crew (*Union Carbide India Ltd v. Industrial Tribunal*, AP 1979 Lab IC 35 (AP) Agreement made out of India) – the master of a ship who is registered at a port outside India and who has made an agreement with the crew made in due form according to the law of that port or of the port in which her crew was engaged is allowed under the MS Act to engage in any port in India a seaman who is not a citizen of India and who holds a continuous discharge certificate or any other document of identity from a country where the ship is registered or a seaman who is a citizen of India and who holds a certificate of discharge or continuous certificate of discharge issued under the MS Act. Such seaman so engaged is allowed under law to sign the agreement (section 102 Amended 1984).

B. Forms and Contents of the Agreement

242. An agreement with the crew shall be in the prescribed form, and shall be dated at the time of the first signature thereof, and shall be signed by the owner or agent and the master before any seaman signs it. Such agreement shall contain particulars as to: the name of the ship on board which the seaman undertakes to serve; the duration of voyage or engagement and the places of the world where the voyage or engagement is not to extend; the number and description of the crew; the time at which the seaman is to be on board and the time of starting its work; the capacity under which he will serve; the amount and scale of wages; the scale of warm clothing and other provisions; regulations regarding conduct on board and the lawful punishment sanctioned by the Central Government; payment of compensation in case of injury or death; and other provisions regarding termination of services of such seamen outside India. The agreement should also contain the clause that in case of any dispute the matter shall be referred to the Indian consular office. It should also be so framed as to admit of stipulations to be adopted at the will of the master (section 101).

II. Recruiting

243. For the recruitment of the seamen, seamen's employment offices are formed to issue a licence to regulate and control the recruitment and placement service. The office also regulates the payment of fees and other charges of recruitment; ensures the investigation of complaints, maintains registers of seamen. Section 95 of the Act which is amended by Act No. 63 of 2002 with effect from 1 February 2003 to redefine the role of the employment office and states that the office shall levy and collect a fee in respect of the issue of licenses to recruitment and placement service. It also explains the expression 'recruitment and placement service' to mean any person, company, institution, agency or other organization, in the public or private sector which is engaged in recruiting seafarers on behalf of employers or placing seafarers with employers and states that 'seafarer' means any person who fulfils the conditions to be employed or engaged in any capacity on board a seagoing ship other than a Government ship used for the military on non-commercial purposes. For recruitment purposes, the Central Government of India may declare in the Official Gazette that no recruitment as a seaman or in any category of seaman shall be made without prescribed qualifications. The prescribed qualification includes the possession of a certificate as to the effect that the applicant is physically fit. The Central Government also reserves the power to make rules to provide for the courses of training to be pursued, the vocational standards to be attained or the tests to be passed by seamen, the standard of physical fitness required of seamen and other matters connected thereto.

A. *Pre-Sea Training Course*

244. Rule 4(5) of the MS (Seaman's Employment Officers) Rules 1986 prescribes the need to undergo pre-sea training courses for those who fall in the category of 'deck and engine trainees' within the age group of 10 and 12 and not ex-naval ratio or ex-navy ratings. The Government of India in supersession of Merchant Shipping (Standard of Training, Certification and Watch Keeping for Seafarers) Rules 1998, formulated the Merchant Shipping (Standards of Training, Certification and Watch Keeping for Seafarers) Rules 2014[21] with the object of giving full and complete effect to the amended provisions of International Convention on Standards of Training, Certification and Watch-keeping for Seafarers 1978 as adopted by Conference of Parties to STCW Convention in Manila on 25 June 2010. It includes relevant national requirements. It contains rules regarding training and assessment centres [Rule 6], and elaborate rules regarding minimum requirements for certification of officer-in-charge of master and deck department [Rule 20-34], engine department [Rule 35-49] radio communication and radio operators [Rule 50,51] special training requirements for personnel on certain types of ships[Rule 52-55], minimum requirements for emergency, occupational safety, security, medical care and survival functions [Rule 56-66].

III. Duties of the Employer and Employee

245. The Central Government makes rules regarding the employment of the seamen by the owner of the ship or by his agent or by the master of the ship. The term 'servant' means a servant in the constant employment of the master or owner of the ship. The mere engagement of a person to supply seamen does not mean servant. The owner of the ship or his agent is under an obligation to the employees as specified by the Central Government regarding their service conditions and welfare as under. The MS Act makes elaborate provisions in this regard.

---

21. *Vide* G. S. R. 546(E) dated 30 Jul. 2014 published in the Gazette of India, Extra, Pt. II Sec. 3 (i), dated 31 Jul. 2014. It came into force on 31 Jul. 2014.

A. General Duties of the Employer

1. Duties Regarding Employment of Young Persons

246. The Child Labour (Prohibition and Regulation) Act 1986 makes certain amendments in the MS Act keeping in view the welfare of young persons. It prohibits the employment of children less than 14 years of age in the engagement to work in any capacity in any ship or to be carried to the sea. The exception allows such children to be engaged when it is a school ship; when the child is with the family; when the ship is the home-trade ship of less than two hundred tonnes gross or where such person is to be employed on nominal wages and is under some guardianship from his family. Young persons cannot be engaged or employed without delivering to the master a certificate granted by a prescribed medical authority as to their physical fitness regarding the employment of such persons in a certain capacity. The master can do away with such certificate if such young person is with family in the ship and where the shipping master has authorized a young person to be engaged or carried to sea on the ground of urgency. A register containing the list of young persons and their personal particulars so employed is to be included in every agreement with the crew of every Indian ship (sections 109, 110, 111 and 112).

2. Duties Regarding Health and Accommodation

247. The MS Act envisages detailed provisions for the welfare and health of the seamen. For this, it imposes certain obligations on the master of the ship to arrange for it accordingly. These are as under.

a. Sufficient Provision and Water

248. Sufficient provision and good quality drinkable water should be provided by the master-owner of the ship for the seamen. In case any complaint is received as to the unhygienic quality of water or provision then an inspection shall be made by an authorized person (under section 17) and once it is declared by the inspecting person that such water or provision is not fit for the use of seamen then it is the duty of the master to see that alternate arrangement of fit quality water and provisions is made. However, if the inspection was made on any complaint by any crew member and it was later found to be frivolous or vexatious then every complaining member is required to forfeit to the owner of the ship out of his wages a sum not exceeding one week's wages.

b. Weights and Measures on Board

249. The master of a ship shall keep on board proper weights and measures for determining the quantities of the several provisions and articles served out and shall allow the same to be used at the time of serving out the provisions and articles in the presence of witnesses whenever any dispute arises about the quantities.

c. Beddings, Medicines

250. The owner of every ship of over five hundred tonnes gross shall supply or cause to be supplied to every seaman for his personal use, beddings, towels, mass utensils and other articles according to such scale as may be prescribed. All foreign-going Indian ships and all home-trade ships of two hundred tonnes gross or more shall have always on board a sufficient supply of medicines, medical stores, appliances and first aid equipment, suitable for diseases and accidents. The Central Government, in order to make the provisions of this section more fruitful, has passed MS (Medicines, Medical Stores and Appliances) Rules 1966 and Seaman (Supply of Articles for Personal Use) Rules 1966 (Gazette of India dated, 11 June 1966, pt. II section 3(i), at 1028).

d. Medical Expenses

251. Whenever the master, seaman, or apprentice of an Indian ship receives any hurt or injury or suffers from any illness, not caused due to his wilful misconduct, the expenses of providing necessary surgical and medical advice, attendance and treatment and medicine, and also the expenses of the maintenance of the master, seaman or apprentice until he is cured or dies are to be borne by the owner of the ship. In case of his death, his burial or cremation expenses are to be defrayed by the owner. In case due to peculiar condition of his illness, the master, seaman or apprentice is made to be removed away from the ship at a port other than his proper port of return, then during his such stay, all the medical expenses, treatment and maintenance are to be borne by the owner in the above manner.

e. Accommodation for Seamen

252. The Central Government passed Merchant Shipping (Crew Accommodation) Rules 1960 (Gazette of India, 1960, pt. II section 3(i), Ext. at 741) regarding making crew accommodation to be provided by the shipowners inside the ship. The owner must make provision for the minimum space for each person which must be provided in the ship for sleeping accommodation for seamen and apprentices and the maximum number of persons by whom any specified part of such sleeping accommodation may be used; the maintenance and repair of such accommodation; prohibition or restriction on the use of such accommodation, and so on.

B. Social Welfare Duties

253. With the advent of times and changing circumstances, the duties of the employer are even extended to the welfare and well-being of the employees. These are:

1. National Welfare Board for Seafarers

254. It is the duty of the shipowner, like most employers, to take care of the post superannuation exigencies of the seamen and the crew members. As provided under section 218 of the MS Act the Central Government shall constitute a National Welfare Board for Seafarers in which even the shipowners are required to pay a fee which would be used by the Board for providing amenities for the seamen and for taking other measures for the welfare of seamen. By virtue of the National Welfare Board for Seafarers Rules 1963, the Government of India constituted a Board which comprises two Members of Parliament, two representatives from Central Government, three representatives each of shipowners and Seafarers, two representatives from Port Trusts, one non-official Member from the field of Seamen's Welfare of Public, one representative from Society interested in Seamen's Welfare including its Chairman and Vice-Chairman.

2. Seamen's Provident Fund

255. The Seamen's Provident Fund Act 1966 (4 of 1966) was made effective retrospectively from 1 July 1964 and started the Seamen's Provident Fund Scheme to provide for the institution of a provident fund for seamen. Under this Scheme, the employers or shipowners are required to deposit the provident fund contributions in respect of seamen employed by them with their matching contribution with the Seamen's Provident Fund organization after the termination of each voyage. All monies belonging to the fund are invested in the Securities as per the pattern prescribed by the Ministry of Finance.

3. Seamen's Welfare Fund Society

256. The Seafarer's Welfare Fund Society (SWFS) is a Central Organization for the Welfare of Indian Seafarers and their families. It is registered under the Societies Registration act 1860 and as a Trust under the Bombay Public Trust Act 1950. Representatives of Indian and Foreign shipowners are in the society and the shipowners are under a duty to make ad hoc grants which along with other funds is used for the welfare of the seamen. Some of the factors added to the funds of the Society when the shipping companies remitted to SWFA, the wage differentials between International wage and Indian wage for Seafarers. The shipowners are also under an obligation to make Welfare Contributions and Unemployment Relief Contributions by virtue of the Agreement under the National Maritime Board. The funds thus reached up to INR 104.94 crore as of 31 December 2004. The funds are being used for various welfare schemes like the Monthly Ex-Gratia Monetary Assistance (MEMA) and a number of other such schemes. For the promotion of the welfare of seafarers, the recruitment and placement service shall pay to the Seafarers Welfare Fund Society, Mumbai, a welfare fund contribution of INR 6,000 per seafarer per annum for every seafarer excluding trainees engaged on board flag ships, on the basis of the actual period of the seafarers employed. (Rule 6: The Merchant Shipping (Recruitment and Placement of Seafarers) Rules 2016).

C. Duties of the Employee

257. The employees engaged in the ship are to be disciplined and in case they are not so they may be booked for misconduct. The master, seamen or apprentice belonging to an Indian ship must not do anything which may cause loss or damage to the ship or endanger the life or cause injury to any person on board the ship and they must not refuse or omit to do any lawful act proper and requisite to be done by him for preserving the ship from immediate loss, destruction or serious damage or for preserving any person belonging to or on board the ship from danger to life or from injury. Neither any seaman nor any apprentice shall desert the ship or shall neglect or refuse without reason to board the ship. Such employees should also not be absent without leave any time within twenty hours of the ship's sailing nor when he is on the ship except without leave or without sufficient reason. In case the ship is unseaworthy then it can be a sufficient reason provided such seaman has reported to the authorities concerned about the unseaworthiness of the ship (sections 190, 191 MS Act).

IV. Termination

258. A seaman, on the termination of his engagement, either in the foreign-going ship or serving in a home-trade ship of two hundred tonnes gross or more shall be discharged in accordance with the provisions of the Act in the presence of a shipping master. At the time of discharge or on payment of wages, the master shall sign and give to the seaman, a certificate of his discharge in the prescribed form specifying the period, time, and place of his discharge. The service book of the seaman should also be returned to him immediately and failure to do so will entitle the seaman to claim damages in a civil suit and not in a petition under Article 32 of the Constitution of India (*KK Puri v. B. M. Engineering Works (P) Ltd*, AIR 1982 SC 1173; (1982) 1 SCC 500). A certificate of discharge where the experience and qualification of the seaman are mentioned and is signed by the master shall not be denied only because it has not been countersigned by the shipping master. At the time of discharge, the master of a ship shall submit a report in the prescribed form to the shipping master mentioning the quality of work of the discharged seaman and also the fact whether the seaman fulfilled his obligations under the agreement with the crew. If the master declines to express an opinion on such matters, then he should mention that too. A copy of such a report may be given to the seaman on his request along with the certificate of discharge. If the seaman so desires he may apply to the shipping master to issue a continuous discharge certificate in lieu of the certificate of discharge or the report by the master mentioning the quality of his work and other particulars as mentioned in the report (sections 118, 119, 120 & 121).

A. Discharge and Leaving Behind of Seamen by Masters of Indian Ships

259. The master of an Indian ship shall not without the authority of an officer discharge a seaman before the expiration of the period for which he was engaged unless the seaman consents to. The master should also not leave behind a seaman or apprentice except in circumstances beyond his control without the authority of the officer specified on this behalf by the Central Government. Such officer shall before granting a certificate in this respect shall investigate the grounds on which the seaman is to be discharged or left behind. Section 121(1) of the MS Act provides for the appointment of an officer to certify an agreement with the crew.

260. The Central Government makes a public notification specifying such officers on whose authority the seamen may be discharged on seamen or apprentices may be left behind (section 121) (S. O. published in Gazette of India dated 17.3.62, pt. II section 3(ii), at 598).

Chapter 4. Liability and Limitation of Liability in Maritime Law

§1. Liability of a Shipowner and the Crew

261. In section 352(d) the term ‘liability’ in relation to the owner of a vessel includes liability of the vessel itself. The section specifies the claims in respect of which an owner of a sea-going vessel may limit his liability under Part XA and the claims in respect of which he cannot limit his liability. The owner, salvor or any person for whose act, neglect or default the owner or salvor are responsible, and an insurer of liability for claims to the same extent as the assured himself, may limit his liability in respect of certain claims as mentioned in section 352(1) provided that such occurrence has not resulted from his actual fault of privity. The burden of proving that the occurrence has not resulted from his actual fault or privity is on the owner himself. The responsibility of the owner is limited only to such act, neglect or default as has taken place in the navigation or management of the vessel, loading carriage or discharge of cargo and embarkation, carriage and disembarkation of passengers.

262. Often the liability of the owner is co-extensive or joint with the master of the ship. Section 432 of the MS Act shows that the liability of the shipowner is either joint with the master or the agent or it is only the shipowner alone who is answerable before law. The shipowner is also made liable for the loss of goods but his liability varies in case of a clean bill of lading and in the case where wrong and misguiding entries are made in the bill of lading. He holds responsibility for the goods in the voyage and is answerable before the consignee where he delivers goods which are different or in worse condition in which he received them but not otherwise. Poorly packed goods should have a mention in the bill of lading but in case the fact of wrong packing is not entered in it then the shipowner is held liable irrespective of the fact that the poor packing of the cargo caused the loss or damage to the goods.

I. Liability of a Shipowner under a Charter Party

263. The owner of a ship is liable for short delivery of cargo unless terms of the charter party exempt him from liability and are incorporated in the bill of lading (*General Traders Ltd v. O Pierce Leslie (India) Ltd* AIR 1987 Ker 62. When the stevedores at the time of loading mishandled the cargo thereby damaging it the shipowner was held not liable (*Union of India v. Transmerine Shipping Agencies* AIR 1979 Guj 57). When under a voyage charter party there is a mention of the specific date and time of the arrival of the ship at the port of loading and the ship fails in it then the charterer can refuse to load even if the failure is due to some excepted peril. However, the exception clause if clearly applies to such condition of time then the shipowner shall not be held liable.

§2. LIMITATION OF LIABILITY

264. Shipowner's liability for loss of life and damage to property are onerous and may involve extra ordinary payments by way of damages especially in the present times where bulk carriers, super tankers and large luxury passenger lines are the hallmarks of the shipping industry. The liability of the shipowner when he is also the charterer is that of a bailee and thus when in spite of taking good care if some loss or damage occurs to the goods then the shipowner is exonerated.

Under the International Convention Relating to the Limitation of the Liability of Owners of Sea-going Ships which is also ratified by India under Article 3 of the United Nations Treaty Series, it is given that a shipowner who has not been guilty of actual fault or privity is entitled to limit his liability regarding: (a) personal claims, the limit shall not exceed 3,100 francs per tonne of the ship's tonnage; (b) property claims, the limit shall not exceed 1,000 francs per tonne on the ship's tonnage; (c) for both personal and property claims an aggregate amount of 3,100 francs per tonne of which the first portion of 2,100 francs is to be exclusively appropriated for the payment of personal claims and the second portion of 1,000 francs appropriated for the payment of property claims. If the first portion is insufficient to pay the personal claims in full, the unpaid balance of such personal claims will rank rateably with the property claims for payment against the second portion of the amount. For purposes of calculating the limits of liability, the ships' tonnage shall be deemed to be net tonnage with the addition, however, of the tonnage attributable to engine space. Limitation of liability can be obtained by applying to the court and the owner can set up a limitation fund in the court when the aggregate claims arising on any distinct occasion exceed the limits of liability. The rupee equivalent of the amounts in francs are mentioned in the convention are notified by the Government of India from time to time.

I. Limitation of Liability under the Merchant Shipping Act

265. The law of limitation of liability under Maritime Law in India has undergone considerable change after the Amendment of 1970 and 2002 in the MS Act 1958. The 1970 Amendment inserts Part XA with section 352 and adding section 352A to 352F. The Amendment in 2002 with effect from 1 February 2003 certain terms like 'convention', 'salvor', 'salvage operations', 'shipowner' and 'SDRs' have been defined in accordance with the International Convention relating to the Limitation of Liability of Owners of Sea-going Ships 1957. After the 1957 Convention, the Convention of LLMC 1976 was adopted. Apart from other improvements the 1976 Convention substantially increases the shipowner's limits of liability arising on any distinct occasion. This convention came into force internationally in 1986. In 2002, amendments were made in the MS Act 1958 with a view to include the proposals of the LLMC 1976. According to this Amendment, section 352B says that the amount to which any person referred to in 352A(1) may limit his liability in accordance with the provisions of the Convention and in cases where the provisions of the Convention are not applicable, the limit shall be in accordance with the rules made in this behalf may prescribe. In exercise of the powers conferred by section 352FA read with section 352B the Government of India has formulated The Merchant Shipping (Limitation of Liability for Maritime Claims) Rules 2015[22] to fix the limit of liability. This liability is subject to the provisions of section 352B and thereby the limit of liability for claims under section 352 A (I) shall be as given in Rule 3 of the said Rules which came into force on 16.2.2015.

§3. Ships for Which the Limitation of Liability Can Be Invoked

266. For the purpose of limitation of liability the term 'ship' has been taken to include 'any structure, whether completed or in course of completion, launched and intended for use in navigation as a ship or part of a ship'. Moreover, the benefit of limitation was extended to all British ships notwithstanding that they have not yet been registered. This was favourable for certain ships who sought registration under section 23 of the MS Act 1894 only for the purpose of claiming limitation of liability. A person who (is the shipowner, salvor or any person for whose act, neglect or default the shipowner, or salvor, as the case may be, is responsible) limits his liability before the Court or seeks to procure the release of a ship or other property or the discharge of any guarantee given within the Indian jurisdiction shall get the benefit of limitation of liability. The Central Government has the authority to specify the vessels on which the provisions of limitation of liability can be extended. The benefit shall not exceed to: ships which are intended for navigation on or around the coast of India and are registered as coastal vessels under the provisions of the MS Act; ships less than three hundred tonnes; air-cushion vehicles; floating platforms which are extended for the purpose of exploring or exploiting the natural resources of the seabed or the subsoil thereof (section 352E MS Act). However, if the Central Government gives notice to the effect, then these can come under the benefit of the limitation of liability.

§4. Claims Subject to Limitation

267. As given under section 352(1) following are the claims which are subject to limitation of liability as given under 352B by the shipowner, salvor, and an insurer of liability for claims to the same extent as the assured himself. These are the claims which are subject to limitation of liability even if brought by way of recourse or for indemnity under a contract or otherwise.

I. Claims for Loss of Life

268. Claims arising from loss of life of or personal injury to, or loss of or damage to, property (including damage to harbour works, basins and waterways and

22. *Vide* G. S. R. 98(E), dated 16 Feb. 2015 published in the Gazette of India, Extra., Part II, sec. 3(i) No. 94 dated 16 Feb. 2015.

aids to navigation), occurring on board or indirect connection with the operation of the ship or with salvage operations, and consequential loss resulting there from. The limit in respect of such loss (as per Rule 3 of *The Merchant Shipping (Limitation of Liability for Maritime Claims) Rules 2015)* will be as follows:

(a) In respect of claims for loss of life or personal injury, -
  - (i) [23] [3.02 million units] of account[24] for a ship with a tonnage not exceeding two thousand tons;
  - (ii) for a ship with a tonnage exceeding two thousand tons the following amount in addition to that mentioned in sub clause (i)
    - (A) for each ton form two thousand and one tons to thirty thousand tons, eight [25][1208 units] of account; will be as follows:
    - (B) for each ton from thirty thousand and one tons to thirty thousand and one tons to seventy thousand tons [26][906 units] of account;
    - (C) for each ton in excess of seventy thousand tons,[27][604 units] of account.

(b) In respect of any other claim, -
  - (i) [28][1.5 million units] of account for ship with a tonnage not exceeding two thousand tons;
  - (ii) for a ship with a tonnage exceeding two thousand tons the following amount in addition to that mentioned in sub clause (b)(i):-
    - (A) for each ton from two thousand and one tons to thirty thousand tons,[29] [604 units]of account;
    - (B) for each ton from thirty thousand and one tons to seventy thousand tons,[30] [453 units] of account: and
    - (C) for each ton in excess of seventy thousand tons [31] [302 units] of account.

II. Delay

269. Claims arising out of loss resulting from delay in the carriage by sea of cargo and passengers or their luggage.

---

23. Substituted by G. S. R. 153(E) dated 21 Feb. 2017 for 'two million units' (w.e.f. 21 Feb. 2017).
24. The Term 'units of account' means the Special Drawing Rights as defined in section 352(j) of the Merchant Shipping Act 1958.
    The Amount calculated under Rule 3 & 4 shall be converted into Indian rupee according to the value of the rupee at the date the Fund is constituted or deposit is made or guarantee is given under Section 352C((2) [Rule 5].
25. Substituted by G. S. R. 153(E) dated 21 Feb. 2017 for 'eight hundred units' (w.e.f. 21.2.2017).
26. Substituted by G. S. R. 153(E) dated 21 Feb. 2017 for 'six hundred units' (w.e.f. 21.2.2017).
27. Substituted by G. S. R. 153(E) dated 21 Feb. 2017 for 'four hundred units' (w.e.f. 21.2.2017).
28. Substituted by G. S. R. 153(E) dated 21 Feb. 2017 for 'for one million units' (w.e.f. 21.2.2017).
29. Substituted by G. S. R. 153(E) dated 21 Feb. 2017 for 'for four hundred units' (w.e.f. 21.2.2017).
30. Substituted by G. S. R. 153(E) dated 21 Feb. 2017 for 'for four hundred units' (w.e.f. 21.2.2017).
31. Substituted by G. S. R. 153(E) dated 21 Feb. 2017 for 'for two hundred units' (w.e.f. 21.2.2017).

III. Infringements of Rights

270. Claims arising out of other loss resulting from infringement of rights other than contractual rights, occurring in direct connection with the operation of the ship or salvage operations.

IV. Other Person

271. Claims of a person other than the person liable in respect of measures taken in order to avert or minimize loss for which the person liable may limit his liability in accordance with the provisions of the Convention or the rules made in this behalf prescribe, as the case may be, and such further loss caused by such measures.

V. Under Contract of Passenger Carriage

272. Claims for the loss of life or personal injury to passengers of a ship brought by or on behalf of any person under the contract of passenger carriage or who is accompanying a vehicle for live animals under a contract in the ship.

§5. Claims Excluded from Limitation

273. Section 352(3) enumerates the claims in respect of which the owner of a vessel cannot limit his liability. These are listed below.

I. General Average

274. Claims for salvage or contribution in general average.

II. Oil Pollution

275. Claims for oil pollution damage within the meaning of the International Convention on Civil Liability for Oil Pollution Damage 1992.

III. Servants

276. Claims by the servants of shipowner or salvors whose duties are connected with the ship or salvage operations.

IV. International Convention

277. Claims subject to International Convention or any law for the time being in force in India governing or prohibiting limitation of liability for nuclear damage; claims against the shipowner of a nuclear ship for nuclear damage.

§6. Counter Claims

278. As per Article 5 of the Convention on Liability for Maritime Claims 1976 (LLMC) when any person who enjoys limitation of liability under the rules of LLMC has a claim against the claimant arising out of the same occurrence then their respective claim shall be set off against each other and the Convention shall apply only to the balance.

§7. Conduct Barring Limitation

279. A shipowner is expected to be a prudent and careful man and thus his conduct which is reasonable shall bring him under the benefit of limitation of liability. The loss should have occurred without the owner's actual fault or negligence. Sea navigation calls for utmost caution including the seaworthiness of the ship, its proper manning, and safety consciousness on the part of the owner. Whether the shipowner is a professional carrier or whether they are only carrying their own products the standard of care remains the same. Excessive speed in fog is the proof of carelessness and as high speed is encouraged by radar, it is the duty of the shipowner to keep special vigilance over it. Failing to take such caution amounts to gross negligence and it is the conduct which bars the benefit of limitation of liability. Where the master failed to use radar in the fog, they were refused to limit their liability as they also failed to show that the collision had occurred without their actual fault or privity (The Lady Gwendolyn: *Arthur Guinness Son & Co. Dublin Ltd v. Owners of Freshfield* ([1965] 2 All ER 283). The Indian MS Act 1958 closely follows the MS Act 1894 (English).

§8. Persons Entitled to Limit

280. According to section 352F the charterer, manager and operator of the vessel, master, members of the crew and other servants of the owner, charterer, manager or operator acting in the course of their employment are the persons who like the owner are entitled to limit liability in respect of personal claims and property, claims arising on a distinct occasion but shall not exceed, the amounts determined in accordance with the provisions of section 352B. The master or a member of the crew of a vessel may limit his liability even if the occurrence which gives rise to a claim against him resulted from the actual fault or privity of the master and the members of the crew or any one or more of them.

§9. General Limits of Liability

281. Section 352B substituted by the MS (Amendment) Act 2002 sets the amounts to which the owner of a vessel may limit his liability. As per the Limitation of Liability Convention, the amounts are expressed in terms of francs and it is the power of the Central Government to specify the equivalent amount of the same in terms of Indian currency. The limit set by this section is regarding claims which are isolated and not for several claims which are combined together. The limit of liability is to be calculated in respect of the tonnage of the vessel and where the tonnage is less than 300 tonnes, the vessel will be treated for purposes of such computation as of 300 tonnes.

§10. Limitation Fund

282. A need arises for limiting the liability of the owner when such liability exceeds the limits provided in section 352B. Thus, section 352 C provides that when such a situation occurs then the owner may apply to the High Court for determining the limit of his liability as provided under the limits of liability in section 352B and for setting up a limitation Fund for the total sum representing the amounts set out in the Convention or the rules made in this behalf under this Part applicable to claims for which that person may be liable together with interest thereon from the date of occurrence giving rise to the liability until the date of the constitution of the Fund. Such High Court shall then require the owner to deposit such amount with the High Court or produce a bank guarantee in respect of the amount as in the opinion of the High Court is satisfactory and such amount or guarantee shall constitute the limitation Fund and shall be utilized for the satisfaction of claims. With the Fund being constituted no claimant can proceed against the assets of the owner in respect of his claim where the Fund is actually available for the benefit of the claimant. The amount of the Fund may be distributed rateably by the High Court amongst the several claimants.

§11. Procedure

283. Regarding the place of the trial, any person who commits an offence under the MS Act maybe tried in any place where he is found. The Central Government also has the power to specify the place of trial which it may publish as a notification in the Official Gazette. The offences shall be tried by a Metropolitan Magistrate or by a Judicial Magistrate of the first class. High Courts also have jurisdiction in this matter and the owner of a ship (under section 352C) may apply to the High Court for determining the amount of his liability in accordance with the limits of liability under section 352B. In case any witness is required in the proceeding under the Act and the accused does not produce such witness then any deposition made by the witness in relation to the same subject matter previously in any other court in India or before any Marine Board or before any Indian consular shall be admissible in evidence after it is authenticated by the signature of the preceding officer (sections 437–439, 442). The LLMC is silent on the point of jurisdiction.

Chapter 5. Charter Parties

§1. Definition and Varieties of Charter Parties

284. A charter party is a contract to let a ship on hire or to provide services of the whole or part of a ship for an agreed time or voyage. Charter parties are contracts of affreightment under which the shipowner, in return for a sum of money called the freight or charter hire, agrees to carry goods in bulk by sea or provide the services of a vessel for the purpose of such carriage. Most of the countries have refrained from giving legislative forms to charter parties. The terms and conditions of charter parties evolved through the growth of maritime commerce and shipping industry. The UK Chamber of shipping and the Baltic International Maritime conference in Copenhagen have played a significant role in evolving internationally accepted charter parties. The Supreme Court of India thus describing the charter party says that 'it is wrong to assume that a charter party has to be an agreement for the carriage of something like goods, passengers, livestock or mail. It is a contract by which an entire ship or some principal part thereof is let to a merchant, who is called the charterer, for the conveyance of goods on a determined voyage to one or more places, or until the expiration' of (specified period, in the former case it is called a 'voyage charter party' and in the latter a 'time charter party' (*Union of India v. Gosalia Shipping (P) Ltd* (1978) 3 SCC 1196). Two kinds of charter parties are commonly followed though the other kinds of charter parties depend on the intention of the parties.

I. Voyage Charter Party

285. When the ship is hired for a determined voyage or a number of voyages then it is called a voyage charter party contract. It is an ordinary charter party and the crew remains the employee of the shipowner. This is a contract under which the owner undertakes to perform a voyage or series of voyages for the carriage of specified goods between named ports (or within certain ranges of loading and discharging ports) with a vessel that is equipped and manned to him for and for the navigation and management of which he remains responsible throughout the performance of the contract. Voyage chartering is usually resorted to when the movement of a shipload of cargo under the rules relating to lay time and demurrage. The hire paid by the charterer is actually the freight on the cargo carried and is directly proportionate to the volume of the cargo. The weight of the cargo to be carried is specified and if the charterer fails to deliver the contracted quantity, the owner may claim dead freight on the quantity short delivered.

II. Time Charter Party

286. This is also known as charter party by demise. In this, the ship is temporarily leased out to the charterer and he becomes the owner not only of the ship but also of the crew and thus becomes answerable for their negligence. This is a contract under which the owner provides the services of one or more vessels to the charterer for a period of time in return for charter hire. The charterer becomes full caretaker of the ship arranges for its men and equipment and takes full responsibility for its navigation, management and operation. Except for the financial commitments of ownership, the charterer acts as the owner for the entire period of charter contract. Often the bareboat charter serves as a hire/purchase contract or the contract for the purchase of a vessel on an instalment basis. The bareboat charter party commonly used in India is the standard Barecon charter party. The important feature of such a charter party is that it includes the following features of; description of the vessel including size, speed, fuel consumption, loading capacity, and so on, on which its performance depends; survey to be carried out on delivery and redelivery; inventories of stores to be taken on delivery and redelivery; charter period is included in the contract which gives the charterer the option of extending the validity of the charter by a specified period; rate of charter hire and mode of payment. This is usually computed on the dead weight tonnage of the vessel per month and is payable every month in advance; maintenance and operation during the period of charter. The vessel has to be at the disposal and under the complete control of the charterer who remains responsible for the supply of crew, officers, stores, provisions, bunkers, and so on, and for all other items of operational costs including insurance. In both kinds of charter parties, sub-chartering is common. This gives the original charterer a double position as though retaining his position as a charterer, he becomes the owner as against the sub-charterer.

III. Position of Charterer

287. This is also known as charter party by demise. In this, the ship is temporarily leased out to the charterer and he becomes the owner not only of the ship but also of the crew and thus becomes answerable for their negligence. This is a contract under which the owner provides the services of one or more vessels to the charterer for a period of time in return for charter hire. The charterer becomes full caretaker of the ship arranges for its men and equipment and takes full responsibility for its navigation, management and operation. Except for the financial commitments of ownership the charterer acts as the owner for the entire period of charter contract. Often the bareboat charter serves as a hire/purchase contract or the contract for the purchase of a vessel on an instalment basis. The bareboat charter party commonly used in India is the standard Barecon charter party. The important feature of such a charter party is that it includes the following features of: description of vessel including size, speed, fuel consumption, loading capacity, and so on, on which its performance depends; survey to be carried out on delivery and redelivery; inventories of stores to be taken on delivery and redelivery; charter period is included in the contract which gives the charterer the option of extending the validity of the charter by a specified period; rate of charter hire and mode of payment. This is usually computed on the dead weight tonnage of the vessel per month and is payable every month in advance; maintenance and operation during the period of charter. The vessel has to be at the disposal and under the complete control of the charterer who remains responsible for the supply of crew, officers, stores, provisions, bunkers, and so on, and for all other items of operational costs including insurance. In both kinds of charter parties, sub-chartering is common. This gives the original charterer a double position as though retaining his position as a charterer he becomes the owner as against the sub-charterer.

IV. Difference between Voyage Charter Party and Time Charter party

288. Difference between voyage and time charter parties is related to the following points:

- Regarding Specified Goods
  In a voyage charter party, the specified goods are taken by the owner to specified ports while under the time charter party no such specific destination is mentioned and the vessel is entirely at the beck and call of the charterer.
- Regarding Delay
  Under the voyage charter party, the charterer assumes responsibility regarding a delay in loading and discharging ports under the rules of lay time and demurrage. Under the time charter party, the charterer gets a better hold of goods and he exercises more control over managing the cargo, its uploading and downloading, and so on.
- Regarding Freight
  In a voyage charter party, the freight is related to the size and amount of cargo while under a time charter party it is related to the time period.
- Regarding Time
  Under a voyage charter party, the time factor is the responsibility of the owner while under a time charter party, the loss of time is borne by the charterer.

§2. Statutory Provisions

289. The Indian Carriage of Goods by Sea Act 1925 is silent on the subject of charter party. It is seen that law relating to charter parties is in disarray as most of the countries including India have refrained from legislative action for regulating chartering practices. The terms and conditions of charter parties have been evolved over a period of years in keeping with the growth of maritime commerce and the shipping industry. Organizations like the UK Chamber of Commerce and Shipping and the Baltic International Maritime Conference in Copenhagen have contributed significantly to evolving internationally accepted charter parties. Apart from these charter parties, there are even private charter party forms evolved by individual commodity producers and merchants. The Uniform General Charter (Gencon) of the Baltic International Maritime Conference is the charter party which is widely used in India and elsewhere and has been designed for general purposes rather than for a particular trade. The other long-standing charter party forms are used in a specific trade. Thus the Mediterranean Iron Ore Charter party, continent grain charter party (Synacomed), Nauyozai charter party, Bulk sugar charter party, North American

Grain Charter party, Baltimore Grain Charter party, are mostly approved by the Baltic International Maritime Conference and the UK Chamber of Shipping. The charter parties commonly used in India's export/import trade for the movement of bulk commodities like iron ore, food grains, fertilizers, and so on, are C (Ore) 7, Ferticon and Baltimore Berth Grain. This explains the heterogeneous character of charter parties. India has been closely following the English traditions in this respect as the subject matter is still to be legislated. As a charter party is basically a contract of affreightment hence it is mainly regulated by the provisions of the Indian Contract Act 1872. When the construction of the contract is such that it is difficult to understand the nature of the instrument, then at such a point, evidence of acts under it serve as a guide to the intention of parties particularly when acts are done immediately after the date of the instrument (*Godhra Electricity Co. Ltd v. State of Gujarat* AIR 1975 SC 32). In India, the common principle applied by the Indian courts in understanding the nature of the contract is that the courts look into the substance rather than the form of an agreement. A party cannot ignore and escape law provisions by reason of the form of the contract or instrument while in reality, the instrument appears to be different in nature (*CIT v. Panipat Woollen etc. Co. Ltd* AIR 1976 SC 640). It is also followed by the courts that the words of a charter party are to be understood in the plain, ordinary and popular meaning.

§3. Duties of the Shipowner

290. India is following the English practice in this respect and the duties and liabilities of the shipowner as they apply to the charter party in the United Kingdom are also followed in India unless they are differently interpreted by the Indian courts. In a voyage charter party where the ship is to arrive at a port at a particular date then the shipowner is under duty to fulfil it failing which the charterer may refuse to load. Again when the voyage charter party contains a clause that the ship shall sail from the port of loading to the port of discharge 'with all convenient speed' then it should be treated as a stipulation and the master of the ship and the crew shall be liable to the charterer in case they fail to comply with the stipulation. The shipowner is also under duty not to deviate from the prescribed route and he is liable if damage or loss to cargo is caused thereby unless he is able to prove that the loss would have occurred even without such deviation or that such deviation is taken to save a life, to avoid imminent danger, as a failure to load cargo or there is an express stipulation to excuse such deviation or delay.

§4. Duties of the Charterer

291. The charterer is under obligation to abide by the terms of the charter party. A voyage charter party contains a description of the cargo and the actual cargo should conform to the given description. When the description is given in general terms then the variety of such cargo can be conveniently be included. The charterer is under duty to ship only that cargo which is strictly in accordance with the description given in the charter party. The charterer is also under duty not to ship dangerous and hazardous goods if they are prohibited under law and if such goods are permissible then their packing, and so on, should be as per the requirement of the nature of the goods so that they are not a risk for others. A voyage charter usually contains a stipulation regarding a specific quantity of cargo and in the absence of such stipulation, the charterer cannot be compelled to ship any particular quantity.

I. Excepted Perils

292. In the contract of affreightment, the shipowner and the charterer both are required to perform their duties unless prevented by certain perils which are excepted in the contract. Such excepted perils are: acts of God, perils of the sea, fire, barratry, pirates, collisions, strandings and accidents of navigation. Leakage and breakage are also often brought under the excepted perils.

Chapter 6. Transport under Bill of Lading

§1. Definitions and Functions of the Bill of Lading

I. Definition

293. The bill of lading is issued to the shipper when the goods are loaded on board by the master as the owner's representative or on the master's behalf by the vessel's agents. It is an acknowledgement of the receipt of merchant's goods which are usually in three parts: one is retained by the consignor of goods; the other is sent to the consignee; and the other is preserved by the master of the ship. The bill of lading is usually preceded by a contract of affreightment and is also evidence of the same. It is a document of title to the goods and serves as a basis for documentary credits in international trade. 'The bill of lading is a typical document of title. Thanks to its character as a document of title, the bill of lading is invested with particular attributes of great practical importance commercially. This enables it to become one of the key instruments in international trade.' (Caslav Pejowic; Documents of title in Carriage of Goods by Sea; Present Status and Possible Future Directions, [2001] JBL 461 at 463).

294. Moreover, for the charterer or the shipper, the bill of lading also serves as the necessary instrument for carrying through the commercial purpose of the transport (Report by the secretariat of UNCTAD, published by United Nations, New York, 1974). It is also held as prima facie evidence in favour of the endorsee that the quantity of goods has been shipped and the shipowners become liable whenever the quantity of goods as delivered is less than the quantity of goods shown in the bill of lading. The Bill of lading is an important document which reflects the contractual relation between the parties and takes effect even after the termination of the contract of carriage. The exclusive jurisdiction clause in the bill of lading has significant importance in international commerce. Where the bill of lading is replaced with two further bills and the claimant delivers goods to the alternative buyer, a dispute arising the place of jurisdiction shall be the one which is given in the exclusive jurisdiction clause given in the bill of lading irrespective of the fact that contract ceased to exist. The exclusive jurisdiction Clause shall survive termination of contract (*AP Moller-Maersk A/S (trading as Maersk Line) v. Soneac Villas Cen Sad Fadoul Christopher Clarke, J.* [2010] Bus LR D 97). In India, according to section 4 of the Indian Carriage of Goods by Sea Act 1925, apart from other similar documents of title, every bill of lading should contain a declaration as to the application of Hague rules as incorporated in the Schedule of the Act. But a bill of lading which does not contain such declaration does not become invalid merely on that ground and it is the only document which creates a relation between the parties as distinct from the exemption and immunities granted by the statute (*Muhammadi Steamship Co. v. Vallabdas* AIR 1957 Trav-Co 133).

295. Another law relating to Bills of Lading which was enacted in India much before the Indian Carriage of Goods by Sea Act, 1925 and which is still in force is the Indian Bills of Lading Act 1856. The object of this Act is to vest in the consignee and every endorsee of a bill of lading all rights that accrue to the shipper as if such consignee or endorsee has himself entered into the contract of affreightment with the carrier. This enables the shipper to get the value of the goods shipped by him on negotiating the bill of lading in favour of the consignee. This Act closely follows the English Bills of Lading Act 1855 is unaffected by the Indian Carriage of Goods by Sea Act 1925.

II. Functions

296. A bill of lading serves three purposes:

> *First,* it is proof of the shipped goods and contains the terms and conditions on which it is received. It operates as a certificate that the goods are received and also constitutes estoppel against the shipowner so that he is precluded from denying the fact of receiving the goods for shipment. The bill of lading thus serves two main purposes. As against the shipowner, it is only prima facie evidence and as against the consignee or endorsee, it is conclusive evidence so that in the event of any damage or loss of goods he can hold the person signing the bill liable.
> *Second,* it is evidence of the contract of goods for their carriage it is not the contract of affreightment in itself but evidence of it.
> *Third,* it is a document of title for the goods which are mentioned therein. It symbolizes the right to property in the goods. Where the defendants neither paid the price nor returned the bill of lading the Delhi High Court held that the property in goods passed to the defendants and they were liable to pay the price of it (*Rudnap Export-Import v. Eastern Associates Co.* AIR 1984 Del 30). But the property in the goods shipped does not pass where the bill of lading is sent by the shipper to his own agent to be delivered to the buyer on payment (Great *India Trading Co. P Ltd v. Nowrangrai Ramniwas* AIR 1983 Cal 237).

297. A Bill of lading is a mercantile document of title which passes to the endorsee the good title to the goods covered by such bill of lading. There is a difference between a clean bill of lading and an unclean bill of lading. A clean bill of lading is one which has no negative remark or reservation as to the apparent good order or condition of either of the goods themselves or their packing and where there is a defect in packing and it is noted in the bill of lading then it is known as an unclean bill of lading (*E & B Steamship Co. v. Bhagojee Sommul* AIR 1961 Mad 442).

§2. Various Types of Bills of Lading and Similar Documents of Title

I. Bill of Lading 'Received for Shipment'

298. Often when the goods are loaded and the bill of lading is to be issued by the carrier or master or agent of the carrier, then on the demand by the shipper, a 'shipped' bill of lading can also be issued in lieu of it. If the shipper has previously taken any other document of title to goods then he shall return the same. A Bill of lading may be of bearer bill or order bill. In the bearer bill, no name of any person is mentioned to whom the goods are to be delivered and the goods are delivered to the bearer of the bill as the name implies. An order bill is one which contains the name of a person on whose order the goods are to be delivered. Such bill of lading is again of two types; in the first one the delivery of goods is made to a named consignee or to his 'order or assigns' or containing similar words implying transferability; in the second one makes the goods deliverable to 'order or assigns' or contains similar words implying transferability but where the consignee is not named.

II. Through Bill of Lading

299. Through Bill of lading is the document which is used to continue when two or more than two modes of transport are employed in carriage of goods. The format of the through bill of lading is similar to the sample ocean bill of lading. A through bill of lading can be issued in a carriage by sea only. The through bill of lading is issued by the carrier which is a title given to the holder of it. A through bill of lading also contains immunity clauses for the carrier exempting him from liability in respect of the cargo he is carrying or even limiting it.

III. Combined Transport Bill of Lading

300. With the changing scenario in the mode of transportation in modern times, there is felt a change in the documentation as well. Nowadays, there is unitization of cargo and before shipment, the cargo is prepared on flats or pallets or in a container. The multimodal (combined) bill of lading is likely to replace the traditional bill of lading as an instrument to prove that: the seller has handed the goods to the transport operator for delivery to the buyer; the transportation takes place on certain terms agreed upon between the seller and the transport operator; the seller is no longer in possession of the goods and can consequently no longer direct the transport operator as to the forwarding of the goods to the buyer; and the risk of loss or damage to the goods has passed from the seller to the buyer. The United Nations Convention on International Multimodal Transport of Goods 1980 influenced by the uniform rules for combined transport made by the ICC earlier has established an international standard for transport documents which is acceptable to all the nations.

IV. Delivery Order

301. Delivery of goods can be refused to a person who does not produce the document of title namely the bill of lading. Delivery of shipped goods at the destined place to the consignee is the sine qua non of performance of the contract of affreightment. Thus it was held by the Privy Council that a bill of lading could not be said to be exhausted until the goods were delivered as per contract and put under the control of the consignee and the agents of both the shipowners and the agents for the consignee were intermediaries until the bill of lading was produced with the delivery order duly endorsed (*Chartered Bank of India v. BI Steam Navigation Co. Ltd, Agarwalia Air Transport v. Mohd. Nasratullah*, AIR 1959 Cal 755).

A. Short Delivery

302. The provisions of the Carriage of Goods by Sea Act 1925 do not apply to the goods where the goods were originated and loaded in a port outside India As the goods were short landed, a suit for damages were filed against the foreign principal. The court held that the Indian agent was automatically discharged from his liability under section 230 of the Indian Contract Act 1872 which says that both the agent and the principal could not be sued (*West Bengal Essential Commodities Supply Corporation Ltd v. Korean Foreign Transportation Corporation* AIR 2002 Cal 211). In the case of a short landing, the short landing certificate is the conclusive document which supersedes any other record regarding the goods. The burden of proving short delivery is on the person who claims it (*Amoco Oil Co. v. Parpada Shipping Co. Ltd* (1989) 1 Lloyd's Rep 369 (CA)).

B. Place of Delivery

303. The normal place of delivery is at the ship's side. The consignee should also be prepared to affect the timely delivery and where it provided lighters but not sufficient men to work them, he was held liable for the consequential delay in unloading. The delivery operation is a joint venture whereas the shipowner and the consignee are required to stand face to face to complete it. Thus the shipowner is required to be on board the ship with the goods in a ready condition to deliver while the consignee must be ready to take the delivery from the side of the ship, or from the other ship, or from the quay or the barge or the lighter as the case may be.

§3. Charter Party and Bill of Lading

304. Contract of affreightment takes two forms; bill of lading and charter party. Under the contract of charter party, the entire ship is booked for the purpose of carrying full cargo. In this type of contract, the ship is hired either fully for one voyage or for many voyages or for a specified time. A bill of lading becomes an acknowledgement of the receipt of goods when the charterer himself sends goods and the bill of lading is taken in his own name. In such a case the contract of carriage is embodied in the charter party alone. A bill of lading cannot override the charter party though parties are at liberty to agree to different terms. However, when the goods are not shipped by the charterer then the entire contract depends upon the nature of the charter party. Thus where the charter party amounts to a demise of the ship, the contract under the bill of lading is between the shipper and the charterer and not between the shipper and the shipowner; but where the charter party does not amount to demise, the nature of contract depends upon the circumstances of the case as to whether the contract is between the shipper and the shipowner or between the shipper and the charterer. The normal practice is that in such a case the contract is taken to be between the shipper and the charterer and the shipowner is exonerated but an express contract in this regard is to be proved. In case of a conflict between the bill of lading and the charter party, the terms given under the charter party should prevail because the bill of lading is not regarded as a subsequent contract which effects a change in the charter party terms.

§4. Hague Rules: Visby Rules

I. National Incorporation of the Hague-Visby Rules

A. Applicability of the Rules

305. The International Law Association held at The Hague in September 1921 a body of interested persons formulated a set of rules called 'Hague Rules 1921'. There followed a recommendation to the states to adopt these rules and incorporate them in the national legislation. The rules were subsequently revised in 1968 and came to be known as 'Hague–Visby Rules' The original text of the rules being in French it is still referred to as the authentic source though the authorized translation of the same is made for the convenience of the states. These rules govern the contract of affreightment and cover major areas of the contract of affreightment. Though Article II allows liberty to enter into a special agreement regarding the contract of carriage of goods by sea, in respect of loading, handling, stowage, carriage, custody care and discharge of goods it retains the application of the responsibilities and liabilities of the carrier and its entitlement to the rights and immunities as given in the Hague–Visby Rules.

306. The delegates attending the diplomatic conference recommended the adoption of the same in their respective countries with such modification as may be found suitable. In India, the same has been adopted in the Indian Carriage of Goods by Sea Act 1925 and a declaration to this effect is made in the Preamble of the said Act. Such adoption has substantially changed the status of the sea carriers under the bills of lading. The Act also restricts the shipowner's right to contract out of their liabilities. Thus the shipowner's way of contracting is a matter of complaint by the consignees and endorsees who were not parties to the contract between the shipper and the carrier (Halsbury's Laws of India, Volume 23: Carriers (45.459) at 228).

B. Areas of Applicability

307. The Indian Carriage of Goods by Sea Act 1925 declares the enunciation of the Rules in the Act as it is the very object of the passing of the 1925 Act. The Act was amended in 1964 and is closely connected with the Indian Bills of Lading Act 1856, the MS Act 1958 and the Coasting Vessels Act 1938. Before the passing of the Act, the common law of England relating to the common carrier by sea was applied and the liability of the common carrier remains unaffected by sections 151, 152 of the Indian Contract Act 1872. The bill of lading relieves the shipowner from any liability to show how the loss had occurred (*B. I. S. N. Co. Ltd v. Sokkalal* AIR 1953 Mad 3).

1. Goods Not Brought to Indian Port

308. Section 2 cannot be invoked regarding the goods which are not brought to the Indian port. Article III Rule 6 shall not apply, in view of section 2 of the Act as it cannot be said that the Act applies only to the carriage of goods by sea in ship carrying goods from any port in India to any other port within or outside India. Section 2 is merely an extension of the application of the Hague Rules to a case of carriage of goods in ship carrying goods from any port of India to any other port in India or outside (*National Insurance Co. Ltd v. Navram Constantza* AIR 1988 Cal 155). The provisions of the Rules apply only to cases where a bill of lading has been issued incorporating the provisions of the Act and do not apply *proprio vigore* to all contracts of carriage by sea (*Far Eastern Steamship Cp. V. Kolka Trading Co.* AIR AP 433). When goods were loaded and carried from a port outside and discharged at a port within India, then section 2 did not apply.

2. Absolute Warranty

309. Absolute warranty of seaworthiness is not to be implied in the contract of carriage of goods by sea to which the Rules apply (section 3).

3. Mentioning of Facts

310. In every bill of lading or similar document of title, there should be clear mentioning of the fact that the contract shall be subject to the Rules (section 4).

4. Goods in Sailing Ships

311. Article VI of the Rules is modified in relation to goods carried in sailing ships and by prescribed routes. Article VI shall in relation to the carriage of goods by sea in sailing ships carrying goods from any port in India to any other port whether within or outside it and the carriage of goods by sea in ships carrying goods from a port in India to a port in Ceylon as though the article referred to goods of any class instead of to particular goods and as though the proviso to the second paragraph of the said article were omitted (section 5).

5. Bulk Cargoes

312. Rules 4 and 5 of Article III has been modified in relation to bulk cargoes. Whenever the weight of any bulk of cargo is either ascertained or accepted by the third party or when it is to be ascertained then irrespective of any Rules the bill is not the prima facie evidence against the carrier of the weight of the goods (section 6).

6. Saving

313. Sections 331 and 352 of the MS Act 1958 (44 of 1958) shall remain unaffected by the provisions of the 1925 Act or by any other legislation (section 7).

II. Transport Period

314. The transport in a carriage by sea starts with the loading of the cargo on board and till the moment they are discharged at the destined port. The liability of the carrier thus spreads over the transport period as usually the contract is explicit about it and the carrier mentions this period clearly in the bill of lading and are thus exempted from liability when the loss to goods results before loading and after the discharge. The 'carriage of goods' covers the period from the time when the goods are loaded to the time when they are discharged from the ship (Article I (e) The International Conference on Maritime Law 1922 incorporated in the ICGSA). This Rule along with others is approved under the Indian Carriage of Goods by Sea Act 1925 by section 2 which says that; 'subject to the provisions of this Act, the rules set out in the Schedule (hereinafter referred to as "the rules") shall have effect in relation to and in connection with the carriage of goods by sea in ships carrying goods from any port in India'.

III. Cargo and Excepted Cargo

315. Cargo in a contract of affreightment forms its subject matter. Several obligations of the carrier are connected with the safety of the cargo failing which he is made liable. The carrier should also give due attention to the nature of cargo while storing it; where the carrier stacked tobacco bags in the deep stowage and near the engine room it was held that he failed to take 'proper' care of the cargo (*AS Navigation Co. v. Jethalal* AIR 1959 Cal 479).

IV. Deck Cargo

316. Schedule of the Indian Carriage of Goods by Sea Act 1925, under Article 1(c) defines a Deck Cargo. Under it, Deck Cargo has been excluded from the definition of 'goods' and the definition says that goods include goods, wares, merchandises, and articles of every kind whatsoever, except live animals and cargo which by the contract of carriage is states as being carried on deck and is so carried. In other words, the Act is not applied to cargo which is stated in the contract as being carried on deck. Deck cargo is to be understood as including anything carried on deck in some space not already included in the measurement of the ship's cargo-carrying capacity ([1908] 1 KB 528 CA per Lord Alverstone at 532). It is a cargo which is carried on any open space on the deck or on a covered space not included in the cubicle contents forming the ship's registered tonnage. The Bombay High Court has held that the burden is on the carrier to prove that the goods were on the deck and a mere mentioning in the contract of carriage is not sufficient to exclude such cargo from the definition of 'goods'. The carrier may exclude liability for negligence regarding loss of such cargo (*Scindia Steam Navigation Co. v. Ismain Lohmed* AIR 1960 Bom 416) (Article 1 Rule (c)).

V. The Description of the Goods in the Bill of Lading

317. At the time of shipment, the shipper should disclose to the carrier the details of the cargo including guaranteeing to the carrier, the accuracy, at the time of shipment of the marks, number, quantity and weight as furnished by him and the shipper shall indemnify the carrier against all loss, damages and expenses arising or resulting from inaccuracies in such particulars. Notice should be given to the carrier regarding the loss or damage caused to the goods but the notice need not be given in case there has been a joint inspection. The master, shipowner or the agent as the case may be after receiving the goods for carriage should hand over the bill of lading to the shipper which should include important declarations about the goods and out of which the rights and liabilities of the shipper and the carrier flow. Some important declarations in a bill of lading related to the goods are as given in The Indian Carriage of Goods by Sea Act 1925 as follows:

> The leading marks to differentiate the goods should be given in writing by the shipper to the carrier before loading. These marks should also be stamped on the goods in a legible manner in a prominent place.
>
> – The weight, numbers of packages, quality and general condition of the goods should also be furnished in writing by the shipper.
> – Where the shipowner, master or the agent is suspicious of the authenticity of the declarations so made by the shipper then they remain not bound by such declarations.

The carrier is also free to surrender either wholly or partially his rights and immunities by entering a clause in the bill of lading to the effect.

A bill of lading or similar documents of title to the goods as issued in India must expressly state that the provisions and rules of the Indian Carriage of Goods by Sea Act 1925 are applicable to them. It was held that under Article III Rule 4 of the Act the shipowner is not given the power to prove that the goods were in apparent good condition when he accepted it as against the persons who accepted the bill of lading on the faith of the statement contained in it (*Canada and Dominion Sugar Co. Ltd v. Canadian National (West Indies – Steamship Ltd)* AIR 1947 Pc 40,228 IC 614)).

VI. Jurisdiction Clauses

318. All the cases concerning the damage caused to the goods and cargo and regarding relief sought by the plaintiff are heard by the concerned High Courts under the admiralty jurisdiction; whether it is marine lien, arrest of ship, or other matters connected with the carriage of goods by sea. This was even declared by the High Court of Calcutta that the admiralty jurisdiction of the court cannot be doubted and when due to lack of care of cargo it is damaged and suit for arrest of the ship was filed by the aggrieved the court could hear the matter (*Paharpur Ceiling Towers Ltd v. Owners and Parties Interested in the Vessel MV Lima 1.* (2001) 2 Cal LT 445 (Cal)).

319. However, recently, many cases regarding goods which were damaged or lost in carriage by sea were taken to the District Forum established under the Consumer Protection Act 1986. Where on refusal by the consignee the consignor ordered the return of the goods and on arrival all the cartons were found empty, it was held that the consignor had the right to approach the District Forum and the same had jurisdiction over the matter (*Paras Mal v. Roshan Freight Carriers*, 1993 CCJ 48 Delhi).

VII. Vessel

320. When any vessel is to be employed under a charter party then the shipowner is under certain obligations regarding the readiness of the ship for the forthcoming engagements. It is required that the ship must be at the place of loading contemplated by the charter party, it must be in such a condition so as to be ready to receive the goods on board. Once the ship is ready, the charterer is to be duly notified about the fact and no demurrage or detention of time can be put against the charterer unless such notice is duly served on him. After making the ship ready the shipowner is also required to take pratique so that the ship is taken to be a disease-free ship allowed to use a port. The seaworthiness of the vessel at the time of loading is also implied in the contract of affreightment.

§5. Duties of the Carrier

Indian Carriage of Goods by Sea Act 1925

321. The article contains the responsibilities and liabilities of the carrier which become operative only when a bill of lading is issued which contains the terms that the rights and liabilities, including the exemption in favour of the carrier, are regulated by the provisions of Article II to Article III (*Province of Madras v. I. S. & C. Machade* AIR 1955 Mad 519).

I. Duty Relating to the Vessel

322. After issuing the bill of lading the carrier is bound, before and at the beginning of the voyage to exercise due diligence to:

(a) make the ship seaworthy;
(b) properly man, equip and supply the ship;
(c) make the holds, refrigerating and cool chambers, and all other parts of the ship in which goods are carried fit and safe for their reception, carriage and preservation *(Article III Rule 1*).

II. Duties Relating to the Cargo

323. Subject to the rights and immunities as given under Article IV, the carrier shall properly and carefully load, handle, stow, carry, keep care for and discharge the goods carried. The amount of care which is to be taken by the carrier depends on the nature of goods shipped (*A. S. Navigation Co. v. Jethalal* AIR 1959 Cal 479). After receiving the goods for shipment, the carrier has to issue a bill of lading which should manifest the following particulars in respect of the cargo booked:

(1) *Leading Marks*: The leading marks necessary for identification of the goods as the same are furnished in writing by the shipper before the loading of such goods starts. Such identification marks should be stamped clearly on the goods and should remain legible till the end of the voyage.
(2) *Quantity*: Either the number of packages or pieces or the quantity or weight, whatever it may be, as furnished by the shipper.
(3) *Apparent Order*: The apparent order and condition of the goods are also to be mentioned clearly.

324. Such declarations made by the carrier are to be accurate and he can always refuse to make any entry if he is of the opinion that they do not accurately represent the goods. The shipper, however, becomes liable for any inaccuracy which may be discovered later. The carrier is not bound to state both the quantity and weight of the shipped goods and he is free to state that the weight is unknown. However, if he declared both then he becomes liable for both. Where the bill of lading acknowledged a number of Indian polythene and as regarding weight noted the heading 'said to weigh' and there being a shortage of weight, the heading was not taken to be a sufficient disclaimer and the carrier was held liable (*Pannalal Krishnalal v. O. S. Kaisha* (1966) 70 Cal WN 307). In the case decided by the Kerala High Court where the bill of lading after stating the weight wrote 'weight declared by the shippers, but not checked', the shipowner was held not liable (*Collis Line P Ltd v. New India Assurance Co. Ltd* AIR 1982 Ker 127). (Article III Rule 2, 3).

§6. Immunities and Limitations of Liability

325. The rule states the extent of liability and the immunity given to the carrier in the following words.

I. Liability and Onus of Proof

326. Neither the carrier nor the ship shall be liable for loss or damage arising or resulting from unseaworthiness unless caused by want of due diligence on the part of the carrier to make the ship seaworthy, and to secure that the ship is properly manned, equipped and supplied, and to make the holds, refrigerating and cool chambers and all other parts of the ship in which goods are carried fit and safe for their reception carriage and preservation in accordance with the provisions of paragraph 1 of Article III. The burden of proving that due diligence was exercised in respect of the goods is on the carrier or on any person who claims exemption under the given clause (Article IV Rule 1).

II. Immunities

327. The rule states that neither the carrier nor the ship shall be responsible for loss or damage arising or resulting from:

(a) Act, neglect, or default of the master, mariner, pilot or the servants of the carrier in the navigation or in the management of the ship.
(b) Fire, unless caused by the actual fault or privity of the carrier.
(c) Perils, dangers and accidents, of the sea or other navigable waters.
(d) Act of God.
(e) Act of War.
(f) Act of public enemies.
(g) Arrest or restraint of princes, rulers of people, or seizure under legal process.
(h) Quarantine restrictions.
(i) Act or omission of the shipper or owner of the goods, his agent or representatives.
(j) Strikes or lockouts or stoppage or restraint of labour from whatever cause, whether partial or general.

(k) Riots and civil commotions.
(l) Saving or attempting to save life or property at sea.
(m) Wastage in bulk or weight or any other loss or damage arising from inherent defect, quality or vice of the goods.
(n) Insufficiency of packing.
(o) Insufficiency or inadequacy or marks.
(p) Latent defects not discoverable by due diligence.
(q) Any other cause arising without the actual fault or privity of the carrier, or without the fault or neglect of the agents or servants of the carrier, but the burden of proof shall be on the person claiming the benefit of this exception to show that neither the actual fault nor privity of the carrier nor the fault or neglect of the agents or servants of the carrier contributed to the loss or damage (*Article IV Rule 2*).

III. Deviation

328. The rule gives another ground of immunity in the form of deviation in saving or attempting to save life or property at sea. The deviation has to be reasonable with reference to the circumstances faced. The House of Lords interpreting the rule held that as the contingencies and emergencies arising in maritime transport are infinite and unpredictable hence no criterion of universal applicability can be laid down. The reasonableness of an act must, however, be judged in relation to the circumstances existing at the time of its commission and not by any abstract standard (*Stag Line, Ltd v. Foscolo, Mango & Company Ltd* [1931] All ER Rep 666: 1932 AC 328). (Article IV Rule 4).

IV. Nature and Value of Cargo

329. According to this rule, the carrier is not liable beyond GBP 100 per package or unit, or the equivalent of that sum in other currency unless the nature and value of such goods have been declared by the shipper before shipment and inserted in the bill of lading. Any such declaration in the bill of lading shall operate as prima facie evidence but shall not be binding or conclusive on the carrier. The monetary limit given in the rule is the minimum one and it can always be increased by mutual agreement. The value of the goods has to be declared by the shipper and it has to be accurate in order to enable the shipper to get over this limitation clause (Article IV Rule 5).

V. Dangerous Goods

330. According to this rule in case the goods are of an inflammable, explosive or dangerous nature to which the carrier, master or agent of the carrier have not consented may at any time before discharge land them, or destroy them, or render them innocuous without compensating the shipper. The shipper may in turn be liable for all damages and expenses directly or indirectly arising out of or resulting from such shipment. However, if such goods are shipped with the knowledge or consent then they may be landed, destroyed or rendered innocuous by the carrier without liability on the part of the carrier except to general average if any (Article IV Rule 6).

§7. Non-negotiable Seaway Bills

331. The non-negotiable sea way bill is marked with the words 'Sea Way bill' on the face of it. The Non-negotiable seaway bill is not considered as a bill of lading. In a negotiable instrument, a bona fide transferee is not affected by any defect in the title of his transferor but a bill of lading passes property to all previous defects in title. Though basically speaking, a bill of lading is not a negotiable instrument, yet it is regarded as a bill of lading in the sense that the property in the goods represented by the bill passes to the person to whom it is transferred. However, in the case of a negotiable instrument transferee is not affected by any defective title of the transferor but a bill of lading is affected in such a situation. Section 1 of the Indian Bills of Lading Act 1856 subsumes this principle. The section thus reads:

> Every consignee of goods named in a bill of lading and every endorsee of a bill of lading to whom the property in the goods therein mentioned shall pass, upon or by reason of such consignment of endorsement shall have transferred to and vested in him all rights of suit, and be subject to the same liabilities in respect of such goods as if the contract contained in the bill of lading had been made with himself.
>
> Hague-Visby Rules as amended in 1968 are adopted by India. Earlier The Indian Carriage of Goods by Sea Act 1925 includes the Hague Rules 1924. Freedom to impose terms and conditions of carriage is subject to these rules which are commonly used by merchants and mariners equally.
>
> A bill of lading in due course of time has not only become a contract of carriage but it has also become a negotiable instrument and a document of title (AK Bansal, 'The Four Pillars of International Maritime Law and Bills of Lading', *Journal of the Indian Law Institute*, Vol. 48:4, New Delhi [2006], page 527).

§8. Hamburg Rules

332. A contract for carriage of goods via international waters involves not only great risks but that partaking in a number of national laws makes the availability of relief very difficult. International efforts continue to evolve a unified solution to maritime matters. The United UNCTAD Working Group on Shipping Legislation and the United Nations Commission on International Trade Law examined the Hague Rules as amended up to 1977 relating to the system of liability for loss of or damage to goods and held the United Nations Diplomatic Conference held in March 1978 (the Hamburg Conference) and adopted the United Nations Convention on the Carriage of Goods by Sea 1978 which are also known as the Hamburg Rules. These

Rules represent the Final Act of the UN regarding carriage of goods by sea. The Rules apply to all the carriages of goods by sea irrespective of the nationality of the ship or of the shipper, carrier or any other person with the object of achieving uniformity in maritime law of carriage. It envisages the duration of the responsibility of the carrier, the basis and limits of his liability and also the grounds on which it may be lost.

I. Bill of Lading under the Hamburg Rules

333. The Rules define 'Bill of lading' as a document which is the evidence of the contract of carriage of goods by sea and in which the carrier undertakes to deliver the goods to the person named in it on the production of such document. At the time of loading, the carrier when taking charge of the goods issues to the shipper a bill of lading after getting it signed by a person having authority to do so and often it is also the master of a ship which carriers the goods who is said to have the authority to sign the bill. The bill of lading contains the particulars which include, among other things, the name and personal details of the shipper, carrier, and consignee if any, the nature, condition, identification marks and quantity of goods in the form of packets. The freight to be payable, the place of loading and the port of discharge, the date of delivery of goods and also the increased limit of liability of the carrier are also mentioned in the bill of lading. On the demand of the shipper, the carrier must also issue a 'shipped' bill of lading which indicates that the goods are on board and the date on which they have been loaded. Where a doubt arises as to the particulars given in a bill of lading or in a 'shipped' bill of lading that the goods or their character may be different from what has been disclosed then the carrier must insert his suspicion in the bill of lading.

§9. Right of Action

334. The cause of action regarding the loss of goods may arise either on the basis of a contract or on the basis of liabilities arising out of alleged tortuous acts of the owner of the vessel and his agent. Thus the suit against the agent was maintainable (*Nepal Food Corporation v. U. P. T. Import & Export Ltd* AIR 1988 Cal 283). A suit for loss or damage of goods should be brought within one year after delivery of the goods or the date when the goods should have been delivered. In case no suit is brought within the stipulated time, then the carrier shall be discharged from liability.

Chapter 7. Piloting

§1. Introduction

335. The job of navigating the ship is entrusted to the pilot who has specialized knowledge of navigation. Section 3(3) of the Indian Ports Act 1908 defines a pilot as to mean a 'person for the time being authorized by the [government] to pilot vessels'. He is the person who is licensed for a zone or a master or a mate with a pilotage certificate. The pilot has got to have the certificate of competency as Master of a foreign-going ship. He normally navigates within the harbour and has special and detailed information about the local signals, lights, depths of harbour, and so on. However, according to the Government of India, the nature and functions of a Pilot and Master are similar and the Union of India has implemented the experience of both the Pilot and the Master together for the purpose of recruitment (*Capt. Karan Vaswani v. Union of India (2000) 3 SCC602* AIR 2000 SC 1446).

§2. Statutory Provisions

336. The Indian Ports Act 1908 contains rules regarding pilotage. Moreover, the UK practice is followed in India regarding the offences committed by the pilot and other situations where Indian law is silent on the subject.

§3. Duties of the Pilot

337. A pilot is a person who has got a license for a zone or a master or a mate with a pilotage certificate. When a pilot has been engaged by a master then he is entitled to pilot facilities for getting on board and for leaving the ship. If the pilot so desires, the master is required to explain to the pilot draught, length and beam of the ship and provide the pilot with such information relating to the ship or its cargo as the pilot specifies which will be helpful for him to carry out his duties. The master is also under obligation to make the pilot aware of the material defects if any in the ship which may affect the navigation and thus may prevent the pilot from discharging his duties.

§4. Pilot to Require Master to Hoist Number

338. Every pilot in charge of a vessel shall require the number of the vessel to be duly signalled. If on such requisition the master refuses to hoist the number of a vessel or to adopt such other means of making her name known as may be practicable as usual, the pilot may, on arrival at the first place of safe anchorage, anchor the vessel and refuse to proceed on his course until the requisition has been complied with (section 52 The Indian Ports Act 1908).

§5. Liability of the Pilot

339. Pilotage may be compulsory or voluntary depending on the law of the port. However, whether compulsory or voluntary a pilot is generally not held answerable for a collision even though it was due to his negligence or fault. Pilots are usually taken as expert advisers while navigation remains the responsibility of the master. The owners are responsible for the negligence of both masters and pilots in navigation.

I. Personal Liability

340. Personal liability of the pilot can arise out of his contract of employment; it may be civil as under the civil law of the country or it may also be criminal.

A. Contractual Liability

341. India follows the UK practice in this respect where the pilot has personal liability regarding certain acts. Thus a pilot shall be held responsible for loss or suspension of license or certificate. A pilotage authority is also generally not liable for the negligence of a pilot licensed but not employed by him.

B. Civil Liability

342. According to the practice followed in the United Kingdom and other countries, the pilot in India shall be liable for corrupt practices, for lending his license, for employing anything extra for the services of the ship, leaves the ship without the consent of the master, refuses to follow any of his duties regarding taking charge or delaying in taking charge of the ship or commits any act which is violative of his duties or against the provisions of the prevailing law.

C. Criminal Liability

343. Where the pilot of a vessel disobeys or abets disobedience to any of the provisions then he is punishable with a fine which may extend to INR 500 for each instance of such disobedience of abetment and shall be liable to have authority to act as a pilot withdrawn (section 53 The Indian Ports Act 1908). The offences committed by the pilot or by any other person are to be tried by a magistrate the magistrate may cause the amount of any fine imposed upon the owner or the master of any vessel for any offence committed on board of the vessel or in the management thereof.

Chapter 8. Towing and Pushing Contract

§1. Introduction

344. Apart from being garlanded by water waves in the southern triangular land, India is also gifted by Nature with sprawling rivers, navigable canals, creeks and backwaters. The water wealth of India can be divided into two broad categories. India is among those rare countries of the world which are blessed both with the boundless oceans and with the river network; both in abundance.

I. Ocean and Sea Wealth

345. While the Arabian Sea, the Bay of Bengal and the Indian Ocean share the waters surrounding from three sides in the southernmost peninsula of India, there are a good number of ports and round-the-clock activity is seen on these ports.

II. Inland Waterways Wealth

346. The transport in these waterways can be divided between inland waterways transport and ocean transport. The waterways in India are restricted to very limited areas like the Ganges in the Eastern Region, Brahmaputra in the North-Eastern region, Goa waterways and canals and backwaters of Kerala, Karnataka, Andhra Pradesh and Maharashtra. Most of these waterways suffer from navigational hazards like shallow water, narrow width during dry weather, bank erosion and inadequate clearances. The main constraints on the inland waterway are that:

- Rivers are not navigable throughout the year.
- Night navigation is not available.
- There is slow speed-high transit time.
- There is non-availability of loading and unloading infrastructure and jetties.
- Vessels are not in a very satisfactory condition.

Normally the contract of pushing and towing is usually entered into by the carriers, shipowners, the port authorities and by the government on two occasions.

§2. Statutory Provisions

347. There is no law on the contract of pushing and towing in India. The MS Act nowhere defines the contract and even the act of pushing and towing is defined nowhere. Whenever the occasion arises the ideal law is the law and practice of the United Kingdom which is closely followed by India especially in the area of marine law. However, some mentioning of the services is found in relevant Acts. The relevant provisions regarding the contracts in the nature of the contracts of pushing and towing, though not mentioned by name, are retrieved from various Acts. Thus such contracts may be entered into by the government authorities either in regular times or as part of rescue operations.

I. At Regular Times

348. Whenever the work is employed by a party keeping in view the unusual sea and port surroundings, there was presumed an implied condition that the person who employs the services of the tug shall see that the towage operation is successfully carried out. Failing this obligation the other party would not be able to render towage services as per the contract and is entitled to compensation. The plaintiffs were once engaged by the defendants to tow a concrete lighter. Though the tug arrived at the coast, yet it could not reach the lighter because of insufficient water except in a high tide. The defendants did not bother to bring the lighter in such a position so as to make them get it towed. Plaintiff's action for damages succeeded because the Court held that the defendants should have made the arrangements for the better and easy towage of the lighter (*Elliot Steam Tug Co. Ltd v. New Medway Steam Packet Co. Ltd* [1907] 59 LIL Rep 35 at 38).

Towage is defined as 'a service rendered by one vessel to aid the propulsion or to expedite the movement of another vessel'.

A. Removal of Obstructions

349. Though the towage and pushing terminology is not used yet in a number of Acts, there has been a mentioning of the services of the tug which are employed. The authorities which are authorized to make contracts for services is the Central Government which has the power to remove or destroy an obstruction in the fairway which may have resulted due to where the vessel was stuck, stranded or abandoned or any fishing stake, timber or other thing is placed or left by causing such timber to be removed or destroyed if the removal is neither possible nor desirable (section 2 The Obstruction in Fairways Act 1881). And thus, these are also taken here to mean the authorities which are engaged in making the contract of towing and pushing.

B. Removal of Obstructions and Other Hazards

350. The State Government is given the power to appoint an officer to have the authority to cause the mechanically propelled vessel to be raised, removed, blown up or otherwise destroyed when any such vessel is wrecked, stranded, or sunk in any inland water or is likely to become an obstruction or impediment or danger to the safe and convenient navigation or use of inland water or the landing place or embankment (section 44A). The Inland Vessels Act 1917). When such obstruction is removed by the State Government then it can recover the expenses of removal from the person who has caused such obstruction or impediment or public nuisance (section 44C). Thus these are the provisions which indicate that the removal of wrecks or obstructions is undertaken by the government authorities and when such services are engaged then these are on the basis of a contract of services. Moreover, it is also mentioned in the Act that the State Government has the power to make rules for protection of inland mechanically propelled vessels from accidents, explosion, fire, collision and other similar hazards including the rules to – regulate the towing of vessels astern or alongside (section 52). The government also has the power to regulate the carriage and exhibition of lights by other vessels on specified inland waters, regulate the navigation of inland 'mechanically propelled vessels' to prevent danger to other vessels or to the banks, channels, navigation marks or any other movable or immovable property.

C. *Board of Trustees*

351. A Board of Trustees formed under the Act is a body corporate and is entrusted with a number of functions in respect of maintenance of ports and other services. The Board executes services and provides appliances to engage in certain services. Thus, section 35 of the Major Port Trusts Act 1963 says that a Board shall execute such work and provide such appliances which it thinks necessary to employ for the maintenance of the ports or appliances or for rendering some services. Section 35(h) of the Act says that such works and appliances may include:

(h) vessels, tugs or other boats for use within the limits of the port or beyond those limits, whether in territorial waters or otherwise, for the purpose of towing or rendering assistance to any vessel, whether entering or leaving the port or bound elsewhere and for the purpose of saving or protecting life of property and for the purpose of landing, shipping or transshipping, passengers or goods under section 12.

(l) dry docks, slipways, boat basins and workshops to carry out repairs or overhauling vessels, tugs, boats machinery or other appliances.

The Board of Trustees Thus the Board is the authority which employs the tugs for maintenance work.

Thus all the debts, obligations and liabilities incurred and all contracts where are supposed to be done by the Central Government are to be done by the Board (section 29 (b) The Major Port Trusts Act 1963).

D. *Inland Waterways Authority of India*

352. The IWAI constituted under the IWAI Act 1985 is the authority which undertakes the jobs on behalf of the Central Government and is authorized to make contracts and engage services connected with the functions of the Authority under the said Act. All the debts, obligations and liabilities incurred and all contracts entered into by the Central Government for the purposes of the IWT Directorate shall be deemed to be on behalf of the Authority (section 11(b)). Thus one of the activities of the Authority is that to Control activities such as throwing rubbish, dumping or removal of material, from the bed of the NWs, and appurtenant land in so far as they affect the safe and efficient shipping and navigation, maintenance of navigable channels, river training and conservancy matters (section 14).

E. The Indian Ports Act 1908.

353. The Central Government is authorized under the Act to make rules regarding rules for:

- For striking the yards and topmasts, and for rigging in the booms and yards of vessels in any such port, and for swinging or taking in davits, boats and other things projecting from such vessels.
- The removal or proper hanging or placing of anchors, spars and other things being in or attached to vessels in any such port.
- For regulating the bunkering of vessels with liquid fuel in any such port and the description of barges, pipelines or tank vehicles to be employed in such bunkering.
- For regulating the moving the warping of all vessels within any such port and the use of warps.
- For fixing the rates to be paid for the use of such moorings when belonging to the government or of any boat, hawser, or other thing belonging to the Government (section 6).

Moreover, the conservator under the Act is also authorized to remove obstructions, timber, raft or other thing floating which impedes or obstructs the free navigation or lawful use of any pier, jetty landing place, wharf, quay dock, and mooring. The owner of any such timber, raft or other thing is required to pay the reasonable expenses of the removal (section 10).

The activities mentioned herein do require the services of hired tugs and other equipment required for towage and pushing purposes.

II. At Rescue Operations

354. Sea perils are part of sea life. Whenever a vessel touches the sea waters, it becomes vulnerable to sea hazards. Such hazards may be the result of accidents involving human agency or it may be a natural calamity such as sea storms, rise and ebb of tides and a number of other sea perils. When humans get stuck in such dangerous situations SOS or other calls for help may be met by a helping hand. It can also be done in an organized manner if time permits. One of these is salvage services.

A. *Salvage Operations*

355. Salvage means giving help to save life and property of the endangered vessel and men. The operation apart from the human agency also requires certain equipment as the size and nature of the obstructions and wrecks is such which calls for specialized rescue operations. Salvage services are paid services and it is often followed by an agreement to measure the contribution of the salvor and then fixing his award as per the contract. All the property which is benefited by the salvage services such as the ship, cargo, people they all contribute to the salvage award. Often important legal issues arise from the breach of such contracts as sometimes it involves the laws of contract and services of two different countries. Often damage is also caused to the equipment which is engaged in such operations. The owners of the salving vessel are liable for the damages caused. Thus when a salving vessel is damaged by collision through the negligence of another vessel, then the salvage expenses cannot be recovered if the salvage is chargeable to improper abandonment. Often the vessel engaged in salvage operations is itself sunk or destroyed by the negligence of another vessel. In such a case a claim is recognized (The Betsey Caines [1826] 2 Hag Adm 28). Once while a vessel was in distress in the Atlantic, another vessel, the Missouri, towed her to Halifax but during the towage operations, the crankshaft of the vessel was damaged. The Court held that in estimating the salvage award, the value of the Missouri and the danger to which she was exposed must be taken into consideration. Courts have shown a tendency to give importance to the rights of the shipowners when their vessel is engaged in salvage operations and order the giving of a liberal salvage award. In another case of 'Tojo Maru' when a driver was operating from the salvor's tug then he negligently fired a bolt gun causing damage. The salvors contended to set off the sum against the salvage award ((1917) 1 All ER 1110). Treaty and agreements with foreign countries regarding matters connected with the salvages services would be effective as per their terms and the MS Act or any other act shall not affect it (section 403).

B. *Collisions*

356. The sea mishap may also be the result of two vessels colliding with each other. As a result loss and damage to life and property ensues. Often certain things which are still floating on the surface can be saved and often it is for the removing or cleaning of obstructions that towing and pushing services are pressed into. Though when there is a collision in the sea, owners of the vessels colliding with each other have mutual rights and liabilities and damages can be recovered in tort. In an old decision when there was a collision apart from the two vessels involved, the third vessel was held three-quarters to blame. The tug was to be blamed for one-quarter. The cargo owner in the tow was only entitled to recover three-quarters of his damage as the owners of the tug were declared to be the tow owners (The Umona [1914] P 141).

357. In India, there is no mentioning of the rescue operations at the time of collision. However, the MS (Prevention of Collisions at Sea) Regulations 1975 do give merely the description of towing and pushing regarding its maintenance. It says that a power drive vessel when towing shall exhibit two masthead lights forward in a vertical line. When the length of the tow measuring from the stern of the towing vessel to the other end of the tow exceeds 20 m, there must be three such lights in a vertical line. It should also have a sidelight, a stern light, a towing light in a vertical line above the stern light. When the length of the tow exceeds 200 m, then it should be of diamond shape and also visible.

358. As regarding pushing vessels too, the Rules give some maintenance directions. It says that when a pushing vessel and a vessel being pushed ahead are rigidly connected in a composite unit, then they shall be regarded as a power-driven vessel and its lighting system should be that of a power-driven vessel. But when the pushing vessel is pushing ahead or towing alongside, then it should have two masthead lights, sidelights and a stern light. The vessel which is being towed should also exhibit sidelights and a stern light. Any number of vessels being towed or pushed in a group shall be lighted as one vessel (Rule 24).

C. Pollution Problems

359. Disturbing the natural ambience of water in the oceans through a human agency is commonly known as pollution of the sea. Environmental pollution is defined as 'substantial physical damage to human health or to marine life or resource in coastal or inland waters or areas adjacent thereto, caused by pollution, contamination, fire, explosion or similar major incidents'.

Pollution of the sea may be caused by spilling of oil, by the discharge of oil contents from the ship itself, by offshore installations and by sewage outlets and by dumping garbage and human waste into the sea. Of these, the oil spilling is the most destructive one.

Whatever may be the source of pollution, havoc is caused in the sea or river as the case may be and as a result manoeuvring of vessels and cleaning of the area can be done only with the help of towing and pushing services. This is yet another occasion where the contracts are made by port authorities to overcome the situation.

§3. Liability and Limitation of Liability

360. No law in India deals specifically with the contract of pushing and towing, though from the above provisions it is quite clear that the pushing and towing services are frequently employed and are not unknown to the marine culture in India. One may thus presume that such contracts are dealt with by the normal contract of service and hire which are commonly governed in India by the Indian Contract Act 1872. Under the Act, the liability of the defendant is restricted up to paying the damages to the plaintiff and making good the loss suffered by him. There is, therefore, no hard and fast rule to measure the damages and it mainly depends on the terms of the contract between the parties.

Moreover, as the contract of towing and pushing is mainly a contract of service in India the applicable law in such situations is also the Consumer Protection Act 1986 which provides for the compensation of the party who suffers under a paid service.

Moreover, the High Courts also have jurisdiction regarding the towing services contract. Thus, a High Court shall have power over (k) any claim in the nature of towage which says '(k) any claim in the nature of towage supplied to any foreign ship or sea-going vessel whether such ship may have been within India or upon the high seas at the time services were rendered in respect of which the claim is made' (section 6, Admiralty Court Act 1840).

I. The MS Act

361. Under the MS Act, salvage operations are payable for saving life, cargo or wreck. The liability of the persons engaging equipment or hiring them is paid in the following manner for tugs and towage (section 402):

- salvage regarding life preservation when payable by the owner of the vessel shall be paid to all other claims as well;
- where the government or the commander or crew of any vessel engages in such services then such government or the commander or crew would be entitled to salvage.

362. By the last clause, it is clear that such towing and pushing services may also arise independent of any contract and it is not only that private salvors are entitled who have a distinct contract of service but even the government units have similar rights and liabilities though they may not have concluded a formal contract.
All the disputes arising from such contracts of services and amounts due under it are to be decided on the application of any of the disputed parties by:

- a Judicial Magistrate of the First Class where the amount claimed does not exceed INR 10,000; and
- where the amount exceeds INR 10,000, the High Court concerned.

The distribution of the salvage award among its claimants shall be done by such courts and the costs of proceedings, persons or property liable to pay them are also to be decided by them.

Chapter 9. Salvage and Assistance

§1. Definition

363. Maritime salvage means saving life or maritime property at sea. The more common kinds of salvage services include: towing a vessel into a port, efforts to refloat a stranded or sunken vessel with its cargo; operations aimed at the recovery of cargo; services rendered in extinguishing fire on board; measures taken to keep a sinking vessel afloat; holding or removing a vessel adrift from her moorings; initiating, procuring or bringing necessary assistance to a distressed vessel.

364. Colliding vessels are also bound to stand by each other under section 422 of the (English) MS Act 1894. Also, ships receiving a wireless distress call are bound to render assistance under section 22 of the (English) MS (Safety Conventions) Act 1949. An international convention for the unification of certain Rules of Law respecting Assistance and Salvage at Sea was adopted in 1910. It lays down international norms for rendering assistance to vessels in distress at sea and for payment of equitable remuneration. It also makes it obligatory for the Master of a ship to render assistance even to an enemy in the hour of peril. India ratified this Convention in 1913. An amendment was made to this convention in the Brussels Conference in 1967–1968 which was mainly to include the warships and other state-owned ships. International Convention on Salvage 1989 which came into force on 14 July 1996 was ratified by India on 18 October 1995.

According to section 3(40) 'salvage' includes all expenses properly incurred by the salvor in the performance of salvage services. It signifies not only the service rendered by a salvor but the reward payable to him for his services. This service actually implies the help and cooperation rendered voluntarily by a person, known as a salvor during ship wreckage, or during sea perils.

§2. Statutory Provisions

365. Sections 402–404 of the MS Act enumerates the rules regarding salvage. According to section 402(4), any dispute arising about the amount due as a salvage award is to be decided by a Judicial Magistrate of First class when the amount is less than INR 10,000 and by the High Court when it exceeds INR 10,000. When there is more than one claimant to the salvage award then the judicial Magistrate of First Class, the Metropolitan Magistrate or the High Court as the case may be shall decide the matter and apportion the amount among them. These courts shall also decide the costs and incidental expenses to be paid in respect of the proceedings. Section 403 protects any treaty or arrangement of the Indian Government with any foreign country regarding the disposal of the proceeds of wrecks on their respective coasts.

366. Section 29 of the Indian Ports Act 1908 penalizes a person who without the permission of the conservator creeps or sweeps for anchors, cables or other stores lost and makes it an offence punishable with INR 100.

Section 403(b) says that section 29 remains unaffected by it and that any person who recovers a property by creeping or sweeping in violation of section 29 of that Act shall not be entitled to salvage. Moreover, section 404 declares that the Central Government of India shall make rules respecting wreck and salvage. In exercise of the powers conferred by section 404 and sub-section (2) of section 458 of the MS Act 1958, the Government of India passed the (Wrecks and Salvage) Rules 1974 as amended 1975 and 1976 (GSR 1218). The breach of such rules is punishable with a fine which may extend to INR 1,000 and if the breach is a continuous one with a further fine which may extend to INR 50 for every day after the first during which the breach is continuous (Rule 29).

The Government of India then passed another set of rules under section 356 of the Act with regard to signals for communicating information regarding dangers to navigation ships in distress, and so on, namely the MS (Distress And Safety communication) Rules 1995.

I. Assistance

367. The master of an Indian ship on receiving a signal of distress or information from any source that a vessel or aircraft is in distress shall proceed with all speed to the assistance of the persons in distress unless under some special circumstances he considers it unreasonable or unnecessary to do so. The law also makes it obligatory upon the master of a ship or person in charge of each ship to, without taking a risk on his own ship, crew or passengers to assist in case of collision. While extending such assistance the master of a ship shall render to such ship such assistance which is practicable to save it and also to stay with such ship until he has ascertained that the ship has no need of further assistance. Such master when giving such assistance shall give to the other ship the name of his own ship and of the port to which she belongs and also the names of the ports from which she comes and to which she is abounding (section 348 MS Act).

368. The master of an Indian ship is also under an obligation to comply with the call of a ship in distress which has requisitioned its assistance. A master who for some special reason is unable to comply with such requisition shall make a statement to that effect in its official log book giving the reason for his not visiting the ship in distress. He should also enter in the official logbook every signal of distress or message that a vessel, aircraft or person is in distress at sea (section 355 MS Act 1958).

369. The master is, however, released from such obligation if:

(a) he is under obligation of rendering such assistance to one or more ships; or
(b) when the master is informed by the persons in distress or by the master of any ship that has reached the persons in distress that the assistance is no longer required.

Apart from the statutory obligation imposed on the Master of the Indian ship to go to the rescue of a ship or aircraft in distress (vide section 355 of the Act), the Government of India has set up an Air-Sea Search and Rescue Organization for rendering assistance when a ship or aircraft is in distress around the coast of India. The organization avails of the services of coastal Radio stations, the Indian Defence Navy, the Indian Coast Guard, the Indian Air Force, the Mercantile Marine Department and the Port Authorities in rendering such service.

Whenever any stranded or vessel in distress receives assistance from the receiver for saving life or property on board including its gear, ankle, boats and other equipment, then the owner of the vessel is under liability to pay to the receiver all expenses incurred in such rescue operation. The receiver has the authority to detain the vessel until the payment of such charges including salvage charges or in the alternative if adequate security is furnished by the owner for payment of any amount due from him.

§3. Salvage Award

370. Salvage is one of the important features of maritime law the world over. Under section 6 of the (English) Maritime Conventions Act 1911(1 and 2 Geo. 5, c. 57), the master of a vessel is under obligation to render assistance to every person who is found in peril at sea and is guilty of misdemeanour in case he fails to do so. Since the time of Romans, the right to reward for the rescue of maritime property has been recognized. The essence of the service of the salvage is saving life and property during tidal waters when the person and property on board are in danger of being lost or damaged and when the salvor does it voluntarily and without legal or official duty. But the person who renders such service becomes entitled to remuneration known as 'salvage reward'. The salvor becomes entitled to salvage remuneration from the owners of the salved ship, cargo or to other property and to this extent they have a lien on the property saved. The salvor becomes entitled to the salvage award only when: the service rendered is voluntary and not as part of a pre-existing statutory duty or contractual obligation; the service rendered must be in respect of some recognized subject of salvage which according to maritime law is vessels, their apparel, cargo and merchandise, bunkers, wreck and the so-called freight at risk and include services for saving life from a ship; the salvors must establish the fact that at the time of rendering the service, the recognized subject or the property was in real and appreciable danger; the service rendered must be successful which rests on the belief that 'no cure, no pay'.

371. Section 402 of the MS Act 1958 as amended in 2002 explains salvage reward and the circumstances under which it will be paid.

I. Where Salvage Is Paid

372. According to it, where services are rendered, wholly or in part within the TW of India in saving life from any vessel, or elsewhere in saving life from a vessel registered in India; in assisting a vessel or saving the cargo or equipment of a vessel which is wrecked, stranded or in distress at any place on or near the coasts of India; or by any person other than the receiver of the wreck in saving any wreck then the owner of the vessel cargo equipment or wreck, shall pay to the salvor a reasonable sum for salvage having regard to all the circumstances of the case. Salvage for preservation of life when payable by the owner of the vessel shall be payable in priority to all other claims for salvage.

II. Where Salvage Is Not Paid

373. Under Indian law, no salvage award shall be paid:

(a) In a case where the property or sale proceeds thereof are claimed by the owner or his duly authorized agent or assign, until the title of the claimant to the said property or sale proceeds thereof is established.
(b) In a case where the property is not claimed by its owner or his duly authorized agent or assign until the said property is sold.
(c) In a case where either party has applied for the appointment of valuer until the valuer's charge has been paid. Where the receiver has made a salvage award, he shall withhold the delivery of the wreck to the owner until the owner obtains a release from the salvor in respect of salvage due to him under the said award; where the receiver has disposed of any wreck he shall settle the salvor's claim in accordance with the award from within the sale proceeds of the wreck and obtain a receipt from the salvor in token of his having received the amount in full and final settlement of his claim before effecting payment of balance sale proceeds to the owner (Rule 23: MS Rules 1974).

§4. Reward of the Crew

374. According to section 402(3),when salvage services are rendered by or on behalf of the Government or by a vessel of the Indian Navy or of the Coast Guard or the commander or crew of any such vessel, the Government, the commander or the crew as the case may be shall be entitled to salvage and shall have the same rights and remedies in respect of those services as any other salvor. Where a tanker was removed from Diamond Harbour to keep a portion of River Hooghly safe for shipping and allied services by the commissioner for the Port of Calcutta and the Commissioner's Officers who rendered service beyond the scope of their normal duties were entitled to salvage reward independently of the commissioner (*Calcutta Port Trust v. Cargo of Benzene* (1977) 2 Cal LJ 554.

Again it was held that a rescue ship when saves the life and property on a ship in distress, then the payment of salvage reward to the commander of that rescue ship cannot be denied merely on the ground that it was the duty of the salvor as coast guard (*K. P. Shashidharan v. Union of India* AIR 2002 Ker 388).

I. Determination of Amount Due as Salvage

375. The amount of salvage due to any person in absence of any express agreement under section 402 of the act shall be determined having regard to the following considerations: the nature and degree of danger to which human life and or property saved was exposed; the aggregate value of the property saved; sale proceeds of the salved property where such property was sold; nature and degree of risk incurred by salvor; the value of salvor's property engaged in salvage service and nature and degree of danger to which it was exposed; responsibilities incurred in the performance of salvage services such as risk to insurance, liability to passengers or cargo or both through deviation of delay; loss incurred in salvage service; expenses properly incurred by salvor; expenses incurred by salvor towards loss of or injury to life or damage to property arising out of salvage service; skill shown by salvor in rendering service and time and labour spent (Rule 21, MS Rules 1974).

§5. Liability and Limitation of Liability of Salvors

I. The Liability of the Salvors

376. The practice of salvage is encouraged by the courts and international society as well. Thus the liability area of the salvors is not very wide. The salvage award is calculated in proportion to the value of the property saved. The Liability is thus of the following extent.

A. Misconduct or Negligence

377. If the salvors are found guilty of misconduct or negligence but not of a flagrant nature then it will tend to diminish the remuneration payable.

B. Underwriters

378. The salvage award is apportioned to salvors over the values of the property saved and on which it has been assessed provided the services were incurred in preventing loss by insured perils, the underwriters ensuring the respective interests would be liable for their proportion of the salvage award. If the salved vessel was imperilled solely owing solely to her unseaworthiness then the salvage charges would be payable by the owners and the underwriters would not be liable as for surcharges as they were not incurred as a result of a peril insured against. In the case of salvage of life, the liability is covered by the Protection and Indemnity Association and not the underwriters.

II. The Limitation of Liability of Salvors

379. Salvors are strictly treated though they are the ones who are engaged in life-saving operations. However, they are also treated by the 'no cure, no pay' principle (1910) and are paid only when positive results are achieved. The International Convention on Salvage 1989 seeks to do away with this principle and is planning to give more incentive to the salvors, though they may be held liable for the negligence committed during salvage operations. The Indian law says nothing specifically about it. The LLMC (section 6 paragraph 4) is applied regarding the limitation of liability of salvors.

§6. Removal of Wrecks

I. Legal Provisions

380. 'Wreck' means property cast ashore within the ebb and flow of the tide after a shipwreck. The property must be part or remains of a ship and not an independent piece of property like a raft of timber (Nicholson v. Chapman [1793] 2 Bl 254). The harbour or conservancy authority is to remove the wrecks which are in its opinion an obstruction of danger to navigation or to the lifeboat service or tidal water under the control of the harbour or conservancy authority.

381. The subject of wreck removal is still without a proper legal framework whether national or international. The maritime states have formulated rules for dealing with vessels which are wrecked, stranded found in distress near their coasts. The International Convention on Maritime Search and Rescue 1979 has come into force in June 1985 was adopted by IMO. India is still considering the ratification of this Convention.

382. The shipowners are under liability for raising, removing or destroying wrecks which they usually insure with Protection and Indemnity Clubs. In India provisions relating to wrecks and salvage are contained in Part XIII of the MS Act. Sections 355, 402 and 403 conform broadly to the provisions of the 1910 and 1989 conventions. The Government of India also formulated MS (Wrecks and Salvage) Rules 1974. Absence of any specific international convention on wrecks has created hardships for national governments as due to the enormity of the wreck the shipowners are also careless and negligent in removing it and usually depend on public authorities. They also shun their liability to pay for the wreck removal. In India, the disposal of wreck is taken care by the receiver appointed under the Indian Ports Act 1908 and the Rules of 1974 as under.

II. Procedure of Disposal of Wrecks

383. The Central Government appoints a person to be a Receiver of Wreck to receive and take possession of wreck and to perform such duties connected therewith as are given under the MS Act or Rules 1974. Such receiver shall then, on receiving intelligence of any vessel having been wrecked or stranded or of being in distress shall communicate the matter to the principal officer and then forthwith proceed there. He shall then take command of all the persons and assign duties and take command of all persons giving them directions to do the needful for the preservation of the ship. But the receiver in doing so shall not interfere between the master and crew of the vessel (sections 391, 392). Moreover, the receiver receives an intelligence that a vessel is sunk or stranded near the coast of India and is abandoned by its owner he on his arrival to the place where the vessel lies, drop a lead line over such vessel declaring his possession over the vessel. If the intelligence relates to a wreck which is not of a vessel then in such a case the receiver shall physically take possession of the wreck.

III. Role of The Receiver

384. The receiver is the person who is specially appointed for the purpose of taking care and disposal of the wreck. So in this respect, he is required to take care by suppressing plunder and disorder by force and for this, he may command any person to assist him. The receiver may also conduct any investigation of certain matters in respect of the wrecked vessels. Thus he may conduct an investigation into the name and description of the vessel, the master and owner of the vessel; the name of the owner of the cargo; the ports from and to which the vessel was bound; the occasion of the wrecking, stranding or distress of the vessel and the services rendered and such other matters which appear to be necessary to understand the entire situation (sections 394, 395).

IV. Action Taken

385. The receiver who takes possession of the wreck before disposing of the wreck is required under the Rules 1974 to take the following steps namely where the wreck consists of a vessel other than an Indian vessel or of parts, articles or equipment of a vessel or of any cargo cast overboard from a vessel other than an Indian vessel then he must send a written intimation of the wrecked vessel to the nearest consular officer of the country in which the vessel is registered. If the wreck consists of an Indian vessel or of any parts, articles or equipment of the vessel or of any cargo cast overboard from an Indian vessel engaged in trading otherwise than in the coasting trade of India then send a written intimation to the owner of the vessel; if the wreck consists of any cargo cast overboard from a vessel other than an Indian vessel. If the wreck consists of any vessel owned and operated by a Government Department or any article of cargo or equipment of such vessel, send a written intimation giving full particulars of such vessel, or the articles of cargo or equipment to the appropriate authorities of the Department concerned. Where the vessel so wrecked, sunken or stranded is likely to cause an obstruction or danger to navigation in a fairway leading to any port or place in India, the receiver shall send a report of such obstruction or danger to navigation to the principal officer in the prescribed form (Rule 6, Rules 1974).

V. Claims of Owners

386. The owner of any wreck in the possession of the receiver, upon establishing his claim of the same to the satisfaction of the receiver within one year, upon payment of the salvage shall be entitled to have the wreck or the proceeds delivered to him. In case of possession of any articles belonging to the wreck of a vessel other than Indian vessel, the consular officer of that country to which the owners of the vessel belong shall, in the absence of the authorized persons of the owner, is deemed to be the agent of the owner in respect of the custody and disposal of the articles. Where the owner of the vessel fails to make a claim within one year of the date of the sale then the balance of the sale shall become the property of the Central Government (section 399).

No doubtful claims, or the claims by agents or assignees, or by the representatives of the deceased owner shall be entertained by the receiver unless he satisfies the receiver by the production of such documentary evidence as the receiver may deem necessary.

VI. Sale of the Unclaimed Wreck

387. The receiver of wreck may sell the wreck under his custody where:

(a) it is under the value of INR 500;
(b) it is of a perishable nature and cannot be preserved for long; or
(c) it is not of sufficient value for warehousing. Proceeds of the sale shall be held by the receiver for purposes under the Act. In case the above conditions do not apply to a wreck then such wreck shall not be sold by the receiver except after taking written instructions from the Central Government (section 398 and Rule 14). The receiver of the wreck shall sell the wreck only by way of public auction which shall be made on 'as is where is' basis and the purchaser shall take full responsibility as regarding taxes payable to the Government and for encumbrances on the wreck such as maritime liens. The public auction shall be made only after a notice for sale of a wreck shall be given for not less than fourteen days in advance of the appointed date of sale, in three consecutive issues of at least two daily newspapers having a wide circulation the Mercantile Department District. Such notice shall include the description of the wreck, the percentage of the auction price as a down payment, the period within which the balanced amount shall be paid by the successful bidder, and so on.

VII. Delivery of Wreck

388. Any rightful owner of a wreck who has established his title to a wreck or any part thereof or the sale proceeds of such wreck or part thereof to the satisfaction of the receiver shall be under obligation to pay to the receiver salvage charges, any other expenditure properly incurred by the receiver for the recovery, preservation or safety of the wreck and fees payable to the receiver. Failing the payment by the owner of the charges mentioned above the receiver shall withhold delivery of any wreck or part thereof.

Chapter 10. General Average

§1. Historical Introduction

389. In maritime matters, there are three separate interests that are exposed to risks which are interest in the ship, interest in the freight and interest in the cargo. Usually, risk related to all these three is covered by insurance. Where the loss sustained by any of these interests falls upon particular interest affected in which case if the loss is total then it is called a 'particular average loss'. Where the loss arises out of a sacrifice made or any unusual expenditure made then it is called a 'general average loss'. It is so-called because the loss is borne proportionately by all (*Birkley v. Pregrave* (1801) 1 East 220).

390. The General average forms an important feature of marine insurance. For long, India remained without proper and specific legislation on the subject. The Twenty-First Report of the Law Commission of India in 1961 admitted the lacuna in Indian law. Certain sporadic legal provisions collectively tried to meet some of the exigencies arising out of marine insurance. The then-existing law in India regarding marine insurance and related matters was scattered and could be retrieved from the following Acts namely the Indian Stamp Act 1899 (section 2(20), sections 7 and 66 and Article 47, sub-divisions A and E of the Schedule to the Act) which also prescribes the duties payable on insurance policies. The Transfer of Property Act 1882 (section 130 Exception and sections 130A and 135A) envisages certain provisions connected with the formalities to be observed in the assignment of marine policies. The Insurance Act 1938 regulates generally the carrying on of the business of insurance by corporations and individuals but not with the contract of insurance between the insurer and the assured. The Commercial Documents Evidence Act 1939 (entry 9 in the Schedule Part I) was also referred to in certain matters.

391. The MS Act 1958 (sections 345–352 and sections 402–404) too does not deal with marine insurance although it provides for certain connected matters like seaworthiness, salvage, collision, and so on. Thus an exhaustive law on marine insurance in India was a desideratum as expressed in 1944 when the Bill of amending the provisions of the Transfer of Property Act relating to the assignment of policy of Marine Insurance was introduced. There was a strong suggestion to adopt the English Marine Insurance Act 1906 as a model law for India in the matter of marine insurance. The reason forwarded for this was that the business in maritime insurance in India closely follows the English pattern that the English Act is based on the 300 years old experience of a maritime nation of UK and that the Act itself has stood the test of time. Based on these recommendations the Draft Bill of the marine insurance law in India was presented by the Twenty-First Law Commission of India under the Chairmanship TL Venkatarama Aiyar on 29 July 1961.

§2. Statutory Provisions

392. Section 66 of the Marine Insurance Act 1963 deals with general average loss and defines it accordingly. The section is fully based on Clause 67 of the Marine Insurance Bill 1961. It says that a general average loss is a loss caused by or directly consequential on a general average act. It includes a general average expenditure as well as a general average sacrifice.

There is a general average act where any extraordinary sacrifice of expenditure is voluntarily and reasonably made or incurred in time of peril for the purpose of preserving the property imperilled in the common adventure. The party on whom the general average loss falls is entitled subject to the conditions imposed by maritime law, to a rateable contribution from the other interested parties.

Where the assured has incurred a general average of expenditure then, subject to the policy contents, the assured can recover it from the insurer in respect of the proportion of the loss which falls upon him. In the case of the general average sacrifice, the assured may recover from the insurer in respect of the whole loss without having enforced his right of contribution from the other parties liable to contribute.

393. In case the assured has paid a general average contribution in respect of the interest insured he may recover it from the insurer. In case there is no express stipulation then the insurer is not liable for any general average loss or contribution where the loss was not incurred for the purpose of avoiding, or in connection with the avoidance of a peril insured against. Where the ship, freight and cargo or any two of those interests are owned by the same assured, the liability of the insurer in respect of general average losses or contributions is to be determined as if those interests were owned by different persons.

§3. Definition and History of General Average

394. The concept of general average is used in varied ways having different shades of meaning which are not the same. First, there is a general average act. Thus at the time of peril, to avoid it there is either voluntary sacrifice or expenditure incurred and this is known as general average act. Second, as a result of such an act, there is a loss. If the loss is caused by or directly consequential on a general average act, then the loss is called a general average loss. Third, to compensate for such a loss, there is contribution from the other parties interested. Such a contribution is called a general average contribution. The chronological order of the various steps is illustrated from the following chart:

General average *act* — (i) sacrifice or (ii) expenditure

General averge *loss*

General average *contribution*

395. The perils of sea often call for certain extraordinary practices which are unheard of in otherwise normal life on dry areas. A sea peril may be foreseen once again it may also be an unforeseen one when a reaction from the one who is the probable victim of such a hazard is quite expected. 'The principle of general average, namely, that all whose property has been saved by the sacrifice of the property of another shall contribute to make good his loss, is of very ancient date and of universal reception among commercial nations.' (Abbot CJ in *Simonds v. White* (1824) 2 B&C 805) In *Johnson v. Chapman* [(91865) 19 CB (NS) 563] the Shooting Star is the ancient example; 'The ship "Shooting Star" sailed with a cargo timber, namely deals and staves. She was broken adrift in consequence of stormy weather. This impeded the navigation and safety of the vessel. A part of the cargo was jettisoned to lighten the ship and to save the adventure.' The decision said that the cargo owner whose cargo was thus lost was entitled to claim general average for his loss as against the shipowner whose ship was thereby saved. It was held that:

> In order to make jettison the subject of a general average contribution two conditions must be fulfilled:
>
> – First of all there must be common danger. It must be a maritime peril and it must be common to the whole adventure which would exclude the case of a subject matter that had within itself the elements of destruction which developed themselves during the storm.
> – Secondly, there must be a sacrifice in the sense of intentional sacrifice.

In this case, there was only one cargo on the ship and the only property saved was the ship itself and the right insured against the shipowner.

General average loss of cargo arises in varied ways; for instance, a portion of the cargo may be jettisoned for saving the rest of adventure but it is necessary that such cargo must be carried there by virtue of some custom or by the agreement of all the interested parties (*Strong Steel & Co. V. A. Scott & Co.* [1889] 4 App Cas 601). When cargo is sold at a port of refuge for the purpose of completing the voyage then it is a general average sacrifice (*Hallett v. Wigram* [1850] 9 CB 580).

396. There is a general average loss of freight (Halsbury's Laws of England, 4th edn, 43, paragraph 745) when in an attempt to avoid the danger to the whole adventure the shipowner damages a portion of the cargo so as to render it unfit to be carried to its destination thereby sacrificing the opportunity of earning freight upon that portion. Where the shipowner, owing to some inherent defect in the cargo abandons it on a port of refuge and does not carry it further then there is no general average sacrifice.

397. After the nationalization of general insurance in 1971, Indian shipowners and cargo interests were made to compulsorily insure Indian ships and cargo with Indian insurance companies. The New India Assurance Company Ltd. (Mumbai), the United Insurance Company Ltd. (Madras), the National Insurance Co. Ltd. (Calcutta) and the Oriental Insurance Co. Ltd. (Delhi) formed with the General Insurance Corporation of India at the apex. Liability for general average loss or contribution may be covered by marine insurance by means of a specific provision to that effect in the policy.

I. Demurrage and Lay Days

398. 'Lay Days' is the time given to the cargo owner to remove the goods after the arrival of the ship at the port of destination, failing which he is required to pay rent called 'demurrage'. Lay days and demurrage are described in the charter parties. 'Lay days' is the term which is described in charter parties in various different ways and is also calculated in different ways. Thus to remove the difficulties arising from multiplicity of meanings attached to the term 'days' the term 'running days' is introduced. 'That is a nautical term, and it can be at once seen what it means. What is the run of a ship? One speaks of the number of days it will take a ship to "run" from the Indies to England, and "running days" were those days on which a ship is running. What are those? Why, all day and every day, day and night.' (*Lord Esher MR in Nielsen v. Wair* [1885] 54 LT 344).

399. Demurrage is payable only when there is an express stipulation regarding it in the contract. When there is no such mentioning about it then the shipowner is not entitled to claim demurrage nor the charterer is justified in detaining the ship beyond the expiration of the time allowed by the charter party for load or discharging and in case he detains it then he may be liable for breach of contract. The liability for demurrage ceases as soon as the charterer has fully performed his obligation of providing or taking away the cargo and no responsibility can be attached to him for any default or detention of ship. An exception clause cannot relieve the charterer from liability for detention of ship unless it is worded clearly. Thus a charter party contained a strike clause stating that the time for discharging should not count against the charterer during continuance of strike. When the vessel at port began to discharge the cargo and when the lay time expired, a strike was called which disturbed further unloading. House of Lords held that the strike clause was not clearly worded and thus it would not have the effect of relieving the charterer from the payment of demurrage (Compania *Naviera Acolus S. A. v. Union of India* [1962] 3 All ER 670).

Again it is held that demurrage is not money payable by a charterer as consideration for the exercise by him of a right to detain a chartered ship beyond the stipulated lay days. By detaining the chartered ship beyond the stipulated lay days the charterer breaches his contract and is liable to pay damages (*President of India v. Lips Maritime Corporation* [1988] AC 395).

§4. Application of the York-Antwerp Rules 1974 (YAR)

400. When a loss occurs in the sea, its effect is enormous. Often there is time to save the unaffected property through various means and ways like jettisoning, making sacrifices and allowing salvage services which are done by a number of functionaries. Once the exercise is successful and the adventure as a whole has been saved then there comes the question of contribution. In case no property is saved for which all the sacrifices were made then there is no general average. Once successful, claimants of different nationalities shall put forward their own law to be applied in calculation and contribution. Diversity in laws relating to the general average among maritime countries led to the formulation and adoption of the York-Antwerp Rules first in 1877. That was an attempt to have a uniform approach for calculation of general average contribution. The Rules since then are being revised and amended from time to time. The York-Antwerp Rules 1994 were adopted during a meeting of the Comite' Maritime International (CMI) held in Sydney, Australia. These Rules become effective to determine a claim for general average when they are placed in a charter party or bill of lading.

The 2016 Amendments

401. On 5 May 2016, a new version of the York-Antwerp Rules was adopted entitled York-Antwerp Rules 2016. These Rules lay down contractual regimes for the determination of general average contributions. YAR 2016 aim at attaining uniformity in the area of general average. The Rules 2016 initiated some minor changes including changes in the numbering system and uniformity in the terms used in the Rules. The CMI has also come up with some non-binding Guidelines. They give details regarding basic principles of general average adjustment and also spell out the role of the average adjuster and the general interest surveyor. These Rules withdraw certain advantages from shipowners (in particular the old commission and interest rate), they also reinstate some of the allowances which had been restricted in the 2004 Rules.[32]

32. Alex Kemp-*York-Antwerp Rules 2016: A Summary*. file:///C:/Users/this%20pc/Desktop/HFW%20_%20York-Antwerp%20Rules%202016_%20a%20summary%20_%20York-Antwerp%20Rules%202016_%20a%20summary. Html.

I. Applicability under Indian Law

402. There is no specific provision regarding 'general average' in the Merchant Shipping Act 1958. The general average area therefore is guided by the common law and on the terms of contract between the parties. The contract or a bill of lading incorporates the York-Antwerp Rules for adjustment of general average and for security and payment of general average contribution.[33]

403. The Marine Insurance Act 1963 of India is almost a verbatim of the UK Marine Insurance Act 1906, and thus it has incorporated the York-Antwerp Rules to the extent the latter has and differs in some points in like manner. The definition of 'general average act' (section 66(2)) under the MIA has the following ingredients:

- First, the existence of 'actual danger' is denoted by the words 'in time of peril' in the section. This apparently marks a departure from the Rules as under the Rules a reasonable mistaken belief in the existence of danger is sufficient to render the act as a general average act.
- Second, there must be some extraordinary sacrifice or danger and it must not fall under the 'ordinary duties of the shipowner'. Thus when a sailing ship which has an auxiliary engine loses her sailing power and has to use steam thereby increasing the expenses, then such expenses are not extraordinary (*Wilson v. Bank of Victoria* [1867] LR 2 QB 203). The 'sacrifice' may consist of 'jettison' that is throwing away of the cargo to lighten the ship, or it may consist of burning the cargo.
- Third, the 'act' must be voluntary and not an act of God or the act of any other person. Rule A of the York-Antwerp Rules speaks of a 'sacrifice' or expenditure which is 'intentionally' made or incurred. The question remains whether the MIA shows a departure as curiously enough the word 'intentionally' is again used in Rule V but the marginal note is 'voluntary stranding'.
- Fourth, the 'act' must be reasonable.
- Fifth, the act must have been done for the preservation of the property. In Rule A of the York-Antwerp Rules, the words 'for the common safety for the purpose of preserving from peril the property involved in a common maritime adventure' are used. Both under the York-Antwerp Rules and under the MIA contribution can be demanded only if the general average act is successful and achieves positive results.

§5. General Average Adjustment

404. The losses admissible in general average are assessed and apportioned over the net arrived values of the property saved plus the value of the sacrificed property and a final balance due to or from each party is arrived at. This assessment is commonly known as general average adjustment.

33. Shardul Thacker – India – Mulla & Mulla & Craigie Blunt & Caroe' – Chapter 25 – ICLG to Shipping Law 2018 at 122.

I. Calculation of General Average Contribution

405. There are certain conditions or requisites to be fulfilled for a general average contribution. These are:

- the interest claiming contribution and the interest from which it is claimed must have been exposed to a common danger;
- the danger must not be attributable to the actionable default of the interest claiming contribution. Where there is default in shipping the goods, or where the shipowner did not take care to make the ship seaworthy, his claim for general average was allowed to be met with a set off with the counter-claim for damages (*Goulandris Bros. Ltd v. G. Goldman & Sons* [1957] 3 All ER 100). When there is no actual fault or negligence of the shipowner or his servants then his claim for general average loss against the cargo was allowed. The owner is made to bear the loss himself in case the loss is due to his own default;
- the danger must be a real one and not merely an imaginary one. The existing danger must entail certainty of loss within a short time unless something which could not be anticipated should intervene;
- the sacrifice made must be for the benefit of the adventure. In case the property which is jettisoned was already a wreck than before it is thrown overboard, then it cannot be termed as 'real' sacrifice. It was held in *Sherpherd v. Kottgen* [(1877) 37 LT 618] it was held that:

> Where a part of a common adventure is abandoned to save the rest, then all those whose property is saved must contribute to compensate those whose have been sacrificed, and the various portions of the ship must be considered as the goods of the master if they are sacrificed to save the cargo. But, where the thing abandoned was in such a condition that it must have been lost anyhow, the hastening of its destruction cannot be sufficient for contribution [COTTON LJ].

- where the claim is for contribution to a general average as opposed to a general average expenditure the property in respect of which general average contribution is claimed must have been saved by reason of sacrifice.

§6. Receiving Fund

406. When the peril befalls, the ship, the cargo and the freight are the possible vulnerabilities. Either of these may be sacrificed or bear the expenses to protect the common maritime adventure. This step is taken in order to save other property aboard which may belong to third parties. The sacrifice or the loss which is undertaken may be later on be made good by the beneficiaries of the crisis. For this where damage is caused to the ship or some extraordinary expenses are incurred to save the cargo then they will be entitled to general average contribution from the cargo and the freight.

407. The YAR 2016 lay down the rules to determine the nature and extent of sacrifice and the contribution so made. When loss of freight has arisen from damage to or loss of cargo then it shall be made good as general average either when caused by a general average act or when the damage to or loss of cargo is so made. Deductions shall also be made from the amount of gross freight loss of the charges which the owner would have incurred to earn such freight though he has not incurred it. (Rule XV YAR 2016). Where the assured has paid for any general average contribution the indemnity by the insurer shall be made on the basis of the full amount of the contribution if the subject matter liable to contribution is insured for its full contributory value (section 73 MIA). Even the cargo which was sacrificed to overcome the crisis shall be made good depending on the value of it at the place of its discharge. As for any cargo which has not either been declared at the shipment or has been wrongly declared then the value of these, according to YAR XIX shall not be declared as general average but if it is partially declared then it will be contributed for at the declared value. Rule I also says that no jettison of cargo shall be made good as general average unless the cargo is carried in accordance with the customs of the particular trade.

§7. Contributing Fund

408. The sacrifices and expenditure in 'general average sacrifices' and the amount to be contributed towards the loss by the respective interests are called a 'general average contribution'. A claim for general average contribution arises only when the danger is real and common; there is a necessity for a sacrifice; the sacrifice is voluntary which is a real one and not an imaginary one; the object of the sacrifice must be the saving of the imperilled property; and the common danger must not be the result of any default for which the interest claiming a general average contribution is liable in law. All the persons whose interest in the adventure is benefited by the general average sacrifice are liable to contribute including the freight which if benefited from it would contribute.

I. General Average Contributions of Salvage Charges

409. Where the assured has paid or is liable for any general average contribution, the measure of indemnity is the full amount of such contribution if the subject matter liable to contribution is insured for its full contributory value; but if such subject matter be not insured for its full contributory value, or if only part of it be insured, the indemnity payable by the insurer must be reduced in proportion to the under insurance. In case of a particular average loss which consists of a deduction from the contributory value, and for which the insurer is liable then that amount must be deducted from the insured value in order to ascertain what the insurer is liable to contribute. The same principle regarding the liability of the insurer shall apply where the insurer is liable for salvage charges (section 73 MIA).

§8. PROCEEDINGS

410. The master of a ship has been assigned certain duties to perform even at the time of crisis or when there is some peril. The owner or the master of the ship which has sustained or caused any accident which resulted in the loss of life or any serious injury to any person or has received any material damage affecting her seaworthiness shall within twenty-four hours after the happening of the accident or damage or at the earliest possible time send a report to the newest officer regarding the damage, the reason thereof, the ship which caused including its details and other necessary information which is relevant. Such duty results when any sea accident, collision or loss of any Indian ship occurs. The report is meant to inform the Central Government (sections 350, 351 MS Act).

411. Moreover, when any shipwreck or any other calamity occurs which necessitates immediate action by the Government then the prescribed officers who are nearest to the spot of the said peril must be informed of it so that subsequent action ascertaining the rights and liabilities of the ship and the cargo and passengers aboard can be taken. The Central Government is empowered to make rules to contain the situation. Such Rules to provide for the procedure to be followed by a receiver of the wreck in respect of the possession or disposal of the wreck, regarding fee payable to them, the procedure to be followed in dealing with the claims relating to ownership of wrecks, regarding appointment of valuers in salvage cases, the principles to be followed in awarding and the apportioning of salvage, the procedure to be followed for dealing with claims for salvage and regarding the detention of property in the custody of a receiver of wreck for the purpose of enforcing payment of salvage (section 404 MS Act).

Chapter 11. Particular Average

§1. General Concepts

412. Particular average is the partial loss caused by any accident is caused by any hazard against which it is insured. Damage by sea water when not amounting to total loss or damage by fire or collision are examples of particular averages. The difference between a general average and particular average is that the general average is voluntary while particular average is accidental and while a general average is undertaken to save property imperilled in a common adventure, a particular average is a loss pure and simple. A Particular charge is incurred by the assured for the safety or preservation of the insured subject matter. Charges are called particular as they apply to a particular interest, for instance, the cost of picking sound cotton from damaged cotton, the cost of 'skimming' cocoa and other re-conditioning charges.

§2. Particular Average of the Vessel

I. Definition

413. The particular average on the vessel means the physical damage suffered by the vessel impairing its machinery, or its body which may be caused by a natural calamity like a storm or by a sudden accident or collision occurring in the sea. According to section 64 of the Marine Insurance Act 1963, a particular average loss is a partial loss of the subject matter insured against, by a peril insured against and which is not a general loss. Expenses which are incurred by or on behalf of the assured for the safety or preservation of the subject matter insured other than general average and salvage charges are particular charges and they are not included in the particular average.

II. Insurance

414. The assured can recover the sum in respect of a loss on a policy by which he is insured and in the case of an unvalued policy to the full extent of the value fixed by the policy. Where there is a loss recoverable under the policy, the insurer or insurers are liable for such proportion of the measure of indemnity as the amount of his subscription bears to the value fixed by the policy in the case of a valued policy or to the insurable value in the case of an unvalued policy (section 67 The Marine Insurance Act 1963). A policy may be either valued or unvalued. When there is a total loss of the subject matter insured then in the case of a valued policy the measure of indemnity is the sum fixed by the policy and if it is an unvalued policy then the measure of indemnity is the insurable value of the subject matter insured. In case of partial loss of a ship the measure of indemnity in case of the repair of the ship the assured is entitled to the reasonable cost of the repairs from which the customary deductions have been made and in case the ship is partially repaired then apart from the reasonable cost he is also to be indemnified for the reasonable depreciation, if any, arising from the unrepaired damage. Where the ship is neither repaired nor sold in the damaged state then the assured is entitled to be indemnified for the reasonable depreciation. Where the ship is repaired but not sold then he is entitled to be indemnified for the reasonable depreciation.

A policy may be either for a voyage or for time.

A. Voyage and Time Policies

415. When a contract of insurance spreads over the voyage from the starting point to the destination point then it is called a voyage policy. A voyage policy has to follow certain rules as given under the MIA 1963. Thus any change in the prescribed route discharges the insurer from liability so also when there is deviation from the destined route the insurer is discharged (sections 47, 48 MIA). When the contract is made to insure the subject matter for a definite period of time then it is known as time policy and there also may be a contract in which both the conditions are present. The time policy is required to be within a span of twelve months. Any policy exceeding this limitation is invalid (section 27 MIA).

III. Settlement

416. The claim settlement process is that if a loss or damage occurs to a property which results in a claim, the assured will request a broker to proceed with the mechanics of the settlement. The claim is then submitted to the claim adjuster who has the responsibility under the policy to pay the claim and shall adjust the claim himself if it is not already adjusted. In case it is already adjusted then he will check it for propriety. Under this settlement, guidance must be taken from law provisions to ascertain whether the loss is included or excluded, whether it is partial or total and whether it is actual or constructive (sections 55–57).

A. Salvage Charges

417. Salvage charges incurred in preventing a loss by perils insured against may be recovered as a loss by those perils. Salvage charges are those charges recoverable under maritime law by a salvor independently of a contract. They are the expenses of services in the nature of salvage rendered by the assured or his agents or any person employed by them. Such expenses are recoverable as particular charges or as a general average loss depending on the circumstances (section 66 IMA).

B. Abandonment

418. Often it happens that there is time to give up and transfer the ensuing damage to the other party by getting rid of the imperilled vessel. If the assured opts for abandoning the vessel to the insurer then he must duly notify him either in writing or orally or partly by mouth and partly in writing. If he fails to do so then the loss is treated as partial loss. The notice should state explicitly the intention of the assured to abandon his insured interest in the subject matter unconditionally to the insurer. When the notice is properly served then the refusal of the notice shall not have any effect on the right of the assured. Acceptance by the insurer also may be either orally or by written words and mere silence does not amount to acceptance. Once the notice of abandonment is accepted it conclusively admits liability for the loss and the sufficiency of the notice. It is useless to give notice when the assured receives the information of the loss. Notice of abandonment may be waived by the insurer. Where the insurer has reinsured his risk then there is no need to give notice of abandonment. After the notice has been accepted by the insurer he is entitled to take over the insured subject matter and the rights connected thereto become his rights. Once the insurer takes over, he is also entitled to the freight subsequent to the loss and he is also entitled to recover from the owner the expenses of carrying his goods after the casualty (sections 62, 63 MIA).

§3. Particular Average on Cargo

419. In commercial insurance, the purchasers of insurance are usually cargo owners in respect of hull insurance or cargo insurance. In the case of c. I. F. contract, the shipper of goods obtains insurance but in the case of f. O. B. contract, the buyer obtains insurance. When the premium rate is fixed factors like the type of cargo, adequacy of its packing, types of ships to be utilized, nature of the voyage, records of claims of the shipper and the commodity is taken into consideration. The contract also contains certain occurrences called insured risks or insured perils for which the insurer undertakes to pay an indemnity.

I. Definition

420. Under a contract of marine insurance for goods, the insurer undertakes to indemnify the assured against loss of goods or other movables in the contract of transport. The risk covers damage or loss to the cargo, financial losses, resulting from loss of freight, passage money and liabilities incurred to third persons. There may be in a contract of carriage for goods a warranty regarding the 'good safety' of the cargo. When it is so and the subject matter insured is warranted 'well' or 'in good safety' on a particular day then it is sufficient if is found safe at any time during the risk (section 40 MIA).

II. Insurance

421. The insurer on ship or goods is not liable for any loss proximately caused by delay unless the policy provides for the same. In the matter of insurance of a cargo, the insurer is exonerated from liability for ordinary wear and tear, ordinary leakage and breakage, inherent vice or nature of the subject matter insured or for any loss caused by rats or vermin or for any injury to machinery not proximately caused by maritime perils. When by a peril insured against the voyage is interrupted and the master undertakes transshipment of the goods to other destinations then it does not affect the liability of the insurer. When goods are damaged in such a way that the marking becomes such that identification becomes impossible then the loss is treated as partial loss and when the damage is such which renders the goods as different from the kind insured or if the assured is irretrievably deprived thereof then such loss is a total loss. There may be constructive loss when the assured is deprived of the possession of the goods and the cost of recovering it may exceed the value of such goods and when the damage of goods caused is such that the cost of repairing or taking them to a proper destination would incur such expense which would exceed the actual value of the goods. In such a case the assured would abandon the goods to the insurer and treat the loss as an actual total loss (sections 55–60 MIA). There may also be some other types of policy.

A. *Floating Policy*

422. A floating policy is one which is described by general terms and the name or names of the ship are left to be settled subsequently. Such subsequent declaration shall be made either by making an endorsement in the policy or by or in other customary manner. Such declaration should form part of the order of dispatch or shipment and must comprise all consignments within the terms of the policy in case of carriage of goods. The details regarding the goods must be honestly stated and if there is any omission or erroneous declaration made in good faith then it may be rectified even after loss or arrival of the cargo. If there has been no declaration of the value of the subject matter, then the policy is to be treated like an unvalued policy regarding the subject matter of the declaration.

III. Settlement

423. In a matter of complicated cargo claims and for most hull claims, the broker submits the claim to an average adjuster who calculates or adjusts the claim according to his professional expertise and in an impartial manner. Then the matter is submitted to the claim adjuster to pay the claim.

§4. Extra Expenses and Financial Losses Sea and Labour Cost, Loss of Freight, Delay

I. Expenses and Labour Cost

424. Where a policy contains a suing and labour clause any engagement thereby entered into is deemed to be supplementary to the contract of insurance and the insurer is bound to pay the sum which is spent in meeting the expenses. General average losses, and contributions and salvage charges are not recoverable under the labouring clause. Where extra expenses are incurred for the purpose of averting or diminishing any loss not covered by the policy is not recoverable under the suing and labouring clause (section 78 MIA).

II. Loss of Freight

425. When there is partial loss of freight, then in case of a valued policy the measure of indemnity is in proportion to the sum fixed by the policy and in case of an unvalued policy as the proportion of freight lost by the assured bears to the whole freight at the risk of the assured under the policy (section 70 MIA).

III. Partial Loss of Goods Merchandise

426. When there is partial loss of goods, merchandise or other movables, the measure of indemnity will be as follows:

- In case of total loss of the part of the goods, merchandise or other movables insured by a valued policy, the measure of indemnity is such proportion of the sum fixed by the policy as the insurable value of the whole as ascertained in the case of an unvalued policy.
- In case of total loss of the part of the goods, merchandise or other movables insured by an unvalued policy, the measure of indemnity is the insurable value of the part lost ascertained as in case of total loss.
- In case of the delivery of the insured goods or merchandise in a damaged from at its destination, the measure of indemnity is such proportion of the sum fixed by the policy in case of an unvalued policy, or of the insurable value in the case of an unvalued policy, as the difference between the gross sound and damaged values at the place of arrival bears to the gross sound value. The term ‘gross value’ means the wholesale price or the estimated value with freight landing charges and duty paid beforehand. Where the goods or merchandise are customarily sold in bonds, the bonded price is deemed to be the ‘gross value’. ‘Gross proceeds’ means the actual price obtained at a sale where all charges on sale are paid by the sellers. The insurer is also liable for successive losses even though the total amount of such losses may exceed the sum insured. In cases where under the same policy a partial loss which has not been repaid or otherwise made good, is

followed by a total loss the assured can only recover in respect of the total loss but the liability of the insurer is not affected by it under the labouring clause.

IV. Delay

427. In a contract of insurance where the subject matter is insured by voyage policy 'at and from' or 'from' a particular place the commencement is impliedly taken to be at a reasonable time and if this fails the insurer is free to avoid the contract. The contract of insurance is affected by a number of factors for instance the alteration of the port of departure, the sailing for a destination different from that as stated in the policy or by change of voyage. When there is a change of voyage which is done deliberately in violation of the policy then the insurer is discharged from liability. Deviation also exonerates the insurer from liability and the intention to deviate is immaterial. Similarly, the insured adventure must be prosecuted throughout the course with reasonable dispatch, and if an unreasonable delay occurs, the insurer is relieved from his liability. However, the delay in voyage or deviation is excused if so authorized by the policy, or when caused by uncontrollable circumstances, or when the delay was necessary for the safety of the ship or subject matter insured, where the delay occurred in order to save human life, or where it was due to obtaining medical care for someone on board the ship or when it was caused by the barratrous conduct of the master or crew if barratry is one of the perils insured against (sections 44–51 Marine Insurance Act).

§5. Recovery Actions against the Sea Carrier

428. Sea is a risky place and so is the journey around it. In fact, all the things connected with the sea, be it the voyage, the carriage of cargo, the commercial ties, the insurance contracts and the ships themselves are all high-risk deals. Thus the sea carrier who undertakes to carry passengers or goods is always at high risk and his liabilities are numerous. They also come up very easily. Ships are the vehicles of international trade, the oldest, and still, the cheapest mode of carriage and the world trade falls into bulk cargo which are homogeneous goods, then liner or general cargo which are of heterogeneous nature and the freight remains stable. Then there are contracts of affreightment in which the owner undertakes to carry on ships owned or chartered by him a specific quantity of cargo for a specific period of time. All this together goes to enlarge and enhance the area of liability of the sea carrier and exposes him to be legally answerable for the; loss or damage of cargo, loss of life or injury to persons, unexpected sea perils, collisions, pollution hazards to name a few. Thus the carrier covers the risk by engaging the insurers so as to minimize his liability. The exercise is commonly known as marine insurance which falls into two broad categories commercial insurance and mutual insurance.

I. Commercial Insurance

429. Commercial insurance involves both cargo and hull insurance. This is of course carried on the basis of contract of insurance on the basis of accepting premiums in advance and retaining it irrespective of the remaining intact or loss of the insured property. Britishers being the starters in the area of shipping and sea carriage, also became the first ones to introduce to the world the concept of marine insurance and soon London became the international market centre of marine insurance. Since the 1950s, the professional insurers started making their presence felt in developing countries, the developed insurance market centres continued to enjoy the dominating position. The Lloyd's in London, the Institute of London Underwriters, United States of America, Netherlands, France, Japan, Norway, became the main markets for commercial marine insurance. The insurance market has now become global and relatively more developed markets are India and Kuwait.

II. Mutual Insurance

430. It involves a group of persons or corporations agreeing in advance to contribute (as against premium in commercial insurance) to offset each other's losses. In short, each member is an insurer of every other member. Such groups are commonly known as Protection and Indemnity (P&I) Clubs. The use of mutual insurance is limited to cover risk property that is, hull insurance to the extent not covered by commercial insurance markets and risks or liabilities in the form of cargo claims, claims for crew sickness or injury, claims for loss of life or personal injury, collision liability, claims for pollution damage, claims for wreck removal, and so on. When there is a loss then all the members contribute rateably according to a predetermined formula so that the loss falls equally on all the members. As against commercial insurance, there is no element of profit in this type of insurance as it is only sharing of the loss by the members.

Chapter 12. Collisions

§1. Definition

431. 'Collision' under admiralty law means the violent encounter of a moving body with another. Maritime safety includes avoidance of collisions at sea. The matter has received considerable attention at international conventions. It constitutes an important aspect of the problem of safety of shipping and measures for the prevention of collision. Collision law as it concerns safety was also an important part of the old Roman law. The Justinian Digest (533 AD) also mentions cases of collision at sea. The three Mediterranean Sea Code on the law of collision namely the (a) Constitutum Usus of Pisa (C.1160); (b) The Statutes of Ancona (C.1350) and (c) the Consolat de Mar of Barcelona (thirteenth Century). The Roles of Oleron is the most important law of collision in the development of English law concerning collision. Sir Walter Scott laid down certain principles relating to collision law in the case of the Woodrop-Sims ((2 Dods 63; 165 Eng Rep 1422 (Adm 1815)).

In India, the collision law is mainly dependent and guided by the English law on collision.

§2. Statutory Provisions

I. Incorporation of Treaty Law

432. The collision regulations play an important role in regulating the road at sea. The earliest regulations namely the Brussels regulations 1910 remained in force till 1953 were formulated to being uniform in the rules regarding collision which was till then mainly guided by customary rules practised by seamen. Then the Brussels Regulations were replaced by International regulations for Preventing Collisions at Sea 1948. This was approved by the International Conference on the Safety of Life at Sea in 1948. The main feature of the 1948 regulations was that their application was extended to sea planes on the water.

Later the International Convention on Safety of Life at Sea 1960 incorporated a recommendation for the use of radar in reduced visibility. Again the international regulations for Preventing Collisions at Sea 1972 was adopted at an international conference held in 1972.

New rules for introducing yellow light for towing vessels, increasing intensity of lights and recognition of electronic aids and radar as means of navigational watch keeping, steering and sailing rules, and traffic separation schemes were adopted. This is in force in the UK. These regulations apply to all vessels upon the high seas and in all waters connected with them navigable by sea-going vessels.

433. Every vessel is required to move at a safe speed so that it can take proper and effective action to avoid collision. In determining such speed, care should be taken regarding the:

– state of visibility;

– the traffic density;
– the manoeuvrability of the vessel;
– at night the presence of background light;
– the state of wind;
– the draught in relation to the available depth of water;
– This convention was entered into force on 15 July 1977 and India ratified it on 30 May 1977.

434. Later, the international community made considerable effort in improving safety conditions at sea and the avoidance of collisions at sea. The most important one is the Safety of Life at Sea (SOLAS) of 1974. The IMO and the CMI promulgated certain International Collision Conventions which are; Convention of the International Regulation for Preventing Collisions at Sea (1972 and 1981), International Convention for the Unification of certain Rules of Law with respect to collision between Vessels; International Convention on certain Rules Concerning Civil jurisdiction in Matters of Collision and International Convention for the Unification of Certain Rules relating to Penal Jurisdiction in Matters of Collision or Other Incidents of Navigation. In India the regulations have been incorporated in sections 285, 286, 287 of the MS Act 1958 which even empower the central Government to frame regulations to prevent collisions at sea.

435. By virtue of these provisions, the Central Government formulated the MS (Prevention of Collision at Sea) Regulations 1962 (Gazette of India 1962, pt. II section 3(i), at 1128 as amended by GSR 1169 published in Gazette of India dated 21 August 1965. pt. II section 3(i), at 1230). When a ship collides, it is the duty of the master to reduce in writing the entire occurrence and its other details and enter the same in the official log book. Such a statement is also to be signed by one of the crew members or the mate.

436. The owner or master of the ship is under obligation to report to the Central Government or to the nearest principal officer, within twenty hours of the occurrence of an accident the details regarding the loss of life, serious injury to any person, or any material damage affecting the seaworthiness or efficiency either to the hull or any serious alteration of the machinery of the ship and must also state the probable reason of the accident. The report should also contain the number of the ship, her official number, her port of registry and the place where she is. The owner or agent of any Indian ship if due to non-appearance of the ship has reason to believe that the ship has been lost then he shall as soon as possible send to the Central Government a written notice about the loss and about the probable cause of it giving the detail about the official number and the port of registry of the ship (sections 350 and 351 MS Act).

A. Indian Law Regarding Collision

1. Precautions for Prevention of Collisions

437. The Central Government may make regulations for the prevention of collisions at sea and may thereby regulate the lights and shapes to be carried and exhibited, the fog and distress signals to be carried and used, and the steering and sailing rules to be observed by Indian ships and sailing vessels registered in India. The collisions rules are given under the MS Act and the collisions regulations are made mandatory to be followed by all foreign ships and sailing vessels within Indian jurisdiction and in case of any dispute, the matter shall be heard by the Indian court of proper jurisdiction against the foreign ship or sailing vessel as if they were registered in India (section 285 MS Act). By virtue of this section, the MS (Prevention of Collisions at Sea) Regulations 1975 was formulated by the Government of India. The day of its enforcement was the day of the enforcement of the Convention on the International Regulations for Preventing Collisions at Sea 1972 which ended in London on 20 October 1972.

438. More emphasis is laid, both at the international and national level on the prevention of collision which only shows that the magnitude of the destruction would be so much that it is better to prevent than to face it. The Regulations of 1975 contain a number of directions and the first liability is thus fixed on the master of the ship to comply with the Rules and to prevent collisions. The responsibility is given to any vessel, owner master or crew not to neglect any precaution which may be required by the ordinary practice of seamen or by the special circumstances of the case to avoid the danger. In the Regulations, there are certain Rules which are adopted in order to prevent collision at sea. These are:

- Steering and Sailing Rules (Rule 4).
- Safe Speed Rules (Rule 6).
- Risk of Collision (Rule 7).
- Action to Avoid Collision (Rule 8).
- Traffic Separation Scheme (Rule 10).
- Sailing Vessels (Rule 12).
- Overtaking (Rule 13).
- Head-on Situation (Rule 14).
- Crossing Situation (Rule 15).
- Responsibilities Between Vessels (Rule 18).
- Conduct of Vessels in Restricted Visibility (Rule 19).
- Light and Shapes (Rule 20).
- Equipment for Sound Signals (Rule 33).
- Manoeuvring and Warning Signals (Rule 34).

439. These are some of the selected Rules which are minutely detailed out in the Regulation and are more helpful in avoiding a navigational danger and collision. Apart from this, the MS Act enjoins the duty upon the master to assist in case of collision. According to it the master or person in charge of each ship shall be under obligation to assist another vessel in distress and to extend every help required by it without endangering his own vessel and passengers aboard. The master should also disclose the name and other details of his own ship to the master of the other ship. In the event of a collision, the master should make an entry about it in the official book meant for it.

440. The owner or master of the ship, in the event of a collision taking place, is required to send the report of the accident with the number of casualties, and so on, within twenty-four hours after the happening of the accident to the Government of India through proper channel (sections 348–350 MS Act). Not only this, the violation of such obligations is made a punishable offence under section 436 of the MS Act. According to Part XVI (Penalties and Procedure) MS Act, neglect or non-compliance with the obligation to assist by the master shall be punishable with imprisonment which may extend to three months or fine which may extend to INR 3,000, or both.

441. Where the master fails to comply with the duty to enter the report of collision in the official log book then he will be punished with a fine which may extend to INR 200. Where the owner or the master fails to send a report of the collision to the Government of India then they are liable to be punished with a fine which may extend to INR 500. The trial may take place at a court in any place in India where he is found or at such a place as notified by the State. The court of the Metropolitan Magistrate or a Judicial Magistrate of the first class shall hold the trial. When a summons is issued to the accused under the MS Act to secure his presence in the respected court, then such summon should specify the offence he is charged with.

2. Observance

442. As regarding the observance of collision regulations, the owner or master of every ship and the owner or tidal of every sailing vessel to which section 285 applies shall obey the collision regulations and shall not carry or exhibit any lights or shapes or use any fog or distress signals, other than those required by the said regulations. Any damage to person or property resulting from non-observance of the said regulations by any ship or sailing vessel shall be deemed to be taken as the result of the wilful default of the person in charge of the ship or sailing vessel. However, if it is shown to the satisfaction of the court that such non-observance or departure from the regulations was necessary then the default may be excused (section 286 MS Act). In order to ensure proper safety and the installation of safety measures on vessels, the Central Government is authorized to appoint inspectors to inspect any port ships or sailing vessels to which the collision regulations apply for the purpose of seeing that such ship or sailing vessel is sufficiently provided with lights and shapes and with the means of making fog and distress signals as required by such regulations. In case the inspector finds that any ship or sailing vessel is not so provided, he shall give to the owner, master or tidal a written notice pointing out the deficiency and suggesting measures to remedy the same. Such notice shall be communicated to the customs collector at any port from which such ship or sailing vessel may seek to clear, and no customs collector to whom such communication is made shall grant such ship a port clearance or allow her to proceed to sea without a certificate being furnished that the said ship or sailing vessel is properly provided with lights and shapes and with the means of making fog and distress signals in pursuance of the said regulations (section 287 MS Act).

II. Damages and Procedure

A. Damages

443. Where the loss is caused by the fault of two or more ships to the cargo or property on board of one or more of them then the liability to make good the damage or loss shall be in proportion to the degree to which each ship was at fault. But the liability shall be apportioned equally if due to the circumstances of the case it is not possible to establish different degrees of fault. However, if any ship has not contributed to the loss then she will not be held liable under these provisions. A person's liability under any contract or his exemption from such liability by any contract shall not be affected by the present section. Damage or loss terms shall be construed as references to any salvage or other expenses which are consequent upon that fault, recoverable in law by way of damages (section 345 MS Act). As regarding damages for personal injury including loss of life shall be borne by the owners of the ship jointly and severally. However, the right of defence and the right to limit liability shall be available to the person against whom the action is brought (section 346 MS Act). Claim of loss of life can be filed in admiralty jurisdiction of the High Court (AIR 1961 Bom 200).

Any person on board who suffers loss of life or any other personal injury due to the fault of that ship and of any other ship or ships, then that person is entitled to recover damages from all such ships who were at fault, the amount of such damages being in proportion to the fault of each ship which caused the collision and loss. But if there is any statutory exemption or contractual limitation then the amount shall not be recoverable. Such person shall be entitled in matters of contribution to same rights and powers as the persons entitled to sue for damages in the first instance (section 347 MS Act).

B. Procedure

444. Some of the selected Rules are minutely detailed out in the Regulation and are more helpful in avoiding a navigational danger and collision.

Apart from this, the MS Act enjoins the duty upon the master to assist in case of collision. According to it the master or person in charge of each ship shall be under obligation to assist another vessel in distress and to extend every help required by it without endangering his own vessel and passengers aboard. The master should also disclose the name and other details of his own ship to the master of the other ship. In the event of a collision, the master should make an entry about it in the official book meant for it. The owner or master of the ship, in the event of a collision taking place, is required to send the report of the accident with the number of casualties, and so on, within twenty-four hours after the happening of the accident to the Government of India through proper channel (sections 348–350 MS Act). Not only this, the violation of such obligations is made a punishable offence under section 436 of the MS Act. According to Part XVI (Penalties and Procedure) MS Act, neglect or non-compliance with the obligation to assist by the master shall be punishable with imprisonment which may extend to three months or fine which may extend to INR 3,000, or both. Where the master fails to comply with the duty to enter the report of collision in the official logbook then he will be punished with a fine which may extend to INR 200. Where the owner or the master fails to send a report of the collision to the Government of India then they are liable to be punished with a fine which may extend to INR 500. The trial may take place at a court in any place in India where he is found or at such a place as notified by the State. The court of the Metropolitan Magistrate or a Judicial Magistrate of the first class shall hold the trial. When a summons is issued to the accused under the MS Act to secure his presence in the respected court then such summon should specify the offence he is charged with.

III. Limitation of Liability

445. 'Both-to-Blame' collision clause implies the division of damages between the carrier and the owner of the goods resulting from loss of cargo in the event of collision through the common fault of the carrying ship and another vessel. Fault or mistake constitutes the basis of liability for collision. There are a number of marine perils like, fog, storm, low visibility which lie beneath the fault. Prudent seamanship, good standard of care and strict compliance of the requirement of safety and precautionary measures are helpful in avoiding collisions. Where the loss or damage is caused to goods on board an unseaworthy ship at the beginning of a voyage but due to the peril of collision and not due to unseaworthiness then the shipowner is not liable. Part X of the MS Act 1958 deals with liability of collisions, accidents at sea. The term 'limitation' was deleted from the title of Part X by Act 25 of 1970, section 15 (w. E. F. 15 September 1972) and the title now reads as Collision. Accidents at Sea and Liability.

Chapter 13. Maritime Pollution

§1. Introduction

446. The unbounded oceans being the purest and cleanest gift of Nature to mankind are subjected to the selfish and careless conduct of man. The modern activities on the High Seas and the increase of sea traffic have interfered with Nature and the result is that the friends of man are turning into its enemies. In post World War II period, soil, air and water pollution have taken formidable dimensions so much so that it has necessitated immediate steps to curb the menace and to rise from the lull of slapdash. Prevention and control of pollution and contamination of the Seas underline the international activities in this area.

447. Several factors are responsible for the present maritime pollution: first, post-war industrial development led to air, soil and water pollution; increasing size of ships which are one of the sources of marine pollution; the pollution casualties of tankers Torrey Canyon in 1967 and Amoco Cadiz in 1976 are the glaring examples of catastrophic marine pollution; increased dumping of municipal wastes into the sea; discharge of radioactive waste; deliberate discharge and dumping of waste by ships; and quite recently the most damaging source of pollution has been the oil spills.

448. The MS Act 1958 imposes civil and criminal liability in respect of oil spills by the owner of an Indian or foreign vessel regarding damages to the environment in the TW or the EEZ. The Act also provides a comprehensive plan for dealing with the civil liability arising from oil pollution damage on no-fault liability basis. To protect the Coastal Resource Zone (CRZ) the Notification of 1991 and the Central Government in its Environmental guidelines for Development of Beaches published by the Department of Environment in 1983 defined the CRZ.

§2. Statutory Provisions: Sources of Law

I. National Legislation

449. The Indian MS Act 1958 gives effect to the International Convention for the prevention of pollution of the sea by oil 1954 as amended 1962 and the Marine Insurance Act 1963. The problem of prevention of such oil pollution is tackled by International Convention, MS Act 1958 and MS (Prevention of Pollution of the Sea by Oil) Rules 1974. Shipping Wing in the Department of Shipping is the nodal authority for Maritime Laws. Part XB of the MS Act 1958 has been amended in 2002 coming into force on 1 February 2003 with the object of defining various expressions on the lines of the Convention on Civil Liability for Oil Pollution Damage 1992. Part XC which is mainly concerned with International Oil Pollution Compensation Fund is also amended by the MS (Amendment) Act 2002. India is a signatory to the Basel Convention on Transboundary Movement of Hazardous

Waste on 15 March 1990 and ratified it on 24 June 1992. The case law declared by the Indian Supreme Court is in line with the Basel Convention.

450. It is not that India awoke to environmental consciousness only recently. The idea of preserving the surroundings and keeping it free from pollution through legislative activity was never at bay. Thus a number of legislations dating back to the nineteenth century have aimed at healthy and pollution-free sea surroundings.

451. The Indian Ports Act 1908 (Act 15 of 1908) under section 6 empowers the government to make rules for keeping the rivers, waterways and canals, and so on, free from environmental hazards. Though the word pollution does not appear in the Act yet its purpose of regulating the activity and movement of boats and other water craft and taking precautions to avoid contamination is mentionable. Thus the Government is empowered to make Rules regarding the following steps to be taken to prevent pollution:

- For regulating the berths, stations and anchorages to be occupied by vessels in ports.
- For the manner of discharge of oil or oil-water mixture in ports.
- For regulating the use of fires and lights within ports.
- For the prevention of danger arising to the public health by making arrangements for it in the vessels.
- For the cleaning, ventilation and disinfection of vessels.

To further strengthen the law regarding the prevention of pollution by ships, the Government of India has introduced in the Upper House of the Parliament *(Rajya Sabha)*, a Bill[34] to amend the Merchant Shipping Act 1958 called the Merchant Shipping (Amendment) Bill 2015. The Bill is yet to see the light of day.

Some of the other relevant Acts are:

- The Northern India Ferries Act 1878 (Act No. 17 of 1878).
- The Indian Fisheries Act 1897 (Act No. 4 of 1897).
- The Inland Vessels Act 1917 (Act No. 1 of 1917).
- The Major Port Trusts Act 1963 (Act No. 38 of 1963).
- The Marine Insurance Act 1963 (Act No. 11 of 1963).
- The Inland Waterways Authority of India Act 1985 (Act No. 82 of 1985).
- TW, Continental Shelf, EEZ Act 1976 (Act No. 80 of 1976).
- The Maritime Zones of India (Regulation of Fishing by Foreign Vessels) Act 1981 (Act No. 42 of 1981).
- Indian Boiler Act of 1923 (Act 5 of 1923).
- The Oil Fields (Regulation and Development) Act 1948.

34. Bill No. 227 of 2015.

II. International Law

452. The international community realized the importance of a pollution-free sea and its exploitation mainly by the developed nations much earlier. The United Nations Organization (UNO) has been active to bring the nations together in making a concerted effort to fight and eradicate the pollution of the sea. For this, there came the important question regarding the ownership, use and control of TW on the global level. The Geneva Convention of High Seas was held in 1958. Articles 24 and 25 of the Convention enjoin duties upon the states 'to draw up regulations to prevent pollution of the seas by discharge of oil from ships or pipelines or resulting from activities regarding the seabed and its subsoil'. Article 25 aims at 'dumping of radioactive waste' by requiring every state to 'take measures to prevent pollution from this source' and 'to cooperate with the competent international organization'.

453. The Law of the Sea Convention 1982 defines marine pollution as:

> the pollution of the marine environment means the introduction by man, directly or indirectly of substances or energy into the marine environment (including estuaries) which results or is likely to result in such deleterious effect as harm to living resources and marine life, hazards to human health, hindrance to marine activities including fishing and other legitimate uses of the sea, impairment of quality sea water and reduction of amenities.

India has a long coastline of over 8,000 km with an associated continental shelf of 0.5 million km and an EEZ of 2.02 million km with its west lands, lagoons, mangroves, sea-grass beds, coral reefs and shallow bays, creeks and estuaries which are very rich in marine biodiversity and natural resources.

India is signatory to the United Convention of Law of Sea of 1982, which gives several coastal states the right to establish their territorial sea up to a limit of 12 nautical miles, the contiguous zone between 12 and 24 miles limits and EEZ up to 200 nautical miles. By virtue of the Territorial water, Continental shelf EEZ and other Maritime Zone Act (MZ Act) 1976, India established a 200 nautical miles EEZ. India also joined the Antarctic Treaty in 1983, the Convention of the Conservation of Antarctic Marine Living Resources of 1985 and is signatory to the Madrid Protocol on Environmental Protection to the Antarctic Protection to the Antarctic Treaty of 1991.

454. The law on Marine pollution is provided by MZ Act 1976 which asserts India's sovereignty over the natural resources in the CS and EEZ. Under the Indian Coast Guard Act 1978 the coast guard patrols the maritime zones by resorting to such means which would preserve and protect the maritime environment and would prevent and control marine pollution.

§3. Sources of Pollution

I. Pollution from Ships

455. Ships have always used sea water to dispose of operational waste, garbage, sanitary waste, bilge water, sludge oily waste and dirty ballast water. With the bulk of sea traffic in the increasing direction, the scale of disposal of operational waste also increased. The source of pollution is either resulting from acts performed in the course of normal ship operations or pollution resulting from accidents. The MARPOL Convention is the most important convention on pollution by ships. Apart from ships, heavy tankers are also a big source of contamination of sea water. Tankers have increased in size for the last fifty years and though they are now levelling out yet the size is enormous enough to cause substantial harm. The International Convention for the Prevention of Pollution from Ships 1973 was modified by the Protocol of 1978. India's draft maritime policy declares that it will scrutinize and ratify necessary Conventions. Revised regulations to prevent marine pollution by ships carrying oil or chemicals were adopted by the Marine Environment Protection Committee (MEPC) of the IMO Conventions.

A. *Oil Pollutants*

456. Increased number of vessels on the surface of the Sea and hectic commercial activities by them makes the situation worse as oil spills prove devastating not only for the sea water but for the endangered sea life, the rare flora and fauna. The oil pollution is caused by: discharge by oil tankers; by ships other than oil tankers; and by the discharge of oil by offshore installation which includes installation whether mobile or fixed used for underwater exploration or exploitation of crude oil, petroleum or other similar mineral oils whether operating under a license or contract. It also includes any installation which could be shifted on its motive power and also a pipeline. 'Oil' includes petroleum in any form, crude oil, fuel oil, sludge, oil refuse and refined products. 'Ship' includes a vessel of any description which floats in the maritime environment and includes hydrofoil boats, air-cushion vehicles, submersibles, floating craft and fixed or floating platforms.

457. The Government of India in supersession of the Merchant Shipping (Prevention of Pollution by Oil from Ships) Rules 1974 has formulated the Merchant Shipping (Prevention of Pollution by Oil from ships) Rules 2010 under which it is the obligation of ships to prevent pollution of sea by oil.[Rule 2]. These Rules [1-39] elaborately deal with the prevention of oil pollutants from ships. In Chapter II the rules regarding survey and certification are given in detail and all the provisions are in conformity with the International Convention for the Prevention of Pollution from Ships 1973. It also provides for oil fuel tank protection, for control and discharge of oil and with other matters connected therewith. These rules are elaborate ones and take care of all the minute technicalities connected with oil pollution by ships.

1. Oil Tankers

458. The oil tankers, whether Indian or foreign, are required not to discharge oil or oily mixture into the sea except; when the tanker is proceeding en route, the on the spot discharge of oil is not more than 60 litres per mile, the total quantity of oil discharge is not more than 1/15,000 part of the total capacity of the tanker, the distance of tanker from the main land is 50 miles, and the tanker is not within the prohibited zone as declared by the TW Continental Shelf EEZ and Other Maritime Zones Act 1976.

459. Regarding ships which are other than oil tankers fitted with cargo spaces which are constructed and used to carry oil bulk of an aggregate capacity of two hundred cubic metres or more the provisions of Rule 16(4) and Rules 29, 30, 31, 32, 34 and 36 shall apply for the construction and operation of cargo spaces in such ships. But in case the aggregate capacity is less than one thousand cubic metres Rule 34(6) will apply. [Rule 2(2)].

460. The provisions of the Merchant Shipping (Prevention of Pollution by Oil from ships) Rules 2010, Rule 29, 31 and 32 shall not apply to oil tankers carrying asphalt or other products which are subject to the provisions of these Rules. As for the oil tankers delivered on or before the 1st June 1982 and which are solely engaged in specific trades between:

(a) ports or terminals within India;
(b) ports or terminals of State Parties to the Convention[35] where –
   (i) the voyage is entirely within a special area;
   (ii) the voyage is entirely within other limits designated by the Organisation.[36]

To such oil tankers as defined in clause (33) of Rule 1A, the provisions of Rule (6) and (8) shall not apply.[Rule 2(5)]

2. Ships

461. Both the Indian and foreign ships are prohibited from discharging oil or oil mixture into the coastal waters of India except when the ship is proceeding en route when the on the spot discharge of oil does not exceed 60 litres per mile, the discharge has less than one hundred parts per million parts of the oily mixture, the discharge is made as far as possible from the mainland as possible and the ship is out of the declared prohibited area as given in the TW, Continental Shelf, EEZ and other Maritime Zones Act 1976.

---

35. Convention means the International Convention for the Prevention of Pollution from Ships 1973 (section 356B The Merchant Shipping Act 1958).
36. Organisation means the International Maritime Organization. [Rule 1A (39) of the Merchant Shipping (Prevention of Pollution by Oil from ships) Rules 2010].

Control of Anti-Fouling Systems on ships

By inserting Part XIB in the MS Act 1958[37] the Government has ensured control of anti-fouling systems in Indian ships which are not entitled to fly the Indian flag but operating under the authority of India are made to comply with the provisions of Part XIB. All other vehicles to which this Part applies are also mandated to comply with requirements given in this Part.

The Government of India has formulated Rules entitled the Merchant Shipping (Control of Anti-Fouling system) Rules 2016[38] to give effect to the provisions of Part XIB.

Prevention of Pollution by Harmful Substances

To give effect to provisions of section 356E, section 356O(ee) of the MS Act 1958 the Government of India formulated rules entitled the Merchant Shipping (Prevention of Pollution by Harmful Substances Carried by Sea in Packaged Form) Rules 2010.[39] These Rules prohibit the carriage of harmful substances by ships except as provided in the Rules itself. There are rules regarding packing, marking, labelling, stowage and documentation of the entire process. [Rules 4-7].

3. Offshore Installation

462. An installation which is used for underwater exploration or exploitation of crude oil, petroleum or other similar oils, whether mobile or fixed, operating under a lease or license or any other contractual agreement is also prohibited to discharge oil or oil mixture.

B. Accident Pollutants

463. Elaborate measures are taken under the MS Act for the containment of accidental pollution. Thus when there is escape or discharge of oil or noxious liquid substance from a tanker, ship or offshore installation which causes pollution in any part of coasts or coastal waters of India then for minimizing or preventing such pollution the Central Government shall require by notice the owner, agent, master, charterer, operator or any other person having hold of such activities to take action to prevent escape of such noxious substance or/in addition to removal of such polluting substance to such place as notified by it. It may also ask to remove the vessel itself or the offshore installation to a notified place or it may require the notified persons to remove or disperse slicks on the surface of the sea it may also give notice to take any other measure not so mentioned. In case the notified persons fail to take

37. Part XIB (containing sections 356P to 356Y inserted by Act 31 of 2014, sec. 2 (w.e.f. 1-4-2015, *vide* S. O. 521((E) dated 16 Feb. 2015).

38. *Vide* G. S. R. 84(E), dated 19 Jan. 2016, published in the Gazette of India, Extra, Pt. II, sec. 3(i), No. 43, dated 19 Jan. 2016. It came into force on 19-1-2016.

39. *Vide* G. S. R. 14(E), dated 7 Jan. 2010, published in the Gazette of India, Extra, Pt. II, sec. 3(i), No. 43, dated 7 Jan. 2010. It came into force on 7 Jan. 2010.

action as given in the notice then the Central Government is empowered to contain the pollution itself and any expenditure made by the Government in this regard is recoverable as debt from the persons concerned (section 356 J-356L MS Act). Empowered by section 356B(h), 356 C (ee), section 356 O and section 457 of the MS Act the Government of India has made rules entitled the Merchant Shipping (Control of Pollution by Noxious Liquid Substances in Bulk) Rules 2010.[40] These Rules elaborately deal with the obligation of ships to prevent pollution of the sea by noxious liquid substances [Rule 2], categorization of noxious liquid substances and other substances [Rule 6],surveys and certification[Rule 7-10], measures of control by Port States[Rule 16] prevention of pollution arising from an incident involving noxious liquid substances[Rule 17] among other relevant matters.

464. Moreover, a Contingency Plan of Action is prepared to tackle spillage, mitigation, containment or any other such problem. The Director General as the Central Coordinating Authority coordinates along with the local coordinating control authorities in the major ports. The Local Action Groups are required to have the attendant infrastructure ready to meet the contingent situation cautiously, promptly and with full success. The Local Action Groups in the major ports of Kandla, Mumbai, Goa, Mangalore, Cochin, Chennai, Tuticorin, Vishakhapatnam, Paradip and Calcutta are to be well equipped. They are notified to have oil reception facilities as required by the Convention and are also required to be well equipped with dispersants, dispersant spraying equipment, crafts, skimmers, offshore books and other materials.

465. According to the Draft Policy, the shipping activities will be included under the relevant provisions of 'The Territorial Waters Continental Shelf, EEZ, and other Maritime Zones Act 1976' so that consequential benefits are available. When notifications are issued under this Act, relevant provisions from maritime legislation will be included in such notifications to promote Indian Shipping and to regulate foreign-owned shipping in the EEZ of India. Various Bilateral and Multi-lateral agreements with other countries would be improved upon for securing and promoting Indian Maritime Interests. Particular Sensitive Sea Areas (PSSA) will be specified especially along the eastern coasts around Andaman and Nicobar Islands with the aim of preserving the natural habitat and environment in these areas. Shipbreaking and Ship-recycling activity being a labour-intensive industry will be further encouraged also considering the employment potential but without compromising on environmental concerns. The Indian law in this respect is that before a ship arrives at a port in India it should have proper consent from the State Marine Board and must declare that it does not contain any hazardous waste or radioactive substances. AERB should be consulted in this matter.

40. *Vide* G. S. R. 15(E), dated 7 Jan. 2010 published in the Gazette of India, Extra Pt. II, Section 3(i), dated 7 Jan. 2010. It came into force on 7 Jan. 2010.

466. To implement the Hong Kong International Convention for the Safe and Environmentally Sound Recycling of Ships, 2009 the Government of India has formulated the Recycling of Ships Act 2019[41] which is a step towards protection of the environment and which aims to avoid unnecessary risk to human health and safety. It aims to cover the areas which were not addressed in the Ship-Breaking Code (Revised) of 2013 as notified by the Government of India. The Act sets down certain standards and a statutory mechanism for enforcement of such standards. It has been made incumbent upon the Ship Recycler to ensure safe and environmentally sound removal of ship hazardous material from a ship [section 21, 22 of the Act]. A violation of such provisions will *inter alia* entail imprisonment up to three months or with a fine of up to five lakh INR [Half a million] or with both [section 31(1)-(6) &section 32].

467. The Central Pollution Control Board guidelines state that the proper authority or the State Marine Board should issue a certificate to the effect that the ship is free from any hazardous substance and that it should not be allowed to breaking unless the provisions of the Environment Protection Act 1986 are complied with. The Supreme Court also has a penalty/enforcement clause which says that whenever illegal import of hazardous waste takes place due to non-fulfilment of the requisite conditions then an inquiry should be conducted against the officer or staff responsible for it and this action should be backed by rules. At the international level, India should participate in international meetings on ship-breaking at the level of the IMO and the Basel Convention's Technical Working Group with a clear mandate for the decontamination of ships of their hazardous substances such as asbestos, waste oil, gas and PCBs prior to exports to India for breaking. Participation should include from Central and State levels.

II. Pollution from Land-Based Sources

468. Land areas inhabiting humans are undoubtedly the home of all commercial and industrial activities. The main areas of concern are chemicals (especially chlorinated hydrocarbons) used for agricultural purposes and emission of metals like lead and mercury from industrial units and the petroleum exploration offshore services. Again the natural radioactivity resulting from the testing of nuclear weapons and dumping of radioactive wastes also accounts for marine pollution.

III. Pollution from Seabed Activities

469. It is an internationally accepted fact that the 'International Seabed Area' is 'the common heritage of mankind' (1970). The Seabed Area comprises the seabed and ocean floor beyond the limits of national jurisdiction. This area is now based on

41. The Gazette of India Extraordinary – Part II – Section I – New Delhi, 16 Dec. 2019. REGISTERED NO. DL—(N)04/0007/2003—19.

the precise definition of the continental shelf. The multimillion-dollar hidden treasure embedded in the deep end of the seas could not escape the lust of man. With technological advancement, it was possible to reach and explore the cached natural riches and to exploit them. One calculation estimates the secreted sea wealth at USD 300 million but truly speaking it is the unfathomable treasures comprising black potato-shaped mineral-rich manganese nodules which are the centre of commercial focus which includes the valuable nickel, cobalt, zirconium and iron.

470. The copper reserves are said to last for 600 years as compared to the forty years reserve on land while nickel is said to last for 150,000 years as compared to land reserve to last for 100 years and aluminium is said to last for 20,000 years as compared to 100 years reserve on land. In an attempt to exploit these great natural reserves advanced and sophisticated technology is required which is the prerogative of a handful of nations. Commercial tycoons have been active in the seabed area and are making lucrative business as the reserves are still beyond the reach of the underdeveloped or undeveloped nations of the world. All this though contributing in a meagre measure to the development side is doubtlessly responsible for disturbing the natural ambience under the sea and thus polluting it profusely.

IV. Dumping and Incineration of Wastes

471. The disposal of domestic and industrial wastes from the seashore, carried by rivers, sewage outlets, or by direct dumping is the largest source of pollution in the seas, especially in the coastal area. In India, the situation apart from commercial exploitation has also been aggravated by some religious activities on the coastal area; like submerging idols into the sea based on religious belief and use of coastal belt for bathing and sanitation purposes during festivities. There have been certain judicial pronouncements by the Supreme Court of India directing the government to put a curb on such activities and looking for an alternative so that even religious sentiments remain unhurt.

Prevention of Pollution by Garbage

472. The Merchant Shipping (Prevention of Pollution by Garbage from Ships) Rules 2009[42]makes obligatory upon all ships to comply with the provisions of these Rules to prevent pollution of sea by garbage. The rules make special requirements for disposal of garbage outside special areas and [Rule 3] and disposal of garbage within special areas [Rule 5].

Prevention of Pollution by Sewage

To give effect to section 356 C (3), section 356 E(ee) and 356 O the Government of India formulated the Merchant Shipping (Prevention of Pollution by Sewage from

42. *Vide* G. S. R., 847(E), dated 26 Nov. 2009 published in the Gazette of India, Extra, Pt. II, Sec. 3(i), No. 679, dated 26 Nov. 2009. It came into force on 26 Nov. 2009.

Ships) Rules 2010.[43] The Rules also provide for surveys [Rule 4] and issue of the Indian Sewage Pollution Prevention Certificate.[Rule 8] among other relevant matters.

§4. Liability for Marine Pollution

I. Civil Liability

473. According to section 352 I of the MS Act 1958 the owner of the ship, at the time of an incident, or at the time of the first occurrence where the incident consists of a series of occurrences, would be liable for pollution damage caused by oil which has escaped from the ship. But in case the pollution damage is caused by; an act of war, hostilities, civil war, insurrection or a natural phenomenon; or by an intentional act to cause such damage by any other person; or was caused by the negligent or wrongful act of any Government or other authority responsible for the maintenance of lights or other navigational aids in the exercise of its functions in this behalf, the owner will be fully exempted from such liability. In case the damage is caused by two or more ships then in that case the owners of all such ships shall be liable jointly and severally in case the damage is not reasonably separable. No claim for compensation for pollution damage may be made; against the servants or agents of the owner or members of the crew; or against the pilot; or against the charterer, manager or operator of the ship; or against any person undertaking salvage operations; or against any person taking preventive measures unless such damage results from the personal act or omission of such person. Moreover, the MS Act prevents the discharge of oil or oily mixtures into the sea anywhere within the coastal waters of India. Violation of this may entail a penalty of up to USD 10,000. The Government of India has formulated rules in supersession of the Merchant Shipping (Form of Certificate of Insurance for Civil Liability for Oil Pollution Damages) Rules, 1985 called the Merchant Shipping (Civil Liability for Oil Pollution Damage) Rules 2008[44] and has set the limits of the owner's liability regarding oil pollution damage as follows.

The liability of any one incident to an aggregate amount shall be:

(a) 45,10000 units of account where the ship's tonnage does not exceed 5,000 units of tonnage;
(b) 631 units of account for every additional unit of tonnage, where the ship's tonnage exceeds 5,000 units of tonnage:

> Provided that the aggregate amount shall not in any case exceed 8,97,70,000 units of account.

---

43. *Vide* G. S. R. 13(E), dated 7 Jan. 2010, published in the Gazette of India, Extra Pt. II, Sec. 3(i) dated 7 Jan. 2010. It came into force on 7 Jan. 2010.
44. *Vide* G. S. R. 219(E), dated 27 Mar. 2008, published in the Gazette of India, Extra Pt. II, which came into force on 27 Mar. 2008.

II. Criminal Liability

474. India ratified the International Convention for the Prevention of Pollution from Ships (ICPPS) in 1986 which introduces criminal liability for shipowners. It imputes criminal liability arising out of pollution by harmful substances in package form, sewage and garbage, and so on. It makes a general declaration that any operational pollution or accidental pollution shall be punishable by the law of the ratifying state within whose jurisdiction such pollution has taken place.

III. Marine Insurance

475. The MS Act in section 352N makes it compulsory for the owner of a ship which carries more than 2,000 tonnes or more of oil to have suitable insurance. The 'contract of marine insurance' is guided by the provisions of the Marine Insurance Act 1963 which should be embodied in a policy. Under the Marine Insurance Act 1963 if the contract of insurance expressly includes any liability to third parties, the measure of indemnity would be the amount paid or payable by the assured to such third party in respect of such liability.

IV. Limitation of Liability

476. The owner is entitled to limit his liability in respect of any one or more incidents unless the incident causing the pollution is proved to result from the owner's personal act or omission done either intentionally, recklessly or with knowledge.

§5. Marine Pollution Control and Cooperation

477. Mentionable legal steps in consonance with international conventions are taken in India to tackle the menace of marine pollution and to control it. The attempt has been to focus mainly on the oil tankers of 150 tonnes gross or more and ships of 400 tonnes gross and the offshore installations while exempting the warships and the government ships involved in non-commercial service from the legal grip. The legal measures fall into two categories: measures to control pollution by oil and measures to control pollution caused by accidents. Oil pollutants are thus controlled in the area of discharge by oil tankers, discharge by normal ships and discharge by offshore installations.

478. Every Indian oil tanker or Indian ship is required to maintain record books regarding details as to the substances they are carrying and they are also subjected to inspection by authorities to see whether these vessels are following the preventive measures and are well equipped to stop any kind of spillage, leakage or damage leading to marine pollution.

I. Oil Pollution Cess

479. In order to make the prevention of pollution by oil even more effective, the Central Government imposes Oil Pollution Cess on every ship calling at any port in India which carries oil as cargo at the rate of fifty paise each tonne of oil imported into India in bulk as cargo and on oil which is shipped from India. The proceeds of such cess shall be utilized by the Government for the purpose of providing oil reception facilities and equipment and materials for combating oil pollution at various ports in India. No port clearance shall be given by the authorities unless the oil pollution has been paid by the ship (section 356M, 356N MS Act).

Chapter 14. The Arrest of Ships

§1. Sources of Law

480. India is not a signatory and did not ratify either the International Convention Relating to the Arrest of Sea-going ships or the International Convention on certain Rules concerning Civil Jurisdiction in Matters of Collision which were signed at Brussels on 10 May 1952.

481. In India, carriage of goods by sea is governed by the Indian Bills of Lading Act, 1856, the Indian Carriage of Goods by Sea Act, 1925, the MS Act, 1958, and general statutes, such as the Marine Insurance Act, 1963, the Contract Act, 1872, the Evidence Act, 1872, the Indian Penal Code, 1860, the Transfer of Property Act, 1882, the Code of Civil Procedure, 1908, the Criminal Procedure Code, 1973, the Companies Act, 1956, and so on, as well as the general principles of law such as the law of tort, public and private international law, and so on. In this connection, reference may also be made to the Indian Ports Act, 1908 and the Major Port Trusts Act, 1963 concerning the administration of the port and the jurisdiction over ships in port, the Customs Act, 1962 containing various regulatory measures affecting ships, goods and persons in connection with importation or exportation of goods, as well as the provisions governing employment of labour.

482. The Indian Bills of Lading Act, 1856 lays emphasis on the negotiable and other characteristics of a bill of lading. The Carriage of Goods by Sea Act, 1925, contains the Hague Rules regulating the respective rights and liabilities of the parties to a contract governed by bills of lading or similar documents of title for carriage of goods by sea 'from any port in India to any other port whether in India or outside India'.

483. The MS Act 1958 embodies provisions which have been adopted from rules formulated by various international conventions such as the IMO or the International Labour Organization (ILO) but many provisions of international conventions regarding arrest of ships, civil and penal jurisdiction matters of collision, maritime liens and mortgage though incorporated by many maritime countries is yet not fully adopted by India and hence does not show much legal activity on this account. Again, the substantive rules concerning the transport of goods are contained in the Indian Bills of Lading Act 1856 and the Indian Carriage of Goods Act 1925, but the jurisdictional question concerning the arrest of foreign ships for enforcement of claims against the shipowner as a transporter of goods which in England are regulated by the Supreme Court Act 1981 are left unregulated by the Indian legislation. All this goes to say that Indian law regarding jurisdiction in matters of substantive rights concerning the arrest of ships is still in a very ambiguous state.

§2. JUDICIAL PROCEDURE FOR CONSERVATORY ARREST

484. Ships on international voyages expose themselves to a number of national jurisdictions while passing through various countries. A ship may get involved in a number of legal actions like violating the customs, safety measures, environmental laws, private and public laws and thus subject itself to the jurisdiction of foreign courts. Such courts then cause the ship to be arrested for the purpose of; acquiring jurisdiction; for obtaining security for the satisfaction of the claims; in executing a decree. Even though there is no claim on merits, there can be conservatory arrest of ship which is an autonomous proceeding. The arrest of a ship is only a temporary remedy to bring the ship under the jurisdiction of a particular court as it brings it under the custody of the marshal or any other authorized officer.

485. It is only a method of safeguarding the interest of the plaintiff and there may be no such arrest if the defendant ship through its lawyer agrees to 'accept service and to put in bail or to pay money into court in lieu of bail'. The court can order the sale of the arrested ship if sufficient bail is not provided or if the cargo is found to be deteriorating after duly notifying the parties. For a court which is issuing the warrant of arrest against a foreign ship, it is proper to see that the ship is at that time within its jurisdiction as it being an action in rem the court order not only affects the parties concerned but also the world at large. In India, the arrest of ship is a two-pronged device whereas the traditional admiralty law and the provisions of the MS Act go together to make ship arrest.

I. Ship Arrest under Admiralty Law

486. The three pioneer High Courts in India namely, Bombay, Calcutta and Madras High Courts, traditionally speaking have admiralty jurisdiction. Thus an action against a foreign ship which belongs to a foreign company and has no place of residence or business in India can lie under the admiralty jurisdiction of these courts regarding a tort or a breach of duty arising from the carriage of goods from a port in India to a foreign port. The decision by the Supreme Court of India while interpreting Article 225 of the Constitution of India allocates original and appellate, inherent and plenary powers to all the High Courts in India and thus High Courts at other littoral States like Gujarat, Goa, Orissa, and so on, have the power to demarcate their own jurisdictional limits (*m. v. Elizabeth v. Harwan Investment & Trading Pvt. Ltd Goa* SC 1993). 'Arrest' of ship signifies merely the detention of ship to satisfy maritime claims and not the seizure of ship in execution or satisfaction of judgment.

487. Though India does not ratify the Conventions in this regard yet the territorial sovereignty and the power to arrest a foreign vessel while in the waters of a coastal state recognized by the generality of maritime States constitutes part of Indian common law. The Mareva Injunction as recognized under section 45 of the Supreme Court of Judicature (Consolidation) Act 1925 is not available to Indian courts having admiralty jurisdiction. 'Attachment' before judgment can be exercised by the Indian courts under ordinary civil jurisdiction regarding claims including claims for charter hire or stevedore services or necessaries supplied provided that the court is assured on the basis of an affidavit that the ship is the only asset of the defendant and that he is about to dispose it off in order to defeat, obstruct or delay the execution of any decree.

488. For quite a long time, courts have been evolving practical procedure devices to render justice in matters of maritime claims and liens, salvage and collisions, and other substantive rights arising from breach of maritime contracts and for which the substantive laws of the country do not provide a remedy. It is thus also within the power of the appropriate Indian courts to deal with such situations in accordance with the general principles of maritime law and the applicability of statutory law regarding persons and property found within their jurisdiction. Thus where a higher court is equipped with certain powers to deal with similar situations coming within their jurisdiction then even in matters of foreign ships, and in absence of any specific provision regarding it the Indian courts can also administer justice and give remedy to the claimant against a foreign ship. This power of the High Court includes the power, in the interest of justice to make interlocutory orders for arrest and attachment before judgment.

489. All the Indian High Courts are courts of record (Article 129 of the Indian Constitution). They have original and appellate jurisdiction including the inherent and plenary powers to administer justice. The protection and determination of rights of shipowners, of other persons connected thereto when ships are arrested in rem by Admiralty court, are innate in the courts having admiralty jurisdiction. In case of a ship being wrongly or improperly arrested there is provision for the aggrieved in advance; the aggrieved can file a praecipe in the prescribed form and obtain the entry of a caveat against arrest in the caveat book kept in the Admiralty Registry/ Prothonotary and Senior Master of the High Court. Though this may not prevent the arrest of the res yet the caveator on a subsequent motion after arrest, may obtain the discharge of the arrest warrant and the condemnation of the arresting party in damages. If a foreign ship is registered in a country and the consulate of that country is in the jurisdiction of the High Court which is ordering for its arrest then prior notice of the arrest must be given to such consulate.

490. The Supreme Court of India thus ruled that the admiralty action is an action in rem and that there is a strong triable case. The ship being a foreign national there are jurisdictional hardships regarding it and once the ship leaves the Indian TW then it becomes impractical to get it back within the jurisdiction and often a successful claim remains ineffective and private international law issues may arise (*Videsh Sanchar Nigam Limited v. Kapitan Kud* (1986)). The Court then says that certain conditions should be put before the foreign ship is released. The conditions imposed in this case were that the respondent shall deposit a sum of INR 10 crore, that the Ukrainian Government shall give an undertaking through its Ambassador attached to its Embassy in India for the compliance of the decree; the undertaking should be around for INR 25 crore inclusive of costs and other expenses. The Court though did not fix any limit for the compliance of these directions yet it ordered that the ship shall not leave Indian waters unless the said amount is deposited and undertaking is given to the satisfaction of the Division Bench of the High Court.

491. In this case, the Bombay High Court framed rules on admiralty jurisdiction in Part III to regulate the procedure and practice thereof. The Rule also binds the claimant to give an undertaking through its advocate to pay such sum as the Court may award by way of compensation should the arrest is declared to be a prejudiced one (Original side, Rule 941). Yet in another case it was held that even a civil court, exercising power under Order 39 Rule 1 while granting interim injunction, the Court can put a condition that the plaintiff should give an undertaking to compensate the defendant in case the case his claim is declared to be baseless without the filing of a separate suit by the defendant for it.

Moreover, Rule 954 of Admiralty Rules provides that subject to the provisions of Rule 952 (caveat property not to be released unless notice is given to the caveator) that the ship (property) arrested under a warrant may be ordered to be released:

(1) at the request of the plaintiff;
(2) on payment of the ordered amount by the defendant in the court;
(3) the defendant giving such security for the amount claimed in the suit as the Court may direct;
(4) on any other just ground as given by the Court (*Mahadeo Savlaram Shelke & Others v. Pune Municipal Corporation & Another* (1995) 3 SCC 33).

II. Ship Arrest Provisions under MS Act

492. The three Indian courts of admiralty jurisdiction have concurrent jurisdiction and territorially extend over the coastline of India. Sections 443, 444 of the MS Act 1958. The Act is a regulatory Act and under section 3(15) High Court means a High Court within whose jurisdiction the port of registry of the vessel is situated; or where the vessel is for the time being found; or where the cause of action wholly or in part arises and a foreign ship is said to be within the maritime jurisdiction of a High Court if above situation arises. Sections 443 and 444 authorize the courts to detain a foreign ship. Thus the power to detain a foreign ship is envisaged in section 443 as under:

(1) Whenever, any foreign ship causes damage to any property belonging to the government of India or to any citizen of India in any part of the world, then at any time thereafter when the ship is found within Indian jurisdiction then on an application of the aggrieved, the High Court shall issue an order to detain the ship. The ship shall remain detained until the claim is satisfied or some security is furnished by the owner, master or consignee of the ship as directed by the court.
(2) In case there is an apprehension before the application as aforesaid is made that the ship is about to leave India or the TW of India then any proper officer may detain the ship until the submission of such application. Such officer shall

not be liable for any cost or damages in respect of the detention unless such detention is without reasonable grounds.

(3) For all the proceedings in this respect, the person furnishing security shall be made a defendant and shall be deemed to be the owner of the ship which has occasioned damage.

493. Section 444 of the MS Act power to enforce detention is given which says that; any commissioned officer of the Indian Navy or any port officer, pilot, harbour master, conservation of port or customs collector may detain the ship. After the ship is formally detained, its movement into the sea without proper authority would render its master or any other person responsible for it guilty of offence under this section. Such person shall also be guilty of an offence if he carries on board any other person on duty to detain the ship and shall be liable to pay all expenses of, and incidental to it. The word 'damages' occurring in section 443 is wide enough to include not only physical damages but also to include all types of maritime questions or claims involving damage caused by unauthorized acts or conduct of the owner, agents, servants, and so on.

494. The section also relates to detention by reason of damage caused in any part of the world by a foreign ship to property belonging to the Government of India or to an Indian citizen or company. Though damage is usually physical in nature, yet damage can also be caused by a breach of contract or the carriers or his servants may also be negligent thereby causing damage; for instance, due to carelessness, exposure of goods to bad weather, theft or other negligent act damage may be caused to the cargo.

495. The English courts have used the expression 'damage done by any ship' as not to apply to claims against the carrying ship for damage done to cargo. It was held the term damage is used in the physical sense and said that 'S. 7 of the Admiralty Court Act 1861 (24 Victoriaec. 10) – The High Court of Admiralty shall have jurisdiction over any Claim for Damage done by any ship.' It is meant to apply only to physical damage done by a ship by way of collision or so. Under the English statutes of 1920, 1925, 1956 and 1981, the English courts did not interpret it to include cargo claims and the like within the term damage.

496. The power to detain, however, extends to any ship which is of any nationality, or the nationality of its owner or the domicile or place of residence or business of the owner or no matter where the cause of action has arisen. This was further put up in the words '… but this question is academic in the light of the fact that jurisdiction in respect of claims for damage to cargo carried in a ship is now expressly given by the Supreme Court Act 1981 section 20(2)(g)'. (Halsbury's Laws of England, 4th edn, Vol. I (i) paragraph 319 No. 12) In India there is no specific statute like that of English law and hence the phrase 'damage caused by ship' is taken widely to cover all maritime questions and claims. Thus when damage is caused to the ship or to the cargo by the negligence of the shipowner or his agents, by physical contact, no matter wherever such ship is registered or the cause of action has arisen, the aggrieved party has a right to invoke the jurisdiction of the High Court and seek remedy as to detaining the ship if found within the jurisdiction of such court, under section 443.

497. In India, regarding the jurisdiction of courts for the arrest of ships, a number of laws like the law relating to contract, tort, crime, mortgage, marine insurance, customs, port operations, and the Civil and Criminal Procedure Codes, as well as the relevant rules of court, govern the claims relating to inward and outward cargo and such claims are enforceable against foreign ships by recourse for arrest and detention when located within the court's jurisdiction.

498. Thus the High Court in the state of Andhra Pradesh does not lack admiralty jurisdiction in respect of claims regarding outward cargo. The admiralty jurisdiction of the High Court is dependent on the presence of the foreign ship in Indian waters and founded on the arrest of that ship irrespective of the residence or place of business of the defendant falling under the same jurisdiction. Once the foreign ship is arrested within the local limits of jurisdiction of the High Court and the owner of the ship has entered his appearance and furnished security to the satisfaction of the High Court for the release of his ship, the proceedings then continue as a personal action.

III. Procedure of Arrest of Ship

499. High Courts having admiralty jurisdiction for ship arrest also subsume certain rules regarding the safety of ownership and private property rights in respect of the ship arrested. For instance, a party wishing to prevent the seizure of property in an action in rem may, by filing a praecipe in the prescribed form, obtain the entry of a caveat against arrest in the caveat book kept in the Admiralty Register or Prothonotary and Senior Master of the High Court. In this way, though the entry of the caveat does not prevent arrest of the res, the caveator, on a subsequent motion after arrest, may obtain the discharge of the arrest warrant and the condemnation of the arresting party in damages, if the latter is unable to show 'good and sufficient reason' for having arrested.

500. The High Court Rules for the High Courts of Bombay, Calcutta and Madras give intricate rules regarding arrest of foreign ships. The Rules require that a notice regarding the institution of the suit be given to the consul of the state to which the foreign ship belongs and a copy of such notice be attached with the warrant. The Rules require that before issuing the warrant of arrest the registrar of the court shall ascertain whether or not any caveat warrant has been entered, Rule 941 of the Bombay High Court Rules additionally require that a certificate of Prothonotary & Senior Master containing the declaration that search has been made in the Caveat Warrant Book and that no caveat has been filed be attached with the affidavit leading to the warrant. Such Rules also require that the affidavit should also state the nature of the claim in the suit and the fact that it has not been satisfied.

501. An undertaking by the plaintiff securing cost and damages should be given to the court at the time of making an application for the arrest of ship. The Calcutta and Madras High Court Rules also require that in a suit for bottomry, a copy of the bottomry bond if in a foreign language then a notarial translation of it should be attached with the affidavit and be produced for the perusal of the registrar of the court. The Rules also require that in the plaint in a suit in rem, the nationality of the ship should also be mentioned which is to be followed by the words 'together with its engines, boats, gear, tackle, apparel furniture and papers and everything belonging to it whether on board or ashore'.

502. The Plaint should clearly mention the maritime claim or lien. The judge's order for the arrest will indicate the day and time of arrest and also a direction that in case the ad valorem court fee and the sheriff's poundage is paid off or the satisfactory security for the claim is furnished then the ship may not be arrested. As regarding the service of the warrant of arrest the Rules particularly state that when it is issued by the court's registry then it will be served by the bailiff of the Marshal of Calcutta and by the bailiff of the Sheriff of Bombay (Mumbai) or Madras (Chennai) who will effect the service by affixing the original warrant of arrest for a short time that is, for about ten to fifteen minutes on any mast of the ship or on the outside of any suitable part of the ship's superstructure, then removing the original and leaving a duplicate thereof affixed in its place. When this mode of service is not followed and the service is affected on the master or a mate of the ship by obtaining his acknowledgement then it is considered as bad service. However, the Rules are silent regarding effecting service on a ship lying at a port other than that in whose registry the writ has been issued namely, Calcutta, Bombay or Madras through the Collector of Customs at such other port. In such situations the plaintiff is required to take the sheriff's substitute to the port where the ship is laying thus the possibility of the ship being carried away in avoidance of the warrant is always there. In such cases, it is advisable that the registry should be requested by a praecipe to give telegraphic or facsimile intimation to the Port Conservator and to the Commissioner of Customs at the particular port of issue giving them the important instructions for not granting port clearance to such ship pending the arrival of warrant.

503. The Calcutta and Madras Rules provide that, after expiration of twelve days from the return of the warrant for arrest the suit should be set down for hearing. The judge being satisfied that the plaintiff's claim is well-founded may order the sale of the ship and the instruction that the proceeds of the sale should be paid into the registry. Warrant of arrest issued by these two High Courts is in the form of a citatory calling upon the owners and all interested parties to appear before the court which is deemed to be sufficient notice to all concerned regarding the suit although it does not require them to file a written statement. The Bombay Rules which came into effect from 1 January 1980 do not contain a citation to the owners or to the interested parties. The Bombay Rules require the service of the writ of summons in the same manner as the warrant of arrest and the writ of summons is in the same form applicable to the suit filed in the ordinary original civil jurisdiction of the High Court. The Bombay High Court Rules are more stringent and lengthy as they require the owners and other parties to file a written statement which takes more time, delaying the date of hearing of the suit; thus, it is a disadvantage of the plaintiff.

504. However, the Rules of all the above-mentioned High Courts require that in a suit in rem no service of warrant of arrest shall be required when the Advocate for the defendant ship agrees to accept service and to give security or to pay money into court. In India, the procedure for initiating an action on a claim under the Admiralty jurisdiction of the High Courts is an ordinary one and differs drastically from the one which prevailed in England in 1890 or even today. It entails only general procedural rules regarding the institution of an ordinary civil suit as given under the provisions of the Civil Procedure Code 1908. It is to be signed by the plaintiff and where he is a foreign plaintiff then it must grant power of attorney to a person, usually at the place where the action is to be instituted.

505. A foreign firm is not recognized in India and thus all the partners should join as plaintiffs and must also give the power of attorney. A power of attorney where the country is a commonwealth country must be executed and authenticated by a notary public and in other cases, the signature of the public notary be authenticated by an Indian consular officer. The power of attorney can also be executed before the Indian consular officer under section 3 of the Diplomatic and Consular Officers (Oaths and Fees) Act 1948. Often this requirement of verification of the plaint causes a harmful delay in the matter of arrest of ship. The application for arrest is moved unilaterally. But the courts before passing an ex parte order in order to avoid wrongful arrest often notify the master of the ship. Such notice often expedites early settlement and furnishing of security.

§3. Ship

506. Ships are the centre point of all the activities which are undertaken by men on sea. However, the word 'ship', though easy to comprehend, has been defined in different words under different legislations in India.

I. The Concept of 'Ship' under Indian Law

507. Section 3(55) of the MS Act substituted ship for vessel and defines 'vessel' as including any ship, boat, sailing vessel or other description of vessel used in navigation. Section 3(45) of the same Act declares that 'ship' does not include a sailing vessel:

- The Indian Ports Act 1908 (No. 15 of 1908) defines 'vessel' as including anything made for the conveyance [mainly] by water, of human beings or of property. [Section 3(7)].
- The Marine Insurance Act 1963 defines 'ship' as to include every description of vessel used in navigation [Section 2 (3)].

- The Sailing Vessels (Members of Crew) Rules 1967 defines 'vessel' to mean a sailing vessel to which Part XV of the MS Act applies. [Rule 2 (g)].
- The Indian Carriage of Goods by Sea Act 1925 defines 'ship' as to mean any vessel used for the carriage of goods by sea. [Schedule Article 1 (d)].
- The Maritime Zones of India (Regulation of Fishing by Foreign Vessels) Act 1981 (Act No. 42 of 1981) defines 'Indian vessel' to mean-
- a vessel owned by government or by a corporation established by a Central Act or a Provincial or State Act or
- a vessel
  a. which is owned wholly by any of the following persons
     i. a citizen of India
     ii. a company which has 60% of its share held by Indians
     iii. a registered society of Indian whose members are all Indian
  b. which is registered under the Merchant Shipping Act 1958 or under any other Indian law.

Thus, the various Acts use the term 'vessel' and 'ship' almost interchangeably.

II. Sistership

508. A 'sistership' though not defined under the Act is a ship in the same beneficial ownership as the ship in regard to which the claim arose. The Bombay High Court observed that 'in view of the decision of the Supreme Court in m v. Elizabeth we are of the clear view that the High Court does have jurisdiction to arrest a "sistership" for securing any maritime claim' (*Mariner IV v. Videsh Sanchar Nigam Limited* BHC 1997 unreported case).

509. Under the international convention, an action in rem can be invoked against the ship which is the subject of controversy and not against the ship which is a 'sistership' or any other ship. If it is owned by the same owner then an action in personam may lie making the owner personally liable. The Indian carriage of Goods by Sea Act 1925 applies to carriage of goods by sea under bills of lading or similar documents of title from a port in India to any other port whether in or outside India.

510. The Act envisages certain rights and immunities upon the carrier (Arts. III & IV) and in respect of a claim relating to an outward cargo, the cargo owner has a right to bring a suit against a shipowner subject to the period of limitation specified under the Act which is one year. The substantial rights recognized by the statute are of equal application to foreign merchant ships as they are to Indian merchant ships. There is no provision in the Carriage of Goods by Sea Act regarding the arrest of foreign vessels in Indian waters and hence there is no effective remedy available to a cargo owner against a foreign owner. The same position is regarding the claims relating to cargo carried under a charter party.

511. As an ultimate resort, the MS Act is applied by the cargo owner to assume jurisdiction over a foreign ship. The Act empowers a High Court to pass orders to arrest a ship in respect of a substantive right. A right conferred by the Indian Carriage of Goods by Sea Act 1925 in respect of outward cargo is one of those rights which can be enforced by arrest and detention of the foreign ship in order to ascertain jurisdiction over the vessel and its owners, just as it can be done in respect of inward cargo by reason of substantive rights conferred by the Admiralty Court Act 1861 read with the Colonial Courts of Admiralty Act 1890 and other rules of law.

§4. Maritime Claims

512. The Indian Parliament passed The Admiralty Jurisdiction and Settlement of Maritime Claims Act 2017 (No. 22 of 2017).[45] As per the Act maritime claim means a claim as referred to in section 4 of the Act.[46] It is a long-awaited law which finally settles the contours of admiralty jurisdiction of Indian courts. The Act thus defines 'maritime claims' in detail which include; disputes regarding vessel ownership or possession, disputes regarding the earnings of the vessel among the co-owners, claims regarding mortgage or charges of a vessel, claims regarding loss or damage of the vessel caused by the operation of the vessel which also includes environmental damage, claims regarding loss of life or personal injury in respect of the operation of the vessel and also claims regarding loss or damage of goods. As per section 4 maritime claims also include claims regarding certain agreements including agreements regarding carriage of goods or passengers and claims regarding hire or use of the vessel. The term also includes claims arising out of supply of goods or services rendered to the vessel for its operation, management, preservation or maintenance and claims regarding payment of wages of seamen and insurance-related matters also fall within the purview of 'maritime claims' so also claims arising under a manning and crew agreement relating to a vessel. Notwithstanding anything contained in sections 150 & 151 of the Merchant Shipping Act 1958, claims regarding disbursement on behalf of the vessel or its owners, particular average and general average and disputes arising out of a contract of sale of the vessel disputes regarding insurance premium, commission, brokerage or agency fee payable in respect of the vessel, damage or threat of damage caused by the vessel to the environment and all the matters related to including loss incurred by the third parties come under the term maritime claims. Also included within the term maritime claims are costs or expenses relating to removal, recovery, etc., of a sunk, wrecked, stranded or abandoned vessel and maritime liens which are a special type of maritime claims which are connected with a vessel in spite of any change in its ownership registration or flag[section 4 (a)–(w)].

513. Although the Hague Rules are embodied in the Carriage of Goods by Sea Act 1925 it did not become a party to the International Convention laying down

45. The Gazette of India Extraordinary – Part II – Section I – No. 32 – New Delhi, Wednesday, 9 Aug. 2017/Shravana 18, 1939(SAKA).
46. Section 2(f) of the said Act.

those Rules and merely incorporated the principles given in the Carriage of Goods by Sea Act 1925 of the United Kingdom. Though the UK repealed its Act of 1924 and incorporated the Hague-Visby Rules in its new law, the Carriage of Goods by Sea Act 1971.

514. Here India did not follow the United Kingdom and has also not adopted the Brussels Convention of 1967 regarding maritime liens and mortgages. But though they are not adopted in the legislation in India; the principles of these important International Conventions to facilitate international trade have become the common law of India and are followed in the enforcement of maritime claims against foreign ships. The LLMC 1976 was adopted by India by an amendment in the MS Act 1958 which safeguarded the interest of the shipowners. Previously the onus was on the shipowner to prove that he is not guilty of negligence. Now the claimant is required to prove that the damage was caused due to the shipowner's negligence.

I. Maritime Claims and Admiralty Jurisdiction

515. The newly enacted Act namely the Admiralty (Jurisdiction and Settlement of Maritime Claims) Act 2017 in its section 5 spells out admiralty jurisdiction. Previously only the High Courts of Bombay, Calcutta and Madras had the admiralty jurisdiction but the new Act enjoins admiralty jurisdiction on various coastal High Courts including the Karnataka High Court, the Gujarat High Court, the Orissa High Court, the Kerala High Court and the High Court of Judicature at Hyderabad for the State of Telangana and the State of Andhra Pradesh High Court [section 2(e)].

516. The admiralty jurisdiction of High Courts in respect of maritime claims is now well settled under the new Act of 2017 which is as follows:

> Arrest of Vessel in rem (Section 5)
> The High Court may order arrest of any vessel within its jurisdiction for the purpose of providing security against a maritime claim if the court has reason to believe that:
>
> – that the owner of the vessel is liable for the claim or
> – the demise charterer of the vessel is liable for the claim and is the owner of the vessel or
> – the claim is based on the mortgage or charge of a similar nature on the vessel or
> – the claim relates to ownership or possession of the vessel or
> – the claim is against the owner, demise charterer, manager or operator of the vessel and is secured by a maritime lien as provided in section 9.[47]

47. *Inter se* priority on Maritime lien. Section 9 of the Admiralty (Jurisdiction and Settlement of Maritime Claims) Act 2017.

Subject to section 5 (1) the High Court may order arrest of any other vessel for the purpose of providing security against a maritime claim *in lieu* of the vessel against which claim has been made. However, no such arrest can be made in respect of a maritime claim under clause (a) of sub-section (1) of section 4. [Proviso Section 5].

A. Admiralty Jurisdiction In Personam

517. Subject to section 7 the High Court may exercise admiralty jurisdiction by action in personam in respect of maritime claim as defined under section 4 of the Act. Section 7 enumerates certain restrictions imposed on High Courts regarding the exercise of jurisdiction in action in personam. Where a maritime claim arose out of collisions between vessels, in carrying out or omission to carry out a manoeuvre of vessels, non-compliance of collision regulations as given in section 285 of the MS Act 1958 by any of the vessels then the High Court shall not take any action against any defendant unless the cause of action arises in India or the defendant at the time of action by the High Court resides in India or personally works for gain [section 7].

518. The High Court also cannot take an action in personam against the defendant in case the plaintiff has previously brought a case against that defendant in respect of the same incident outside India and such case has not been discontinued or terminated [section 7].

519. The Indian Courts possessing Admiralty jurisdiction have jurisdiction over the following claims and to hear and determine any questions with regard thereto. According to section 5 of the Act, the Indian courts which exercise admiralty jurisdiction have jurisdiction over the following maritime claims and have the power to hear the matter related thereto. These are:

- Any claim for damage done by any ship. The High Court has exclusive admiralty jurisdiction in respect of damage caused by a ship on the high seas.
- Any claim for damage received by any ship or sea-going vessel whether such a ship or vessel may have been in India or upon the high seas when the damage was received.
- Any claim in the nature of salvage services rendered to a ship, whether such ship or vessel may have been within India or the high seas at the time when its services were rendered in respect of which the claim is made. Section 402 of the MS Act also enumerates the rules relating to salvage services.
- Again any claim by a master or crew for wages or for any money or property which under any statutory provisions is recoverable as such comes under the Act.
- Any claim by a master in respect of disbursements made on account of a ship.
- Any claim arising out of bottomry.

520. In this respect the Maritime Conventions Act 1911, in so far as it extended to and operated as part of the law of India, was repealed by section 46(2) of the MS

Act, 1958, with effect from 1 January 1961 and it is still to be considered whether after this date such a claim for damages for loss of life or personal injuries will fall within the section. The Supreme Court Act 1981 of England has catalogued maritime claims with reference to the unified rules adopted by the Brussels Convention of 1952 on the Arrest of Sea-going Ships. India has not adopted the various Brussels conventions. The internationally unified laws on maritime were evolved out of the national legislations of various countries and are helpful for the courts for supplementing the MS act and other enactments connected with maritime laws.

521. Several times in Bombay, using the section 443(2) provisions there has been temporary detention of a foreign ship and the shipowners are found to quickly settle the claim. In this section, the term 'High Court' in relation to a vessel is defined by the act to mean the High Court within the limits of whose appellate jurisdiction the vessel is found. This gives jurisdiction to the High Courts of all littoral states of India jurisdiction in respect of claims which come under section 443. Section 402 of the Indian MS Act 1958 enumerates any claim in the nature of salvage services. In such cases, the claim is settled by a judicial magistrate of the First Class when the claimed amount is less than INR 10,000 and by the High Court when the said amount exceeds INR 10,000.

522. Thus ultimately a plain interpretation of the section explains that all the High Courts and not only should those having admiralty jurisdiction entertain the claim relating to salvage services. Whenever any ship shall be under arrest by the court or the proceeds of any ship having been so arrested shall have been brought into and be in the registry of the said court a claim and cause of action of any person. The High Courts under the admiralty jurisdiction can hear claims for which there is no maritime lien but only a right in rem while it can also hear some cases of maritime lien. Under Indian rules of conflict of laws, a foreign maritime lien may not be recognized and enforced by Indian courts although the native law gives it a maritime lien status. In India, in case of claims under contractual documents such as bill of lading or charter parties where they contain a clause as to resorting to arbitration where even the court while acting under the Arbitration and Conciliation Act 1996 which contains the provisions of the New York Convention, such court may order a stay on an application being made by the owner of the arrested ship. Thus a maritime claimant while starting to sue under admiralty jurisdiction of any court in India must ascertain the viability of the ship arrest as in case of any failure or wrongful arrest the legal procedure is a complicated one.

§5. Security and Counter Security

523. Security is insisted upon by the court to be furnished by the plaintiff to compensate the defendant in case the arrest is wrongful or is declared to be mala fide. This practice of obtaining a security is followed in the United States, Japan and other countries because a wrongful arrest may cause irreparable loss to the shipowner in whom he is required to be compensated by the party seeking arrest. When a trading ship is arrested it is always advisable that the security fixed by the court must be complied with and thereafter the ship is released so that detention loss is avoided. In case there is a caveat release outstanding in the Caveat Release Book then a notice will have to be issued to the caveator. In this respect, the High Court Rules of the High Courts of Bombay, Calcutta and Madras which have admiralty jurisdiction come into play. Giving of security shall not amount to submission to court's jurisdiction. Where the amount of security to be deposited is excessive, then an application, before or after furnishing the security can be made for its reduction. Security for the claim in the suit is furnished by means of a case deposit in the registry or a bank guarantee for the amount stated in the warrant of arrest. The bank guarantee is required to be from a nationalized bank in India or a foreign bank carrying on business in India and having an office in Calcutta, Bombay or Madras where the warrant of arrest is issued. The bank before furnishing its own guarantee to the court may accept a counter-guarantee from a foreign bank.

I. Security for Costs and Damages

524. At the time of applying for arrest, an undertaking is required to be given in writing to pay such sum by way of damages as the court may award as compensation in the event of a party affected is prejudiced by the arrest. There hardly comes a situation when payment of damages is ordered to the owner of an arrested ship unless the arrest is mala fide and the court's process is misused.

II. Security for the Claim In Suit

525. Security for the claim in suit is deposited by means of a cash deposit in the registry or a bank guarantee for the amount stated in the warrant of arrest. The Bank guarantee has to be either from a nationalized bank or from a foreign bank which has a branch at Calcutta, Madras or Bombay. The bank giving the guarantee will itself require an acceptable counter-guarantee from a bank abroad before furnishing a guarantee to the court. The bank guarantee is continued until the final disposal of the suit and for another year after its disposal. Where there is a cash deposit, the usual practice is that the said amount is saved in an interest-bearing term deposit till the final disposal of the suit. The ship is released from arrest after security in respect of it has been paid either by the shipowner or by any other interested party. Such security may be in the form of a bail bond, payment of money in the court or a bank guarantee or a letter of undertaking (LOU) from the shipowner's protection and indemnity club (P&I Club). Such security also avoids re-arrest. The amount of security is set by the court in its discretion, but generally speaking, it is a sum sufficient to cover the claimant's 'reasonably arguable best case' together with the interest and costs but not exceeding the value of the arrested vessel.

III. Counter Security

526. As a practice though, the arrest of ship may incur huge financial losses to the shipowner yet the courts usually do not ask the plaintiff or the claimant to put up countersecurity as a guarantee against such losses. However, the court may order counter security under Order XXV Rule 1 of Code of Civil Procedure 1908 for Security for Cost. Security for cost may be required by the court from the plaintiff at any stage of the suit, either suo moto or on the defendant's request. This will be done by the court when it appears that the plaintiff/plaintiffs are foreign residents and have no immovable property in India. The court's order shall fix a time limit within which security for the cost incurred or likely to be incurred by the defendant is to be furnished by the plaintiff and should also record reasons for such order.

§6. Subsequent Arrest

527. There is no explicit mentioning of this action under Indian law.

§7. Lifting of the Arrest

528. Once the security is furnished for the plaintiff's claim the ship is released. Often due to the owner's bankruptcy or the master and crew having abandoned the ship, the ship is not released and the marshal/sheriff in whose charge the ship is given makes all sorts of arrangements including providing a skeleton crew for the maintenance of the ship. As the marshal/sheriff is without man and money to take care of the ship the arresting party is ordered by the court to provide all facilities and funds to the sheriff to maintain the ship. Where such arresting party fails to do the needful a report may be sent by the sheriff giving an account of the failure.

529. On the basis of the report, the court after notifying the arresting party shall then order the release of the ship. Often other interveners like a high ranking mortgagee may volunteer to provide the marshal/sheriff with funds to engage a caretaker and the court should be moved for the appointment of such caretaker. To prevent the release of any property under arrest a person so interested may file a praecipe in the registry signed by himself or by his advocate. It should include that a caveat be entered against the release of the said property. A caveat against the release of the said property shall thereupon be entered in a book to be kept in the registry called the 'Caveat Release Book'.

530. The master of an arrested ship can represent the ship while taking steps to get the ship released. The bank guarantee remains intact until the disposal of the case and one year thereafter. In case there is a cash deposit instead of a bank guarantee, then it can be invested as a term deposit until the final disposal of the case. The property so detained under a warrant may be ordered to be released at the request of the plaintiff or by the defendant when he either pays into the court the claimed amount or gives security for it.

§8. Remedies for Wrongful Arrest

531. Often the arrest of a vessel may be replete with mala fide or inadvertence of the aggrieved party. The practice itself is one and a half-century old and the Privy Council laid down the test of wrongful arrest. To succeed in a claim for wrongful arrest the owners must demonstrate that there is either mala fide or crassa negligentia (The Evangelismos (1858) 12 Moo PC 352). Anyone who invoking the admiralty proceedings of the court gets a ship arrested maliciously and without reasonable and probable cause then he is liable to pay damages to the person aggrieved. A new suit has to be filed for wrongful arrest proving and contending that the arrest was malicious. This will result in the condemnation of the claimant for damages only if the court is satisfied regarding the bad faith or gross negligence. An erroneous arrest would not normally entitle the defendant to claim damages, although he might then be able to recover costs.

I. Detention of Unsafe Ships by the Central Government

532. The Central Government has the power to detain ship where it is found unsafe by reason of the defective condition of her hull, equipment or machinery, or by reason of overloading or improper loading and is posing a danger to human life and is unfit to proceed further then it may order its detention. But in case it appears that there was no reasonable and probable cause of detention then the Central Government is liable to pay to the owner of the ship and also compensation for any loss or damage sustained by him by reason of the wrongful detention or survey (section 337 MSA).

§9. Judicial Sale and Ranking

I. Judicial Sale

533. The Admiralty Rules of the three High Courts of Bombay, Calcutta and Madras provide for the sale of the ship either during the pendency of the suit or after the adjudication on the plaintiff's suit. The sale is carried out by the marshal or the Sheriff as it is done in the sale of a movable property under an ordinary suit. Unlike the English practice, neither there is provision for appraisement nor there is provision for any reserve price. In order to get the ship sold at a reasonable price which would fetch its real value, the courts have recently adopted the trend of ordering to get the ship to be valued by a ship valuer. The price then should not be below the valued price. However, if the bidding does not reach up to the appraised value, then on the Marshall or Sheriff's application the court can order its sale even below it.

534. The sale of a ship normally takes place by a public auction by advertising about it in the newspaper as ordered by the court. Though there is no mentioning of it in the Rules, yet there is no sale by private treaty. The court can order sale of perishable goods, goods which are likely to deteriorate easily or goods which are specially considered by the court due to some special reason. All the property aboard the ship which belongs to the shipowner is subject to sale.

A. *Conditions of Sale*

535. When a sale is executed in this manner, then under the terms and conditions of the sale the successful bidder is required to pay a percentage usually 15% of the purchase price. The balance is settled to be paid within a specified period which is usually fifteen days from the date of sale. The payment is made through banker's draft or a certified cheque. The sale is subject to sanction by the court under the Rules.

536. The sale is confined to property which is under arrest. Thus when there is cargo which is not under arrest then the court shall discharge such cargo from being sold along with the ship. The sale shall be ordered by the Admiralty Court when an application is made for it either by the party bringing action or by the Marshall or the Sheriff. During the pendency of a suit, a sale is ordered on the ground that the detention of the property shall cause financial loss to the plaintiff as the security will diminish. Application is served on any person who has obtained judgment against the ship and to all caveators.

The Marshall or the Sheriff can sell the ship in foreign currency and the proceeds of the sale shall be paid into the court. The sale so taking place under the Court's Order gives an encumbrance free title to the purchaser.

II. Ranking

537. A mortgagee may have a high ranking priority and in the event of the arresting party being failed to provide the sheriff with man and money to maintain the ship then he may apply to the court to allow him to provide a caretaker for the mortgaged ship. Expenses incurred for this purpose shall form the first charge on the proceeds of the sale and regardless of the priority ranking of its claim and irrespective of the result of its own suit.

Chapter 15. Carriage of Passengers

§1. Introduction

538. It being a matter of great safety, the carriage of passengers is governed strictly by the national law of a country. It is also for the general welfare and well-being of the fellow passengers and the ship that a passenger is required to be a fit person and must not be a risk aboard. Where the passenger's conduct is anti-law, the master or other authorized officers are usually empowered to take control of him and bring him before a law court. Generally, in the carriage of passengers, the rights and obligations of the parties to the contract of carriage are governed by the law of the country to which they agree. In the absence of such agreement, the intention of the parties is inferred from the circumstances of the contract and there is a prima facie inference that such a contract is governed by the law of the country where the country is entered into. The passenger is required to pay passage money. A ship was captured as a prize and though the passengers were released it was held that the passage money is not payable until the verdict of the court (*Mulloy v. Baker* (1804) 5 East 316). When the passage money becomes payable, the master shall have a lien over the passenger's luggage (*Wolf v. Summers* (1811) 2 Camp 631). When the passage money is paid in advance then it is not recoverable unless the ship is lost before the commencement of the voyage.

§2. Statutory Provisions

539. Sections 219–282 of the MS Act 1958 deal with various aspects of the carriage of passengers, of pilgrims, of their safety and other matters related thereto. No ship is allowed to carry passengers without a certificate of survey. Part VII titled Passenger Ships applies only to sea-going passenger ships fitted with mechanical means of propulsion and the provisions of this Part relating to special trade passenger ships shall not apply to any such ship which is not carrying more than thirty (subs by Act 69 of 1976, section 2 for 'unberthed passenger ships' (w. E. F. 1 December 1976)) or to any such ship not intended to carry to or from any port or place in India (subs. By Act 69 of 1976 section 2 for 'unberthed passengers' (w. E. F. 1 December 1976)). Thus the section declares the above categories of passenger ships as being excepted from the application of Part VII (section 219 as amended 1976). The Central Government also made MS (Form of Passenger ships' Survey certificates) Rules 1964 (Gazette of India dated 11 April 1964, pt. II, section 3(ii), at 629) and also MS (Construction and Survey of Passenger Ships) Rules 1981 (Gazette of India dated 27 July 1981, pt. II, section 3(i), Ext. P. 1362). The statutory provisions relating to the carrying of passengers is enumerated as below.

I. Certificate of Survey

540. It is compulsory for a ship which carries more than twelve passengers within ports and places in India and to any ports or places outside India to have a certificate of survey applicable to the voyage or service which it has undertaken. But a ship which has been granted a certificate under section 235 is exempted from having such a certificate of survey. But if it appears from such a certificate that it is inapplicable to the voyage on which the ship is about to proceed or the service on which she is about to be employed, or there is reason to believe that after the grant of certificate, the ship has sustained some injury or damage or been found unseaworthy or inefficient, then such ship is required to have a certificate of survey. Customs Collector shall not grant a port clearance or assign a pilot to any ship which does not produce a certificate of survey which is required by law to be kept by such ship. Where such ship leaves or attempts to leave any port of survey without a certificate, then the Customs Collector or any pilot on board the ship may detain her until she obtains a certificate (section 220 MS Act).

541. The surveyor of a ship shall be allowed by the owner or agent of every passenger ship to inspect the ship or any part thereof. Such surveyor shall enter the ship for the purpose of making a survey at any reasonable time and shall inspect any part of the ship, machinery, articles on board thereof and shall not unnecessarily hinder the loading or unloading of the ship nor shall it detain or delay it to proceed on the voyage.

542. The owner, agent, master and every officer of the ship shall give all facilities to the surveyor and should also furnish him with all possible information regarding the ship and her machinery and equipment as asked by the surveyor. Before such survey, the owner, agent or master of the ship to be surveyed shall pay to the officer as appointed by the Central Government. Such fee shall be calculated on the tonnage of the ship according to the prescribed rates; and when the survey is to be made in any port of survey other than Bombay, Calcutta or Madras, such additional fee, in respect of the expense if any of the journey of the surveyor to the port as the Central Government may by order directs (sections 221, 222 MS Act).

II. Declaration of the Survey

543. On the completion of the survey and on the full satisfaction of the surveyor, he shall deliver to the owner, agent, or master of the ship surveyed a declaration of the survey in the prescribed form containing the particulars; that the hull and machinery of the ship are sufficient for the service intended and in good conditions; that the equipment of the ship and the certificates of the master, mates, engineers or engine-drivers and of the radiotelegraphy operators are as per the Act; that the time for the hull, machinery and equipment of the ship (if less than one year) will be sufficient; that the ship is fit to ply; that the number of the passengers distributed over being carried on the deck or in the cabins is fit in his opinion. Such declaration, within fourteen days of its receipt, shall be sent by the owner, agent or master of the ship to the Central Government failing which the defaulter shall be liable to pay a penalty of INR 500 for each day of delay and shall pay any sum so forfeited on the delivery of the certificate of survey. On receiving such receipt of declaration of survey, the Central Government shall, through an officer duly appointed for this purpose shall deliver a certificate in duplicate to the owner or agent or master of the ship surveyed on payment of amount if any due as penalty. Such certificate shall be in the prescribed form stating that the related provisions have been complied with (sections 223–225 MS Act).

III. Second Survey

544. Whenever the surveyor refuses to give a declaration of survey or when the owner, agent or master of the ship surveyed is dissatisfied with the declaration, then on an application made by the owner, agent or master the Central Government shall order a second survey on twice the payment of the first survey. The second surveyor shall then make the survey and his decision in this respect shall be final. The certificate of survey shall expire on completion of one year from the date of issue or; when the period is less than one year then on the expiration of the period for which the hull, boilers, engines or any of the equipment have been stated in the certificate to be sufficient or; after receiving notice from the Central Government that such certificate has either been cancelled or suspended. When at the time of the expiry of the certificate the passenger ship is absent from India then it will not be held liable for contravening any provisions of Part VII unless she first begins to ply with passengers after her next return to India (section 227 MS Act).

IV. Cancellation of the Certificate

545. The Central Government may cancel or suspend a certificate of survey if it is satisfied that the declaration by the surveyor of the sufficiency of the hull, boilers, engines or any of equipment of the ship has been fraudulently or erroneously made or that the certificate has been issued upon false or erroneous information. But before making a final decision in this respect the holder of the certificate shall be given a reasonable opportunity to show cause unless the Central Government is of the opinion that it is not reasonably practicable to give such opportunity to the holder of the certificate (section 228 MS Act).

V. Alteration of Ships

546. Whenever there is an alteration in the ship's hull, equipment or machinery which affects the efficiency thereof or the seaworthiness of the ship, the owner, agent or master of the ship shall give written notice to a person duly appointed for this purpose by the Central Government detailing all the alterations. On the satisfaction of the Central Government that such alteration has been made or that the hull, equipment or machinery of the ship has sustained injury or is otherwise insufficient, then it may require the ship to be again surveyed to such extent as necessary and if such requirement is not complied with then it may cancel the certificate of survey. The expired or cancelled certificate shall be delivered to the authorized person. Whenever any certificate has been issued then the owner, agent or master of the ship shall paste a copy of it on some conspicuous part of the ship. No ship shall carry or attempt to carry passengers in contravention of section 220 or violate the given number of passengers. In case such a violation is done by a licensed pilot then his license is liable to be cancelled (sections 228–232 MS Act).

VI. Special Trade and Pilgrim ships

547. The MS Act makes elaborate arrangements for the safety of passenger ships which undertake the task of carrying passengers to a special voyage or to some pilgrim. For this, an amendment is made in section 237 where the term 'special trade passenger ships' is inserted in the section (Subs. By Act 69 of 1976 section 2 for 'unberthed passenger ships' (w. E. F. 1 December 1976)) The section specifically makes it compulsory that any special trade passenger ship or a pilgrim ship shall embark or discharge at such a port in India which is specially appointed for this purpose by the Central Government.

A. Undertaking the Voyage

548. The master, owner or agent of such a ship shall notify the officer specially appointed for this about the proposed time of sailing and about the destination of the ship. In the case of a special trade ship the notice should be given not less than twenty-four hours before the time of sailing and in case of pilgrim ship, at the original port of departure if in India not less than three years and at all other ports not less than twenty-four hours before that time. On receiving such notice the officer shall have authority to enter on the ship and inspect her and her fittings and the provision stores on board. Before sailing, the master of such ship shall hold; a passenger safety certificate, an exemption certificate, a special trade passenger ship safety certificate and a special trade passenger ship space certificate. The Customs Collector shall not give port clearance to a ship unless it holds these certificates.

549. The MS Act requires that out of such certificates there shall be certificate A which would mention the seaworthiness of the ship and a statement to the effect that the ship is properly equipped, fitted and ventilated, the number of passengers which are to be carried by it and certain other particulars. Certificate A shall remain in force for about a year.

B. Journey Safeguards

550. Then the Act also requires that one of the Certificates called Certificate B shall be in the prescribed form and shall contain; the details of the voyage, the name of the intermediate ports, the declaration that it has the proper complement of officers and seamen, a declaration that food, fuel, pure water proper medical facilities, proper protection against weather like substantial bulwarks and a double awning, and so on, have been arranged in the ship for the safety and comfort of the passengers. Certificate B should also contain a statement that the master holds certificate A apart from a passenger ship safety certificate and a nuclear passenger ship space certificate.

551. Sections 241, 242 and 244 are amended in 1976 and they are of a consequential nature. It makes it clear that for the purpose of these sections a nuclear passenger ship safety certificate would in the case of nuclear ships have the same effect as a passenger ship safety certificate would have in the case of non-nuclear passenger ships. An officer specially appointed by the Central Government shall survey the ship and shall give his opinion whether the ship is seaworthy, properly equipped, fitted, well ventilated or not. Such officer may refuse to grant certificate B in case he has reason to believe that the weather conditions are likely to be adverse or that the ship has on board such cargo which may be harmful or injurious to the passengers.

552. The master or any contractor employed for the purpose shall not omit to make the special arrangements for the food, fuel or water and in case of pilgrim ships the prescribed allowances of food and of water for the passengers on board. The ship shall not carry passengers more than the prescribed numbers and in case there are passengers exceeding the number then the authorized officer shall make arrangements for their disembark and may forward them to any port for which they have contracted and shall recover the cost of such forwarding from the master, owner or agent of the ship.

553. Unless required by the perils of the sea or due to some unavoidable accident or unless consent is given in this respect, the master, owner or agent of a ship shall not land any passenger or pilgrim at any port or place other than the one such passenger or pilgrim has contracted for. In case the passenger without his own neglect or default finds himself at any place or port outside India which is also not a place of his destination then the India consular at such port shall forward him to his port of destination. In case within forty-eight hours of the arrival of such passenger the master, owner or agent of the ship gives an undertaking to the consular to forward the passenger within six weeks to his original destination.

C. Steps Taken by Authorities

554. The expenses incurred by the Indian consular in forwarding the passenger shall be considered as a debt due to the Central Government jointly and severally from the owner, charterer, agent and master of the ship. Unless perils of the sea or other unavoidable accident calls for, the master, owner or agent of the ship shall not make the voyage in contravention of the contract.

555. An officer specially appointed on this behalf shall send information to the ports of embarkation and discharge regarding any particulars of the ship regarding the number of passengers and about the compliance of the provisions of the MS Act in this respect regarding the well-being and safety of the passengers. This he will do after making an inspection of the ship. Such report, in any proceeding for the adjudication of any penalty in any judicial court, shall be received as evidence. The master, owner or agent of the ship shall issue an advertisement containing certain details about the date of sailing of the ship and other details connected thereto. The particulars of the ship namely; the name, tonnage and age of the ship, the details about the tickets, and the details about the voyage and the destination should be supplied to the officer who is specially appointed for this purpose. The section deals with the advertising by the master, owner or agent of the ship about the date of sailing, about the price of the tickets which should be within the prescribed limit and the provisional date of sailing from the port or place and also the final date of sailing not less than fifteen days before such date. The section also prohibits the advertising of any ship for the conveyance of pilgrims, or any price of tickets by the master, owner or agent of the ship. The master, owner or agent of the ship shall not omit to supply any important information, without reasonable cause which he is under the law bound to give (section 255).

556. When the ship takes additional passengers at intermediate ports then the master shall obtain from the certifying officer a supplementary certificate stating the number of passengers so taken and that the declaration that food, fuel and pure water over and above what is necessary have been placed on board. The master is required to obtain a fresh certificate B from the certifying officer where after a pilgrim ship has departed or proceeded on her voyage any additional pilgrims are taken on board at a port or place within India appointed under this Part for the embarkation of pilgrims; or if a pilgrim ship upon her voyage touches or arrives at any such port or place and shall make an additional statement specifying the number and the respective sexes of all the additional pilgrims.

The MS Act also requires that the master of a trade passenger ship shall sign a statement in duplicate and shall give full details of all the passengers, including their number, sexes, number of additional passengers if any taken, number of passengers embarked and other details.

1. Death of a Passenger

557. When during a voyage, any passenger on board dies, then it becomes incumbent on the master of such special trade passenger ship or pilgrim ship to make a statement regarding the date and supposed cause of the death and when the ship arrives at such port or place which is in India, then he should produce the statement to the certifying or any other officer appointed on this behalf by the Central Government.

2. Medical Care of Passengers

558. Every special trade passenger ship carrier shall have on board one medical officer as part of her complement when the number of passengers and crew is within one thousand and when such number is more than one thousand, then, in addition to the medical officer, she shall have such number of medical attendants as may be prescribed. Every such ship shall be provided with medical stores and equipment as may be prescribed. Similarly, every pilgrim ship should also have a medical attendant when the number of pilgrims and crew is within one thousand and where the number is more than one thousand then a second medical officer and other medical attendants must be on board. Such medical officer is not to charge any passenger or pilgrim for his services, and he should perform his duties, keep diaries and submit reports and returns as is prescribed by law.

559. Where the special trade passenger ship carries more than one hundred passengers and is on a voyage for more than forty-eight hours, then it shall have a hospital on board offering such conditions relating to security, space, health and sanitation and capable of accommodating such proportion of the maximum number of passengers as the ship is certified to carry (section 269).

3. Passenger Welfare Cess

560. All the passengers are required, as stated in the Official Gazette to pay a Cess on the passage money paid by every passenger carried by special trade passenger ship. The Cess called passenger welfare Cess should not be more than 5% of passage money depending on the different classes of passengers. Such cess when collected by the owner or charterer or by their agent shall be paid to such authority as the Central Government specify. The proceeds of such welfare cess shall be utilized for the purpose of providing amenities to passengers. Special welfare arrangements are made under the MS Act for the comfort of the passengers. Ships going on a voyage for less than seventy-two hours shall provide space for each passenger and where the voyage time exceeds seventy-two hours then bunks should be provided for each passenger. Passengers are also to be provided with open airing space on the deck, day and night and which should not be less than 0.37 sq. m.

4. Bond

561. For the security of the pilgrims on board and for the strict compliance of the provisions of the MS Act the master, owner or agent are required to execute a bond. When the pilgrim ship proceeds on outward voyage then port clearance shall not be given to them unless such bond is produced. The joint or several bond is to be executed by either the master, owner or agent of the ship along with two sureties resident in India in favour of the Central Government, for the sum of INR 10,000 or has given such other guarantee or security as may be acceptable to that Government covering all voyages which may be made by the ship in the current pilgrim season. The bond shall be about the strict compliance of the provisions of the act and the undertaking by the master, owner, or agent to pay any sum which is claimed by the Central Government under the provisions of the act.

5. Medical Inspection of Pilgrims

562. The MS Act makes provisions for the medical inspection of the pilgrims before and after embarkation. Before embarkation, as according to rules prescribed in this respect by the Central Government every pilgrim shall be inoculated against cholera and vaccinated against smallpox and shall carry a certificate to that effect by the medical officer concerned before getting on board. In the opinion of the medical officer if a pilgrim is found to suffer from cholera or choleric indisposition or any dangerously infectious or contagious disease or shows any signs of the same then such pilgrim shall not be permitted to embark. The articles on board used by such pilgrims as found to be suffering from any contagious disease shall be disinfected under the supervision of the medical officer. Where after embarkation any person is found to be suffering from cholera or any dangerously contagious disease then a medical inspection of all persons on board shall be done. In case any person is found to be suffering from any dangerous disease then he shall be at once removed from the ship (sections 271, 272).

563. Pilgrims are also required to board the ship with the return ticket in their possession and or with such amount deposited with the authorized officer to defray the cost of his return ticket. The officer may exempt such pilgrim from the above requirement if he thinks proper. The pilgrim, after making all payments is entitled to have a ticket which he is required to show to the officer when asked for. Such ticket will also entitle the holder to receive food, water, medicine and other amenities on board.

6. Refund

564. Every pilgrim undertaking a voyage as mentioned above is entitled to refund of his passage money when he is prevented from embarking on grounds of illness or being medically unfit. Any pilgrim, within one year of his sailing from India, satisfies to Indian consular officer at Jeddah that he intends to return to India by a route other than the route by which he came from India shall be entitled to a refund of any deposit made by him for defraying the return ticket. On the death of such pilgrim, his representatives would be entitled to such refund. Where any pilgrim fails to return to India within one year from sailing from India or comes to India by any other route then any person nominated by him would be entitled to the refund. Refunds may be subject to certain conditions. Where the refund of passage money remains unclaimed even after the prescribed period then the amount shall be made over to such authority administering any fund maintained for the assistance of pilgrims as the Central Government may specify (section 276).

§3. Liability and Limitation of Liability

565. Though a shipowner is not an insurer of the safety of the passengers yet his responsibility is limited by the terms of the contract of carriage and by his implied undertaking to take all due care including the exercise of reasonable skill and foresight by him. When a passenger is injured due to the negligence of the shipowner or his employees acting within the course of their employment then the liability of the shipowner extends even to a passenger on another ship who may be injured by reason of such negligence (*Mills v. Armstrong, The Bernima* (1888) 13 App Cas 1 (HL)). In the absence of any contract, the shipowner is liable on the basis of negligence and is liable for the luggage of the passenger in the same manner like that of the other carriers. The MS Act in Part VII details out the rules regarding the safety, welfare and security of the special trade passenger ships and pilgrim ships and the liability of the master, owner or agent of the ship in this respect. The act also takes care of the financial security of the pilgrims. For this, the following liability is fixed.

I. Liability Regarding Return Journey

566. The master, owner or agent of every pilgrim ship shall make all arrangements for ensuring the return of all pilgrims in possession of a return ticket issued in India who are carried to the Haj pilgrim by such ship, within a period of ninety days after the Haj day. Where any pilgrim notifies to the authorities his desire to embark for the return journey and due to his inability to obtain accommodation within the period ninety days aforesaid in a ship for which the return ticket is available, detained at Jeddah beyond the said period, then the master, owner or agent of the ship are liable to pay to the Central Government a sum not exceeding double the sum received by the master, owner or agent in respect of the return ticket as the Central Government claims as to the costs of repatriating the pilgrim, together with a sum of INR 5 for each day after the expiry of the period. A certificate of such detention by the Indian consular officer at Jeddah shall be received in any court in India as evidence.

II. Compensation

567. Where the ship fails to proceed from any port or place on the date as advertised for sailing, then the master, owner or agent of the ship are liable to pay as compensation to each pilgrim who has paid his passage money on or before such date the sum of INR 3 for each completed day during which the sailing of the ship is delayed after that date. But such compensation shall not be payable in case the delay is caused not due to the default of the master, owner or agent. Where the compensation has been paid to any pilgrim in respect of delay in the sailing and there is a further delay then the pilgrim is entitled to compensation only in respect of any period by which the duration of such further delay exceeds the duration of the delay in respect of which he has already received or become entitled to compensation. Thus when the ship fails to sail on the advertised date then master, owner or agent shall be bound forthwith to inform the pilgrim officer at the port or place at which the delay occurs of the number of passage tickets. The amount of compensation shall be paid to the pilgrim officer at the port where the delay has occurred and where such officer specifies to the master, owner or agent of the ship the amount payable.

§4. Maritime Security

568. Security assumes great importance in the present global surroundings. It is relevant, important and worthy of attention never as before. Whether land, air or seas, the world is no longer security-proof. Keeping this in mind, suitable amendments are made in the decades-old merchant law in India and the MS Act 1958 (44 of 1958) is passed to update Indian merchant law to include provisions of the International Code for the Security of Ships and Port Facility (ISPS Code). ISPS was introduced as an amendment to the International Convention on Safety of Life at Sea 1974 (SOLAS). Thus the MS (Amendment) Act, 2007 (40 of 2007) is passed which also makes amendments in the Indian Ports Act 1908 (15 of 1908). The Act applies to ships engaged in international carriage, including passenger ships, cargo ships and mobile offshore units, and ports serving such ships. Government can also extend it to the ports that are occasionally required to serve ships on international voyages.

The highlights of the new law are as follows:

- The long title has been amended in which the words 'registration, certification, safety and security' have been substituted for the word 'registration'.
- The word 'security' has been defined as maritime security and includes any measure to protect ports or ships or any person or thing relating to maritime navigation against terrorism, sabotage, stowaways, illegal migrants, asylum seekers, piracy, armed robbery, seizure or pilferage (section 44A MS Act).[48]
- Ship Identification Number (SIN) will now form part of the entries in the Register Book (31(aa) MS Act).
- Seafarers are not to be engaged without identity document (section 99A MS Act).
- Insertion of a new Chapter 9B entitled *Security of Ships and Port Facilities* (section 344 J-344 T MS Act).

I. On the High Seas

569. The new Chapter 9B entitled Security of Ships and Port Facilities the chapter applies to the following types of ships:

(1) Passenger ships including high-speed passenger crafts.
(2) Cargo ships including high-speed crafts of five hundred gross tonnages and above.

48. By virtue of this section, the Director General of Shipping stipulated the security Measures on 5 May 2009 regarding Laning of Fishing Vessel in Major and Non-Major Ports (Nautical Surveyor cum DDG (Tech).

(3) Mobile offshore drilling units. (It can be extended to those ships which are exclusively engaged on coastal voyages.)
(4) The Port facilities serving ships as referred to in section 344J(a).

The Central Government has been authorized under the amendment Act 2007 to set a security level which means the qualification of the degree of risk associated with the threat or unlawful act against a ship, or against a port facility (section 344K(g)); to take proper security measures after taking into consideration the human element, it should provide information to all the Indian ships and to port facilities within India and to every ship before entering any Indian port (section 344M). For identification purposes, every Indian ship of one hundred gross tonnages and above and every Indian cargo ship of three hundred gross tonnages and above shall be given a ship identification number which conforms to the relevant scheme formulated by the IMO by the Central Government or by the authorities concerned (section 344L).

The Government or the authority concerned will issue to every Indian ship an International Ship Security Certificate (ISSC) (section 344Q). Every Indian ship shall be provided with a Ship Security Alert System (section 344R).

To ensure the application of Part IXB, the government is authorized not only to make Rules but also to prescribe control measures (section 344S). For this, it has been made the obligations of companies and Port Facility to comply with the Rules and directions issued by the government (section 344O & 344P).

II. At Ports

570. As a sequel to the security-related legislation, the Indian Ports Act 1908 (Act 15 of 1908) has also been amended in which a port facility in India is made to comply with the Chapter 9B of the MS Act 1958 as amended 2007 (section 68D – Maritime Security – The Indian Ports Act, 1908 (Act 15 of 1908)).

Part III. Other Transport

Chapter 1. Transport by Road

§1. Introduction

571. 2017-2020 can be termed as the watershed years in the history of road development in India. A number of unprecedented innovations are introduced and the government budget towards road construction and upgrading has also been unprecedented. Earlier the Central Road Fund Act 2000 was formulated with the object of having a sustained financial arrangement for the development and maintenance of national highways, state roads, rural roads, construction of overbridges, underbridges, etc. Consequently, the Central Road Fund (State Roads) Rules 2014[49] were made for better utilization of the Central Road Fund in respect of specified projects, schemes and activities relating to development and maintenance of State roads including roads of interstate connectivity and economic importance. No other means of communication make such indenting inroads into the main heartland as the roadways. Roads are the oldest and most popular means of communication and transport anywhere in the world including India. India being predominantly a rural country the roadways have been the lifeline of the common man. Trucks are the main plank of transporting goods even to thousands of km within the country and perishable commodities of daily use like vegetables; milk and fresh fruits are mainly carried by trucks. With the signing of the 1998 Agreement of WP-29 (World Forum for harmonization of vehicles regulations) on 21 April 2006, India entered into a new phase of participation in global norms for road safety and regulations of motor vehicles. It has helped the country to benchmark the safety and convenience of the passengers travelling by road. With the introduction of bus services between Amritsar–Lahore and Amritsar–Nankana Sahib India has crossed national borders by road with all modern amenities. The country has made striking progress in the development of road and transport in the country in the last decade and efforts are in progress to modernize the infrastructure along with modern technology. To enhance transport connectivity in South Asia India was a signatory of the third meeting of SAARC Transport ministers held at New Delhi on 23 November 2010. In the meeting plans were chalked out to have container train run between India and Bangladesh, Ocean Ferry Service covering India, Sri Lanka and the Maldives and the initiatives to implement the intra-regional transport projects were endorsed by the

49. *Vide* G. S. R., 531(E), dated 24 Jul. 2014 published in the Gazette of India, Extra, Pt. II section 3(i), No. 381, dated 24 Jul. 2014 and which came into force on 24 Jul. 2014.

representatives of SAARC countries. While making certain improvements within the country in the area of RT the Department of Road, RT and Highways also addressed the transport concerns like congestion on roads, environmental impact, ageing infrastructure, changing demographics and the climate factor. For this, international cooperation was sought and the country signed various MoU with the foreign countries. These are:

- On 10 May 2010, a Memorandum of Cooperation was signed between the Transport representatives of the Republic of Finland and the Government of India in the field of RT.
- On 27 September 2010, an MoU was signed between the Government of the United Kingdom of Great Britain and Northern Ireland on Cooperation in the RT and Road Sector.
- On 21 December 2010, an MoU was signed between the Government of Malaysia and the Government of India on cooperation relating to the provision of technical assistance services and highways management and development.

572. Information Technology has also hit Indian roads with the introduction of issuing smart card-based driving licenses (DL) and registration certificates (RC). This step is already taken in the four states of Delhi, West Bengal, Jharkhand and Tripper. The developmental efforts have been eco-friendly and road safety has been elevated to number one position in all considerations regarding roads as the Road Safety Week from 1–7 January 2007 had the theme of 'Road Safety is Life Safety' and was observed nationally and the Road Safety was reiterated in the Road Safety Week held again from 1–7 January 2011 in which the theme was 'Road Safety is a Mission, Not an Intermission'.

573. The Energy and Resources Institute (TERI) recommended the establishment of a separate body on road safety and traffic management. The main legislation, an archaic law; the Carriers Act 1865 which has governed the transportation by road in India for more than a century was a subject of criticism in legal circles on the ground of being outdated that being more than a century old law, discrepancies and anomalies hampered its proper implementation in modern surroundings. The following can be enumerated as the reasons behind bringing a new Act:

- The Carriers Act 1865 was originally enacted to cover various means of transportation which have now separate enactments like the Railways (The Railways Act 1989) hence it was necessary to have a separate law for the RT.
- The Carriers Act 1865 became insufficient to deal with the complexity and sophistication of the modern world.

In the modern transportation system middlemen like brokers and agents emerged which were hitherto uncovered by the Carriers Act 1865.

- The liability of the common carrier was grossly inadequate under the Carriers Act (INR 100) which also demanded a change.

- Thus a new legislation to replace it was tabled in the Upper House of the Parliament in December 2005 titled Carriage by Road Act 2005. The Bill was referred to the Parliamentary Standing Committee on Transport, Tourism and Culture which made some recommendations. The Bill ultimately saw the light of the day in the form of The Carriage by Road Act 2007 (41 of 2007) (hereinafter called the 'Act of 2007') when it received the assent of the President of India on 29 September 2007.[50]

– *Introduction to the Act of 2007*

The newly introduced Act is a long-awaited one and replaces the Carriers Act 1865 (section 22). There were many legal hassles in its way of implementation but at last, it became active on 28 February 2011. By virtue of section 20 of the Act, the Carriage by Road Rules 2011 has been made by the Central Government which ultimately tighten the legal noose around transporters. So far 75%–80% of the goods transported originated from the Small & Medium Enterprises (SME). Thc Act of 2007 is an epoch-making one in as much as it deliberates largely on the liability of the carrier and it brings standardization and accountability to the RT industry in India.[51] The highlights of the said Act are as follows:

- The Act of 2007 defines the relation between all parties, from the consignor to the booking agent.
- The Act ensures statistical reporting in the transport sector by transporters and intermediaries and by other persons involved in the transportation business.
- It provides for the registration of common carriers.
- The aim of the Act is to regulate common carriers, to limit their liability regarding loss of or damage to goods caused by their negligent or criminal act.
- It has a provision for penalizing the defaulting transporter.
- It has the effect of bringing all the units of the transport industry within the Tax Net.
- It also initiates the onset of the General Sales Tax (GST) regime that the State plans to activate in 2012.
- It gives rule-making power to the Government so as to make it suitable for the changing demands of the transport industry.
- It abrogates the Carriers Act 1865.

By virtue of the power conferred by section 20 of the Carriage by Road Act 2007 (41 of 2007), the Government of India made the Carriage by Road Rules 2011[52] to supplement the said Act.

50. *The Gazette of India*, Extraordinary, Part II –s. I, New Delhi. Monday, 1 Oct. 2007/ASVINA 9, 1929. Registered No. DL-(N) 04/0007/2003-07.
51. Amarnani Shalini, *Road Transport to be More Accountable* (India Transport Portal – India's Transport News and Analysis, 25 Mar. 2011).
52. *Vide* G. S. R. 176 (E), dated 28 Feb. 2011, published in the *Gazette of India*, Extra, Part. II, s. 3(i), dated 1 Mar. 2011 read with Corrigendum G. S. R. 205(E), dated 10 Mar. 2011. The Rules came into force on 1 Mar. 2011.

Apart from the above important legislation, the transport industry is also regulated by the RT Corporations Act 1950 (which is mainly a law to regulate RT corporations) and the Motor Vehicles Act 1988. Steps are being taken by the Government to revise this law. A Committee in the month of June 2009 proposed certain amendments in the said Motor Vehicles Act 1988 to meet modern-day requirements and to construct it on the pattern of best vehicular practices of countries like China, Japan, and so on. The Committee submitted its report on 2 February 2011 and which is under consideration by the Government.

§2. Liability of the Carrier under General Law

574. A carrier is a person who transports goods from place to place by land or inland navigation under a multimodal transport document or under a contract. All carriers by land except railways come under the definition of common carriers. Thus a steamship company carrying goods by river is a carrier, a licensee of a ferry, a person carrying goods from a jetty to a ship, or the owner of a public lorry are all common carriers. Common carriers are now rare. Due to their strict position nowadays the carriers disown the title of common carriers in their contracts and courts also show the tendency of not considering a carrier as a common carrier. However, the common carriers are not extinct. But this position existed in The Carriers Act 1865 as based on the common law of England which aims to fix the liability of carriers and is now repealed and instead The Carriage by Road Act 2007 (Act 41 of 2007) now defines common carrier as a person who is engaged in the business of collecting, storing, forwarding or distributing goods which are carried by goods carriages under a receipt. It also includes a person who transports for hire of goods from one place to another through any motorized transport on road and includes goods booking company, contractor, agent, broker and courier agency engaged in the door to door transportation of documents or goods which utilizes the services of a person to carry goods. The definition excludes 'government' from its purview (section 2(a)).

Registration Law

However, the new Act makes it compulsory for all the persons who are engaged in the business of common carriers to get themselves registered.[53] (section 3) This is the hallmark of the Act of 2007 and it deals elaborately with the registration of common carriers. It also sets the procedure for grant or renewal of registration by the issuance of appropriate certificate for carrying on the business of common carrier. Such registration can be done in any one state of India and its validity period will be one year (section 4). However, the registration shall be done on certain conditions and if the incumbent does not comply with or violates such conditions then

53. The registration has to take place within ninety days from the date of commencement of the Carriage by Road Act 2007(41 of 2007).

his registration will be suspended or cancelled (section 5; the Carriage by Road Act 2007). Non-registration or carrying of dangerous or hazardous goods is made a punishable offence[54] (section 18).

The Act of 2007 also makes it for the first time the submission of annual return by the State Transport Authority in each State or Union territory to the Ministry or Department of the Central Government dealing with RT and highways. This is a new provision which is for statistical purposes.

The Act not only protects the interest of the consignor it also limits the liability of the carriers who ran great risk while carrying bulky goods and were unable to convince the consignor regarding the limits of their liability. The common carrier is made to follow the Rules[55] while carrying goods of dangerous and hazardous nature and the consignor is also to indicate the details of the goods in the goods forwarding note.

I. Liability of the Carrier

575. Every carrier is liable for loss of or damage to any property delivered to him for carriage purposes. There has been a sea change in matters of liability of the common carrier under the new The Carriage by Road Act 2007 though in some respects it corresponds to section 3 and some other provisions of the Carriers Act 1865. However, the liability of the common carrier under the erstwhile and present law is drastically different as follows:

The Carriers Act 1865	*The Carriage by Road Act 2007*
1. Compensation was not limited to multiples of freight.	1. Compensation is increased to ten times the freight charges.
2. Compensation was according to value of goods as declared.	2. Compensation can never exceed the value of goods.
	3. Transporter must register themselves and if fail to pay twelve times the freight charge their license will be suspended for a week.
	4. The Act also fixes the liability of the carrier in case of delay as agreed upon between himself and the carrier.

54. The punishment is pecuniary one entailing a fine of INR 5,000 for the first offence and for the second or subsequent offence the fine may extend to INR 10,000 (s. 18(1) the Carriage by Road Act 2007).

55. A common carrier should comply with the procedure and safeguards specified under Rules 130,131,132,133,134,135,136 and 137 of the Central Motor Vehicles Rules, 1989 (Rule 12(1), the Carriage by Road Rules, 2011).

There is a provision (like the Carriers Act 1865, section 4)) that the carrier has to follow a procedure for payment of higher risk rate for undertaking higher risk goods (section 11, Carriage by Road Act 2007). The common carrier would be liable to the consignor for the loss or damage on account of his criminal act. He would be liable to compensate the consignor and that the onus of proving the negligence or criminal act of the common carrier would not be on the plaintiff. However, if any consignment goods which have been detected by the competent authority (The *Explanation* to section 12 clarifies that any person who is authorized to examine the goods under the law is a competent authority) and regarding which the consignor in his forwarding note has made a description (Non-disclosure of the special nature of goods may be taken to be fraud on the part of the consignor in which case he is not entitled to get the price of the goods (*River Steam Navigation Co. v. Jamnadas Ram Kumar* AIR 1932 Cal 344) then the common carrier shall be exonerated from liability if such goods are found to be of prohibited nature (section 12, Carriage by Road Act 2007).

Liability in respect of goods hazardous to human life

The Act has been stringent in respect of carriage of goods which are hazardous to human beings. This arises from increased risk to national safety in the background of sabotaging activities. The Central Government has been empowered to declare in public interest, the goods or class of goods which are listed as prohibited for carriage (section 14, The Carriage by Road Act 2007). The common carrier is not to accept the goods dangerous for human life except in accordance with the prescribed procedure. The Act also provides for the insurance of such hazardous goods before they are accepted for movement and a list of such goods to be displayed on the motor vehicle itself (section 13, The Carriage by Road Act 2007).

Limit of Liability

The liability of the common carrier in case of loss or damage to the consignment is limited to ten times the freight paid or payable. The amount shall be calculated by Government approved valuer or surveyor but it should not exceed the value of the goods as declared in the forwarding note.

The delivery of the consignment to the consignee shall be prima facie evidence of delivery unless the consignee in written form notifies the common carrier about the general nature of loss or damage to the consigned goods.

The common carrier is under obligation to ensure that in case of a vehicle carrying or meant to carry dangerous or hazardous goods that such goods are insured under the Public Liability Insurance Act 1991 (6 of 1991). In case of any loss or damage to the consigned goods the limit of the monetary liability shall be of the following extent depending on the nature of goods consigned:

- *Common Goods*: In case of partial damage or loss to the goods evaluation shall be done by a Government approved valuer or surveyor.
- *Documents*: In case of loss of documents sent along with consignment order the liability shall not exceed INR 500.
- *Perishable Goods*: In case of perishable goods the consignor or consignee should, within twenty-four hours of the report of loss or deterioration of the goods select

the Government approved valuer failing which the common carrier shall be free to select his own valuer to assess the quantum of loss and the extent of liability shall be vis-à-vis such evaluation.

II. Duties of Carrier

576. The liability of the carrier arises from his duties which are; to accept and carry the goods as per his contract and the duty to deliver the goods at the destination in the same condition as they were handed over to him at the time of consignment. Normally a carrier cannot refuse to accept goods for carriage except in very rare cases where there is extraordinary risk involved due to the nature of the goods or when it is beyond his professional potency to deliver the goods at the required destination. Through judicial pronouncements, there are many duties which are being attached to the carrier and the violation of which give rise to liability. Thus a carrier has a duty to follow the instructions of the consignor as regarding the goods and the delivery of goods; there is a duty to deliver within reasonable time; duty to not to deviate; duty to deliver goods against documents only and there is duty under emergency to take a decision in respect of the goods in order to save them from spoiling. In fact, a common carrier is regarded as the insurer of goods and thus either the delivery of goods or their compensation is the only option before a carrier. Before delivering the goods the carrier is under strict obligation to see that it is being delivered to the rightful person and must inquire satisfactorily about the reliability of the person who presents the consignor's note for receiving delivery.

III. Principle of Absolute Liability

577. The liability of the common carrier under the Carriers Act 1865 was stringent and his liability was not regarded as a bailee of goods but his liability can be described as absolute and statutory not arising out of any contract (*Irrawady Flotilla Co. Ltd v. Bugwandas* (1891) 18 1A 121, PC: 18 Cal 620). India closely follows the English law in which it is ruled that the liability is so absolute that even in the case of theft 'a common carrier must make good the loss though even robbed' (*Gibbon v. Paynton* (1769) 4 Bur 2298:98 ER 199). It is held that the carrier must treat the consigned goods as his own and he is liable for loss or damage caused due either to the negligence or criminal act of either himself or that of his agent or servant. The court refused to accept the plea that the goods were destroyed in a fire in spite of taking good care and held that the duty of a carrier under the Carriers Act 1865 is different from the duty of a bailee under the Indian Contract Act 1872 (*Nath Bros. Exim International Ltd v. Best Roadways Ltd* (2000) 4 SCC 553). This ruling was again followed where short delivery of coconut was pleaded to be excused on the ground of some accident. The court also refused the plea that the consignment was being carried on the consignor's risk (*South Eastern Carriers P. Ltd v. Oriental Fire & General Insurance Co.* AIR 2004 Ker 139). However, such absolute liability has undergone a change under the new law and now it is based on rationality.

IV. Exceptions

578. Though the liability of the carrier is said to be absolute yet it cannot be limited by a special contract except for non-scheduled goods. There are certain factors which stand as an exception to the general rule. These factors so far were mainly developed by the Indian courts on the pattern of English law but now they stand statutory under the Carriage by Road Act 2007. On the basis of judicial pronouncements, the Carriage by Road Act 2007 has now subsumed most of these factors. Thus liability of the carrier is excused when the damage or loss to the consigned goods is caused by an act of God. The term 'act of God' was strictly construed to mean any natural or divine happening without the agency of the human hand (*RRN Ramalinga v. Narayana* AIR 1971 Ker 197). Loss caused by the act of national enemies is considered as a ground to exempt the carrier from his liability. There being any inherent defect in the goods and the loss or damage being caused thereby absolves the carrier from his liability. When goods are improperly packed and thus they are lost or damaged for that reason only then the carrier can set up this as a defence to excuse him from liability. Again the carrier may be excused from his liability towards the consigned goods if the consignor who is under obligation to disclose the peculiar or dangerous nature of goods does not do so (in such a case it is the consignor who should compensate the carrier should such goods cause any harm to the carrier). Where the consignor does not give proper address of the place for delivery of goods then the consignor cannot be held liable for non-delivery or late delivery. Again when the goods are accepted by the carrier at 'owner's risk' then it exonerates the carrier from his liability provided any loss or damage caused to such goods is not caused by the negligence or criminal act of either himself or by that of his agent or servant. Presently the liability of the common carrier is limited by the following conditions.

Force Majeure Conditions:

> Though the law imposes stringent liability on the common carrier yet there are a number of such force majeure or necessary conditions which exonerate the common carrier from liabilities so imposed. These conditions are: act of God, acts of war or public enemy, riots and civil commotion, arrest, restraint or seizure under legal process and order or restriction or prohibition imposed by the Central or State Government or by persons authorized by such Government (section 17, Carriage by Road Act 2007). However, the exoneration clause is conditional upon the fact that such loss or destruction or non-delivery is not the result of the conduct of the common carrier and that the common carrier exercised due diligence and care in the carriage of the consignment (Proviso to section 17, Carriage by Road Act 2007).

V. Commencement and Duration of Liability

579. The Liability of the carrier begins the moment the goods are accepted for transit either by the carrier himself or by his agent. An implied acceptance takes place when the carrier instructs the consignor to leave the goods at a certain place awaiting transit. In such a case the carrier is liable if any loss occurs though the goods are not transited. The carrier's liability continues until he delivers the goods to the destined place of delivery at the given time. It is the job of the carrier to undertake all pains to see that goods are transited in proper condition at the proper time and place. However, if the consignor himself undertakes to receive delivery of goods at a given place and time and fails to appear at the place within a reasonable time then the carrier is held not liable. The Carriage by Road Act 2007 explicitly explains the commencement and duration of liability of the common carrier. The liability of the common carrier shall be only for the transit period from the date of taking over the goods in his or her charge from the consignor to the date of arrival at the destination point plus three calendar days. The date of arrival of the consignment shall be taken as the day on which the goods physically arrive at the destination or the day when the consignee or consignor is informed of the arrival of the goods whichever is later (section 12(7) Carriage by Road Act 2007).

§3. Liability of the Carrier under the CMR Convention

580. The Convention on the Contract for the International Carriage of Goods by Road (CMR) was held in Geneva on 19 May 1956. It was held with the object of standardizing the conditions governing the contract for the international carriage of goods by road regarding the documents used in such contracts and regarding the carrier's liability. The Convention is applied when in the contract the consignment and delivery take place in two different countries one of these being the contracting party. It, however, gives no importance to the nationality of the parties and includes the carriage carried out by States or by governmental institutions or organizations.

I. The Consignment Note: Waybill

581. The contract of carriage under the CMR is confirmed by a consignment though the absence or irregularity of the consignment shall not affect the contract and shall continue to be guided by the CMR provisions. The consignment note which is the prima facie evidence of the contract of carriage is prepared in three original copies signed by the sender and by the carrier which may be printed or have stamps of the sender if the law of the country so requires and are given to the sender and carrier of the goods while the third copy accompanies the goods. Where the goods are transited by different vehicles, are in different kinds or are sent in different lots then if the sender or carrier so desire each of these vehicles, lots or kinds may have a separate consignment note.

582. Such consignment note shall contain; the date and place of the consignment, the name and address of the sender and the carrier and the consignee, the place and date of booking of the goods and the place of delivery, the disclosure regarding nature, and way of packing the goods, the number of packages including their special marks and numbering, the gross weight of the goods or their quantity, charges relating to the carriage, the requisite instructions for Customs and other formalities and a statement declaring that the carriage is subject to the Convention (Article 6 paragraph 1). It is, however, optional to declare in the consignment note, a statement that transshipment is not allowed, the charges to be paid by the sender, the amount of 'cash on delivery' charges a declaration regarding the value of the goods, instruction regarding the insurance of the goods, the time limit of the carriage, and a list of the documents handed to the carrier (Article 6 paragraph 2).

II. Rights and Obligations

583. Under a contract of carriage, the contracting parties shall have rights and obligations as follows.

A. Carrier

584. In case the sender asks the carrier to enter in the consignment note the particulars related to the name and address of the sender and the consignee, the date and place of delivery of goods, a disclosure regarding the nature of the goods, their packaging, and so on, then such declarations would be deemed to be done by the sender. Where the consignment note does not contain the statement that the contract shall be subject to the provisions of the Convention then the carrier is held liable for all expenses, loss and damage sustained due to such omission. It is the duty of the carrier to check the accuracy of the statements in the consignment note, the apparent conditions of the goods and their packaging, and so on. In case the carrier fails to check the nature of the goods due to lack of reasonable means to do so or if he has some reservations regarding the goods then he is required to insert it in the consignment note. However, the sender is bound by such reservations only if he expressly agrees to them. When the carrier is asked by the sender to make certain checks regarding the goods, then he is entitled to get the cost of such checking from the sender. The liability of the carrier arising from the inaccuracies or incorrect use of the document shall be that of an agent and compensation paid by him shall be less than the amount of that which would be payable in case of loss of the goods. Where the carrier is unable to carry out the new instructions given in the first copy of the consignment then he is required to inform the person who has given the instructions to him. If the carrier does not carry out the instructions then he becomes liable to the person who has a right to make a claim for any loss or damage caused thereby. If for some reason it becomes impossible to carry out the contract in accordance with the terms of the consignment note then the carrier should seek instructions from the person entitled to dispose of the goods. However, if the contract can be carried out, though not strictly according to the original terms, and the carrier is unable to obtain instructions, then he should act on his own and shall take such steps which would be in the best interest of the person entitled to dispose of the goods (Article 14). Where the carrier is unable to deliver the goods as per contract then he should seek the instructions of the sender and if the consignee refuses the goods the sender shall be able to dispose of them without producing the first copy of the consignment note. The carrier is also entitled to recover the cost of his request for instructions provided such expenses were not the result of his wrongful or negligent act. The carrier shall unload the goods for the person who has a right to dispose them off and with that, the carriage shall come to an end. The carrier shall then entrust the goods to the third party and would exercise reasonable care regarding the goods. In case the goods are of perishable nature or the storage expenses are too much, then the carrier, without waiting for the instructions from the sender, shall himself dispose them off. In case no instruction is received from the rightful person then the carrier shall himself sell off the goods after a reasonable period of time. When such sale takes place then the proceeds of the sale shall be kept for the rightful person and if there is any excess amount then the carrier is entitled to it. The sale shall be determined by the law or custom of the place where it takes place (Article 16).

B. Sender

585. The sender shall be responsible for all expenses, loss and damage sustained by the carrier where the sender has committed a mistake or has omitted to write something regarding the name and address of the sender and the consignee, date and place of delivery of goods, a disclosure regarding the nature of the goods, the number and description of the package and gross weight of the goods, and the required instruction for customs and other formalities. He is also responsible for committing any mistake regarding the optional declarations made in the consignment note. The sender has a right to ask the carrier to check the gross weight and the contents of the goods and shall not be liable for any loss or damage or for any expenses due to defective packing of the goods in case the carrier omits to make any reservations regarding them at the time of accepting the goods (Article 10). To make a convenient delivery the sender is under duty to attach all the necessary documents to the consignment and shall furnish him with all the information which the carrier would be needing at the time of delivery and he should also see that such documents are without mistakes failing which he shall be liable to the carrier in case any loss or damage is suffered thereby. The sender has a right to dispose of the goods by asking the carrier to stop the goods in transit, alter the place of delivery, change the consignee. After this, the consignee shall take over and the carrier comes under his orders.

C. Consignee

586. The consignee is entitled to require the carrier to deliver the goods to him on production of the receipt or the second copy of the consignment note. The consignee may also have the right of disposal of the goods from the time when the consignment note was drawn if it is so declared by the sender. The consignee can, in the exercise of his right of disposal order the delivery of the goods to another person who shall not have the right to name other consignees. The exercise of the right of disposal shall be subject to the condition that the sender or the consignee produces the first copy of the consignment note containing new instructions to the carrier and indemnifies the carrier against all expenses, loss and damage involved in carrying out such instructions; that such instructions do not interfere with the normal working of the carriers' undertaking or prejudice the senders or consignees of other consignments and that; the instructions do not cause a division in the consignment. Where the delivery does not take place due to the loss of goods or if the goods do not arrive even after the expiry of the scheduled time –limit (As given in Article 19) then the consignee becomes entitled to enforce in his own name against the carrier any rights arising from the contract of carriage and shall then be liable to pay the charges as mentioned in the consignment note. The consignee has the right to take delivery of the goods even though he has refused them once if till that moment the carrier has not received any instruction from the sender.

III. Liability of the Carrier

587. Liability of the carrier begins at the time he accepts the goods until he makes the delivery to the one who is entitled to take whether on time or after delay. Liability extends to the total or partial loss of the goods or damage caused thereto (Article 17).

A. *Presumption of Fault*

588. Where the carrier establishes that the loss or damage to the goods was caused due either to the instructions given by the sender or due to the defective packing, or due to the way the handling or loading is done by the sender or his agent, or due to the nature of the goods (Article 17 paragraph 4) then it will be presumed that the loss or damage was so caused. There shall be a presumption of fault against the carrier when the use of unsheeted vehicles led to an abnormal shortage or loss of any package or the loss occurred even though especially equipped vehicles were used. But there shall be no presumption of fault against him if the carrier is able to prove that the loss occurred in spite of taking all reasonable steps to maintain the equipment (Article 18).

B. *Exoneration of Liability*

589. The carrier is relieved of the liability if the loss, damage or delay was caused by the wrongful act or neglect of the claimant, or by the instructions of the claimant, or by the inherent vice of the goods or due to such circumstances which could not be avoided or prevented by the carrier. Thus where on the instructions unsheeted vehicles are used, when there is defective packing of goods and when they are inadequately marked, when the handling loading, stowage or unloading is done by the sender or anyone acting on his behalf when the nature of the goods is such which renders damage or partial or total loss of the goods by breakage, rust, decay, desiccation, leakage, normal wastage, or the action of moth or vermin, and when there is carriage of livestock then the carrier is exonerated from liability provided he himself discharged his own duties to take care of the consigned goods (Article 17). The carrier is not relieved of liability if he uses a defective vehicle or hires one and the loss or damage is caused by the neglect or wrongful act of such person or by his agent or servant unless he himself contributes, to the loss or damage caused to the consigned goods where such loss is caused due to some act of the sender.

C. Sharing of Liability Between the Claimant and the Carrier

590. When the claimant receives the compensation for the missing goods then he can make a written request that in case the goods are recovered within one year then he should be notified. If such notification is received, then within thirty days of it, he may ask for the delivery of the goods on payment of the charges given in the consignment note and he should also refund the compensation. But such payment shall not affect the compensation which is received by him for the delay in delivery either under Article 23 or 26 of the Convention. Where the claimant fails to give notification for delivery of lost goods if they are recovered within a year or when he fails to ask for the delivery of goods within thirty days as mentioned above and they are not recovered even after a year of payment of compensation then the carrier gets the right to dispose of the goods in accordance with the law. The carrier shall also be liable to the sender in case he fails to collect cash from the consignee as per the contract to compensate him up to the amount of charge. The carrier shall have a right to unload, destroy or render harmless any such dangerous goods, the nature of which was not disclosed to him by the sender and need not compensate the sender. The sender shall be liable for all expenses incurred by the carrier in handling such dangerous goods. The liability of the carrier in respect of the total or partial loss of goods is calculated with reference to the value of the goods prevailing at the place and time where the goods were accepted for carriage. The value of the goods is fixed with reference to either the commodity exchange price or current market price or according to the normal value of the goods but which should not exceed 25 francs per kg of gross weight, the sender can on payment of a surcharge declare the value of the goods exceeding this limit. In case of a total loss of goods, the carrier is liable to refund even the custom duties and other expenses in respect of carriage of goods. Where damage results from delay then the carrier is liable to pay compensation for damage not exceeding the carriage charges. The carrier is liable to pay higher charges according to the value of the goods declared and where a special interest in the delivery has been shown by the sender on payment of a surcharge. Where the goods have been damaged then the carrier shall be liable for the amount by which the goods have diminished in value, calculated with reference either to the exchange price or current market price or according to the normal value of the goods and where the customs duties and other charges must also be considered. In such a case the compensation should, however, not exceed the amount payable in case of total loss and the amount payable in the case of loss of the part affected. The sender can also declare special interest in delivery and in case of loss or damage caused to such goods the compensation amount shall be declared in the consignment note. Compensation up to the total amount of interest declared can also be claimed irrespective of the compensation provided as per the market value of the goods, the amount exceeding the prescribed limit of 25 francs and the amount by which the goods have diminished in value. The claimant shall be entitled to claim interest on the amount of compensation which is calculated at 5% per annum and which shall accrue from the date on which the written claim was sent to the carrier and if no such claim is made from the date of institution of legal proceedings. If such amount is not mentioned in the currency of the country in which payment is claimed the conversion rate of exchange shall be such as prevailing at the place of payment of compensation. In case of an extra-contractual claim, the carrier or the persons to whom the carrier is liable may avail such provisions of the Convention which exclude their liability or which fix or limit the compensation due. However, if the damage was caused by the wilful misconduct or default of the carrier or of his agent or servant then he will not be allowed to benefit from the provisions of the Convention (Articles 20–28).

IV. Time Limits for Complaint and Action

591. If within thirty days of the date of delivery or if within sixty days since the goods were accepted for carriage, the goods are not delivered then it will be taken as lost (Article 20). The consignee has a time limit to register his reservations regarding the loss of goods or delay in delivery. Thus, when the loss is apparent then the consignee should have expressed his reservations at the time of delivery, and if the loss is not apparent then within seven days of delivery excluding Sundays and public holidays and the date of delivery. In cases where the goods are found damaged even after the checking then any objection challenging the result of such checking shall be admissible in evidence only if the written reservations were sent to the carrier within seven days of checking excluding Sundays and public holidays and the date of checking. As for the delay of delivery, a reservation should be sent to the carrier within twenty-one days of putting the goods at the disposal of the consignee excluding the date of such disposal (Article 30).

592. As for bringing action in law in any court or tribunal the time limit is one year. In the matter of wilful misconduct or default, the period of limitation is three years depending on the law of the court or tribunal. Such limitation shall start in case of partial loss, damage or delivery from the date of delivery; in case of total loss from the thirtieth day after the expiry of the time limit if any and from the sixtieth day from the date on which the goods were taken by the carrier. In the rest of the cases, the period of limitation shall start from the expiry of three months from the making of the contract excluding the date of start of a period of limitation. A claim can suspend the period of limitation up to such a date as the carrier rejects the claim by a written notification. The extension of the period of limitation depends upon the law of the court or tribunal where the case is pending.

V. Jurisdiction of Courts

593. An action can be brought regarding the disputes related to the carriage under the Convention, in any court or tribunal of a contracting party as agreed in the agreement or in the courts of tribunals of a country within whose territory the defendant ordinarily resides, or has a principal place of business or where the branch of the agency is situated, or either at the place of acceptance of goods for carriage or at the place where delivery was destined. In this respect, no new action is permissible if the matter is already pending in a court or has been decided by it in any of such places unless the judgment of such court or tribunal is devoid of enforcement in such place. The judgment becomes enforceable in such country and in the Contracting States, after completing the formalities if it is a judgment after trial or judgments by default or settlements confirmed by an order of the court but shall not be so enforceable if it is an interim judgment or for award of damages or for costs against the plaintiff.

Chapter 2. Transportation by Rail

§1. STATUTORY PROVISIONS: LEGISLATION

594. Railway lines appeared on the Indian map in 1849 when the then East India Company undertook the construction of railways. Within two decades the isolated lines started developing into a network and from 1869 onwards the spread of railway lines became mentionable though the work was mainly undertaken by private companies. The Indian Railways Act 1989 was the pioneer legislation governing the railways in India. The Act was amended several times but with the mammoth expansion of the railway network and it becoming part of the Government of India undertaking a need was badly felt for a law which should be more responsive to the modern requirements of changing times. The idea was slated in 1986 and consequently, after hectic legislative activity, the Railways Act 1989 was passed which replaced the Act of 1890. The Act mainly aimed at; constitution of new railways zones; empowering the Central Government to fix the rates for the carriage of passengers and goods by railways; to ensure statutory recognition of the railways receipt as a negotiable instrument; limiting the monetary liability of railway administration regarding payment of compensation for loss, damage, and so on, of goods; and the rationalizing and inclusion of certain offences in the Act. With all such objectives, the Bill was passed and it became law on 1 July 1990. The Act has since been amended in 1994, twice in 2003 and lastly in 2005.

595. The liability of a carrier as recognized under the Carriers Act 1865 is not extended to the Railways. Based on English law the Carriage Act 1865 thus excludes Railways from the term ‘common carrier’ and regards it as a bailee which meant to absolve the Railways from the basic liability of a common carrier (*Choggalal v. Secretary of State* AIR 1933 Nag 261).

§2. THE CIV: CONVENTION (PASSENGER AND THEIR LUGGAGE)

596. The Uniform Rules Concerning the Contract for International Carriage of Passengers and Luggage By Rail (CIV) as formulated in the Convention concerning International Carriage by Rail (COITF) of 9 May 1980 regulate all carriage of passengers and luggage including motor vehicles, under international transport documents made out for a journey over the territories of at least two States and exclusively over lines or services included in the list provided for in Articles 3 and 10 of the Convention. They also apply to carriage treated as carriage over a line. The Rules also cover the liability of the railways in case of death or personal injury to passengers and also to persons accompanying a consignment.

I. Exceptions from Scope

597. The Uniform Rules shall not apply to carriage between stations situated in the same State and only passes through the territory of another State: if the lines or services on such territory through which transit takes place is operated by the State of departure or; if both the States have mutually agreed not to regard the carriage as international. Where carriage takes place between stations in two States or two adjacent States and the transit takes place through the territory of a third State then if any one of the States regulates the entire carriage and there is nothing contradictory in the laws of these States then it will be governed by internal traffic regulations of the railway which operates the carriage exclusively.

II. Liability Towards Passengers

598. The provisions regarding liability of the railways in the event of death, personal injury to passengers may be restrained by a State the nationals or residents of which are involved in the accident. This can be done by the State at the time of signing the Convention or at the time of depositing its instrument of ratification, acceptance, approval or accession. The reservation so made can be withdrawn by the State by informing the Depository Government and it shall take place a month after the Swiss Government has notified it to the Member States.

III. Obligation to Carry

599. The Railways is under obligation to carry the passengers and luggage as per Uniform Rules if; the passenger complies with the Uniform Rules, supplementary provisions and the international tariffs; where the carriage can be undertaken by normal staff and transport resources; and the carriage is not prevented by such circumstances which are unavoidable for the railway. The discontinuance or suspension of the service shall be notified to the public and to the railway which shall then inform the railway of another State.

IV. Tariffs, Private Agreements

600. The international tariffs shall contain all the special conditions applicable to carriage including the information regarding calculation of fares and charges and also the conditions necessary for the conversion of currencies and should not derogate from the Uniform Rules. The conditions for the application of international tariffs to all users must be uniform. Railways may also enter into private agreements for reduced fares and charges and it can also grant reductions in fares and charges for the purpose of railways, or for public services, charitable or instructional purposes. Publication of international tariffs is compulsory in those states which are parties to such tariffs and shall be effective on the date of publication and in case of any hike in the fares and charges it shall become effective after six days of its publication. Other modifications in fares and charges shall be effective from the date of publication. The prices for international tickets and luggage charges should be displayed for public view on every station of international traffic.

V. Unit of Account Rate of Exchange

601. The unit of account as given in the Uniform Rules shall be the SDRs as defined by the IMF. The value in SDRs of the Member State of the IMF shall be calculated in accordance with the method applied by the IMF while in the case of a non-Member State the method of calculation shall be decided by the state but which should be as closer to the method applied by the IMF. Where in a non-Member State none of the foregoing rules applies, the unit of account as referred to in the Uniform Rules shall be deemed to be equal to 3 francs gold which is defined as 10/31 of a gram of gold of millesimal fineness 900. The conversion so reached must be as close to the one as reached according to the method applied by the IMF. Every time a change occurs in the method of calculation or in the value of the national currency in relation to a unit of account the States should notify the Central Office which shall notify it further to the States concerned. The Railways should also publish the rate of conversion of foreign currencies and also the rate of acceptance. Two or more States may make supplementary provisions to execute the Uniform Rules but which should not derogate from them and must be published as per the laws of their own country and should notify the Central Office. Where the Uniform Rules are silent and a situation arises, then the national law of the State in which the claimant asserts his rights and the rules relating to conflict of laws should apply. For the application of provisions relating to the liability of the railways in matters of death or personal injury to the passengers, the national law of that State shall apply where the accident happened.

§3. CIM: Convention (Carriage of Goods by Rail)

602. The Uniform Rules Concerning The Contract For International Carriage of Goods By Rail (CIM) apply to all consignments of goods under a consignment note for a route over the territories of at least two States and exclusively over lines or services included in the list given in Articles 3 and 10 of the CIM Convention and to carriage as in accordance with Article 2 second subparagraph of the Convention. These Rules shall not apply to consignments between sending and destination stations situated in the territory of the same State and which pass through the territory of another state only in transit if the railways are operated by a State of departure or if both the states refuse by agreement to regard the consignment as international. Where the consignments are between two adjacent States or between two States but passing in transit through the territory of a third State and are operated by any of these three States then if the sender wishes the consignment shall be governed by the internal traffic regulations.

I. Obligations to Carry

603. The railways shall be bound to undertake all carriage of any goods in complete wagonloads if the sender agrees to comply fully with the Uniform Rules, the normal staff and transport resources undertake the carriage and which is sufficient to meet the usual traffic requirements, and the carriage is not prevented by circumstances which the railway cannot avoid and which is not in a position to remedy. The railways are not under obligation to accept such goods the loading and transshipment and unloading of which require special facilities and would accept only those goods which can be delivered without delay. Where the authorities decide that there will be any change in the nature of any service or that certain goods shall be accepted or refused for transportation, or that certain goods would be given priority then this will be done only after public notification. There can also be a joint agreement regarding concentration of goods traffic between specified frontier points and transit countries. Such measures shall be notified to the Central Office and entered by the railways in the special lists and published in the manner laid down for international tariffs and would be effective a month after the notification to the Central Office.

II. Articles Not Acceptable for Carriage

604. The CIM Convention does not allow the carriage of following articles by railways; articles prohibited by any one of the territories; articles forming the monopoly of the postal department in any one of the territories; articles which are unsuitable for carriage due to their dimension, mass or packaging; substances and articles which are prohibited under the Regulations concerning the international carriage of dangerous goods by rail (RID) (Annex 1 to the Uniform Rules, Exceptions given in Article 5, section 2).

A. Articles Acceptable Subject to Conditions

605. The Convention allows the carriage of the following goods for carriage subject to conditions; funeral consignments, railway rolling stock running on its own wheels, live animals and certain other consignments which due to their size, dimension or packaging pose greater hardships for the transport authorities are accepted with conditions and the normal Rules do not apply to them. Thus two States or two railways can enter into an agreement to include conditions for consignment of goods with special descriptions which are given in RID as not to be accepted for consignment.

B. Tariffs and Private Agreements

606. Carriage Charges and supplementary charges are to be calculated according to the tariff prevailing in each State. The tariffs must declare not only the special conditions applicable to the carriage but also the guidelines for calculating the charges, rules governing the conversion of currencies and must not violate the Uniform Rules unless so expressly provided. The tariffs must have uniform conditions applicable to all users. Railways may also enter into private agreements for reduced charges and other concessions either for public or for charitable purposes. The application of international tariffs must be made compulsory for international traffic but it can be made conditional if it is so inserted in the consignment note. Publication of tariffs and their amendments must be duly published and the publication of international tariff shall be regarded compulsory only in those States where the railways are parties to such tariffs as railways of departure or destination. An increase in the international tariff which tends to make conditions of carriage harder shall come into force only after fifteen days of its publication unless the international tariff when it makes provision for extending the internal tariff to cover the whole route then the period of publication of such internal tariff shall apply; where an increase in the charges in the international tariff comes after an increase in the internal tariff then they will be effective on the following day of their publication provided that such increase in the international tariff is made at least fifteen days in advance; where the carriage and supplementary charges in the international tariffs are amended so as to adjust with the changes in the rates of exchange then such changes shall be effective from the next day of publication.

States which do not make it compulsory to publish certain tariffs may not consider the rules given under the Convention for this purpose as binding on them. Railways should not charge any amount as above the one mentioned under the tariff and the amounts charged should be duly mentioned and inserted in the consignment note with relevant information.

C. Unit of Account, Rate of Exchange

607. The unit of account in the Uniform Rules shall be SDRs as defined by the IMF. In a Member State of the IMF, the value in SDRs of the national currency of that State shall be calculated in accordance with the method of valuation applied by the IMF. Where the State is not a Member State the value shall be determined by the method determined by that State. Such calculation must express in the national currency a real value approximating as closely as possible to that which would result from the application of the rule applicable to the Member State. Where the State is not a Member State and where these foregoing rules do not apply then the unit of account as mentioned in the Uniform Rules shall be deemed to be equal to 3 francs gold. The gold franc is defined as 10/31 of a gram of gold of millesimal fineness 900. The conversion of the gold franc must express in the national currency a real value approximating as closely as possible to that which would result from the application of the rule applicable to the State which is a Member of the IMF. The method of calculation by the States should be notified to the Central office every time a change is made therein. The railways should also publish the rates at which it converts sums expressed in foreign currencies and the rates of acceptance.

D. Special Provisions

608. Special provisions are laid down in the Regulations concerning the international haulage of private owners' wagons by rail (RIP) (Annexure II to the Uniform Rules) For the carriage of containers, special provisions are laid down in the Regulations concerning the international carriage of containers by rail (RICo) (Annexure III to the Uniform Rules). In the case of express parcels traffic, railways may, by tariff clauses, agree on special provisions in accordance with the Regulations concerning the international carriage of express parcels by rail (RIEx) (Annexure IV to the Uniform Rules) Two or more States may enter into a special agreement or two or more railways may agree by supplementary provisions or by tariff clauses to derogate from the Uniform Rules in matters of consignments under cover of a negotiable document; consignments to be delivered only against the return of the duplicate of the consignment note; or consignments of a newspaper; consignments for fairs or exhibitions; or consignments for loading tackle and equipment for protection of goods in transit against heat or cold; consignments over all or part of the route under cover of consignment notes which are not used for charging and billing; or consignments sent under cover of an instrument suitable for automatic data transmission.

609. Two or more States or two or more railways may make supplementary provisions for the execution of the Uniform Rules and should not derogate from the Uniform Rules unless expressly provided by the Rules. The national law of the State in which the person entitled asserts his rights or the rules relating to conflict of laws must be applied where the Uniform Rules, supplementary provisions or international tariffs do not provide for the given situation.

§4. Contract of Carriage by Rail Subject

610. In the Railways Act 1989, there is provision for the establishment of a Rail Land Development Authority which is endowed with the power to discharge functions under the Act. Such authority has the power to enter into agreements on behalf of the Government and the power to execute contracts. The Railway makes a contract for the carriage of passengers and goods by the railway administration. The goods are carried under a consignment contract under which they are entrusted to the railways for carriage (section 2, 4E).

§5. National Transportation

611. Railways form the backbone of the transport network of India. Known as 'the thread which binds the nation together', the Indian Railways have come up as an integrating force during the last 165 years of their formidable existence in the country. Not only as a means of transport the railways have social, cultural and developmental aspects and they augment the spirit of nationalism as they touch the farthest fringes of the vast subcontinent. The massive network spreads over a route length of 67,415 km, running track length of 95,981 km, total trackage of 1,23,542 km, 7,321 stations and a fleet of 12,147 locomotives as in 2019.[56]

The national transport system in India is shared unequally by the road, rail and air to some extent. In India, 60% of goods and 80% of passenger movement takes place through roadways. The National Highways constitute just 2% of the country's road network but carry 40% of the traffic load. 20% of freight and 40% of passengers' movements takes place through railways while only a very insignificant part of passenger and cargo movement depends on airlines. Thus the following explains the working of the Indian Railways.

Passenger Traffic

There has been phenomenal growth in passenger traffic in the railways since it's gearing up in 1950. The passenger originating figures have gone up from 1,284 million in 1950–1951 to 8,439 million in 2019 and passenger kilometre from 66.52 billion in 1950–1951 to 1,157,174 million in 2018–2019. Despite all the constraints the Indian Railway has shown a gradual increase in the progress graph and is one of the departments which copes easily with the population growth and remains popular among the masses.

Freight Traffic

A good number of heavy industries like coal, iron, steel ores, petroleum products and essential commodities like food grains, fertilizers, cement, sugar, salt, edible oils depend largely on railways for transportation. The revenue freight traffic increased from 73.2 million tonnes in 1950–1951 to 1,221.48 million tonnes in 2018–2019.

Revenue Finance

Since 1924–1925, railway finances remain separated from general revenues due to the mammoth financial engagements.

A Paradigm Shift

There has been a major turn in the presentation of the central budget by the Government. In the financial year 2017–2018, the present Government has changed the trend and now the Railway Budget is merged with the General Budget with an aim to give impetus to the transport growth. As per the Government sources, the merger shall bring the Railways to the centre stage of the Government's fiscal policy and would facilitate multimodal transport planning between railways, highways and inland waterways. However, the functional autonomy continues as before. The Railways contribute to the National Budget. There is a Parliamentary Convention Committee which periodically reviews the quantum of contribution by the railways.

Metro Rail

Metro Rail in India is emerging as an important mode of urban transportation. This is helping the urban population as well as taking off the burden of city roads and

56. 2018–2019 Year Book of Indian Railways – Ministry of Railways –Government of India at page 3.

helping the daily commuters. The success of Metro Rail has urged the Government to come up with a new Mero Rail Policy and also a new Metro Rail Act will be enacted by enacting the existing laws. This is aimed at facilitating greater private participation and investment in construction and operation.

612. According to the National Transport Policy Committee (NTPC), Fair Weather Roads (FWR) connect only 55% of the villages and a big amount of capital is required to cover all the villages by All-Weather Roads (AWR). The national transport is at the low priority of the State and needs greater attention. The rural areas in the country mainly depend on the RT and still look up for improvement, road wise and vehicle wise. A study conducted by the Indian Institute of Management (IIM) at Bangalore and the National Council for Applied Economic Research at New Delhi for the period 1979–1989 and has given the conclusion that carts play a predominant role in movement within the villages in India while trucks and tractors dominate outflow. Passenger transport is mainly by bicycles and motorized vans in FWRs and buses of various sizes and capacities in AWRs.

Work is started for a 150 km stretch of FWRs in the State of Uttarakhand which is likely to be completed by 2019. This is part of the AWRs and will be extremely helpful for the Armed forces to mobilise troops and armaments towards the Indo-China border.

Chapter 3. Inland Navigation

§1. Carriage of Goods by Inland Waterways

613. India has a dense river network which is also useful for the movement of cargo within the boundaries of India and also to neighbouring countries. Apart from a formidable coastline, India is also gifted with great rivers which have helped the country to utilize it for transportation and navigation purposes and up to the nineteenth century and half of the twentieth century, the IWT was dominant. With the advent of railways and the massive development of roads, the IWT sector is marginalized. Except for NWs in the states of Assam, Goa, Kerala, and West Bengal and in Mumbai the other rivers require development and betterment of infrastructure for full utilization of the waterways for beneficial trade and transport. The chief authority which takes care of this movement is the Central Inland Water Transport Corporation Limited (CIWTC) which was inaugurated on 11 February 1967 and which took over all the assets of the erstwhile River Steam Navigation Co. Ltd. and liabilities to the State Bank of India and Government of India under a Scheme of Arrangement, approved by the Calcutta High Court on 3 May 1967. The main activities of the Corporation are the transportation of cargo through Inland Waterways in the country and routes identified in the Protocol on IWT between India and Bangladesh. The Corporation is under the administrative control of the Ministry of Shipping RT & Highways, Department of Shipping, Government of India and which has its corporate office at Kolkata and various branch offices at Guwahati, Karimganj, and Patna, and so on. The Corporation has presently River Service Division (RSD) operating vessels owned by it for movement of cargo. Its head office has two divisions namely, Corporate Personnel Division and Corporate Finance Division. After Independence (15 August 1947) there has been a constant movement to upgrade the waterways. To achieve this goal the National Transport Policy Committee (NTPC) in its report (1980) recommended the formation of an authority to regulate waterways and as a result, the IWAI was formed in 1986. The IWAI has been making constant efforts since to develop the waterways of India and its works include:

– Development of infrastructure of NWs.
– Undertakes techno-economic feasibility studies.
– Prepares proposals for the development of other waterways as NWs.
– Advises the Central Government on the improvement of waterways.
– Assists states in the IWT sector.

All this has resulted in considerable upgrading of the waterways. The result is also shown in the area of cargo transportation which has risen from 1.63 billion tonne-km (BTKM) in 2003–2004 to 3.6 BTKM in 2008–2009. The target is to increase the modal share of IQWT to 20 BTKM by 2025.

I. Cargo Transportation by Inland Waterways

(Data Collected as per Annexure to the Annual Report 2008–2009 By Inland Waterways Authority of India)

614. There has been a steady increase in cargo transportation on inland transportation and it rose from 6.59 million tonnes (MT) in 2014–15 to 72.31 MT in 2018–19.[57]

615. On NW-1 and NW-2, the cargo moved was edible oil, cement, silica sand, stone chips, food grains, POL products, fly-ash, coal, and so on. On NW-3, the main cargo transported was rock phosphate, Furness oil, POL, sulphur, and so on. On Goa and Mumbai waterways, iron ore is the main cargo transported by IWT mode. The riverine inlets along the coast, near the ports and the canal systems as part of larger water resource development offer potentially navigable waterways. The ferry operations across rivers are the main passenger movements by inland waterways.

616. During the earlier times, industrial activity was influenced by the logistical convenience of riverine transport possibilities as the roads and rails were not so developed. Goods movement using IWT is influenced by technological and physical viability, commercial potential and operating policy of carriers and associated agencies. In IWT, the availability of the waterway, terminal facilities like jetties and ports, barges and other vessels capable of navigation and finally the management component affect the economies and operation of transport. The Holy Ganga is the river which provides the earliest organized transport movements over considerable distances from ancient times. Goods like tea, jute and spices are the first commodities which attracted transporters from Kolkata in the pre-independence period. The pace of development in the NWs and other waterways is negligible with the exception of the tidal river-canal system in Goa where the growth has been phenomenal and some 30 MT of iron ore moved by barges on the Mandovi–Zuari–Cumburjua system in 2003–2004.

617. The use of waterways as a mode of transport is cost-effective and environment-friendly as well. Where there is demand for construction material or project requirements which is river-based, then there is an additional advantage to use the waterways. The mode proves advantageous where there are large customers with regular demands like iron ore export requirement from north and south Goa, or where there is potential traffic in oil refineries in the north-east or those located at the banks of Rivers Haldia and Barauni, thermal power plants located at Barh and Bandel for carrying away fly-ash and coal. The export-import traffic through ocean-going liners, iron ore from Mormugao and Panaji ports is fed by barge traffic are good users of IWT. As IWT is generally slow in movement, expensive cargo is rarely moved through it.

---

57. https://psuwatch.com/cargo-transport-on-national-waterways-rose-10-times-in-5-years/.

Developments in 2017

In the year 2017, there has been increased activity by the Government to tap the highest potential of Inland Waterways in the country. The movement of cargo has been the main focus of energy as a good number of Terminals are being developed along the Inland waterways. A pilot run of defence cargo transportation on IWAI's *Ro-Ro* vessel on National Waterway 2 in Assam was conducted successfully in April 2017. It was part of the IWAs efforts to promote IWT in the North-eastern Region of India. IWAs cargo vessel MV V. V. moved 240 MT of bagged cement of a prominent manufacturer moved from Lola Ghat (West Bengal) to Bhagalpur. There was also reported 50,610 tonnes of cement from Gaighat (Patna) to Bhagalpur and 73,400 tonnes stone chips from Sahibganj to Manihari was completed by April 2017 by a bareboat charter agency. [58]

International Movement of Cargo

In September 2017, an international movement of cargo commenced on NW-16 (River Barak). The first consignment of 200MT Limestone was transported by Bangladeshi vessel M. V. Mia Mou from Karimganj (Assam) to Ashuganj (Bangladesh).

A. River Craft: Definition

618. River craft denotes any vessel which is used for navigational purposes in a river including boat launches and timber rafts. In the Agreement on the Kosi Project 1954 between the Government of India and the Kingdom of Nepal, it was inserted that use of river craft within two miles of the barrage and headworks will not be allowed except by special license and any unauthorized river craft found there would be subject to prosecution. Apart from this the word 'vessel' is said to include every description of watercraft, including non-displacement craft and seaplanes, used or capable of being used as a means of transportation on water (Rule 3 – The MS (Prevention of Collisions at Sea) Regulations 1975, Government of India).

B. Owner's Legal Liability

619. The owner's legal liability where the river craft, watercraft is co-existence with the shipowner's liability in respect of ships and the cargo carried by them. This results from the charter party clauses as well as from the various law provisions like the Carriage of Goods Act 1865 and the MS Act 1958. Where the owner is required by the terms of the charter party to 'full and complete cargo', then he is liable if he fails to provide space in the ship for the determined amount of cargo. When there is grain cargo in the ship the owner is required to follow the grain loading plan as approved by the Government of India failing which he is liable and shall be found guilty of an offence under the law (Article 331A). Apart from this, the shipowner is

58. Ministry of Shipping – 2017 – Year of Consolidation. Posted on: 20 Dec. 2017 by PIB, Delhi.

required to provide the river craft and watercraft well fitted for the purpose and when it is a ship he is required to provide a ship which is 'tight, staunch and strong and every way fitted for the voyage'. Where the owner fails to comply with the 'sea-worthiness' requirement of the ship then the ship, on the complaint being received is liable to be detained by the authority prescribed for this purpose by the Central Government. When the ship is finally detained then the owner is liable to pay to the Central Government the cost of survey and detention before the ship is released (section 338 MS Act).

C. Charter Party and Carriage of Foods

620. The contract to ship cargo from point of departure to point of destination by sea voyage is a charter party. Varieties of charter parties have evolved depending on the nature of the transaction to undertake the consignment of cargo, for example, time charter party is a contract where the entire ship is leased out to the charterer who becomes the owner of the ship so long the undertaking persists while voyage charter party is one which comprises a normal course of handing over the cargo to the shipowner or to the master of the ship with the purpose of delivering the same at a destined place.

621. Moreover, there may be a port charter party, dock charter party or berth charter party which means that the contract which simply states or names a port where the ship is required to be, or where it is required to be at a particular spot at a port for loading is called berth or dock charter party.

622. Usually, cargo is consigned by means of a voyage charter party. Parties are free to include in the charter party any lawful terms which later operates as conditions or warranties depending on the intention of the parties to regard any part of the contract as such. Often at the time of carriage of cargo the clause 'full and complete cargo' appears in the charter party in which case the charterer is bound to occupy the maximum capacity of the ship so as to avoid the loss of freight. Carriage of foods is also common under the charter parties.

1. Carriage of Grains

623. A charter party may be for the carriage of food like the grains in which case there is the duty of the parties engaged in such contract to abide by the provisions of the MS Act to avoid liability under the Act. Thus the grain cargo which includes wheat, maize, oats, rye, barley, rice pulses and seeds cannot be loaded without proper instructions under the Act as follows.

2. Grain Loading Plan

624. A grain loading plan which includes the stability of the ship and the circumstances of loading on departure and arrival as approved by the Central Government is to be followed when it is being loaded on board an Indian ship. The Central Government may also request a country to which the Safety Convention applies to approve the grain loading plan of an Indian ship and it shall at the request of the other country to which the Safety Convention applies approve the grain loading plan of that country and notify it properly. The statement containing such approval by the Central Government shall be one of the important documents of the ship which even the master is required to hand over to his successor when he is being removed or superseded. When grain is loaded on board a ship as per the grain loading plan then whether it is an Indian ship or a ship which is loaded outside India all necessary and reasonable precautions are required to be taken to prevent the grain from shifting and if the master or the owner fails to take such precautions then he shall be found guilty of an offence. When a ship arrives in India loaded with grain, then the master of the ship shall hand over to the customs authorities a statement specifying the draught of water and freeboard of the ship and the quality and quantity of grain stated in cubic feet, quarters, bushels or tonnes weight which shall then be inspected by the authorities (331A MS Act).

D. Limitation of Liability

625. The liability of the owner of a ship shall be limited by certain circumstances some of which may form part of the charter party itself. Thus a charter party may have an exception that in the matter of 'perils of the sea' where the goods are lost on account of a peril of the sea then the shipowner shall not be held liable. Then again if due to a certain act of God or due to the 'national enemies' any loss is caused then the owner is not liable. In this context, it should also be seen whether the 'excepted perils' resulted due to some act of the owner or whether he could do something to avoid the perils. If he could avoid it or it is his act which exposed the vessel to such peril then in that case he is not exonerated from liability. Frustration of the charter party may be caused when due to certain occurrences like the blowing of the auxiliary boiler; the running aground of the ship renders the charter party frustrated thus also absolving the parties from liability.

E. Towage

626. Towage is a service rendered by one vessel to aid the propulsion or to expedite the movement of another vessel (*Elliott Steam Tug Co. Ltd v. New Medway Steam Packet Co. Ltd* [1907] 59 Lil Rep 35 at 38). A power-driven vessel when towing shall exhibit two masthead lights forward in a vertical line. In case the length of the tow measuring from the stern of the towing vessel to the other end of the tow exceeds 20 m, then it should exhibit sidelights, a stern light, and a towing light in a vertical line above the stern light.

F. Pushing

627. When a pushing vessel and a vessel being pushed ahead are rigidly connected in a composite unit they shall be regarded as a power-driven vessel and exhibit a masthead light, a second masthead light, sidelights and a stern light. A power-driven vessel when pushing ahead or towing alongside shall exhibit two masthead lights forward, sidelights a stern light. Any number of vessels being towed or pushed in a group shall be lighted as one vessel. In case for any sufficient reason the vessels are unable to exhibit light in any of the foregoing ways, then all possible measure is to be taken to light the vessel or object towed.

G. General Average

628. In a voyage, certain factors may cause the loss, impairment or destruction of the craft or ship and extraordinary expenses may be incurred by the owner or other interested persons to put it right. The unusual expenses so incurred and the sacrifices made to save the craft or the ship is general average and which should be shared proportionately among the various interested persons.

H. Freight Market Regulation

629. Freight movement in India through IWT though quite old is not that popular as the government shows lethargy in investing it. The sector investment by the government in the 9th Plan is INR 308 crores (INR 1,701 crores, proposed and in the 10th Plan (INR 5,665 crores, proposed) which is not viable commercially. An increase in the bulk of cargo is required to give incentive to larger investments.

The IWAI is required to expedite development schemes to make full use of the potential of waterways and waterway systems in India. The freight market has better potentials in India because of the interface with ports and the larger marine supply chain. Vessels having both land and coastal operation capabilities, or good interface between the vessels of these two sectors, tidal river systems with good draft availability are enough incentives for the government to invest as in future the possible driving cargo is bulk for export or import through ports of Mormugao, Cochin, Haldia, and Kolkata; coal to Bangladesh, coal to and fly-ash from thermal power plants, construction material for the North-east (dams and other large projects) and Agri exports. IWAI needs to initiate a revenue model based on a combination of usage fees, cess and explicit subsidy needs to be in place.

§2. Statutory Provisions

630. India is a country blessed with legendary rivers which are even extremely useful for navigation purposes and for irrigation as well. The inland water systems of the country contribute to national life in a number of ways through commercial potentialities that are not so commendable. As these water systems are active as waterways since the British period some of the legislations are very old and have not been properly updated.

631. The matters connected with the transportation of passengers and cargo, the insurance of interests in inland navigation, the trade relation with neighbouring countries, prevention of pollution in the waterways are the subjects which are not hitherto covered under single legislation but is sporadic and found in the major legislations covering these subjects individually. Thus the statutory provisions can be divided into the following categories.

I. Constitutional Provisions

632. The Constitution of India distributes legislative power between the Centre and the States (Article 246) The Centre has the power to legislate with regard to regulation of interstate waters and river valleys while the states can legislate on the topic of water supplies, irrigation, canals, drainage, water storage and waterpower.

633. The States have jurisdiction of only local nature and cannot legislate on topics having effects beyond their boundaries. The law made by the Centre has dominance over the law made by the state so far it infringes with the Central law. As regarding the disputes arising out of the interstate rivers or river valleys, the Parliament is empowered to make a law to provide for the adjudication of such disputes which relate to the use, distribution or control of the waters. For this, the Parliament is competent to form a tribunal to hear such disputes.

634. The Inter-State Water Disputes Act 1956 was passed by the parliament to form a tribunal to adjudicate such disputes. The River Boards Act 1956 was also passed with the object of regulation and development of interstate rivers and river valleys by the River Board established under the Act. The River Board so formed has advisory functions and the preparation and implementation of schemes to develop the interstate rivers. Apart from other powers, the River Board has the power to conduct and coordinate research on various aspects including conservation and utilization of water sources and navigation.

II. Other Laws

635. There are no constitutional provisions regarding transportation or navigation. However, The Northern India Ferries Act 1878 (Act XVII of 1878),The Inland Vessels Act 1917 (1 of 1917) and The Inland Waterways Authority of India Act 1985 govern to some extent the navigation and transportation in the rivers though they are far from satisfactory as being old and outdated. The Parliament has enacted the new National Waterways Act 2016 which has declared 111 inland waterways as

National Waterways.[59] The Marine Insurance Act 1963 is applied to the insurance interest and protects the assured against losses on inland waters risks which are identical to any sea voyage. The Damodar Valley Corporation Act 1948 named after the Damodar River, was enacted to establish the Damodar Valley Corporation for controlling floods, generating electric power and work to promote the economic development of the Damodar Valley and adjoining areas and promotion and control of navigation in the Damodar River and its tributaries apart from doing many other functions.

III. IWAI

636. The Inland Waterways Authority of India Act 1985, after prolonged deliberations by the Centre, was passed with the object of establishing an IWAI which would work for the development, maintenance and regulation of NWs for shipping, and navigation. The Act, however, does not affect the provisions of the Indian Ports Act 1908 and the Major Port Trusts Act 1963 and is declared not to be in conflict with the powers and functions of the judicial authorities recognized and established under these Acts.

637. The IWAI Act is a major Act governing the inland waterways in the country. The functions of the IWAI established under the Act mainly aim at; better utilization of the NWs, taking measures for safety and convenience of shipping and navigation, control activities to stop pollution and make shipping and navigation safe and efficient, remove hindrances which come in the way of safe navigation, provide for regulation of navigation and traffic, disseminate navigational meteorological information, study the water transport requirement with a view to coordinating IWT on NWs with other modes of transport, establish and maintain pilotage on the NWs, develop consultancy services with foreign countries regarding planning and development of waterways for shipping and navigation, conduct research for development of IWT, techniques of towage and other facilities, arrange for the training of the IWT personnel (section 14 of the IWAI Act).

A. IWT in India

638. The Ministry of Shipping and the Planning Commission Working Group on IWT in its Policy Document (2001) made some recommendations and statements of initiatives which includes; measures to develop IWT by taking developmental activities to improve the IWT system; to accord the IWT the status of infrastructure to enable it to make use of the concessions applicable to other infrastructure sectors, an outlay of INR 408 crores was provided in the 9th Plan, it also aimed at enhancement of depreciation rate for inland vessels, to encourage IWT fleet expansion, to give vessel building subsidy for shipowners for inland waterways built in

59. INDIA 2018 – Publications Division-Ministry of Information& Broadcasting – Government of India – New Delhi.

Indian shipyards, and so on. The Tenth Year Plan also aims at the accelerated growth of the IWT by planning for stabilizing, strengthening and upgrading the infrastructure on the existing three NWs in terms of river management and control, provisions of required navigable depth (LAD), terminals with added facilities, navigational aids, declaration of new waterways, expanding and improvising the work and activities of the IWAI apart from a number of other developmental projects.

§3. Treaty Law

639. India entered with its neighbour countries into a number of international treaties regarding the use and distribution of water namely; the Agreement on the Kosi Project 1954, Agreement on the Gandak Irrigation and Power Project 1959, Indus Waters Treaty 1960 and Farakka Treaty 1996. These treaties though do not aim at the improvement of IWT yet they are somehow helpful in the utilization of the waters of these rivers. The Agreement on the Kosi Project is between the Government of India and the Government of Nepal and is undertaken to construct a barrage, head works and other activities for the purpose of flood control, irrigation, generation of hydro-electric power and prevention of erosion of Nepal areas on the right side of the Kosi River.

640. It also aims at construction and maintenance of roads, tramways, ropeways and railways but this did not confer any right on the Government of Nepal for commercial or non-commercial use of it and was meant only for departmental use. The same was true when the treaty allowed the Government of India to make use of the roads, waterways and other ways of transport but only for the bona fide purpose of construction and maintenance of barrage and other connected work.

641. The Agreement on the Gandak Irrigation and Power Project was also made between India and Nepal in 1959 and involved the construction of a barrage, canal and other works and the construction and maintenance of the portion of the main Western Canal. The object of the Indus Waters Treaty 1960 which concluded between India and Pakistan aimed at the complete and satisfactory utilization of the waters of the River Indus by classifying the Indus system of Rivers into 'Eastern Rivers' and 'Western Rivers'. The Farakka Treaty 1996 was entered between Bangladesh and India with the object of the sharing of waters of the River Ganges at Farakka apart from taking other steps for the release and distribution of these waters.

Chapter 4. Air Transport

§1. Introduction

642. India is a signatory to the Warsaw Convention of 1929. Consequently, the Warsaw Convention has been given effect in India by the enactment of the Indian Carriage by Air Act 1934 (20 of 1934) in respect of international carriage. The contents have also been extended to the domestic carriage with certain exceptions, adaptations and modifications by virtue of a Notification which was issued in 1964. Later when the Hague Protocol was adopted by the International Civil Aviation Organization (ICAO) conference held at Hague in September 1955, certain provisions of The Hague Convention were amended. While the provisions of the Convention regarding non-international carriages were included in section 4 of the Indian Carriage by Air Act 1934 subject to certain exceptions, adaptations, and modifications a need was felt to include the rules contained in the Warsaw Convention as amended by the Hague Protocol 1955 to non-international carriages in a new law. With this object the country geared up to pass the Carriage by Air Act 1972. This Act replaces the old Act of 1934 and is mainly governed by international conventions.

Airport Authority of India

AAI is the principal aviation services provider in the country. It came into existence on 1st. April 1995 as a statutory authority under the Airports Authority of India Act 1994. The AAI results as a merger of the then International Airports Authority of India and National Airports Authority. The main functions of the Authority are:

- Control and management of the Indian Airspace.
- Providing communicational, navigational and surveillance aids.
- Expansion and improvement of operational areas like runways, aprons, taxiways, etc., and provisions for landing and movement control aids.
- Design and development of passenger terminals.
- Development and management of cargo terminals.
- Provision of passenger facilities in the passenger terminals.

AAI in 2017

There has been a remarkable 21% growth in the traffic in the Indian airspace in 2017 and India is tipped to be the third aviation market in the world by 2020. The National Civil Aviation Policy (NCAP) 2016 aims at flying the common Indian by implementing the flagship schemes of UDAN (Ude Desh ka Aam Nagrik) and Regional Connectivity Scheme (RCS). India became the fourth country in the World to commission a regional satellite-based augmentation system namely GPSAided Geo Augmentation Navigation (GAGAN) and all the new aircraft registered in India are required to be GAGAN compliant by 2019. GAGAN facilitates improved operational efficiency, reduced fuel burn and enhanced capacity.

Montreal Convention

643. The 1999 Montreal Convention unified the rules on international carriage by air and modernized the provisions on limitation of liability for international air carriers. The Convention safeguards the interest of the consumer. Countries which account for the maximum share in international air transport have ratified and though India was a signatory to the 1929 Warsaw Convention and the 1955 Hague Protocol, it is only recently that India ratified the Montreal Convention.

However, India embraced the International civil aviation legal regime by passing *The Carriage by Air (Amendment) Act 2009 (28 of 2009).* The main objective of the amending law is to incorporate the Montreal Convention. Thus India became the 91st country to ratify the Montreal Convention 1999. The Director General of Civil Aviation (India) deposited with International Civil Aviation on 1 May 2009 the Instrument of Accession by India to the Convention for Unification of Certain Rules for International Carriage by Air done at Montreal. The Convention becomes effective in India on 30 June 2009 being the sixtieth day after depositing the Instrument in accordance with Article 53 paragraph (7) of the Montreal Convention. The ICAO has declared that India has ratified in all forty-three International Air Law Instruments. Under Article 253[60] of the Constitution of India Parliament can give effect to any treaty, agreement or convention by legislating on the subject (Entry 13,[61] 14[62]). By virtue of this power and as a sequel to the signing of the Montreal Convention, on 20 March 2009 the Parliament amended the Carriage by Air Act 1972 (69 of 1972) and passed the Carriage by Air (Amendment) Act, 2009 ((28 of 2009) hereinafter called the 'Amending Act 2009') which became law on 30 June 2009. This amendment shall be helpful in the following ways:

(a) Solving complex jurisdictional discrepancies regarding carriage of passenger and goods disputes.
(b) Providing a two-tier liability system. There is strict liability up to a fixed amount and unlimited presumptive liability for air carriers.
(c) Providing compensation for death and personal injury and in this way, it is in harmony with several quasi-legal instruments which eliminated the ceiling on liability for personal injury.
(d) Liability limit has been enhanced thereby manifesting care towards passengers. These are:
  - Death or personal injury – 100,000 SDR.

---

60. 253 – Legislation for giving effect to International Agreements – Notwithstanding anything in the foregoing provisions of this Chapter, Parliament has power to make any law for the whole or any part of the territory of India for implementing any treaty, agreement or convention with any other country or countries or any decision made at any international conference, association or other body (Constitution of India).
61. Under the List I – Union List, there are ninety-seven entries which subsume subjects on which the Parliament can legislate exclusively.
   Entry 13 – Participation in international conferences, associations and other bodies and implementing of decisions made thereof.
62. Entry 14 – Entering into treaties and agreements with foreign countries and implementing of treaties, agreements and conventions with foreign countries.

   - Passenger Delay – 4,150 SDR.
   - Loss, destruction of baggage – 1,000 SDR.
   - Loss, destruction of cargo – 17 SDR per kg.

   These monetary limits are made subject to review by the ICAO every five years.

(e) Jurisdictional ease – Earlier a claimant could bring an action for damages in a state which was a signatory to the Warsaw Convention which was based on:
   - Carrier's place of domicile.
   - Carrier's principal place of business.
   - Place where the ticket was issued or contract of carriage was made.
   - Carrier's place of destination.

(f) Now the Montreal Convention adds the fifth place of jurisdiction that is, the place of domicile of passengers provided the airlines have a presence there. This will help an Indian to file his claim in India even though the ticket was purchased and the journey was taken outside India, provided the carrier has a presence in India.

I. Application of Warsaw Convention to India

644. Section 3 of the Carriage by Air Act 1972 declares that the rules regarding the liability of the carrier for injury or death of passengers or loss of or damage to goods as declared by the convention are contained in the First Schedule relating to the rights and liabilities of carriers, passengers, consignors, consignees and other persons shall, subject to the other provisions of the Act and would apply to India irrespective of the nationality of the aircraft performing the carriage.

645. By virtue of section 4, the amended Convention rules are contained in the Second Schedule of the 1972 Act and they apply to India in respect of the rights and liabilities of carriers, passengers, consignors, consignees and other persons, subject to the other provisions of the Act of 1972 and shall have the force of law in India regarding any carriage by air to which such rules apply irrespective of the nationality of the aircraft performing the carriage. Moreover, section 5 declares the exclusive application of the Convention to India with the exclusion of the Fatal Accidents Act. The First Schedule of the Act lays down the liability extent while the Second Schedule mentions the persons as to by whom and against whom such liability is to be owed. The Convention thus applies by imposing certain statutory terms upon a contract of carriage (*Grien v. Imperial Airways Ltd* [1936] 2 All ER).

II. Application of Montreal Convention to India

646. The Preamble to the Carriage by Air Act 1972 as amended by the Carriage by Air (Amendment) Act 2009 declares that the Act gives effect to the Montreal

Convention[63] signed on 28 May 1999 and it makes provision for applying the rules contained therein subject to exceptions, adaptations and modifications to non-international carriage by air and for other related matters. The Rules contained in the Third Schedule being the provisions of the Montreal Convention relating to the rights and liabilities of carriers, passengers, consignors and other persons shall have the force of law in India in relation to any carriage by air to which those rules apply. These rules will apply irrespective of the nationality of the aircraft performing the carriage (section 4A –Inserted by the Amending Act 2009). The State Parties and the date of enforcement of the said Montreal Convention are given in Part III of the Annexure to the Third Schedule (section 4A(2) of the Amending Act 2009).

The New Amendments: 2015 & 2016

The Carriage by Air Act 1972 has further been amended in 2015 and became effective in 2016. The Principal Act aimed at giving effect to the Warsaw Convention 1929, the Hague Convention 1955 and the Montreal Convention 1999, the Warsaw Convention. The Amending Act (Act No. 12 of 2016) revises the limits of the air carriers *visa vis* the loss caused to the passengers in case of death, injury, loss or damage of cargo, etc.

Previously the Government of India did not have the power to make rules under the Act but could only monitor the applicability of such rules but now by adding Section 8A the Amendment Act of 2016 empowers the Central Government to make rules to carry out provisions of the Principal Act.

Earlier, the Air Carriage Amendment Bill 2015 promised increased compensation to flyers in case of death, injury, loss or damage of baggage and inordinate delay in flights. The carriers are made to pay a compensation amount which is equivalent to their global counterparts.

The Rules given in Schedule III of the Carriage by Air Act 1972 shall apply to all international carriage of persons, baggage or cargo performed by aircraft for reward. The Rules also apply to gratuitous carriage performed by an air transport undertaking (Rule 1, Schedule III). If a carriage is performed by many successive carriers and the parties regard it as a single operation then for the purposes of these Rules it will be regarded as one undivided carriage and in such case, it will not lose its international character merely because the series of contracts is performed within the territory of the same State. The Rules shall also apply to carriage performed by the State or legally constituted bodies if it fulfils the conditions laid down in Rule 1 (Rule 2, Schedule III). However, these Rules shall not apply to the carriage of postal items except those rules which are applicable to the relationship between the carriers and the postal administration.

---

63. 'Montreal Convention' means the Convention for the unification of certain rules for international carriage by air signed at Montreal on the 28 May 1999. Section 2(iii) of the Carriage by Air (Amendment) Act 2009.

§2. General Scope of the Warsaw Convention

647. The Warsaw Convention (WC) of 1929 marked the turning point in the law relating to Air on the international level. The Conference concluded on 12 October 1929 and signed by twenty-three countries came into effect ninety days after the deposit of the fifth instrument of ratification with the government of Poland (Warsaw Convention Article 37(1) and (2)). The Convention was open to denunciation by the High Contracting Parties through a notification to the effect addressed to the Government of Poland. The main object of the Convention is thus to remove conflict in laws of various countries regarding carrier's liability; settling jurisdictional questions and ensuring a uniform limitation period. The other main feature of the Convention was a reversal of the burden of proof where it shifted it from the plaintiff where the passenger or the owner of cargo need not have to prove negligence on the part of the carrier. Under the convention, it remained a fault-based liability.

648. The liability of the carrier regarding payment of damages was fixed to 1,25,000 francs gold in the case of injury to the passenger. More than this amount could be recovered by the plaintiff if he discharged the burden of proof wilful misconduct on the part of the carrier, his servants or agents (see Articles 21, 22, 23, Warsaw Convention). The Warsaw Convention 1929 itself enabled the high contracting parties to take initiative and call upon the Government of France to convene a fresh international conference to revise the convention. This has been done a number of times and the most important has been the Hague Protocol of 1955 which made formidable changes in the original convention.

649. The principal amendments were:

- First, the maximum financial limit for the death of or bodily injury to a passenger was doubled.
- Second, the expression 'wilful misconduct' was redefined as 'intentional or reckless misconduct'.
- Third, the carrier's employees and agents, as well as the carrier himself, could avail themselves of the limits of liability imposed by the convention. The Convention applies to 'all international carriage of persons, baggage or cargo performed by aircraft for reward' and also to 'gratuitous carriage by aircraft performed an air transport undertaking'.

I. Applicability in India

650. There is no statute for internal air carriage in India. The Indian Airlines Corporation is a common carrier in India but it is not a 'common carrier' within the meaning of Carriers Act 1865 (Now Repealed by Carriage by Road Act 2007 (41 of 2007)) thus the liability of the corporation as a common carrier is governed by the English common law as administered in India (*National Tobacco Company of India Ltd v. Indian Airlines Corporation* AIR 1961 Cal 383). The Carriage by Air Act 1934 though replaced by the Carriage by Air Act 1972 envisaged the rules relating to the rights and liabilities of carriers, passengers, consignors, consignees and other persons as being the provisions of the Warsaw Convention 1929 and had the force of law in India in relation to any carriage by air irrespective of the nationality of the aircraft performing the carriage.

651. It was replaced by the Carriage by Air Act 1972 on 1 April 1973. Between 1972 and 1 April 1973 Schedule 1 to the Carriage by Air Act 1972 was applicable. The Act applies to international carriage of goods and passengers. Though there is no law relating to home carriage by air, section 4 of the Act empowers the Central Government to extend by Notification the provisions of the Act to carriage by air which is not international carriage. Thus a Notification was issued on 17 December 1963 and the provisions of the Carriage by Air Act of 1934 have since then also become applicable to home carriers by air in India.

§3. General Scope of the Montreal Convention

652. Montreal Convention applies to all international carriage of persons, baggage or cargo performance by aircraft for reward. The Convention also applies to gratuitous carriage by aircraft performed by an air transport undertaking. The Montreal Convention 1999 supersedes all previous international instruments on air carrier liability. International carriage means any carriage in which the place of departure and the place of destination are situated:

(1) within the territories of two State Parties, or
(2) within the territory of a single State Party if there is an agreed stopping place within the territory of another State, even if that State is not a Party to the convention.

The Convention gives up the archaic way of 'compensating by weight' and adopts a more progressive way to consumer-friendly internationally recognized 'compensate by passenger' system in case of delay, loss or damage of baggage.

I. Applicability in India

653. The ultimate purpose of the Carriage by Air (Amendment) Act 2009 (28 of 2009) is to incorporate the Montreal Convention into air carriages in India. Ninety-one countries of the world have so far ratified the Montreal Convention and since Indian carriers are operating in most of these countries they are required to maintain the required insurance and pay a higher premium. To protect the baggage of the air travellers and to ensure them proper compensation the Carriage law is amended in 2009.

A. International Transport

654. Public International air transportation on a commercial basis started in 1920. At the time of air crisis, the international air transport scene remained spotted with laws of different countries with contrasting legislation giving rise to legal chaos. The Warsaw Convention 1929 made a formidable effort towards making uniformity in rules and it is said to apply to international carriage. The term in common parlance is understood to mean a commercial carriage of persons or cargo that may transcend national boundaries. The Warsaw Convention, however, does not import the commercial notion of 'international' either in meaning or in spirit and has the definition of the term with specific purpose and implication.

The relationship of 'international' is established under the Convention to denote to have a relation with certain countries known as High Contracting Parties and other countries do not come under it and any transit with them does not come under the expression 'international carriage'.

655. Thus under the Warsaw Convention the expression 'international carriage' means any carriage in which according to the contract made by the parties, the place of departure and the place of destination, whether or not there be a break in the carriage or transshipment, are situated whether within the territories of two High Contracting Parties or within the territory of a single High Contracting Party, if in the case of a single High Contracting Party there is an agreed stopping place within a territory subject to the sovereignty, suzerainty, mandate or authority of another Power, even though that Power is not a party to the Convention (Article 1(2)). Thus according to the convention 'international carriage' applies even to such contracts where the carriage originates and ends in the same country if it provides also for an agreed stopping place in the territory of another Power. 'International carriage' according to the Convention constitutes and comprises carriage of persons, baggage or cargo performed by aircraft for reward or gratuitously by an air transport undertaking or a state or a legally constituted public body between territories of two or more High Contracting Parties.

656. Thus by this definition, it can be said that under the British empire, carriage between England and the other British colonies was domestic carriage unless there was a stopping place in the territory which belonged to another Power. The definition thus was originally conceived to cover the earlier situation when there were colonies, dominions and territories of European powers spread to far-flung continents of Asia and Africa.

657. The Hague Convention later gave a more relevant expression in the context of the present political scenario and simply used the term 'territory of a High Contracting Party or another state'. Thus the term under the Warsaw Convention denotes that the nature of the carriage depends on the intention of parties and any deviation in the actual carriage or its part performance or non-completion does not deprive such carriage of its international character.

658. Thus a carriage is international if the contract stipulates that; a break in the continuity of carriage or transshipment whether on the territory of the departure state or that of the destination state does not alter the international disposition of the carriage provided other conditions are also met; that transportation remains international if the total transit is undertaken by several successive air carriers who individually perform carriage within the territory of their own state only, provided that the contract intended or referred to and formed parts of the complete transit as a single transaction; that where there is a mixed mode of transportation then the definition of 'international carriage' under the Convention is applicable only to the particular portion of transit by air provided such portion takes place between two High Contracting Parties or within the territory of the same Party with an agreed stopping place outside that state. Thus the character of 'international carriage' is revealed either by the contractual implications or by the geographical location of the places of origin of the transportation and that of its destination within the territories of the High Contracting Parties to the Convention. Even if it is a case of intra-state transit that is, between two points located within the same state being a High Contracting Party, there must be an 'agreed stopping place' outside that state in order to give international character to such carriage.

659. Montreal Convention: The expression 'international carriage' means any carriage in which, according to the agreement between the parties, the place of departure and the place of destination, whether or not there be a break in the carriage or a transshipment, are situated either within the territories of two State Parties or within the territory of a single State Party provided there is an agreed stoppage within the territory of another State whether or not that is a State Party. But for the purposes of these Rules if there is no agreed stoppage then a carriage between two points within the territory of a single State Party shall not be considered as international carriage (Rule 1(3) Schedule III).

B. Carriage of Aircraft

660. The Convention applies to international carriage performed by aircraft irrespective of the nationality of such aircraft or its place of registry. The use of the term 'aircraft' restricts its applicability. Only a liberal interpretation can bring 'helicopter' under the term 'aircraft', but space shuttles which operate and land like 'aircraft' are beyond this definition.

C. Carriage of Persons, Cargo or Luggage

661. The Warsaw Convention applies to all international carriage of persons, cargo or luggage performed by aircraft for reward. In respect of the carriage of passengers, a passenger ticket shall be issued which would contain *inter alia* the names of the places of departure and destination and the details regarding their stoppage and application of the Convention in matters of limiting the liability of the carrier in the event of the death or personal injury and in respect of loss of or damage to baggage. The passenger ticket shall constitute the prima facie evidence of the conclusion and conditions of the contract of carriage. An airway bill is delivered in respect of the carriage of cargo which is the record of the carriage which shall be made out by the consignor in three original parts; the first one marked as 'for the carrier' is signed by the consignor, the second one marked as 'for the consignee' is to be signed by the consignor and the carrier and the third part shall be signed by the carrier to be given to the consignor after the cargo has been accepted.

662. Montreal Convention-Documentation:

- for the carriage of passengers, a document shall be delivered to the passenger which should contain among other necessary information, the names of the departure and destinations points, if they are within the territory;
- of the single State Party where one or more agreed stoppages are within the territory of another state, then the document should contain the name of these stoppages, an identification tag for each of the checked baggage, information regarding the extent of liability of the carrier in respect of death or injury; and
- for destruction, loss or delay in respect of the baggage.

663. The airway bill and the receipt shall contain the point of departure and destination, indication of the weight of the consignment. The airway bill should be prepared as per the provisions of the Convention and the non-compliance shall not negate the existence of a contract of carriage. Every declaration made in the airway bill or the receipt for the cargo is the prima facie evidence of the facts stated therein.

For the luggage or carriage of registered baggage, a baggage check shall be issued and which if not combined with the passenger ticket shall contain the details of places of departure and destination and such other details which would explain its stoppages and the application of the Warsaw Convention. The baggage check shall constitute prima facie evidence of the registration of the baggage and the conditions of the contract. Any irregularity in the baggage check shall not negate the validity or existence of the contract of carriage and the carriage shall continue to be governed by the Convention.

664. Montreal Convention: For the carriage of cargo an air waybill or cargo receipt shall be delivered which shall indicate the points of departure and destination, if the names of the departure and destinations points are within the territory of the single State Party where one or more agreed stoppages are within the territory of another state then the document should contain the name of at least one of these stoppages, the indication of the weight of the consignment. The consignor may be asked by the authorities to give in written form the nature of the cargo and the liability of the carrier shall remain unaffected by such declaration (Rules 4, 5, & 6, Schedule III).

D. Carriage for Remuneration

665. The Warsaw Convention applies to international carriage by air undertaken for reward or performed gratuitously. The French term in the text of the Convention is contre rèmunèration which means gratuitously. When the carriage of passengers or transportation of cargo is on payment then the passenger ticket or the consignment note is the proof of the contract of carriage and many rights and liabilities of the passenger, consignor and carrier flow from it. However, an irregularity or omission of particulars entered in a passenger ticket or consignment note does not invalidate the contract and the provisions to protect the carrier under the Convention are still available to him.

The remuneration is often paid by a non-passenger for instance when the master is paying for his servant or the host is paying for his guest. Similarly, an army officer travelling under army concession is considered as a 'fare-paying passenger'.

E. Successive and Combined Transport

666. In the international carriage arena often a single carrier is not enough. The lack of service in a given route, non-service or suspension of a flight, mutual reciprocal booking schemes or adjustment of cargo loads for optimal utilization of freighters and other aircraft are the factors which necessitate the engagement of different carriages. Thus the same passenger or the cargo may pass through successive or combined carriages from the originating point to the destination point. In such cases, the contract may be formulated with one carrier or separately with a number of carriers.

Often the first carrier contracts for the total carriage but often different carriers are involved in connecting phases of the carriage and thus remain liable only to that portion of the journey with which they are entrusted. In such successive carriages, the mode of carriage is changed from air carriage to rail, road or sea carriage where the air carrier is given the responsibility to get the cargo transported to the consignee at the purported destination to carry it further.

The Warsaw Convention covers the successive stages of such kind of transportation. Intention of parties plays a vital role in rendering a carriage as successive transport and not only the fact that a single cargo from the point of consignment to the point of delivery has utilized different carriers.

667. The Warsaw Convention defines successive transport as:

> a carriage to be performed by several successive air carriers is deemed for the purposes of this Convention, to be one undivided carriage if it has been regarded by the parties as a single operation, whether it had been agreed upon under the form of a single contract or of a series of contracts, and it does not lose its international character merely because one contract or a series of contracts is to be performed entirely within a territory subject to the sovereignty, suzerainty, mandate or authority of the same High contracting Party.

668. Thus the international carriage by air need not be performed fully by a single carrier; that if intended so the entire carriage is regarded as an undivided one, and it can also be regarded as a single contract or a series of contracts and that the carriage does not lose its international character merely because one or more contracts were performed within the territory of the same State.

The liability of such carriers is governed by the provisions of the Warsaw Convention which assumes that the liability is co-extensive with the role of the carrier in the performance of the contract. It is also possible that the first carrier takes up responsibility on behalf of other carriers. As regarding the liability for baggage and cargo, the Convention states that 'the carriers will be jointly and severally liable to the passenger or to the consignor or consignee'.

1. Combined Carriage

669. Carriage may be spread over a number of modes of transportation in addition to the air carriage. The air carriers accept to combine in the air tickets or air waybill certain portions of the journey by sea, river, rail or road as a package deal to the tourist or otherwise to the public for the latter's convenience. In this way, there is a 'package deal' by the air carrier to take the cargo to the ultimate destination even by employing different modes of transport.

The Warsaw Convention sanctions such mode of combined carriage provided it includes international carriage by air. The Convention also allows parties to insert in the documents of air carriage certain conditions pertaining to other modes of transport in the continuance of the air carriage but which do not violate the provisions of the Convention.

Moreover, the Convention applies to the air carriage portion of such combined carriage and that even if it is of international character. Intention of the parties is given due importance and if parties do not intend then the contract no longer remains a contract of combined carriage but becomes a series of disjointed contracts.

Montreal Convention –Combined Carriage

670. Where the carriage which comes under the meaning of Rule 1 (International carriage of persons, baggage or cargo performed by aircraft for reward and also for gratuitous performance by an air transport undertaking) is performed partly by air and partly by any other mode of carriage then the Rules subject to Rule 18(4)[64] shall apply only to the carriage by air. Such parties can in their document of

64. Rule 18(4) – The period of the carriage by air shall not extend to any carriage by land, by sea or by inland waterway performed outside an airport. If, however such carriage takes place in the performance of a contract for carriage by air, for the purpose of loading, deliver or transshipment, any damage is presumed, subject to proof to the contrary, to have been the result of an event which took place during the carriage by air. If a carrier, without the consent of the consignor, substitutes carriage by another mode of transport for the whole or part of a carriage intended by the agreement between the parties to be carriage by air, such carriage by another mode of transport is deemed to be within the period of carriage by air.

air carriage which is in consonance with these Rules insert conditions relating to the carriage of such cargo by any other mode (Rule 38, Chapter 4, Schedule III).

F. Mandatory Applicability

671. The Warsaw Convention applies to all international carriage of persons, luggage or goods performed by aircraft for reward. It does not apply to gratuitous carriage. If the passengers are appropriately notified then even the gratuitous international carriage can be performed according to the Warsaw limits of liability by the carrier.

The Convention applies only to the High Contracting Parties which are certified and notified in the official gazette as such by the government of a state. Such publication in the official gazette is for administrative convenience and for judicial notice and is not conclusive proof of the status of a state as a High Contracting Party. Once the status is so declared, it cannot even be looked into by the courts (*Parsram Parumal Dabrai v. Air India Ltd* AIR 1955 NUC (Bombay) 18).

672. It also applies to the international carriage of persons, luggage and goods performed by aircraft. Thus it denotes the application of the convention to international carriage between states which are High Contracting Parties or within the territory of the same High Contracting Party provided there is a stopping place outside this territory as per the contract. It applies to international carriage by air of persons, luggage and goods whether it is undertaken for reward or performed gratuitously.

When transportation is for payment of passenger fare or freight charges the ticket or consignment is the evidence of contract but in case of gratuitous travel, no such legal contract is said to take place. Reward may also be paid by anyone and not necessarily by the passenger. The Convention also covers carriage by 'an air transport undertaking' and they also apply to 'carriage performed by the state or legally constituted public bodies', for example, *Air India.*

1. Limits of Applicability

673. The Convention does not apply to 'carriage performed under the terms of any international postal convention'. It also does not apply to 'international carriage by air performed by way of experimental trials conducted by air navigation undertakings with a view to the establishment of a regular line of air navigation'. International carriage by air 'performed in extraordinary circumstances, outside the normal scope of an air carriers' business', for instance, aircraft used for military troops, for rescue operations, and so on do not come under the Convention. All kinds of state aircraft do not come under the provisions of the Warsaw Convention, for instance, military aircraft and aircraft in police and customs duties.

§4. Parties to the Contract of Carriage

674. The contract of carriage by air, by its very nature, is international in character. This necessitates the existence of a number of national laws and the presence of foreign components in the transaction giving rise to contrasting situations. The Warsaw Convention attempts to solve the situation by putting forward certain uniform rules to govern such contracts as also it attempts to demarcate the liability arising out of such contracting ties. Air consignment note is the prescribed document for the carriage of goods and constitutes 'prima facie evidence of the conclusion of the contract of the receipt of goods and of the conditions of carriage'.

675. The contract of carriage by air is in the form of a passenger ticket, baggage check and an air waybill for carriage of passengers, accompanied baggage and cargo respectively. These documents embody inter alia the conditions of carriage and the liability of the carrier. Such documents are required by the Convention to contain a statutory notice purporting to inform the other party about the extent of the liability of the carrier as per the Convention and the carrier cannot use such notice to limit or negate his liability.

676. The parties to such a contract are the air carrier or the contracting carrier and the passenger, consignor or his agent. Though the Convention does not define the term 'carrier' it denotes the operator of an aircraft and they usually constitute public bodies or private companies that undertake transportation by air. A carrier normally solicits the patronage of travelling public, advertise routes and time schedules, fares and baggage allowances and hold out as a common carrier as such (*Ziser v. Colonial Western Airways* 10 NJ Misc. 1118 162 Atl. 591).

Another party to the contract is the passenger or person who has taken a place in a public conveyance by virtue of a contract for the purpose of being transported from one place to another in consideration for payment of fare or its equivalent. An entry into the aircraft of the carrier having obtained a valid ticket or even with the intention of purchasing a ticket creates the relationship of passenger and carrier (*Wabash etc. Ry. v. Rector* (104 III, 296) &*Norfolk & Western Ry. v. Galliher,* 89 Va, 639, 16 SE 935). A person travelling free or on a pass or a person who charters an aircraft for himself alone are all passengers (*Stoll v. Curtis Flying Service* (1930) US Av R 148).

§5. The Carriage of Passengers

I. Ticket

677. The Air Carriage Act 1972 recognizes two types of tickets under the documents of carriage. These are Passenger Tickets and Luggage Tickets.

A. Passenger Ticket

678. According to Rule 3(1) of the First Schedule, the carrier must deliver a passenger ticket which should contain the following details:

(a) the place and date of issue;
(b) the place of departure and destination;
(c) the agreed stopping places, provided that the carrier may reserve the right to alter the stopping places in case of necessity and that if he exercises that right, the alteration shall not have the effect of depriving the carriage of its international character;
(d) the name and address of the carrier or carriers;
(e) a statement that the carriage is subject to the rules relating to liability contained in this Schedule.

(2) The absence, irregularity or loss of the passenger ticket does not affect the existence or the validity of the contract of carriage, which shall nonetheless be subject to these rules. Nevertheless, if the carrier accepts a passenger without a passenger ticket having been delivered he shall not be entitled to avail himself of those provisions of this Schedule which exclude or limit his liability.

As according to Rule 3(1) of the Second Schedule a ticket will be delivered which shall disclose not only the places of departure and destination but if the places are within the territory of a High Contracting Party there should also be an indication of at least one such stopping place if there are many. The ticket is also required to mention the fact that in case the passenger's journey involves an ultimate destination or stoppage in the country other than the country of departure then the amended convention shall apply which shall also limit the liability of carriers for death or personal injury and in respect of loss of, or damage to baggage.

B. Luggage Ticket

679. According to Rule 4 of the First Schedule of the 1972 Act, as for the luggage other than the personal belongings of the passenger, the carrier must deliver the luggage ticket to the passenger. Such ticket should contain the following particulars:

(a) the place and date of issue;
(b) the place of departure and destination;
(c) the name and address of carrier and carriers;
(d) the number of the passenger ticket;
(e) a statement that the luggage will be delivered to the bearer of the luggage ticket;
(f) a statement that the carriage is subject to the 1972 Act.

The Rule also clarifies the fact that the loss of the luggage ticket shall not affect the contract of carriage. In case the carrier accepts the luggage without a ticket and if the luggage ticket does not contain the mandatory particulars, then the carrier shall not be able to avail of the liability exclusion provisions of the Act.

According to Rule 4 of the Second Schedule regarding the carriage of registered luggage, a baggage check shall be delivered, which shall unless combined with the Passenger Ticket should contain an indication of the places of departure and destination; if the places of departure and destination are within the territory of a single High Contracting Party but some of these are in other State then an indication should be made regarding at least one of such stoppages; it should also contain a notice to the effect that if the journey contains an ultimate destination or stoppage in a country other than the departure country, then the amended convention shall govern and limit the liability of the carrier regarding the loss or damage to the baggage.

The baggage check shall be the prima facie evidence of the registration of the baggage and any loss or damage to the baggage check shall not affect the contract between the carrier and the passenger. In case the carrier takes charge of the luggage without a baggage check then unless combined with the passenger ticket, the carrier cannot avail of the liability exclusion clause of the Act.

II. Liability of Carrier

680. Rules 17–30 of the First Schedule given in Chapter 3 envisage the liability of the carrier. The Carrier as such is liable in the following cases:

(1) The carrier is liable for any accident occurring onboard the aircraft or in the course of any of the operations of embarking or disembarking in the event of the death of the passenger or the wounding or any bodily injury caused to him.
(2) The carrier is also liable for damage caused to the luggage or for its loss which occurred during the carriage by air. The period of carriage by air comprises the period during which the luggage is in charge of the carrier whether in the aerodrome or on board the aircraft. However, this period does not extend to any carriage by land or sea unless such a carriage takes place as a contract for carriage by air.
(3) The carrier is also liable for the damage caused by delay in the carriage by air of passengers, luggage or goods.

Montréal Convention – Liability of Carrier

681. The Montreal Convention is a consumer-friendly convention and India with the Amendment Act of 2009 has brought Indian Carriage Law in line with the international standards and the carrier is made mindful of 'Duty to Care' towards its passengers. The liability of the carrier has been elaborated in terms of compensation and it extends both to the passenger and the baggage. In the Amendment Act 2009, it has been included in Chapter 3 of Schedule III which is as follows.

Liability Towards Passenger

If the death or injury to the passenger is caused on board then the carrier shall be liable only if the accident which caused the death or the injury occurred on board or during the course of any of the operations of embarking or disembarking (Rule 17, Schedule III).

Liability Towards Baggage

The carrier shall be liable for any loss or destruction to the checked baggage provided such loss or damage took place on board or during the period when the baggage was under the charge of the carrier.

Liability in matters of Delay

Liability of the carrier in matters of delay in the carriage by air of passengers, baggage or cargo is conditional upon the fact that the servants and agents of the carrier took all reasonable measures to avoid the damage but it was unavoidable in which case the carrier shall not be held liable for such delay (Rule 19 Schedule III).

A. *Exoneration from Liability*

682. The carrier is not liable if he is able to prove that:

(1) The damage was occasioned by negligent pilotage or negligence in the handling of the aircraft or in navigation and that he and his agents took all necessary steps to avoid the damage.
(2) That the damage was caused by or contributed to by the negligence of the injured person then he may be fully or partially exonerated from liability by the court.

Montreal Convention

683. The carrier is exonerated from his liability towards the passenger, baggage or cargo if he is able to prove that the loss or damage resulted from any of the following conditions:

- Any inherent defect in quality or vice of the cargo.
- Defective packing not done by the carrier.
- An act of war or armed attack.
- An act of public authority carried out in connection with the entry, exit or transit of the cargo (Rule 18(2) Schedule III).

– If the damage was the result of the negligence or other wrongful acts of or omission of the claimant and the carrier is able to prove it, then he will be exonerated from the liability (Rule 20, Schedule III).

B. Extent of Liability

684. The Extent of liability is pecuniary which is as follows:

– *Towards Passengers*

Unless settled under a contract to pay higher, the liability of the carrier to pay damages to each passenger is limited to FRF 1,25,000. Even when the damages are settled to be paid by way of periodical payments the sum total of these payments should not exceed FRF 1,25,000.

– *Towards Luggage*

In respect of registered luggage and goods, the liability of the carrier is limited to FRF 250 per kg unless the special nature of the luggage was declared at the time of registration and the supplementary sum if so required has been paid in which case the liability will be co-extensive with the value declared.

As regards the personal belongings of the passenger carried with him, the liability is limited to FRF 5,000 per passenger.

The sums mentioned in this rule shall be deemed to refer to the French franc consisting of sixty-five and a half milligrams gold of millesimal fineness 900.

685. Montreal Convention-Extent of Liability:

– *Towards Passenger*

Death or Injury

> The liability of the carrier under Rule 17(1) is fixed and for damages not exceeding one lakh (SDR)[65] per passenger the carrier shall not be able to exclude or limit its liability. But the carrier shall not be liable for each passenger the damages exceeding 1,00000[66] SDRs if he proves that either the damage was not due to his own negligence or wrongful act or it was solely due to the negligence or wrongful act or omission of a third party (Rule 21, Schedule III).

65. Special Drawing Rights (SDR) are currency conversion measures. It is an interest-bearing international reserve asset created by the International Monetary Fund (IMF) in 1969 to supplement other reserve assets of member countries. One SDR is equivalent to INR 75.
66. Conversion of Special Drawing Rights–Any sum in SDRs as mentioned in Rules 21 and 22 of the Sch. III shall be converted into rupees at the rate of exchange prevailing on the date on which the amount of damages to be paid by the carrier is ascertained by the Court (s. 6A) the Carriage by Air Act 1972, inserted by Amendment Act 2009 (28 of 2009) (s. 8) w.e.f. 1 Jul. 2009.

Delay

> In case of damage caused by delay in carriage of persons the liability of the carrier for each passenger is limited to 4,150 SDRs (Rule 22, Schedule III).

– *Towards Baggage*

The liability of the carrier in case of destruction, loss or delay shall be limited to 1,000 SDRs. If the passenger has made a special declaration of interest in delivery at destination and has also paid a supplementary sum then in such a case the carrier shall be liable to pay a sum not exceeding the declared sum unless it proves that the sum is greater than the passenger's actual interest in delivery at destination (Rule 22(2) Schedule III).

– *Towards Cargo*

In case of destruction, loss damage or delay of the cargo the liability of the carrier is limited to a sum of 17 SDRs per kg. But if the consignor has made at the time of handing over the cargo to the carrier, a special declaration of interest in delivery at destination and has paid a supplementary sum then the carrier shall be liable to pay a sum not exceeding the declared sum unless it is proved that the sum is greater than the consignor's actual interest in delivery at destination (Rule 22(3) Schedule III).

In case of delay, destruction, loss or damage of part of the cargo the total weight of the package should be taken into consideration while limiting the liability of the carrier (Rule 22(4) Schedule III).

§6. The Carriage of Foods or Baggage

I. The Airway bill

686. According to Rule 5(1), every consignor should make out and hand over a document called an 'airway bill' to the carrier and he has got a right to require the carrier to accept this bill. This airway bill should be made out by the consignor in three original parts and be handed over with the cargo; the first part marked as 'for the carrier' shall be signed by the consignor.

The second part marked as 'for the consignee' should be signed both by the carrier and the consignor and shall accompany the cargo; the third part being signed by the carrier should be handed over to the consignor after the cargo has been accepted. The signature of the carrier should be given prior to the loading of the cargo and should be stamped. The airway bill is the prima facie evidence of the contract, of the receipt of the cargo and of the conditions of the carriage.

However, the absence, irregularity or loss of the airway bill does not affect the existence or the validity of the contract of carriage which shall be subject to the Rule 9 of Schedule II will be guided by other rules of Part III relating to air waybill.

687. Montreal Convention In respect of carriage of cargo an airway bill shall be delivered. The carrier may also deliver a cargo receipt instead which contains a record of the carriage and identification of the consignment if so requested by the consignor. The airway bill shall be made out by the consignor in three original parts; the first one to be marked as 'for the carrier' and it shall be signed both by the consignor and the second part shall be marked as 'for the consignee' and it shall be signed by the consignor and by the carrier (Rule 7, Schedule III) Such signature may be printed or stamped.

However, non-compliance with the above rules will not affect the existence or validity of the contract of carriage and the parties shall remain subject to the rules given in Schedule III. Such airway bill or the cargo receipt shall be the prima facie evidence of the conclusion of the contract, of acceptance of cargo and of the conditions of carriage as mentioned therein. Even statements relating to the weight, dimensions and packing of the cargo and the number of packages rare the prima facie evidence of the facts given and they do not constitute evidence against the carrier unless the airway bill or the cargo receipt is checked by the carrier in the presence of the consignor.

A. Contents of the Airway Bill

688. The airway bill, according to Rule 8 of the Second Schedule should contain the following particulars:

(a) an indication of the places of departure and destination;
(b) if the places of departure and destination are within the territory of a single High Contracting Party and one or more of the agreed stopping places are within the territory of another State then it should mention at least one such stopping place;
(c) Moreover it should notify the consignor that if the carriage involves a destination or stop in a country other than the country of departure, the amended Convention will apply and that the amended Convention governs and in most cases limits liability of carriers in respect of loss of or damage to cargo.

In case if with the consent of the carrier, the cargo is loaded without an airway bill or in case the airway bill does contain such notice then the carrier shall not be liable to avail himself of the provisions of sub-rule (2) of Rule 22 which limits the liability of the carrier in case of registered baggage and cargo, to 250 francs per kg and in case of loss or damage or delay of part of registered baggage or cargo or of any object contained therein, the weight to which the carrier's liability shall be limited shall be only the total weight of the package or packages.

1. Contents of the Airway Bill

689. Montreal Convention – The airway bill according to Rule 5 Schedule III should contain the following particulars:

- An indication of the places of departure and destination.
- If the places of departure and destination are within the territory of a single State Party and at least one agreed stoppage is within the territory of another State, then indication of at least one such stoppage.
- An indication of the weight of the consignment.

The consignor may be asked to meet the formalities of customs and other public authorities and shall be asked to deliver the nature of the cargo. This will not create any duty or obligation for the carrier (Rule 6, Schedule III).

II. The Baggage Check

690. In Part II of the Second Schedule under Rule 4, some changes regarding baggage checks are made. It says that for every registered baggage, a baggage check will be delivered which should contain certain particulars regarding; the places of departure and destination; a declaration of at least one stoppage if such places are within the territory of a single High Contracting Party; a declaration that the amended Convention shall apply in case an ultimate destination or stop is in a country other than the country of departure.

The baggage check shall be the prima facie evidence of the registration of the baggage and of the conditions of the contract of carriage. In case of the non-delivery of the check, the carrier cannot avail himself of the benefits of the Schedule (*Patricia D Furlong v. MD East West Airlines* [2004] 2 CPR 60 (Hyd).

III. Rights and Obligations of the User

A. *Rights of Consignor*

691. Subject to the contract of carriage, the consignor has the right to dispose of the cargo by withdrawing it at the point of departure or at any subsequent stop. He may also require it to be delivered at the destination to any person other than the consignee or by requiring it to be returned to the aerodrome of departure. In case the carrier is not able to comply with such requirement then he may inform the consignor accordingly. If the compliance is made without the production of the way bill then the carrier shall be responsible in the event of its being lost. Right of the consignor ends when the rights of the consignee begin provided the consignee accepts the way bill or cargo. In case he does not accept then there will be the revival of the rights of consignor. In case the consignee declines to accept the goods then the consignor gets the right of disposal notwithstanding the fact that the consignee's rights had begun. However, the consignor cannot exercise his right in such a manner as to prejudice the interest of the carrier or of other consignor (*G. G. Pvy. Ltd v. PAW Airways*, Delhi AIR 1983 Del 357).

Montreal Convention – Rights of Consignor

692. The consignor has full rights over the consignment so much so that he can dispose of the cargo by withdrawing it at the airport or departure or destination, he can stop it during the journey, he can also ask for the delivery of the cargo to any person other than the original consignee (Rule 12, Schedule III). However, the carrier may express his inability to follow the instructions of the consignor. If the carrier delivers the cargo to any other person on consignor's instructions but without the production of the airway bill or the cargo receipt then this will entail his liability towards a claimant who is the holder of such airway bill or cargo receipt. Consignor's right ends where the consignee's right begins but if the consignee declines to accept the cargo then the consignor may resume his right of disposition.

B. Rights of Consignee

693. Then the goods reach the destination then the consignee has got a right to have the possession of the goods but only on production of the way bill and after the payment of the outstanding charges. In case the carrier admits that the goods are lost or if the delivery of the goods is not made within a week then the consignee can exercise his rights thereafter.

694. Montreal Convention; Rights of Consignee – On the arrival of the cargo at the destination point the consignee has a right to receive the cargo on payment of the due charges and on complying with other conditions. For this, it is the duty of the carrier to notify the consignee about the arrival of the cargo. However, if the cargo is lost or it is not reached on the expiration of seven days of the notified date then the consignee gets a right to enforce the contract against the carrier (Rule 13, Schedule III).

1. Position of the Owner

695. Often it happens that the owner of the goods who is neither designated as consignor nor as the consignee is interested in enforcing the contract. The point was discussed in a case which involved the consignment of chrysanthemums. The plaintiff acquired ownership of the delivery of the goods to the carrier. When the consignment reached Heathrow, it was in a bad condition. The carrier's plea was that the plaintiff, being neither the consignor nor the consignee is precluded by the Warsaw Convention as amended at the Hague and as implemented by the Carriage of Air Act 1961 from bringing an action against the carrier though the Common Law permits an owner to bring an action in such cases. Reference was made to Article 30(3) of the Convention which lays down rules regarding the action to be brought exclusively either by the consignor or by the consignee under the circumstances given therein (*Gatewhite Ltd v. Iberia Lineas Aereas de Esparia SA* [1989] 1 All ER 944). In a later case the restrictive approach was rejected (*Tasman Pulp and Paper*

Co. Ltd v. Brambles JBO' Loghlen Ltd [1981] 2 NZLR 225 (NZ HC) where the court refused to reject at the instance of the carrier a claim by the owner about whom the court said that he had an arguable case against the carrier as per the Warsaw Convention. It was later concluded that the Convention does not recognize the right of the owner who is neither formally a consignor nor a consignee and it was said that 'It should be recognized that in practice the consignee will often be a forwarding agent or the buyer's bank; it would be undesirable that the buyer's remedy should depend upon the ability and willingness of the actual consignee to bring ac action against the carrier.' (Comment on the case by N. E. Palmer and Robert Merkin, Commercial Law, and All ER Annual Review 1989 at 24).

696. Whenever a complaint is to be made about the damaged goods it should be made within fourteen days of the arrival of goods. In air carriage the time factor plays an important role and delay is said to occur when the delivery is made beyond the period settled in the contract. In the absence of any such stipulation regarding the time, the delay must be addressed with reference to air journey as commonly understood. The Warsaw Convention as amended by The Hague Protocol; a complaint for delay should be made within twenty-one days since the goods were handed over to the carrier. The complaint when made in writing is admissible also as evidence.

IV. Liability of the Carrier

A. Presumption of Fault

697. There is presumption of fault against the carrier when goods are damaged, destroyed or lost during the air transit.

The liability of the carrier regarding the carriage of foods and baggage is governed by the provisions of Rule 17 onwards of the Second Schedule which is as follows. The guiding rules regarding the liability of the carrier are the same though the extent of liability has been enhanced. The immunity given to the carrier in such cases is the same as it is in respect of the carriage of passengers.

B. Liability in Case of Death

698. The carrier is liable for the death or wounding of a passenger if the accident which caused it occurred on board the aircraft or in the course of any of the operations of embarking or disembarking.

C. Liability Regarding Luggage

699. The carrier is liable for damage sustained in the event of the destruction or loss of or of damage caused to any registered baggage or any cargo if the occurrence which caused the damage so sustained took place during the carriage by air which comprises the period during which the baggage or cargo is in charge of the carrier whether in an aerodrome or on board an aircraft or in any place if the landing is outside the aerodrome. The period of the carriage does not extend to any carriage by land, by sea or by river performed outside an aerodrome subject, however, to the terms of the contract.

700. The liability under Rule 18 arises only in respect of registered luggage and not to unauthorized delivery made without bank release order and is not considered as damage during carriage by air and hence the two year limitation period prescribed by Rule 30 would not be applied and the ordinary period of three years of limitation as prescribed under the Limitation Act 1963 is applicable (*Federal Chemical Works Ltd v. NUTSO (Nigeria) Ltd* AIR 2001 Delhi 25).

The liability of the carrier also extends to the delay in the carriage by air of passengers, baggage or cargo. There was a delay in carrying pathological material booked by air and thereby the material was rendered useless for test purposes. When exorbitant damages were demanded by the plaintiff then it was held by the Consumer Forum that for this the regular court should be moved. As the pathological material belonged to the consignor's wife hence she was the consumer as she was the beneficiary of services by her husband (*Greta Rain v. Air Freight Ltd* (1992) 1 CPR 526 NC).

D. Contributory Negligence

701. The carrier can be exempted from liability if it proves that it took all necessary steps to avoid the damage or the situation was such that it was not possible to avoid the damage so caused. However, if the carrier proves that the damage was the result of the contributory negligence of the injured person then on such ground the Court may exonerate him fully or partly from his liability.

E. Limits of Liability

1. Passengers

702. The limit of liability of the carrier in respect of persons given under Rule 22 of the Second Schedule remains subject to the exceptions, adaptations and modifications made in 1980 (S.O. 1885; Ministry of Tourism and Civil Aviation, New Delhi the 5 July 1980). The amended rule describes the kind of physical damage suffered by the injured person in relation to his age. Thus in case of any permanent disablement incapacitating the injured from engaging in or being occupied with his usual duties the liability is INR 2,00,000 in case the injured is above 12 years of age and INR 1,00,000 if the passenger is below 12 years of age.

In case of any temporary disablement, the liability is limited to INR 200 per day so long the disability continues or INR 40,000 whichever is less.

According to Rule 22(1) in the carriage of persons, the liability of the carrier for each passenger is limited to the sum of 2,50,000 francs.

2. Registered Baggage or Cargo

703. Liability regarding registered baggage and of cargo the liability is limited to 250 francs per kg whereas for the words 250 francs the words 'INR 160' are substituted by the Notification of 1980 supra but in case the contract envisages then on extra payment the liability limits could be higher. As regarding the objects which the passenger is carrying with himself the liability is limited to '5,000 francs' per passenger whereas for the words '5,000 francs' 'INR 1,000' are substituted by the Notification. As the liability of the carrier arises in respect of registered luggage only hence the term 'registered luggage' came up for consideration as traditionally speaking there is no 'registration' of the luggage by any airlines as on receiving the customer's luggage an identification card is tagged to the luggage and its counterpart is delivered to the customer. The court held that the check-in procedures as universally followed in the entire civil aviation amount to registration (*Collins v. British Airways Board* [1982] 2 WLR 165).

When the carrier fails to issue a baggage check or airway bill then he is precluded from limiting his liability. He will also not be allowed to exclude or limit his liability if the damage is caused by his wilful misconduct or by such default on his part which is also considered as wilful misconduct or default under the law of the country which where the case is instituted (Article 25 WC).

F. Liability of Different Carriers

704. The goods in this case were directed to be delivered to the bank for collection of payment of the goods but the carrier's agents delivered them to the consignee. In this case, Air India carried the goods to be delivered to a New York buyer. A New York bank was named as the consignee in the airway bill. Air India carried the goods up to Paris and there entrusted them to the Trans World Airlines (TWA) for carriage to New York and the TWA wrongfully delivered the goods to the buyer at New York without obtaining the payment for the goods. Air India was accordingly held liable as under section 30 of the Carriage by Air Act 1972 the liability of the different carriers with regard to the goods remains joint and several. As the action was brought by the consignor hence action against the first carrier that is, Air India is justified. It was held that the goods were delivered without formalities which amounted to fraud (*Anil & Co. v. Air India* AIR 1986 Del 312). In another case, the goods were handed over to the carrier for delivery in the United States and the carrier forwarded the goods to another carrier as the first one was not operating up to the United States. The goods were delivered by the second carrier but in violation of the instructions given. The first carrier disowned any liability as he said that the consignment was handed over to the second carrier in a proper manner, but the court rejected the contention and held that in such cases the entire carriage is a single operation and the liability of the different carriers who appear in it is joint and several (*Rajasthan Handicrafts Emporium v. P. A. World Airways* AIR 1984 Del 396).

§7. PROCEDURE

I. Right of Action

705. Every High Contracting Party (State which has ratified or is adhered to the Hague Protocol 1955) to the Warsaw Convention 1929 or the Hague Protocol 1955 who has not availed itself of the provisions of the additional protocol thereto will be able to enforce a claim in the courts in India. For this purpose, any such state which brings a suit under the First or Second Schedule of the Carriage by Air Act 1972 to enforce a claim in respect of a carriage undertaken by him shall be deemed to have submitted to the jurisdiction of that court and shall also be governed by the provisions of the Code of Civil Procedure 1908.

A. Applicability of Section 86(1) of CPC

706. Section 86(1) is not impliedly superseded by the Carriage by Air Act 1972 as the Act does not contain any provision regarding sovereign immunity. Thus while the Act allows suits to be filed in civil courts the major governing law is the Code of Civil Procedure 1908 (*Mansoor Mumtaz v. Sandi Arabian Airlines Corporation* AIR 2002 Del 103).

The High Court is empowered by section 7 of the Act to make rules of procedure for the institution and carrying of such suits. Rule 7(3) also bars the attachment or sale of property of any High Contracting Party by any court in India.

II. Time Limits

707. In Rule 30 of the Second Schedule, the right to damages will be extinguished if the action is not brought within two years. The two year period is to be calculated either from the date of arrival at the point of destination; or from the date on which the aircraft ought to have arrived; or from the date on which the carriage stopped while the method of calculation shall be determined by the court which is seized of the case.

The two year period of limitation is not applicable in case of unauthorized delivery made without bank release. The Rule is applicable to 'any registered luggage or any cargo' only and the loss or damage must be to the goods and not to the air carrier or the consignee (*East and West Steamship Co. v. S. K. Ramalingam Chettiar* AIR 1960 SC 1058).

Again it was decided by the court that when the unauthorized delivery was made by defendant 2 to defendant 1 without bank release order then it was not taken as 'destruction or loss of or of damage to' the consignments in question within the meaning of Rules 18 and 30 so as to render the suit being barred by time as having been instituted beyond two years (*Vij Sales Corporation v. Lufthansa German Airlines*, ILR (1981) 2 Del 749).

III. Jurisdiction of Courts

708. According to Rules 18, 19, 24(1) and 29(1) contained in the Second Schedule (Chapter 3) to the Act, only those courts have jurisdiction to entertain an action against a carrier in whose jurisdiction: the carrier is ordinarily resident; has his principal place of business; has an establishment by which the contract has been made; or the court has jurisdiction at the place of destination. The question of jurisdiction was elaborately discussed in *Gulf Air Company v. Nahar Spinning Mills Ltd* ((2000) 2 CLT 388 (P&H)).

In this case, the carrier was a resident of Bahrain, the principal place of office was Delhi, and the destination of the consignment was Manchester (UK), and the agreement was concluded at Delhi. A suit for recovery of a sum was filed by the plaintiff company at Ludhiana court. This was challenged by the defendant saying that in view of Rule 29 of the Second Schedule court at Ludhiana has no jurisdiction.

709. The decision went in favour of the defendants on the ground that the Carriage by Air Act 1972 is a special Act and thus prevails over the Code of Civil Procedure 1908 which is a general Act and thus the proper court in this case would be the one in Delhi. The court also held that the Act of 1972 was enacted to give effect to the amended Convention.

This was done by virtue of Article 253 of the Constitution of India which empowers the Indian Parliament to have legislation for giving effect to international agreements and the courts should thus be mindful of this fact and should not attach extra meaning to the words used in the provisions.

Montreal Convention – Jurisdiction of Courts

710. The Montreal Convention has gone a step further in helping the aggrieved consumer and has enlarged the area of jurisdiction. Under it, the passenger has the ease to file a suit within his place of domicile provided the carrier has a presence there. Accordingly, India has included it in its amendment act.

A. Judicial Pronouncements on Airline Services

711. With more and more passengers ready to fly, there are multiple increases in air traffic and in the corporations operating them. Attractive and economical schemes are launched by the airlines to lure the customers. There is therefore an increase in the litigations coming to the courts as the pressure of work often results in mismanagement. The Montreal Convention gives more safeguards to the passengers and has elaborate provisions for compensating the passenger. Thus a recent judgment by the German Supreme Court is in compatibility with the Montreal Convention as the court granted the plaintiff's claim for compensation for inordinate delay in air journey. The delay was treated at par with the cancellation of the flight and where the carrier is unable to show extraordinary circumstances responsible for the delay (*Sturgeon v. Condor Flugdienst GmbH* (2010 Bus LR 1206 (ECJ))).

In India, suits for compensation for deficient services are now frequently decided by the National Commission established under the Consumer Protection Act 1986 which is a consumer forum and acts as a court.

712. The Commission while adjudicating upon Rule 12 in Part III of Chapter 2 of the Carriage by Air Act 1972 held that the rule does not give any right to the consignor to ask the carrier for reshipment of goods to some other destination. Though the carrier is bound to follow the instructions of the consignor at the time of transit yet it is not so bound once the goods reach their destination. The carrier is under obligation to inform the consignor that no one as instructed by him came to take the delivery of the goods. When he fails in his duty then only he can be held liable for loss or damages caused to the goods during that period. But the Commission held in this case that here the carrier is not liable because there is also negligence noted on the part of the consignor who did not care to inquire about the non-delivery of goods due to the absence of any taker at the destination point (*Air India v. N. Divan* (1995) 1 CPJ 68 NC). When due to the enormous amount of the cargo it could not be airlifted for a considerable period and thereafter the owner took back his cargo without giving the carrier yet another opportunity to send the goods by another airliner. Held, it was found that as time was not made the essence of the contract and as safety of the airliners was also in the consideration of the carrier hence there cannot be said to be any deficiency in service (*S. L. Exports v. Singapore Airlines* (2003) 3 CPJ 58 (NC). The loss of the cargo was not shown to be due to the 'wilful misconduct' as within the meaning of Schedule 1 Article 25(1), the carrier was held liable as per the tariff (INR 160 for every kg lost) specified in Regulation 5 of the Air Corporation Act 1954 (*Jindal Photofilms Ltd v. Indian Airlines* (1996) 2 CPJ 168 NC).

A complaint that there was negligence on the part of the carrier in delivering the consignments in time as a result of which important business profits were lost and hence the consignee cancelled the order was allowed both by the District Forum and the State Commission but the National Commission held that there was no wilful negligence nor there was omission or recklessness. The Commission took the view that the complainant failed to mention that there was any wilful misconduct (Rule 25 of the First Schedule of WC). Or that the damage resulted from the intentional causing of damage (Rule 25 of the Second Schedule of the Hague Protocol). The NC took the view that the relief which it could give was the only one as specified in Rule 14 of the Act. It thus reached the decision that the case fell under Rule 22 of the First Schedule or the Second Schedule of the Carriage by Air Act and the respondent-complainant would be entitled to relief of USD 4,180 @ USD 20 per kg, for its weight of 209 kg of the cargo (*Rajasthan State Industrial Development and Investment Corporation Ltd v. Premier Paints* [1991] 2 CPJ 599 (NC).

It is the duty of the carrier not to deliver the goods without the production and surrender of carriage documents which shown his entitlement to the consignment.

Thus when the carrier flouted the established procedure and in a casual, cavalier and negligent manner handed over the goods to a foreign buyer, the NC inflicted heavy penalty and held that the carrier's conduct was quite unbecoming of an international carrier and deserves the severest condemnation (*Presidency Kid Leathers Ltd v. Singapore Airlines Ltd* (1995) 1 CPJ 459).

Air India informed the consignee about the arrival of goods but he did not take the delivery. The consignors instructed the carriers to reship the goods but did not pay the requisite retransportation charges which were to be paid as in foreign or Indian currency after the approval of the Reserve Bank of India (RBI). The Supreme Court held that Air India (carrier) is at no fault and there was no deficiency in service (*Soddler Shoes (P) Ltd v. Air India* [2001] 3 CPJ 1; (2001) 8 SCC 390).

The passenger was allowed compensation when tickets were allowed on a date on which there was no flight (*Mohinderjit Singh Sethi v. Indian Airlines* [2003] 2 CPJ 205 (NC).

There was a question regarding settlement of a claim for death in an air crash, complainants being ignorant of the Rules under IATA (IIA) and MIA (inter-carriage agreements on liability) facing dominant position of the Airliner (Kenyan Airways) signed discharge voucher. The NC held that in India there are a number of legislations like the Fatal Accidents Act 1855, Motor Vehicles Act 1988 and various decisions of the Supreme Court for the guidance of courts (*Anita Bhatia v. Kenyan Airways* [2004] 1 CPJ 58 (NC).

Chapter 5. Multimodal Transportation

§1. Definitions: An Introduction

713. Multimodal transportation is the movement of cargo from the point of origin to the final destination, outside India, by using two or more modes of transportation. Multimodal transportation by land, sea and air is always concerned with the import and export of goods to and from the country. There are more than three hundred Multimodal Transport Operators (MTOs) of which one hundred and twenty are registered with the Association of Multimodal Transporters of India (AMTOI). The idea of multimodal transportation started with the container revolution in the late 1950s by Malcolm Mclean and his trucking operations. Technology has also revolutionized the international transport structure and the use of containers is on the increase to transport goods from one country to another using more than one mode of transportation.

The important feature of multimodal transportation is the uninterrupted and unbroken transportation of goods in the international chain under one single transport document. As a consequence, the multimodal transport operator remains liable to the cargo owner. India too joined the practice of multimodal transportation of containerized cargo along with the developed countries. To meet this India geared up for the challenge by developing its major ports, container railway flat wagons, inland container, depots and container freight stations.

According to section 2(k) of the MMTG Act, multimodal transportation means carriage of goods by at least two different modes of transport under a multimodal transport contract, from the place of acceptance of goods in India to a place of delivery of the goods outside India.

Earlier the goods to be rendered as 'exported' had to undergo many formalities The recent concept of 'MULTIMODALISM' regards a consignment as 'exported' when it is loaded into a container and it has been sealed by the customs authorities irrespective of the fact that it is in the port or in the inland container depot (ICD) which may be even hundreds of kilometres away from the port. In spite of the increasing popularity of multimodal transportation, no international legal regime has been evolved yet thus important legal issues are often raised as the exercise involves a good number of laws from various countries, often there is no legal backup at all thereby making the situation more challenging for the entire trade. The crucial question lies in the liability of such carriers as there is always seen a tendency to avoid it or to transmit it to other carriers.

There have been genuine efforts by the UNO to solve the complexities involved but the outcome is not very convincing. The United Nations Convention on International Multimodal Transport of Goods 1980 failed to attract sufficient ratifications. The UNCTAD/ICC Rules of Multimodal transport Documents which came into force in January 1992 has no legal force.

In 2001, a UNCITRAL Working Group on Transport Law was established by the UNCITRAL Commission to consider the elaboration of a new international instrument focusing on port – to port transport which is a remarkable step. The Working Group which met in April 2002 started considering creating a 'Draft Instrument on Transport Law' (Draft Instrument) which has been prepared by the CMI. The Draft

Instrument subsumes the subject of maritime liability hitherto covered under the Hague-Visby Rules and the Hamburg Rules. Apart from this certain subjects yet have no proper legal coverage like delivery, freight and transfer of the right of control and right of suit. The Draft also gives recognition to e-transactions to replace the existing paper regime. The Draft thus covers all multimodal contracts for the international carriage of goods includes a sea leg.

§2. Statutory Provisions

714. India is one of the rare countries that have a separate law for multimodal transportation. The Government of India, with a view to liberalize controls, simplify procedures, facilitate smooth flow of international trade and promotion of exports, avoiding delays and improving the quality of transport services proposed a legal regime for it. It thus set up a Working Group to examine the then-existing condition of transportation and cargo trade in India. The Group made certain proposals which were based on the rules framed by the ICC.

It also considered the provision of the United Nations Convention on Multimodal Transport of Goods 1980 and also made certain proposals for making amendments to the Carriers Act 1865, (Now repealed by The Carriage by Road Act 2007 (41 of 2007)), The Indian Carriage of Goods by Sea Act 1925 (26 of 1925) and the Sale of Goods Act 1930 (3 of 1930).

Consequently, the President of India thus promulgated the Multimodal Transportation of Goods Ordinance on 16 October 1992.

That being a temporary law soon it was given a permanent form and the Multimodal Transport of Goods Act 1993 was passed to streamline multimodal transportation in India. Its aim was also to regulate the unorganized multimodal operations MOTs though it failed to please them; and to provide for the regulation of the multimodal transportation of goods, from any place in India to a place outside India on the basis of a multimodal transport contract and related matters.

The Director General of Ship (DGS) which is the nodal authority for registering the MTO did not have much power to enforce the law provisions. It suffered from two lacunae; *first,* it preferred and favoured the shippers over the multimodal transporters and *second*, it was not compulsory for multi transporters to register themselves with the DGS. The Act of 1993 obtaining the prior approval of the Ministry of Surface Transport prescribed the Multimodal Transport Document under Rule 3 of Multimodal Transport Document Rules 1994.

Before the enactment of this Act, the law relating to multimodal transportation received attention in a sporadic and insufficient manner as various laws like the Railways Act and other laws touched upon it only in a very brief manner. For instance, in the Railways Act 1989, it is said that the Railway administration has the power to provide other transport services for the purpose of facilitating the carriage of passengers or goods or to provide integrated service for such carriage or to provide any other mode of transport (section 183). The Act of 1993 presents exhaustive law on multimodal transportation.

I. The Multimodal Transportation of Goods Act 1993: Statutory Provisions

715. The 1993 Act is a comparatively short law with barely thirty-two sections and a Schedule showing relevant amendments which are made to the Carriers Act 1865, the Indian Carriage of Goods by Sea Act, 1925 and the Sale of Goods Act 1930 supplemental to the 1993 Act.

The Statutory provisions are summarized as follows.

A. Interpretation Clause

716. Section 2 of the 1993 Act contains various definitions. In the section, the term multimodal transportation means carriage of goods by two or more modes of transport from the place of acceptance of the goods in India to a place of delivery of the goods outside India and the term multimodal transport contract means a contract entered into by the consignor and the multimodal transport operator for multimodal transportation (section 2(k) and (l)).

The term *multimodal transport operator* means any person who: (i) concludes a multimodal transport contract on his own behalf or through another person acting on his behalf; (ii) acts as principal and not as an agent either of the consignor or of the carrier participating in the multimodal transportation, and who assumes responsibility for the performance of the said contract; and (iii) is registered under section 4.

In the section, *Negotiable multimodal transport document* means a multimodal transport document which is either made out to order or to bearer or is made out to order and is transferable without endorsement and 'non-negotiable multimodal transport document' means 'a multimodal transport document' which indicates only one named consignee.

B. Regulation of Multimodal Transportation

717. The Act of 1993 contains certain rules regarding the regulation of multimodal transportation. It lays down the rule that the business of multimodal transportation cannot be carried out without registration. The procedure of registration says that the application for the registration of multimodal transportation must be accompanied by a fee of INR 10,000.

The applicant being a shipping company or a company engaged in the business of freight forwarding in India or abroad with a minimum annual turnover of INR 50,00,000 during the preceding three financial years as certified by a chartered accountant within the meaning of Chartered Accountants Act 1949 (38 of 1949) is eligible for applying for registration. In case the company is a company other than a company as mentioned above then the prescribed share capital of such company should be not less than INR 50,00,000. A certificate so granted remains valid for one year to be renewed thereafter.

The registration can be cancelled on the ground of making false declarations in the application, or in violation of any provisions of the Act, or when the multimodal operator has not entered into any contract for about two years after his registration. However, anyone being aggrieved by the cancellation order may appeal to the Central Government according to the prescribed procedure (Chapter 2).

C. Multimodal Transport Document (MTD)

718. The Act of 1993 also makes provisions for multimodal transport document related rules. Once a contract has been concluded between the consignor and the multimodal transport operator then the multimodal transport operator shall issue a negotiable or non-negotiable multimodal transport document duly signed by the operator or by any authorized person as opted by the consignor.

The multimodal transport document, being regarded as a document to title must contain the following particulars namely; the general nature and character of goods, number of packets or units and its weight or quantity; the apparent conditions of the goods; the name of the principal place of business of the multimodal transport operator, the name of the consignor and the consignee, date and place of taking charge and delivery of the goods; declaration as to whether the document is negotiable or negotiable; the signature of the multimodal transport operator, the intended journey route, terms of shipment and other details which the parties may intend to insert.

Where the multimodal transport operator is of any doubt as to the declaration made by the consignor regarding the state and conditions of the goods then he is authorized to enter a reservation in the document specifying the inaccuracies and the grounds of suspicion.

The multimodal transport document is the prima facie evidence of the fact that the multimodal transport operator has taken charge of the goods and no proof to the contrary is admissible if the multimodal transport operator has issued the document in negotiable form. The consignor is also under the responsibility to state the accuracy and adequacy of goods while handing over the same to the multimodal transport operator (Chapter 3).

D. Responsibilities of the MTO

719. The multimodal transport operator shall be responsible for the loss resulting from any loss or damage to the consignment, for the delay in the delivery of the consignment and any consequential loss or damage when such loss occurs when the goods are in his charge. But he is exempted from liability when the loss occurs due to no fault or neglect on his part or that of his servants or agents.

The multimodal operator shall not be liable for loss or damage arising out of delay if the consignor has not expressed his interest in timely delivery. The 'delay' caused shall make the transport operator liable only when the consignment has not been delivered within the expressed time or within reasonable time. The claimant shall regard the consignment as lost if it is not delivered within ninety consecutive days from the date of delivery.

E. Limits of Liability

720. The liability of the multimodal transport operator shall, according to the provisions of the 1993 Act vary in the following situations:

(a) Once the multimodal transport operator becomes liable for any loss or damage to any consignment the nature and value of which has not been declared and stage of transport where loss or damage occurred is not known, then the liability of the multimodal transport operator shall not exceed 2 SDRs per kilogram of the gross weight of the consignment lost or damaged or 666.67 SDRs per package or unit lost or damaged, whichever is higher.
(b) However, whenever, the multimodal transportation does not, according to the multimodal transport contract, include carriage of goods by sea or by inland waterways, the liability of the multimodal transport operator shall be limited to an amount not exceeding 8.33 SDRs per kilogram of the gross weight of the goods lost.
(c) Where the MTO becomes liable for any loss of or damage to, any consignment, where the nature and value of the consignment have not been declared by the consignor before such consignment has been taken in charge by the MTO and stage of transport where loss or damage occurred is known then the limit of the liability of the MTO for such loss or damage shall be determined in accordance with the provisions of the relevant law applicable in relation to the mode of transport during the course of which the loss or damage occurred and any stipulation in the multimodal transport contract to the contrary shall be void and unenforceable.
(d) Where the delay in delivery of the consignment occurs beyond the time expressly agreed upon or if the delivery has not been made within ninety consecutive days following the date of delivery then the liability of the MTO shall be limited to the freight payable for the consignment so delayed.

The MTO shall not be entitled to the limit of liability if it is shown that the delay or loss occurred with the intent to cause loss, damage or delay recklessly and with the knowledge that such loss, damage, or delay would probably result. The MTO shall not be liable, in any, case for an amount greater than the liability for the total of goods for which a person will be entitled to make a claim against him under the 1993 Act.

Assessment of compensation shall be made with reference to the value of such consignment at that place where, and the time at which such consignment is delivered to the consignee or at the place and time when according to the multimodal transport contract it should have been delivered (Chapter 4).

F. Miscellaneous

721.

- The consignor is under obligation to declare the nature of dangerous goods to the MTO and must take precautions regarding the transportation of such goods. In case the consignor fails to make such declaration then he will be liable to the MTO for all loss resulting from the multimodal transportation of such goods and such goods would at any time be unloaded, destroyed, or rendered innocuous without any payment for compensation.
- The MTO shall have a right of lien on the consignment and on the document in his possession in case he is not paid the amount of compensation as stipulated.

  The period during which the MTO is withholding the goods in his possession in the exercise of his right of lien shall not be calculated in computing the time of delay in delivery of goods.
- The parties to the multimodal transport contract can lawfully include in the multimodal transport document any provision relating to 'general average'. The term 'general average' implies a loss, damage or expense reasonably incurred in order to avert danger to property in common peril and in the common interest involved in the multimodal transport.
- Action can be brought in a law court against the MTO within nine months of; the date of delivery of the goods, or the date when the goods should have been delivered, or the date on and from which the party entitled to receive delivery of the good has the right to treat the goods as lost.

  The court in which action can be brought must be a competent one and within whose jurisdiction the following places are situated namely; the principal place of business or habitual residence of the defendant or the place where the multimodal transport contract was made provided that the defendant has a place of business, branch or agency at such place or the place of taking charge of the goods the multimodal transportation or the place of delivery thereof or any other place specified in the multimodal transport contract and evidenced in the multimodal transport document.
- The Government of India is empowered under the Act of 1993 to make rules for carrying out the provisions of the Act. The government shall notify the rules in the Official Gazette. The rules include rules regarding the draft and form of applications made under the Act, the period of appeal and the form and fees of the same, rules regarding the dangerous goods and any other matter relevant thereof. Every rule so made shall be laid before each House of the Parliament for a total period of thirty days. The opinion of the Houses regarding the validity, modification or effect of the rule shall be final and such modification or annulment of the rule shall not affect the validity of anything previously done under that rule.

Relevant Amendments – To give fuller effect the Act of 1993 amendments is made in certain enactments which are shown in Parts I, II and III of the Schedule of the Act as follows.

Part I – The amendment is made in the Carriers Act 1865 (3 of 1865) whereas in the definition of the term 'common carrier' the words 'transporting property under multimodal transport document' is included.

Part II – The amendment is made in the Indian Carriage of Goods by Sea Act 1925 (26 of 1925) whereas, in the Preamble, the words 'And where as the said rules were amended by the Protocol signed at Brussels on 23 February 1968 and by the Protocol signed at Brussels on 21 December 1979' are inserted.

In section 7 of the Act, sub-section (1) for the words and figures 'sections 331 and 352', the words, figures and letters 'section 331 and Part XA' is substituted.

In Article 1 of the Schedule after the words 'merchandises' the words 'containers, pallets or similar article of transport used to consolidate goods if supplied by the shipper', are inserted. Certain other amendments are made in the said Act regarding the admissibility of the bill of lading which has been transferred to a third party acting in good faith., regarding the extension of the period within which action will be brought in a law court and regarding the amount exceeding per package per unit where m for the words and figures 'amount exceeding 1001 per package or unit', the words and figures 'amount exceeding 666.67 SDRs per package or unit or 2 SDRs per kilogram of gross weight of the goods lost or damaged, whichever is higher' shall be substituted. There has also been amendment pertaining to the number of packages or units enumerated in the Bill of lading and regarding the limitation of liability of the carrier where he is not allowed to take the benefit of such limitation in case the damage resulted from the act or omission on the part of the carrier done with the intent to cause damage or recklessly and with the knowledge that damage would probably result.

Part III – In this part amendment is made in the Sale of Goods Act 1930 (3 of 1930) under which in section 2 of the Act after the words 'railway receipt' the words 'multimodal transport document' is inserted.

Construction of Multimodal Terminals

722. The year 2017 saw immense activity regarding the extension of multimodal trade along the inland waterways. Thus the Multimodal Terminal Varanasi (2018), the Multimodal Terminal Sahibganj scheduled to be completed by 2019, Multimodal Terminal Haldia scheduled to be completed by 2019 and construction of New Navigational Lock, Farakka is also scheduled to be completed in April 2019.[67]

§3. Treaty Law

723. Multimodal transport system was developed with the advancement of technology and the modernization of shipping industry. As a result of the bulk carrier trade, unitization of cargo aiming at the economy in the transport of goods, 'containerization' emerged as a modern concept.

The concept was soon accepted and adopted by the international trading community including India because of the movement of cargo containers from door to door without intermediate loading and unloading of goods, the quicker transport, cheaper packing and less susceptibility of cargo to damage and pilferage.

67. Ministry of Shipping 2017 -Year of Consolidation – Posted on 20 Dec. 2017 by PIB Delhi.

As such trading is cross-border hence the international community agreed to undergo a number of conferences and conventions, treaties and agreements regarding rules to govern the upcoming modern concept of multimodal transportation. As containerization needs huge capital outlay to bear the expenses of the different modes of transportation at a time hence the shipowners and consortia belonging to developed countries have introduced container services.

Even the overseas trades of developing countries like India are being facilitated by container ships with the ports, roads, rails, and so on, being streamlined and modernized to meet the growing demand for multimodal transportation. Each form of transport is governed by a separate international convention. Efforts were started to unify the disjointed set of rules in this regard. Two international conventions were adopted at the International Conference on Container traffic held in Geneva in 1972. A gist of each and its adoption by India are given in the following paragraphs.

I. Customs Convention on Containers 1972

724. The main purpose of this Convention is to facilitate temporary importation of containers, component parts, accessories and equipment free of customs duty and other restrictions. The convention provides regulations on technical conditions applicable to containers which may be accepted for international transport under Customs seal. It also lays down the procedure for the approval of Containers for transport either at the manufacturing stage or at a stage subsequent to manufacture. India though did not ratify this Convention but the customs authorities in India have been allowing temporary duty-free import of containers subject to their re-export within a stipulated period.

II. International Convention for Safe Containers 1972

725. The Convention provides structural requirements to ensure safety in the handling, stacking and transporting of containers and lays down regulations for the testing, inspection and grant of approval of containers by contracting States for which the States are required to establish an effective procedure or entrust such work to organizations duly authorized by it. The Convention became enforceable on 6 September 1977 and India too has ratified it. In India, the Indian Registrar of Shipping has been designated by the Government of India as the authority to approve containers manufactured in India and grant approval plates.

III. International Convention on Facilitation of International Maritime Traffic 1965

726. The purpose of this Convention was to simplify and shorten the formalities, documentary requirements and procedures on arrival, stay and departure of ships engaged on international voyages. This covers all documents pertaining to the ship and its passengers, baggage, crew, cargo and mail which are required by Customs. India ratified this convention on 25 May 1976.

A. The MT Convention

727. In 1980, the United Nations Convention on International Multimodal Transport of Goods (the MT Convention) was held. In this, the limit of liability of the MTO was set at 920 SDRs per package or unit or 2.75 SDRs per kilo of the gross weight of goods if the stage of loss/damage is not known; if the stage of loss/damage is known, then the liability is to be determined as per the convention of law applicable to that stage.

In April 1991, UNCTAD/ICC Rules on Multimodal Transport Document were set up by its joint group to govern multimodal transport. These Rules have followed the Hague/Visby Rules for the limit of liability at 666.67 SDRs per package or unit or 2 SDRs per kilo of gross weight whichever is higher if the stage of loss/damage is not known and if the ship is one of the modes of transport in multimodal transport. If the multimodal transport does not involve carriage by sea and when the stage of loss/damage is not known the limit of liability is fixed at 8.33 SDRs per kilo of the gross weight of goods. However, the Rules provide that when the stage of loss/damage is known then the law/convention relevant to that stage will specify the liability of the MTO.

India has adopted these rules whereas under section 14 of the MMTG discussed *supra*, where the liability of the MTO to pay compensation where the stage of loss or damage is not known, is fixed at not more than 2 SDRs per kilogram of the gross weight of the consignment lost or damaged or 666.67 SDRs per package or unit lost or damaged whichever is higher. Under the Indian law, section 15 of the said Act mentions that where the stage of transport at which such loss or damage occurred is known, the limit of liability of the multimodal transport operator shall be determined according to the relevant law applicable in relation to the mode of transport.

B. The Hamburg Rules

728. The Hamburg Rules is a final Act of the United Nations Conference on the Carriage of Goods by Sea held in Hamburg in 1978. Its aim was to achieve a 'common understanding' regarding certain rules relating to the carriage of goods by sea. It applies to all contracts of carriage by sea between two different States irrespective of the nationality of the ship, the carrier, the shipper the consignee or any other interested person. The Rules also apply to the future shipments of goods.

The term 'contract of carriage by sea' under the Rules means a contract of carriage, on payment of freight to carry goods by sea and when a contract is to employ the other modes of transportation as well then the Rules shall apply to the extent the goods are carried by sea and is to be regarded as a contract of carriage by sea. Thus the Hamburg Rules shall apply to the sea leg of the transaction whenever there is a multimodal transportation of goods. The Rules are not applicable to the charter party but where a bill of lading is issued pursuant to the charter party, then the bill of lading part of it shall be governed by the Rules. The Rules also permit the Contracting States to go ahead with international conventions which are already effective and which apply mandatorily to contracts of carriage of goods by a mode of transportation other than transport by sea.

C. The Warsaw Convention

729. The Warsaw Convention 1929 (As amended at The Hague 1955 and by Protocol No. 4 of Montreal 1975) though mainly applicable to international carriage by air yet it does not prohibit the parties from entering into a contract which partakes of various modes of transportation in one deal.

The condition for the applicability of the Convention to multimodal transportation is that the air leg which forms part of the entire multimodal transportation must be international in nature and if it is not an international carriage by air then the Convention has no application. The Convention also allows the contracting parties in such a contract to insert conditions pertaining to other modes of transport to that of air carriage but without derogating from the provisions of the Convention regarding carriage by air (Article 31).

India is a signatory to the Warsaw Convention 1929 as amended by The Hague of 1955 and has imported the Convention in the Carriage by Air Act 1972 (No. 69 of 1972).

D. The CMR Convention

730. CMR (Geneva, 19 May 1956) shall apply to the whole of the carriage which consists of a journey by sea, rail, inland waterways or air and the goods are not unloaded from the vehicle.

Where any loss or damage or delay occurs during the carriage not due to the act or omission of the carrier by road but for the peculiar reason which is typical of the mode of transportation during which such loss, damage or delay occurred then the liability of the carrier by road shall not be determined by the CMR Convention. In such cases, the liability of the carrier by the other means of transport shall be taken into consideration as per the contract for the carriage of goods between the sender and the carrier considering the conditions as given under such law which governs that kind of transportation and the liability of the carrier by road shall be fixed accordingly.

The provisions of the Convention shall apply to fix the liability of the carrier by road only when there are no such conditions prescribed under that particular law. Such rules will also apply where the carrier by road is himself a carrier even in other modes of transport in the same carriage but in such a situation he will be treated as two different persons.

E. The CIM Convention

731. In the Uniform Rules concerning the Contract for International Carriage of Goods by Rail (CIM) 1980 the term 'station' covers railway stations, ports used by shipping services and all other establishments of transport undertakings which are publicly open for making a contract of carriage. In the CIM special provisions are made for certain types of transport and in the case of multimodal transportation of the carriage of containers special provisions are laid down in the Regulations concerning the international carriage of containers by rail (RICO). Annexure III to the Uniform Rules. The Convention also mentions the liability of the carrier by rail by laying down the rule that where there are more than two modes of transportation and railways is one of those then the carrier by railways shall be responsible for the entire carriage (Articles 35, 1, 36 1). In the CIM the railways do not regard the containers as packing but as a transportation unit (Articles 1, 2 RICO) and the carriage continues from door to door or from the time of uploading to the time of the dismantling of the container.

F. The UPU Arrangements

732. Sporadic and isolated arrangements continued between various countries to deliver posts in each other's country which was not only insufficient but was full of hardships. The Universal Postal Union (UPU) can be dated back to 1857 to form a united body to overcome the situation and to erect a global panoply of the postal system. The United States called for an international postal congress which was held in 1863.

The present UPU was established under the name of Global Postal Union in 1874 as a result of the Treaty of Berne signed on 9 October 1874. It got its present name UPU in 1878. The United Nations strived to bring the nations of the world together and encouraged international cooperation in the field with the object of achieving certainty and regularity in postal services As a result, the UPU came to be attached with the UNO by a special agreement in 1947. It was open to all sovereign states and for the admission of a new member, a two-thirds majority of the existing members of the UNO was required.

733. The UPU established that there should be a more or less uniform flat rate to mail a letter anywhere in the world, that postal authorities should give equal treatment to foreign and domestic mail and that each country should retain all monies it collected for international postage. A mentionable contribution of the UPU is that it stopped the practice of affixing stamps of all the countries through which the letter passed and it rendered sufficient to put the stamp of the member nations for the entire international route. In 1969 the UPU introduced a system by which fees were required to be paid between different countries according to the difference in the total weight of mail between the respective countries which were called 'terminal dues'.

734. However, this practice did not suit the postage of periodicals and hence the new ‘threshold’ system was devised in 1991. Under this practice, different rates are set for letters and periodicals for countries which receive around 150 tonnes of mail per annum while the countries with less quantity of mail retained the original flat rate. The United States maintains a special terminal dues formula with thirteen European countries that include a rate per piece plus a rate per kilogram and has a similar arrangement with Canada.

735. The UPU also operates the system of International Reply Coupons and addresses concerns with ETOEs. The UPU is also active on the philatelic side and in partnership with the World Association for the Development of Philately (WADP) has developed the WADP Numbering System (WNS) which was launched on 1 January 2002. All the members of the UN are the UPU members with the exception of Andorra, Marshall Islands, the Federal States of Micronesia and Palau. India has a postal arrangement with the Royal Government of Bhutan signed in 1967 for the regular exchange of registered and unregistered letters, letter cards or aerogrammes, single postcards, reply postcards, printed papers, samples of merchandise, small packets and literature for the blind.

§4. Commercial Practices and Private Initiatives

I. Through Bill of Lading

736. Through Bill of lading is used to cover at least two different modes of transportation. It has become common with multimodal transportation but its drawbacks have started surfacing. This document is used in a restricted manner where the carriers which issued it utilized it for their own use and also demarcating their liability by putting a disclaimer in it. Article 7 of the Hague-Visby Rules read with Article 11 of the Hamburg Rules do give the carrier an opportunity to plead exemption from liability to goods before the loading and after the discharge.

II. Combined Transport Documents

737. The concept of ‘Combined Transport Documents’ (CTD) was born with the development of international multimodal transport. It is a single document which covers the different modes of transport over which the goods move and which benefits the MTO, the shipper or consignees, the insurer and the banks. It is issued by the MTO at the time the goods enter the transport system or at the time they are received by him for dispatch. It is similar to the traditional bill of lading in the sense that it gives commercial security to the parties concerned and is evidence of the contract of carriage. It can be used as a receipt for identified goods and a negotiable document of title to the goods. Under the Act of 1993, it is called ‘Multimodal Transport Document’ which is negotiable or non-negotiable and which is signed and issued by the MTO or by any authorized person opted by the consignor. It contains the particulars regarding the transported cargo. The CTD or the combined transport document used by the shipping lines and the FIATA documents used by the freight forwarders follow the Hague-Visby Rules suggesting that the carriers are not responsible for the resulting loss caused by the delay.

738. In India, the MMTG also includes the multimodal transport document in Chapter 3. Under it, once the contract to carry goods through multimodal transportation is concluded between the consignor and the MTO, the MTO shall issue a negotiable or non-negotiable multimodal transport document duly signed by the operator or by an authorized person as opted by the consignor.

Selected Bibliography

Government Publications/Other Reports

Annual Report – 2006–2007 – Ministry of Road Transport & Highways Government of India, New Delhi.

Annual Report – 2008–2009 – Ministry of Shipping, Road Transport and Highways.

Annual Report 2018-2019, Ministry of Road Transport and Highways, Government of India.

Constitution of India – (As on 1 September 2010) – Government of India, Ministry of Law and Justice.

Halsbury's Laws of India – Vol. 23. New Delhi: Lexis Nexis, Butterworths, 2005.

India 2007 – A Government of India Publication. New Delhi, 2007.

India 2011 – A Government of India Publication. New Delhi, 2011.

India 2018 – A Government of India Publication. New Delhi, 2018.

India 2021 – A Government of India Publication. New Delhi, 2021.

Indian Railways Year Book 2019-2020 – Published by Directorate of Statistics and Economics-Ministry of Railways (Railway Board), Government of India, New Delhi

India Code Vol VII – 6th Replacement Series. Ministry of Law, Justice and Company Affairs.

Report of the First ATS Coordination Meeting of Bay of Bengal, the Arabian Sea and Indian ocean (bobasio) Region – New Delhi. India. May 2011.

The *Gazette of India* – Extraordinary, Part II – section I, New Delhi. Monday, 1 October 2007/ASVINA 9, 1929. Registered No. DL-(N) 04/0007/2003-07.

Yojana – A Development Monthly – August 2007, vol. 51. Special Issue, Ministry of Information and Broadcasting.

Books, Journals and Papers

Bhatt P. N., Mari. *Indian Demographic Scenario 2025*. Institute of Economic Growth, New Delhi, Discussion Paper No. 27/2001.

Bhatt, S., V. S. Mani & V. Reddy Balakista (eds). *Air, Law and Policy in India*. New Delhi: Lancers Books, 1994.

Chronicle Year Book 2007. Noida: Division of Chronicle Publications, 2007.

Gill, J. S. *Manual of Merchant Shipping Act 1958*. Mumbai: Bhandarkar Publications, 2006.

Selected Bibliography

Gupta, S. P. *The Outlines of Maritime Law*. 1st edn Allahabad: Allahabad Law Agency, 2004.

Hathi, S. *Maritime Practice in India.* 4th edn maritime practice. Com.

Jain, M. P. *Indian Constitutional Law*. 5th edn Wadhwa Nagpur, 2006.

Kapoor, S. K. *International Law – Central Law Agency*. 12th edn (1998).

Manorama Year Book 2018-Malayala Manoram Co. Ltd. 53rd. Edition.

Nehru, J. *Jawaharlal Nehru – The Discovery of India*. 14th edn Jawaharlal Nehru Memorial Fund, 1994.

Rangaraj, N. & G. Raghuram. *Viability of Inland Water Transport (IWT) in India.* Ahmedabad: Indian Institute of Technology, Bombay & Indian Institute of Management, 2006.

Sachdeva, G. S. *International Transportation.* New Delhi: Deep & Deep Publications, 1987.

Saharay, H. K. *The Law of Carriage of Goods by Sea and Air*. Calcutta: Eastern Law House, 2004.

Shetye, C. M. *Maritime Law of India in International Context.* 2nd edn. Mumbai: Bhandakar Publications, 1998.

Shukla, D. S. *Manual of Merchant Shipping Laws*. 3rd edn. Allahabad: Dwivedi Law Publications, 2006.

Singh, A. *Law of Carriage Air, Land & Sea*. 4th edn. Lucknow: Eastern Book Company, 2005.

Singh, A. *Mercantile Law*. 8th edn. Lucknow: Eastern Book Company, 2006.

Thacker, S. India. Mulla & Mulla & Craigie Blunt & Caroe. Chapter 25, 122-128. *The International Comparative Legal Guide to Shipping Law 2018*. 6th edition.

Articles

Bansal, A. K. 'The Four Pillars of International Maritime Law and Bills of Lading'. *Journal of the Indian Law Institute* 48, no. 4 (New Delhi, 2006).

Comah, R. R. York-Antwerp Rules 2016– A Summary of the Changes. Richard Hoggs Lindley. 10 May 2016.

Kemp, A. York-Antwerp Rules 2016: A Summary. file:///C:/Users/this%20pc/Desktop/HFW%20_%20York-Antwerp%20Rules%202016_%20a%20summary%20_%20York-Antwerp%20Rules%202016_%20a%20summary. Html

Saurabh, S. 'A Comment on the Concept of Maritime Lien'. *Journal of the Indian Law Institute* 48, no. 4 (New Delhi, 2006).

Vasishtha, G., Mohanty, S. K., Mishra, U. S. *et al.* Impact of COVID-19 infection on life expectancy, premature mortality, and DALY in Maharashtra, India. *BMC Infect Dis* 21, 343 (2021). https://doi.org/10.1186/s12879-021-06026-6).

Index

The numbers here refer to paragraph numbers

Index